SNAKES
AND OTHER REPTILES
of Zambia and Malawi

Darren Pietersen
Luke Verburgt
John Davies

SNAKES
AND OTHER REPTILES
of Zambia and Malawi

Published by Struik Nature
(an imprint of Penguin Random House South Africa (Pty) Ltd)
Reg. No. 1953/000441/07
The Estuaries No. 4, Oxbow Crescent, Century Avenue, Century City, 7441
PO Box 1144, Cape Town, 8000 South Africa

Visit **www.penguinrandomhouse.co.za** and join the Struik Nature Club for
updates, news, events and special offers.

First published in 2021
1 3 5 7 9 10 8 6 4 2

Publisher: Pippa Parker
Managing editor: Roelien Theron
Editor: Heléne Booyens
Designer: Dominic Robson
Proofreader: Emsie du Plessis

Printed and bound in China by Toppan Leefung Packaging
and Printing (Dongguan) Co., Ltd

ISBN 978 1 77584 737 3 (Print)
ISBN 978 1 77584 738 0 (ePub)

Front cover: Katanga Bush Viper (Frank Willems), Anchieta's Chameleon
(Darren Pietersen), O'Shaughnessy's Thick-toed Gecko (Gary Brown),
Leopard Tortoise (Errol Pietersen)
Half-title page: Speckled Thick-toed Gecko (Luke Kemp)
Title page: Marbled Tree Snake (Luke Verburgt)
Contents page: Rhombic Egg-eater, Flap-necked Chameleon (Luke Verburgt)
Spine: Rhombic Egg-eater (Luke Verburgt)
Back cover: Olive Sand Snake, Nile Crocodile (Luke Verburgt)

DEDICATIONS

To my parents, Errol and Michèle, and my brother Ryan. Thank you for all your love and for always supporting my ideas, no matter how crazy they were.

– Darren Pietersen

To Peter Snyman, who fuelled my passion for herpetofauna and shared his immense knowledge with me. And to my mom, Janine, my wife, Ursula, and my best friend, Sam – none of this would have been possible without you, and I am forever grateful for the love, support and opportunities you've given me.

– Luke Verburgt

To my parents, Peter and Ona, who inspired so much of my passion for nature; my sister Lynne, for putting up with my obsessive birdwatching; and my partner, Lindy, for all her love, patience and support.

– John Davies

ACKNOWLEDGEMENTS

A field guide of this nature would not have been possible without the assistance of numerous individuals and organisations.

We gratefully acknowledge the following parties for sharing their data with us: Ditsong National Museum of Natural History (South Africa), specifically Lauretta Mahlangu; Port Elizabeth Museum, Bayworld (South Africa), specifically Werner Conradie; and the Bulawayo Museum (Zimbabwe), specifically Shiela Broadley. The Biodiversity Institute, specifically René Navarro and Les Underhill, are thanked for sharing the ReptileMAP data with us. Werner Conradie, Johan Marais, Colin Tilbury, Norman Barrett, Gary Brown, Frank Willems and Paul Lloyd are also thanked for sharing their personal data, and many photographs, with us. Thanks to the many people who took the time to share their reptile observations on ReptileMAP and other public citizen science platforms: you have greatly contributed towards shaping the geographic distributions that we present in this field guide.

We are very grateful to the team at the Vegetationmap4Africa project (vegetationmap4africa.org) for allowing us to use their vegetation map in the predictive modelling of the species geographic distributions.

Gary Nicolau is thanked for drawing the excellent scale diagrams included throughout this field guide.

For allowing us to use their photographs, we thank André Coetzer, André van Hecke, Bill Branch, Carl Huchzermeyer, Caspian Johnson, Colin Tilbury, Derek Solomon, Errol Pietersen, Fabio Pupin, Frank Willems, Gary Brown, Gary Nicolau, Harald Hinkel, Johan Marais, Joseph Zulu, Laurent Chirio, Lesley Reynolds, Liam Baisley, Luis Ceriaco, Luke Kemp, Matej Dolinay, Michele Menegon, Mike McLaren, Nick Evans, Norman Barrett, Paul Lloyd, Ronald Auerbach, Stephen Spawls, Tomáš Mazuch, Tyrone Ping, Warren McCleland and Werner Conradie. If we have missed anyone, we sincerely apologise – it was not intentional.

Aaron Bauer, Bill Branch, Werner Conradie and Colin Tilbury are thanked for assisting us in obtaining many obscure scientific publications.

We are extremely grateful to Pippa Parker, Heléne Booyens, Dominic Robson and the entire team at Struik Nature for their help and guidance.

Finally, we thank our families, friends and partners for all their love, support and understanding.

Contents

Preface

Zambia and Malawi are somewhat of a herpetological enigma, at least in the public sphere. They are too far north to be included in southern African field guides, yet too far south for East African field guides. As such, Zambia and Malawi have remained veritable herpetological 'black holes'. Until now, no detailed field guide that covers the entire region has been published.

The idea behind this book originated during a trip to Zambia, when we became increasingly frustrated at the difficulty of identifying reptiles without a suitable consolidated resource. Once back home, we started digging, and realised that although there was a wealth of information regarding the rich reptile diversity of Zambia and Malawi, it was scattered across dozens – if not hundreds – of often obscure publications. Most casual nature enthusiasts wouldn't know where to start, and many of these publications are difficult to obtain.

We decided to consolidate as much of the available information as we could. So began an endeavour that was to last several years. We have done our utmost to ensure that the information contained in these pages is as accurate and up to date as possible. It often necessitated us to track down the original descriptions of species or reviews of genera, and to update this information if anything additional has been published subsequently. Through the field trips we undertook and the data and records we reviewed, several new discoveries were made for both Zambia and Malawi. Some of these discoveries have already been documented, while some newly discovered species remain to be formally described.

It is our hope that this field guide will enable people to identify the wealth of reptiles that surround them in Zambia and Malawi, dispel the myths about all (or even most) snakes being venomous, and generally instill a deeper appreciation for reptiles, which play important roles in the ecosystem. We also hope that this book will stimulate further research into the reptiles of Zambia and Malawi by professionals and amateurs alike, and consequently assist in the conservation of these wonderful creatures.

Although we have made every effort to ensure that the information in this field guide is error-free, any mistakes or oversights contained in these pages are our own. If you notice any inaccuracies or have any questions, you are welcome to contact us.

Darren Pietersen
pietersen.darren@gmail.com

Luke Verburgt
luke@enviro-insight.co.za

John Davies
johnpeter.davies@gmail.com

Foreword

In 1910, FW Fitzsimons wrote *The Snakes of South Africa*, the first guide of its kind. Some three decades later, it was followed by Vivian F Fitzsimons's comprehensive *The Lizards of South Africa*. Other classics on African herpetology include Captain Charles RS Pitman's *A Guide to the Snakes of Uganda* (1938), Margaret Stewart's *Amphibians of Malawi* (1967) and RCH Sweeny's *Snakes of Nyasaland* (1961).

Today, there are plenty of social media pages where snakes (and other reptiles, to a lesser extent) feature daily. Much of what is posted is inaccurate, however, and websites circulate a great deal of misinformation.

I was delighted to hear that Darren Pietersen, a well-known and respected South African herpetologist, was working on a book on the reptiles of Zambia and Malawi with the help of John Davies, who works with avifauna at the Endangered Wildlife Trust. Luke Verburgt, another respected South African herpetologist, soon joined the team. It was an ambitious project, as much of the information on the herpetofauna of Malawi and Zambia was scattered across various scientific papers.

With their combined skills, and over many years, they have produced a comprehensive book that will not just appeal to the layman wanting more information on the interesting reptile diversity of Zambia and Malawi, but will also become the go-to reference for experts in the field and required reading for those studying African herpetology.

The authors chose well when they teamed up with Struik Nature, one of the world's finest natural history publishers. The design and layout of the book is exceptional and makes for easy reading, while the contents are well researched and accurate. Distribution maps are vitally important in any field guide, and here the authors used their vast experience and knowledge of reptile distribution in the region as well as a clear understanding of the diverse habitats to produce maps that will be of great use to herpetologists.

The book covers 117 snake species, 108 lizard species, 13 terrapins and tortoises and two crocodiles. It is lavishly illustrated with over 380 colour photographs. In an age of mediocrity and misinformation, it is great to see a herpetological book of this calibre. It will fit in well with other classics on African herpetology.

Johan Marais
African Snakebite Institute

Introduction

Zambia and Malawi are landlocked African countries in the southern hemisphere. Perhaps their best-known geographical features are the Zambezi River (the longest east-flowing river in Africa), which arises in Zambia, and Lake Malawi (Nyasa), an East African rift lake that covers more than 20% of Malawi. The region's tropical climate, diverse landscape features (ranging from towering inselbergs to lake shores) and wide range of vegetation types are among the primary driving forces behind a high reptile diversity. To date, 240 species have been recorded in these two countries: 117 snakes, 108 lizards, 13 terrapins and tortoises, and two crocodiles. New species are continually 'discovered' using genetic techniques, as widespread species in fact often comprise various closely related and similar-looking species.

ABOVE Eastern Bark Snake
BELOW Mount Mulanje in Malawi

Gary Brown

Tyrone Ping

O'Shaughnessy's Thick-toed Gecko

Eastern Hinged Tortoise

WHAT ARE REPTILES?

Reptiles are a diverse group of vertebrates that belong to the class Reptilia. They come in an extraordinary array of shapes and sizes, with extant reptiles including serpentes (snakes), saurids (lizards), chelonians (tortoises, terrapins and turtles), crocodylians (crocodiles) and sphenodonts (tuataras). Reptiles are characterised by a dry, keratinous skin, usually modified into scales or plates, although in some species, such as the Zambezi Soft-shelled Terrapin (*Cycloderma frenatum*), the scales are covered in leathery skin. Scales consist of a horn-like structure called keratin, and provide protection from predators, injuries and moisture loss.

All reptiles are ectothermic, relying on outside energy sources (such as the sun) to heat up.

This is why they are often seen basking on cold mornings, and why reptile activity decreases during cold periods. Because they rely on external heat sources rather than metabolic heat, reptiles also eat less than mammals or birds of a similar size.

Most reptiles reproduce sexually through internal fertilisation and lay fluid-filled, self-contained eggs that usually incubate unguarded outside the mother's body. The eggs are either soft- or hard-shelled, and in most species are abandoned after being deposited. Eggs are usually laid in a sheltered, warm, moist spot, and in many species the sex of the offspring is determined by the incubation temperature. When they hatch, the young are smaller replicas of their parents – hatchlings of venomous snakes, for example, are just as venomous as their parents.

André van Hecke

The Nile Crocodile is one of two crocodile species found in the region.

TAXONOMY, CLASSIFICATION AND NOMENCLATURE

Taxonomy is the branch of science that assigns names to organisms and documents how they are related to each other. Organisms are grouped by traits that unify them and distinguish them from all other organisms. These traits can be morphological (i.e. external), internal, genetic, or even behavioural. Taxonomic classification is a hierarchical system, meaning that each group higher up on the taxonomic ladder is more inclusive than the one below it. As such, several species form a genus (in a few instances, a genus may contain a single species), several genera are grouped together to form a family, several families form a class, and so on.

Scientific (or Latin) names are those by which an organism is known to the scientific community. Binomial nomenclature is the convention of assigning two-part names consisting of a genus and species name, developed by the Swedish naturalist Carl von Linnaeus in 1735. This approach forms the basis of modern taxonomic classification. Common (or vernacular) names do not follow any specific convention and generally differ between languages and sometimes between regions.

Taxonomy is dynamic, and the scientific names of species continually change as new data become available. This can take several forms: a simple name change; one species being split into two or more species; or forms thought to be different species being synonymised (treated as the same species).

This book has been arranged to largely reflect the taxonomic relationships of families and genera within each order or suborder, with families and genera that are most closely related following each other, using the most recent large-scale phylogenetic studies as a baseline. In a few instances, we feel that the presented evidence does not sufficiently support the proposed taxonomic changes and elect to use the previously accepted taxonomy. Within each genus, species accounts are arranged alphabetically.

Several ongoing studies will affect the taxonomy of reptiles in the region, and more studies are sure to follow. For the most recent taxonomy of the species featured in this book, we direct the reader to The Reptile Database (www.reptile-database.org), a useful online platform that captures updated reptile taxonomy.

Where possible we standardised our use of vernacular names based on the most recent regional reptile guides. We also consulted The Reptile Database for vernacular names of species not occurring in existing guide books, and to see additional vernacular names in use. We generally settled on the most frequently used names, modifying some where appropriate and to reflect recent taxonomic changes.

The Leopard Tortoise, Common Tropical House Gecko and Southern African Python all belong to the same phylum (Chordata) and class (Reptilia). They are known to the scientific community by the binomial names *Stigmochelys pardalis*, *Hemidactylus mabouia* and *Python natalensis*.

Leopard Tortoise

Common Tropical House Gecko

CLASSIFICATION OF REPTILES WITHIN THE ANIMAL KINGDOM

PHYLUM	The animal kingdom is divided into approximately 35 phyla, with reptiles belonging to the phylum Chordata. Members of this phylum have, during some period of their development, a notochord, a dorsal nerve chord, pharyngeal slits and a post-anal tail. Most chordates belong to the subphylum Vertebrata, which is characterised by organisms having a vertebral column (backbone comprising bony vertebrae) and a distinct skull.
CLASS	There are seven classes of chordates, including Reptilia (reptiles), Aves (birds), Amphibia (amphibians), Mammalia (mammals) and three classes of fish.
ORDER	Reptiles are divided into four orders, namely Testudines (tortoises, terrapins and turtles), Crocodylia (crocodiles), Squamata (scaled reptiles) and Sphenodontia (tuataras), the latter found only in New Zealand. The order Squamata is further divided into the suborders Sauria (e.g. lizards, chameleons and agamas) and Serpentes (snakes).
FAMILY	There are 92 reptile families globally, 32 of which occur in the region.
GENUS	At present, some 1,206 reptile genera are recognised worldwide, 97 of which have been recorded in the region.
SPECIES	Currently, 11,341 reptile species are recognised globally, of which 240 have been recorded in the region. Over time, the number of recognised species will continue to increase both regionally and globally.

Evolutionary relationships within the class Reptilia

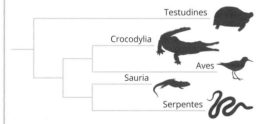

From an evolutionary perspective, birds ought to be included in the class Reptilia, but are traditionally placed in a separate class, Aves, a convention followed in this guide. Crocodylia is most closely related to Aves, while Sauria and Serpentes are more closely related to each other than to any of the remaining reptiles.

Southern African Python

HABITAT TYPES IN ZAMBIA AND MALAWI

Forests

Forests consist of tall, thick trees with interlocking crowns. They are usually rich in plant species, but owing to geological and hydrological characteristics the species composition and height of the forest can vary over short distances. Forests are broadly categorised into two types: moist forests and dry forests. In the region, moist forests are most prevalent in the east where the higher moisture content (from frequent rain and/or mist) sustains them. They usually have a cool, moist and relatively dark interior and the mid- and lower storeys (including climbers or lianas) may be poorly to well developed, depending on the forest type. Moist forests are generally fire-sensitive and thus often occur in isolated patches in gullies, along rivers or other landforms providing protection from fire. They are also generally intolerant of frost. Of the moist forests, **Afromontane rainforests** ① are restricted to high-elevation, high-rainfall regions, particularly on mountain slopes and plateaus. **Swamp forests** or *mushitu*'s ② occur mainly at the headwaters of larger rivers and along smaller streams in north-western Zambia, thinning out to riparian forest in the middle and lower stretches of these rivers. Swamp forests are characterised by tall, dense evergreen trees, often with a well-developed understorey. Many of the trees and shrubs may be seasonally or permanently submerged in shallow water, resulting in a very marshy habitat. **Riparian forests** ③ occur in isolated pockets along some of the larger rivers, usually not extending far into the surrounding vegetation and often forming a relatively abrupt boundary with it. Dry forests are restricted to the drier western regions. In the region, they are represented by the *Cryptosepalum* dry forest (also known as *mavunda*) in north-western Zambia and adjoining Angola. This forest is nearly impenetrable, and many interesting discoveries undoubtedly await the intrepid explorer. In many areas, forests are heavily impacted on by human activities, which include felling for timber, charcoal production and clearing land for agriculture.

Grasslands

Grasslands are characterised by the absence or near-absence of woody plants. They are prone to fire, which maintains them by preventing the encroachment of woody plant species from adjoining habitats. Depending on the region, grasslands can be either short (ankle-height) or tall (taller than a person standing upright). Various grassland types are recognised in the region, largely defined in relation to elevation and geology. **Montane grasslands** 4 occur on mountain summits and plateaus. They are characterised by short grasses and are usually kept moist by frequent rain and/or mist. Owing to their high elevation, montane grasslands can be quite cold (seasonally so in places). **Seasonally flooded grasslands** and **floodplain grasslands** 5 typically occur along rivers, at the edges of pans and in other moist environments. The frequent flooding precludes the establishment or persistence of woody plant species. In places these grasslands are maintained by grazing pressure from large mammals. Palm wooded grassland also usually occurs in moist locations such as in the floodplains of large rivers. This habitat is dominated by grass but is punctuated by palm trees or palm stands, usually Wild Date Palms (*Phoenix reclinata*), Vegetable Ivory Palms (*Hyphaene petersiana*) or Rhun Palms (*Borassus aethiopum*) to varying degrees.

Thickets

The only thickets forming a distinct vegetation type in the region are the Itigi Thickets, situated between Lakes Mweru and Mweru Wantipa in extreme northern Zambia. This vegetation is primarily deciduous and occurs on alluvial soils, and is best characterised by its nearly impenetrable, dense vegetation. However, thickets are a common local feature in many habitats, especially at forest edges and along watercourses 6 . The thicket habitat is characterised by a dense growth of shrubs, trees and grass which often intertwine, making this habitat impenetrable or nearly so.

Woodlands

Woodlands generally consist of tall to stunted trees on a variety of soil types. The trees are spaced relatively close together (sometimes touching), but do not interlock and are not as dense as forests nor as open as savannas. Owing to their more open nature, woodlands are not as moist or dark as forests, and the grass and shrub layer varies from poorly to well developed. Numerous woodland types exist, largely defined based on the dominant plant communities. **Miombo woodland** 7 consists of broad-leaved, deciduous trees mostly belonging to the genera

Brachystegia, *Julbernardia* and *Isoberlinia*. It is an open woodland, occurring in high-rainfall areas on nutrient-poor soils at moderately high elevations.

Mopane woodland 8 usually occurs in relatively hot and dry regions and is characterised by broad-leaved deciduous trees, predominantly Mopane Trees (*Colophospermum mopane*). The growth form (and hence canopy height) varies significantly and is largely dependent on geology, with short, stunted mopane woodland occurring on heavy clay soils, while tall cathedral mopane occurs in sandier areas and along some large rivers. The understorey can be quite well developed (especially the grasses) or nearly absent, and this is also a function of grazing pressure.

Zambezian Kalahari Woodland 9 is restricted to the Zambezi peneplain in western Zambia, where it occurs on Kalahari sands. It varies quite markedly in structure across its range: from tall, broad-leaved *Baikiaea* woodland to short woody shrubland. The shrub layer is generally quite well developed.

In many areas the riverine forests are quite open and are best described as **riverine woodland** 10. These riverine woodlands are generally restricted to the immediate vicinity of the river, sometimes broadening into the adjoining floodplain. The trees are usually a variety of deciduous broad-leaved species, although stands of palms, especially Rhun Palms (*Borassus aethiopum*), can occur.

Undifferentiated woodland consists of a variety of tree types, with no one species dominating.

Waterbodies and wetlands

Various waterbodies occur in the region, ranging from the expansive Lake Malawi and the mighty Zambezi River to temporary pans. The most striking waterbody in the region is undoubtedly the vast **Lake Malawi** 11, which forms most of the eastern border of Malawi with Mozambique and Tanzania. Lake shores vary considerably along their lengths, variously consisting of open sandy beaches, rocky shorelines, rock outcrops on sandy beaches, or well-vegetated shores. The lake itself is an immense open expanse of water, occasionally punctuated by islands. Most reptiles that rely on Lake Malawi occur in relatively close proximity to the lake shore and islands. Other large natural lakes that occur in the region include the southern tip of Lake Tanganyika, Lake Mweru, **Lake Bangweulu** 12, and Lake Mweru Wantipa. Large man-made waterbodies include Lake Kariba and the Itezhi-Tezhi Dam.

Several large rivers occur in the region, including the Zambezi, Kafue, Luangwa, Kalungwishi and **Shire** . These vary markedly in their habitat and morphology along their lengths and some undergo marked seasonal changes. Most of these rivers have associated **floodplains** 14 and wetlands, while some decrease considerably in flow rate seasonally or even stop flowing entirely on occasion. The riverbanks vary significantly along the course of the river, and can successively consist of swamp forest, rock outcrops, riparian forest, woodland, floodplain grassland and marshes, amongst others.

Swamps and marshes usually occur within rivers (such as Elephant Marsh in the Shire River) or in the floodplains of rivers. They are usually relatively large in extent and are characterised by grasses or papyrus stands that are seasonally or permanently inundated to varying depths. These swamps and marshes provide particularly suitable habitat for many amphibian species which, in turn, are preyed on by a variety of reptile species. Pans are usually located away from large rivers and are usually shallow depressions in woodlands that are seasonally inundated by rains. The vegetation varies from being completely absent to inundated grasses or a mosaic of inundated grasses and shrubs. Pans typically remain inundated for only a relatively short period of time (a few months at most), and thus represent an ephemeral habitat. Some pans are, however, quite extensive and can retain water for extended periods of time or may even be permanent (excluding drought years). **Dambos** are shallow grassy wetlands that occur in drainage lines  . The central dambo is fed by a number of drainage lines that vary from being very short to relatively long. Dambos are rain-fed and are thus also largely an ephemeral habitat. Both the dambo and its feeding drainage lines are usually surrounded by trees.

Rock outcrops

Rock outcrops occur in any of the vegetation types and vary greatly in shape and size. They consist predominantly of rocks: either individual rocks that are stacked on top of one another or large, continuous sheets or domes of rock. Because of the general absence of soil, **rock outcrops** are usually largely devoid of vegetation . They can be dominant features in the landscape, rising high above the surrounding regions, of moderate size 17, or may be very small and nearly insignificant.

BIOGEOGRAPHY

Zambia and Malawi together comprise 12 terrestrial ecoregions with several large river systems and Afrotropical lakes. Marked variation in elevation occurs across both countries, the lowest elevations being associated with the Zambezi Valley (~330m a.s.l.) and the highest with Mount Mulanje (~3,000m a.s.l.). Several low-lying regions and high-elevation plateaus occur in both countries, the former generally associated with Mopane (*Colophospermum mopane*) woodlands and the latter with montane grasslands and/or forests. The interaction between elevation, rainfall gradients and a complex geology has resulted in very high diversity of vegetation types,

characterised by 45 regional vegetation types in Zambia and 24 in Malawi.

Subsets of reptiles show similar distribution patterns within the region, which largely reflect the interplay of vegetation, climate, elevation and geology. A species' occurrence is predominantly governed by its habitat preferences and ecology, although habitat connectivity also plays a role. In this regard, the Zambezi River appears to be a substantial dispersal and migration barrier to reptiles in the region, while the Luangwa Valley is apparently a barrier of lesser importance. The geographic distribution patterns of the reptiles in Zambia and Malawi can be grouped into seven regions, which are defined on p. 19.

Terrestrial ecoregions of Zambia and Malawi

Afrotropic Lakes and other large waterbodies
Central Zambezian Miombo Woodlands
Eastern Miombo Woodlands
Itigi-Sumbu Thicket
South Malawi Montane Forest-Grassland Mosaic
Southern Miombo Woodlands

Southern Rift Montane Forest-Grassland Mosaic
Western Zambezian Grasslands
Zambezian and Mopane Woodlands
Zambezian Baikiaea Woodlands
Zambezian Cryptosepalum Dry Forests
Zambezian Flooded Grasslands

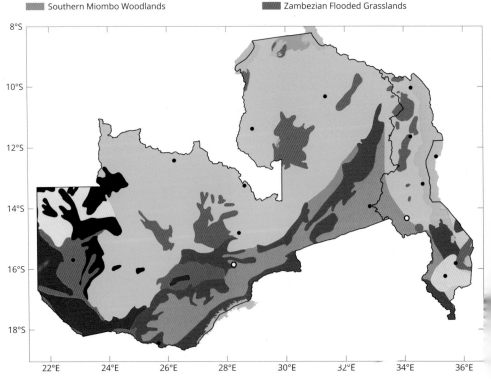

Guinean-Congolian Region

The Guinean-Congolian species are restricted to the Ikelenge Pedicle and surrounding regions in north-western Zambia, as well as extreme northern Malawi. They are predominantly lowland forest species that have a wider distribution in Central Africa, and often into West Africa, with some species also entering woodlands. Examples are the Multi-scaled Forest Lizard (*Adolfus africanus*), Angolan Giant Blind Snake (*Afrotyphlops angolensis*), Katanga Purple-glossed Snake (*Amblyodipsas katangensis*), Forest Night Adder (*Causus lichtensteinii*), Poroto Single-Horned Chameleon (*Kinyongia vanheygeni*), De Witte's Five-toed Skink (*Leptosiaphos dewittei*), Western Forest File Snake (*Mehelya poensis*), Katanga Thick-toed Gecko (*Pachydactylus katanganus*) and Forest Vine Snake (*Thelotornis kirtlandii*).

Zambezi Peneplains Region

These species occur in the Zambezi Valley and surrounding regions. Most of this area consists of deep Kalahari sands, often with well-developed woodlands, although the areas immediately adjoining the Zambezi River are punctuated by a variety of wetlands. Many of the species in this group occur only west of the Zambezi River, often extending into adjoining Angola, while several species are endemic to Zambia. Examples include Barotse Legless Skink (*Acontias jappi*), Schmitz's Legless Skink (*Acontias schmitzi*), Barotse Cat Snake (*Crotaphopeltis barotseensis*), Barotse Worm Lizard (*Dalophia ellenbergeri*), Roux's Dart Skink (*Typhlacontias gracilis*) and Black Dwarf Worm Lizard (*Zygaspis nigra*).

Highlands Region

This region is a composite of various plateaus and mountains. The species found here occur in forests or highland grasslands. The Highlands Region can be further subdivided into: Southern Malawi Highlands (including Mount Mulanje, Dedza Mountain and Zomba Highlands, among others), which has elements of East Coast/Mozambique

Regional map of Zambia and Malawi

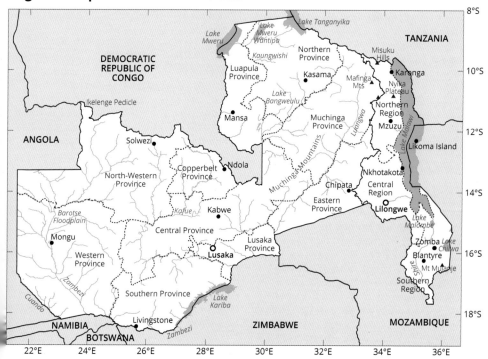

fauna; Nyika Plateau, which has some Tanzanian elements but also elements of the central region and some unique species; and the Misuku Hills complex, which has more Tanzanian elements. The Highlands Region contains the majority of the endemic species and is therefore of great conservation importance. Species representative of this region include Anchieta's Chameleon (*Chamaeleo anchietae*), Nyika Girdled Lizard (*Cordylus nyikae*), Cross-barred Tree Snake (*Dipsadoboa flavida*), Shire Slug-eater (*Duberria shirana*), Mulanje Chameleon (*Nadzikambia mlanjensis*), Mitchell's Flat Lizard (*Platysaurus mitchelli*), Mulanje Montane Skink (*Proscelotes mlanjensis*) and Montane Three-striped Skink (*Trachylepis hildae*).

Eastern Region

Some species occur widely in eastern Africa, including Mozambique and Tanzania. Some are widespread in savannas while others show more specific habitat requirements and are restricted to forests or wetlands, and in the region most of these species are largely restricted to Malawi. Some examples are the Slender Giant Blind Snake (*Afrotyphlops obtusus*), Mozambique Agama (*Agama mossambica*), Black Centipede-eater (*Aparallactus guentheri*), Zambezi Soft-shelled Terrapin (*Cycloderma frenatum*), Green Mamba (*Dendroaspis angusticeps*), Eastern Saw-tailed Lizard (*Holaspis laevis*), Eastern Hinged Tortoise (*Kinixys zombensis*), Forest Marsh Snake (*Natriciteres sylvatica*), Eastern Vine Snake (*Thelotornis mossambicanus*) and Boulenger's Skink (*Trachylepis boulengeri*).

East African Savanna Region

Several East African species enter the region in north-eastern Zambia. Some of these are widespread across Central Africa and into West Africa, while others have their distribution predominantly associated with East Africa. Species typical of this region include Smooth Chameleon (*Chamaeleo laevigatus*), Tornier's Cat Snake (*Crotaphopeltis tornieri*), Tubercled Fragile-skinned Gecko (*Elasmodactylus tuberculosus*), Slender Gracile Blind Snake (*Letheobia gracilis*), Pancake Tortoise (*Malacochersus tornieri*), Speckled Green Snake (*Philothamnus punctatus*) and Grey Hook-nosed Snake (*Scaphiophis albopunctatus*).

Zambian Region

A few species have the majority of their range confined to Zambia, while one species, the Kafue Dwarf Worm Lizard (*Zygaspis kafuensis*), is endemic to this region. Other species include Rasmussen's Night Adder (*Causus rasmusseni*) and Zambian Sand Snake (*Psammophis zambiensis*). These reptiles typically inhabit woodlands on a variety of soil types.

Southern African Savanna Region

This region lies in extreme southern Zambia, becoming slightly wider in eastern Zambia, and encompasses much of south-central and southern Malawi, excluding the highlands. It consists of mainly savanna, woodland or rupicolous species that are widespread in southern Africa, some of which also extend into Zambia and/or Malawi. Examples of these include Reticulated Centipede-eater (*Aparallactus lunulatus*), Rough-scaled Plated Lizard (*Broadleysaurus major*), Incognito Thread Snake (*Leptotyphlops incognitus*), Peters' Thread Snake (*Leptotyphlops scutifrons*), Variegated Wolf Snake (*Lycophidion variegatum*), Mozambique Spitting Cobra (*Naja mossambica*) and Bicoloured Quill-snouted Snake (*Xenocalamus bicolor*).

Widespread species

Many of the species occurring in Zambia and Malawi are common, widespread species that are found across most, if not all, of the above biogeographical regions. Some of the widespread species, such as Brown House Snake (*Boaedon capensis*), Northern Boomslang (*Dispholidus viridis*) and Spotted Bush Snake (*Philothamnus semivariegatus*), are believed to comprise several distinct species and are the subjects of further taxonomic research. Others appear to have wide habitat tolerances and/or a generalist diet, such as Zambezi Giant Blind Snake (*Afrotyphlops mucruso*), Common Purple-glossed Snake (*Amblyodipsas polylepis*), Flap-necked Chameleon (*Chamaeleo dilepis*), Black-templed Cat Snake (*Crotaphopeltis hotamboeia*), Rhombic Egg-eater (*Dasypeltis scabra*), Black Mamba (*Dendroaspis polylepis*), Speke's Hinged Tortoise (*Kinixys spekii*), Common Dwarf Gecko (*Lygodactylus capensis*), Olive Sand Snake (*Psammophis mossambicus*) and Southern African Python (*Python natalensis*).

VENOM TYPES AND SNAKEBITE TREATMENT

Of the 117 snake species recorded in the region, only 35 have venom considered to be either life threatening or dangerous to humans. Several species are considered mildly venomous. Here, 'mildly' refers to the venom's effect on most humans, as it may be potently effective against the snake's typical prey. For most people, a bite from a mildly venomous snake will have no effect, but people with venom sensitivities may find themselves in a life-threatening situation. Venom sensitivities appear to be pre-existing in some people, while gradually developing in others through repeated exposure. Someone who initially shows no reaction to the bite of a mildly venomous species may, over time, become so sensitive that a bite from the same species results in the rapid onset of anaphylactic shock. As such, all snakes should be treated with caution, even those that are considered to have venom that is not dangerous to humans, and bites should always be avoided.

There are three basic venom types among the snakes in the region, namely cytotoxic, haemotoxic and neurotoxic venom. Most snake bites do not require antivenom and can be treated symptomatically. However, in the case of a severe adder bite as well as with some cobra and mamba bites, the use of antivenom greatly reduces the extent of tissue damage and may immediately reverse the effects of neurotoxic venom. Because of the way that antivenom is produced, however, the antivenom itself holds a high risk of inducing

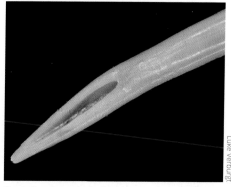

The hollow fang of a Puff Adder

Luke Verburgt

anaphylactic shock and should be administered only by a medical practitioner and ideally in a hospital environment where there is capacity to deal with potentially fatal side-effects.

Cytotoxic Venom

Most adders, vipers and burrowing asps (*Atheris*, *Atractaspis*, *Bitis*, *Causus* and *Proatheris*) have cytotoxic venom, while the two spitting cobras (*Naja*) have cytotoxic properties to their venom. The three garter snakes (*Elapsoidea*) are also believed to have mild cytotoxic venom that may require medical attention in the event of a bite, although bites are not believed to be life threatening to most people. Cytotoxic venom affects the soft tissue

The Black Mamba is the largest venomous snake in the region. Its venom is potently neurotoxic and cardiotoxic and is produced in large quantities.

Venom classification

Each snake species account in this field guide is accompanied by an icon indicating the danger its venom poses to humans.

🕱 Life threatening

🕱 Dangerous

🕱 Mildly venomous

🕱 Harmless

🕱 Unknown

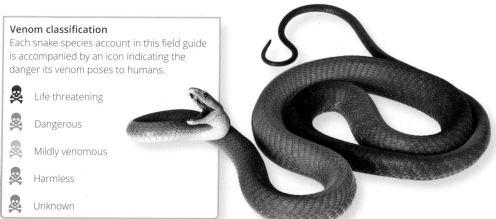

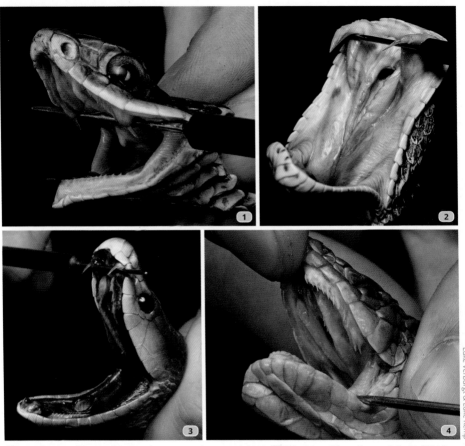

Luke Verburgt & Luke Kemp

1 The fixed rear fangs of the Northern Boomslang, a colubrid. **2** The hinged front fangs of the Puff Adder, a viperid. **3** The fixed front fangs of the Black Mamba, an elapid. **4** The enlarged teeth of the Mole Snake, a colubrid.

cells and blood vessel walls, resulting in leakage of fluid into the intracellular space which results in swelling and may also lead to local necrosis. In the event of a bite, the patient should be reassured and kept calm. The limb should be elevated but a pressure bandage should not be applied, as this localises the venom and increases tissue damage. Polyvalent antivenom may be required, especially for the bites of large adders (*Bitis*) where antivenom may limit the amount of tissue damage. In the event of venom being squirted into the eyes (spitting cobras), the patient's eyes should immediately be flushed with copious amounts of running water. If running water is not immediately available, any benign liquid should be used.

Haemotoxic Venom

Boomslangs (*Dispholidus*) and vine snakes (*Thelotornis*) have haemotoxic venom, while the Gaboon Adder (*Bitis gabonica*) has a predominantly cytotoxic venom with some haemotoxic properties. Haemotoxic venom destroys the red blood cells and prevents blood clotting, resulting in internal and subcutaneous bleeding as well as uncontrolled bleeding from orifices and any open wounds. In the event of a bite, the patient should be calmed and reassured, and the affected limb immobilised. A pressure bandage, strapped to the same pressure as for a sprained ankle, should be applied to the affected limb, starting at the bite site and working up the limb and then down over the bite site again. The limb should then be immobilised using a splint. The patient should be transported to a medical facility where they should remain under observation for at least 48 hours: haemotoxic venom is usually very slow acting and symptoms may take up to 48 hours to manifest (although in very rare cases symptoms may appear within 20 minutes). A monovalent antivenom for boomslangs is currently available only from producers in South Africa.

Neurotoxic Venom

Mambas (*Dendroaspis*), cobras (*Naja*) and Blanding's Tree Snake (*Toxicodryas blandingii*) have neurotoxic venom. Neurotoxic venom is probably the deadliest of the three venom types, as it predominantly affects the nervous system and in a rapid manner, although it usually affects other tissues to a lesser extent as well. In the event of a bite, the patient should be calmed and reassured, and the affected limb immobilised. The limb should be bandaged using a pressure bandage strapped at the same pressure as would be used for a sprained ankle, starting at the bite site and working up the limb before proceeding down the limb and over the bite site. The limb should also be immobilised using a splint. The patient should be transported to the nearest medical facility as quickly as is safely possible. If the patient experiences difficulty breathing, mouth-to-mouth resuscitation or a bag-valve mask can be used to assist them, although the use of the latter requires training. CPR can be used successfully to keep patients alive who have stopped breathing and whose hearts have stopped. Once started, CPR needs to be continued until medical assistance is obtained. Polyvalent antivenom may be required, especially in the case of mambas and non-spitting cobras.

The reader is also directed to the books *Snakes and snakebite in southern Africa* (Marais, 2014) and *The snakes of Zimbabwe and Botswana* (Broadley and Blaylock, 2013), which provide treatment protocols for many of the snake species that occur in Zambia and Malawi.

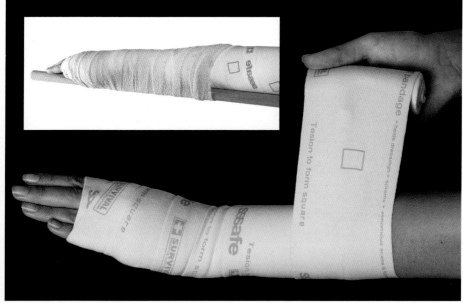

The correct way to apply a pressure bandage. Bandage the bitten limb starting from the bite site (likely the extremity) and working your way up the limb towards the body. Apply the bandage at the same pressure as for a sprained ankle. Note that some bandages have rectangles printed on them that must be tensioned until they form a square, which indicates the correct application pressure. Once the limb has been bandaged, splint it to further minimise movement.

REGIONAL ENDEMICS

Schmitz's Legless Skink *Acontias schmitzi* 1
A medium-sized legless skink with a flattened and pointed snout. The back is blue-grey to dark, and the lower half of flanks and ventrum are yellow-white to light orange. It is known from only three specimens. **Range:** Western Zambia, east of the Zambezi River.

Nyika Girdled Lizard *Cordylus nyikae* 2
A medium-sized cordylid with a stocky, flattened body and a broad, triangular head covered in rough scales. This diurnal lizard inhabits narrow rock cracks and small rock outcrops in montane grassland. **Range:** Nyika Plateau and Misuku Mountains.

Cross-barred Tree Snake *Dipsadoboa flavida flavida* 3
A slender snake with a broad, flattened head and a long tail. The head is bright yellow, with red-brown mottling. This nocturnal, predominantly arboreal snake is mildly venomous. **Range:** The typical subspecies is endemic to Mount Mulanje.

Nyika Serpentiform Skink *Eumecia johnstoni*
A long, serpentine skink known only from the type specimen, which was collected in 1896. Given that this species has not been observed in more than 120 years, it may be extinct. **Range:** The exact collecting locality is debated and was originally given as the Nyika Plateau, although some authorities believe that it may have been collected near Livingstonia.

Mulanje Dwarf Gecko *Lygodactylus bonsi* 4
A robust dwarf gecko with a pair of lateral clefts in the mental. The body is olive-brown, with scattered pale spots. It inhabits rock outcrops in high-elevation montane grassland and boulder-fields with scrub-heathland. **Range:** Mount Mulanje.

Mulanje Chameleon *Nadzikambia mlanjensis* 5
A small chameleon with a cranial crest. The body is green to orange, usually with blue infusions on the lower back and two pale triangular bars on each flank. This arboreal chameleon favours sub-montane evergreen forest. **Range:** Mount Mulanje.

Mitchell's Flat Lizard *Platysaurus mitchelli* 6
A large flat lizard that usually forms small colonies. Adults are most often found on vertical cliffs, but also inhabit boulders at the forest edge and in grassland on the valley floor. **Range:** Mount Mulanje.

Mulanje Montane Skink *Proscelotes mlanjensis* 7
A small skink with smooth, close-fitting scales and
a brown body. It is fossorial and probably diurnal,
inhabiting montane grassland and evergreen forest
and hunting in leaf litter and under rotting logs.
Range: Mount Mulanje.

Chapman's Pygmy Chameleon
Rhampholeon chapmanorum 8
A small chameleon with a laterally compressed body
and a very short tail. The body is a mottled pale brown,
becoming paler ventrolaterally. It inhabits lowland
seasonal rain forest, and is usually encountered
perched on leaves, twigs or moss in the understorey.
Range: Natundu Hills Range in southern Malawi.

Mulanje Pygmy Chameleon
Rhampholeon platyceps 9
A fairly large pygmy chameleon with a laterally
compressed body and a very short tail. The body is
grey-brown to olive-brown, sometimes with a darker
head. This terrestrial chameleon spends most of its
time on leaf litter or in low shrubs during the day, and
sleeps in low shrubs at night. **Range:** Mount Mulanje.

Montane Three-striped Skink *Trachylepis hildae* 10
A small, robust skink with numerous dark speckles and
streaks that usually form two broad bands either side
of dorsal midline. It inhabits open montane grassland
and rock outcrops. **Range:** Nyika Plateau in northern
Malawi, and adjacent Zambia.

Mulanje Skink *Trachylepis mlanjensis* 11
A relatively small, montane skink. The back is dark
brown with numerous lighter flecks and three equally
sized pale dorsal stripes. This active, diurnal skink
inhabits montane grassland and rock outcrops.
Range: Mount Mulanje and Dedza Mountain.

Roux's Dart Skink *Typhlacontias gracilis*
A small, slender skink that lacks external limbs. It
resembles Rohan's Dart Skink (*T. rohani*) and is found
in woodland on Kalahari sands. **Range:** Western
Zambia, west of the Zambezi River.

Kafue Dwarf Worm Lizard *Zygaspis kafuensis* 12
A large worm lizard with a rounded head and fairly
long tail. It is a uniform purple-brown above and paler
below. It is fossorial, and is often found in the top layer
of soil or under suitable cover. **Range:** Kafue Flats.

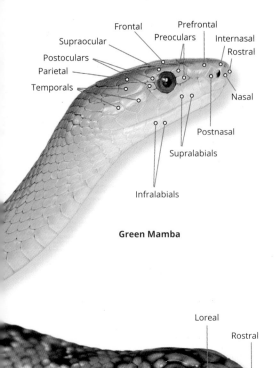

Green Mamba

Labels: Frontal, Prefrontal, Preoculars, Internasal, Supraocular, Rostral, Postoculars, Parietal, Temporals, Nasal, Postnasal, Supralabials, Infralabials

REPTILE IDENTIFICATION USING SCALES

Scale type and arrangement are important features in reptile identification. When identifying snakes and lizards, head scales are of particular importance, as are the number of scale rows at midbody, along the belly and under the tail.

The start of each order and suborder account (and some family accounts) includes head diagrams indicating scales that are important when identifying the relevant reptiles. As a starting point, some of these are discussed below. Further scale terminology appears in the **Glossary** (p. 366).

Snakes and lizards

Snakes and lizards have many scales in common and are thus dealt with simultaneously. The **rostral** is the scale on the tip of a reptile's snout. Some species (especially burrowing species) have an enlarged rostral, which may also contain a **sulcus**: a groove or furrow that extends from the nostril to the posterior margin of the rostral. **Nasals** either enclose or touch the nostrils. If there is more than one nasal, the uppermost nasal is called the **supranasal** and the lower one is called the **infranasal**. The scale bordering the nasal posteriorly is the **postnasal**. The scales between the nasals are called **internasals** and may be discrete or fused.

The **frontal** is situated more or less in the middle of the head and is usually a single, large scale. Separate or fused **prefrontals** are situated immediately in front of it.

Labials are, by definition, always in contact with the mouth. **Supralabials** and **infralabials** are usually enlarged and form a row along the upper and lower lip respectively. Supralabials may enter the orbit (i.e. be in contact with the eye), or be separated from the eye by the **subocular**.

Supraciliaries are located immediately above the eye, while **supraoculars** are situated between the supraciliaries and the frontal. **Frontoparietals** are situated between the frontal(s) and the **parietals**, which are situated towards the back of the head and are in contact with the frontal or frontoparietal(s) anteriorly.

The **preocular** borders the eye anteriorly in those species with an exposed eye. In those species where the eye is covered by the **ocular**,

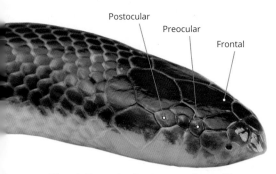

Labels: Loreal, Rostral, Nasals

The **Mole Snake** has a slightly hooked snout with an enlarged rostral. The nostril is usually situated between two nasals. A loreal is present.

Labels: Postocular, Preocular, Frontal

Bibron's Burrowing Asp has a small eye, with one preocular bordering it anteriorly and one postocular bordering it posteriorly. A single, large frontal is situated in the middle of the head.

the preocular is situated immediately anterior to the ocular. The **postocular** is in contact with the posterior border of the exposed eye, and immediately posterior to the ocular when the eye is not exposed. The **subocular** is in contact with the lower border of the eye (or the ocular, when the eye is not exposed) and in some species is also in contact with the mouth. **Loreals** are situated on the side of the head between the nostril and the eye but do not contact either.

Temporals are situated on the side of the head, behind the postoculars and above the supralabials, and can be single or paired. There are usually between one and three sets of temporals (in one species, the temporals are fragmented into numerous smaller scales).

The anterior-most scale on the lower jaw of a reptile is called the **mental**, and is often enlarged. The mental is bordered on each side by the infralabials, which extend posteriorly along the lower lip. The enlarged scales immediately behind the mental and in contact with the infralabials along their sides are termed **sublinguals**, and there may be up to three pairs extending posteriorly. In geckos, the small scales bordering the mental are called **postmentals**.

Chameleons and agamas

Chameleons and agamas have certain features that require their own terminology. In chameleons, the **casque** is the raised, helmet-like structure found on the back of the head while the **saggital crest** is a raised bony projection at the back of the head that is in line with the vertebral midline. **Occipital lobes** (or ear flaps) are bony projections on the sides of a chameleon's head which are attached to the casque medially but are unattached posteriorly and laterally. The **supraorbital crest** is a small, raised ridge above the eye. In both chameleons and agamas, the *canthus rostralis* refers to the angular region between the top and side of the head, between the eye and the snout.

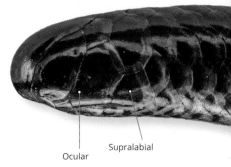

An ocular covers the eye of the **Incognito Thread Snake**, bordered posteriorly by a single large supralabial.

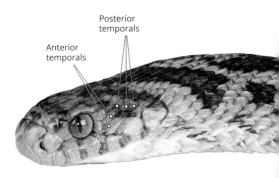

The **Rhombic Egg-eater** usually has two anterior and three posterior temporals.

The **Flap-necked Chameleon** has a casque that is slightly raised posteriorly, as well as prominent supraorbital crests and large occipital lobes.

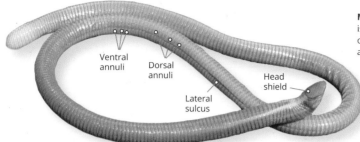

Maurice's Worm Lizard is covered in rings of non-overlapping scales known as annuli.

Ventral annuli

Dorsal annuli

Lateral sulcus

Head shield

Worm lizards

The scales of worm lizards differ from those of other lizards, and have terminology unique to them. Many worm lizards have one or two enlarged bony plates on their head, which aid in digging. These are called **head shields**. Body scales are known as **annuli** (singular: annulus), and can be further separated into dorsal and ventral annuli depending on whether they occur above or below the thin, unscaled dividing line on the flanks (the **lateral sulcus**). In addition to annuli, many worm lizards have dorsal half-annuli: incomplete annulus rings that are present only on one side of the body. Some worm lizards have 1–3 pairs of enlarged **pectorals** in the 'neck' region, starting on the belly and extending to the lower flanks.

Dorsal annuli are counted in a straight line from the first scale above the lateral sulcus on the one side of the body to the last scale above the lateral sulcus on the other side of the body. **Ventral annuli** are counted from the first scale row below the lateral sulcus on one side of the body to the last scale row below the lateral sulcus on the other side of the body. Many worm lizards have dorsal

annuli that are narrower than the ventral annuli, and in some the dorsal annuli may also only be present on one side of the body. Because of this, **body annuli** are counted from the 3rd infralabial, over the top of the enlarged pectoral scales (when present) and then along the lower margin of the lateral sulcus.

Tortoises and terrapins

The individual hard plates that cover a chelonian (tortoise and terrapin) shell are termed **scutes**, and the central portion of each scute is termed the **areolus**. The anterior-most scute on the carapace is the **nuchal**. The median row of enlarged dorsal scutes are termed **vertebrals**, the large scales on the sides are termed **costals**, and the lower-most row of smaller dorsal scales are termed **marginals**. The posterior-most marginal scales above the tail are also referred to as **supracaudals**. See the figure on p. 339 for detailed shell illustrations.

Chelonian beaks can have a single anterior point (**unicuspid**), one point on either side (**bicuspid**) or a single anterior point and an additional point on each side (**tricuspid**).

In worm lizards the eye is covered by the ocular.

Luke Verburgt

The beak of the Eastern Hinged Tortoise is unicuspid.

SCALE TYPES

There are various scale types, all of which can aid in the identification of reptiles. Most chelonians have large, fairly thin scales (scutes) overlying their bony shells. Crocodylians and some lizard species have osteoderms, which are bony plates ensconced in their scales. Squamates can have either abutting or overlapping scales (the latter termed imbricate scales), and they can further be drawn into a terminal spine (mucronate). Abutting scales can be rectangular or granular, and small or enlarged (termed tubercles). Overlapping scales usually resemble fish scales, with the posterior portion overlapping the anterior portion of the next scale. Scales can be smooth, rough or keeled (having one or more raised ridges), and some scales may have up to seven rows of parallel keels.

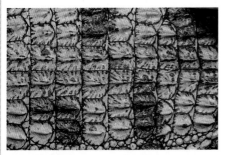

Enlarged osteoderms (scales with bony plates inside of them) of a Nile Crocodile.

Abutting granular tubercles (rounded scales) of a Kalahari Thick-toed Gecko.

Overlapping mucronate scales with a central keel (ridge), as found in Puff Adders.

Close-fitting, smooth and overlapping scales are found in many lizard species.

Smooth, overlapping scales are found in many snake species.

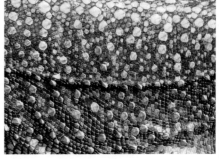

Most agamas and many geckos have a mosaic of enlarged and small scales.

Counting body scales

Various scale counts are useful when identifying reptiles. Counts may refer to ventrals (the scales on the belly), dorsals (those on the back), or subcaudals (those on the underside of the tail). Scale rows are often defined relative to their position to the cloaca, the common cavity at the end of the digestive system that is used to excrete waste products and provides access to the genitalia. The cloaca also marks the end of the body and the start of the tail.

The counts done and methodology followed may depend on the information available – perhaps only one side of the body is visible in a photograph, or just a section of the tail.

In snakes, **midbody scale rows** are counted at a position midway between the snout and the cloaca. The ventral scale row is not included in this count. Instead, scales are counted from the first scale bordering the ventral on the one side of the body to the last scale bordering the ventral on the opposite side. See the section and figure unpacking the different ways to determine the number of midbody scale rows opposite.

In some snake species, the **anterior/posterior scale rows** need to be counted. This is done using the same methodology as for midbody scale rows, but these values are counted one head length posterior to the head and one head length anterior to the cloaca, respectively.

The number of ventrals and subcaudals are also key identification features for many snake and some lizard species. Most herpetologists have adopted the Dowling system of counting **ventrals**, whereby ventrals are defined as those scales that are bordered by a dorsal scale on each side. Counts run from the first ventral to the last scale bordering (but not including) the cloacal scale. **Subcaudals** are counted from the first scale posterior to the cloaca to the tip of the tail. In those species with paired subcaudals, only one of the two rows are counted.

In blind snakes, **middorsal scale counts** are used, as these reptiles do not have distinct ventral scales. Middorsal scale rows are counted from the first scale posterior to the rostral to the last scale before the terminal tail spine.

Many lizard species do not have distinct size or shape differences between the dorsal and ventral scales, and in these cases **midbody scale counts** are the total number of scales counted in a straight line around the whole body at a position midway between the front and hind limbs.

Some lizards do have enlarged ventral scales, the number of which can assist with identifying the species. In lizards, ventrals are defined as the first row of belly scales that are bordered by dorsal scales on both sides. **Longitudinal ventral rows** run from the head to the cloaca, and are thus counted across the body. **Transverse ventral rows** run across the body from one side to the other, and are counted from the first row of scales anteriorly that are bordered by dorsal scales on both sides to the last full row before the cloacal scale. **Subcaudals** are counted from the first scale posterior to the cloaca to the tip of the tail, usually along the medial scale row.

The Brown House Snake has smooth, overlapping dorsals that are usually in 23–35 rows at midbody.

Frank Willems

Ventrals are defined as those scales bordered by a dorsal scale on each side. In the case of the Eastern Striped Swamp Snake, the yellow ventrals are easy to distinguish from the dark dorsals.

Holub's Scrub Lizard has granular, flattened dorsals, which are usually in 41–65 rows at midbody.

Counting midbody scale rows

The schematic figure on the right shows the ventrals (enlarged belly scales) on either side and the single dorsal midline row in the middle, i.e. if you were to skin a snake along the belly and lie the skin flat. In this case, there are 19 dorsal scale rows (this number is almost always odd in snakes because of the single row at the dorsal midline).

There are three ways to determine the number of midbody scale rows: **A** count in a zig-zag pattern directly across the body; **B** count diagonally to the midline and then reverse the direction of counting (i.e. if you were counting diagonally towards the front on the one side, you switch to counting diagonally towards the back on the other side); **C** count diagonally across the body.

If only one side of a body is visible, the scale rows can be counted using any of these methods, starting at the first scale bordering the ventral and ending at the last scale bordering (but excluding) the dorsal midline. Double this value, and add one ([side one count x 2] + 1).

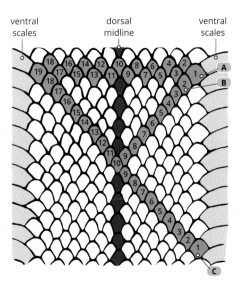

ventral scales   dorsal midline   ventral scales

HOW TO USE THIS BOOK

This field guide describes every species of reptile currently known to occur in Zambia and Malawi. Newcomers to the subject may find it difficult to distinguish species within a group. With practice, however, identifying reptiles to species level can become second nature.

When you spot a reptile, try to photograph it or make field notes of any morphological characteristics and behaviour that you can see: shape, size, colour and patterns, as well as location and habitat. Some features offer simple clues, such as the presence of an external shell, indicating a tortoise or terrapin. The presence of legs would suggest a lizard (not all lizards have legs, but no snakes have legs).

Identification keys

To make this book useful to both the novice and the experienced herpetologist, we provide different tiers of dichotomous identification keys based predominantly on morphological differences. There is a key at the start of the snake, lizard, chelonian and crocodile section to help you determine the genus a reptile belongs to. Keys consist of numbered pairs of choices (labelled option 'a' or 'b') that branch to either the next pair of choices, or the genus/species name. Read option 'a' and see whether your reptile matches this description. If not, proceed to 'b' and see whether it matches better. Once you determine the genus, proceed to the relevant genus account and a further key will help you to identify the particular species.

After you have identified your reptile using the key, read the description in the species account and check whether it matches your reptile. If it does not, go back to the key. There was possibly a step where you were unsure of which option to choose – try the alternative option. Always bear in mind that reptiles can show variation in colour, scale arrangements and counts, and so on, though we have tried to use characters in the keys that are uniform within each species to minimise these instances.

Look at the known and predicted distribution of that species and compare it to where you saw your reptile. Owing to the limited data available, predicted distributions may not be entirely accurate, but they will give a good indication of which species are most likely to occur in a particular area. If the species you have identified is not known or predicted to occur where you observed it, it does not necessarily mean that you have incorrectly identified your reptile. Even in countries that are well surveyed, geographic range extensions of species frequently occur. It may also be a human-assisted translocation.

Sharing knowledge

If you have recorded a species outside of its known geographic distribution, it is important to make this information available in the public domain. Many species' conservation assessments (commonly known as the IUCN Red List Assessments and available on www.iucnredlist.org) rely on species distribution to determine what threats they face. Infrastructure developments use this information for impact assessments, and conservation interventions for threatened species also rely on having accurate distribution data. If you find a species where it has not been recorded before, a good starting point is taking a photograph and uploading it to a citizen science platform such as the ReptileMAP Virtual Museum (vmus.adu.org.za) or iNaturalist (inaturalist.org). See also **Useful Contacts** (p. 372).

KEY Regional *Leptotyphlops* species

1a Discrete prefrontal separates rostral from supraoculars 2
 b Rostral fused with prefrontal, in contact with supraoculars 3

2a Cloacal scale triangular; 198–244 middorsal scales; nostril separated
 from rostral by longer suture . . . . *L. emini* (p. 46)
 b Cloacal scale heart-shaped; 209–267 middorsal scales;
 nostril separated from rostral by shorter suture . . . . *L. kafubi* (p. 48)

3a Rostral barely extends past posterior border of eye; rostral less
 than a third of head width at level of eye . . . . *L. incognitus* (p. 47)
 b Rostral extends well past posterior border of eye; rostral more
 than a third of head width at level of eye . . . . *L. scutifrons* (p. 48)

Adders and Vipers
Family Viperidae

1 The members of this family are characterised by large, erectile fangs in protective membranous sheaths, situated in the front of the mouth. The fangs are swung forward and locked into position when the snake strikes or eats and folded back against the roof of the mouth when not in use.

Puff Adder

These snakes generally have a squat body and most species have a large, triangular head that is distinct from the body (it is fairly narrow and only slightly distinct in night adders [*Causus*]). The head is covered in numerous small, non-overlapping and asymmetrically arranged scales (in night adders, there are usually nine large scales). The body scales are relatively small and strongly keeled in most species, but smooth and appearing velvety in night adders.

Most species are terrestrial, although some species are arboreal while others are semi-aquatic and a single species is fossorial. They are predominantly nocturnal or crepuscular, but also display a fair amount of diurnal activity. They prey on a wide variety of vertebrates, mainly small mammals, amphibians and lizards, which are killed by envenomation. Hunting is mostly done from ambush, relying on superb camouflage to escape detection. Females either lay eggs which develop outside of their bodies, or retain the eggs within their bodies until the embryos complete their development.

The family consists of two well-defined radiations, namely pit vipers (Crotalinae), which mainly occur in the Americas and Asia, and Old World adders (Viperinae), which largely occur in Western Europe and Africa. There are 331 species in 35 genera which occur near-globally (they are absent from Australia, Antarctica and many oceanic islands). A total of 11 species in four genera occur in the region (with one species that is claimed to occur but lacks supporting evidence).

FLOODPLAIN VIPERS *Proatheris*

2 Small adders with a moderately robust body. The dorsal head scales are small and keeled, except for a pair of large, rugose supraoculars. The nasals are in broad contact with the rostral. There is no duplication of transverse dorsal scale rows. The subcaudals are paired. This genus contains a single species.

3 Floodplain Viper   *Proatheris superciliaris* **4**   **5**

6 Max. SVL ♂ 513mm ♀ 600mm

7 A small, moderately robust snake with an elongate and depressed head that is distinct from the neck. Snout short, rounded. Head covered in small keeled scales, except for supraoculars, which are large, rugose. Nostrils large, directed dorsolaterally. 1–3 internasals; 5–7 interorbitals; 8–14 circumorbitals. 8–11 supralabials; 10–13 infralabials, first 4 in contact with single pair of sublinguals. Dorsals strongly keeled, imbricate, in 27–29 (rarely 26 or 30) rows at midbody; no duplication of transverse dorsal scale rows. Outermost dorsal scale row enlarged, feebly keeled to smooth. 131–156 ventrals; 32–45 paired subcaudals; cloacal scale entire. Body pale grey-brown to brown, with numerous dark spots or blotches along back. These correspond with dark spots or

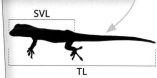

Annotation key (right sidebar)

1 Family account
2 Genus account
3 Common name
4 Scientific name
5 Venom classification
6 Size (max/average)
7 Species description
8 Footer: Family name

Abbreviations
SVL = Snout–vent length
TL = Total length

SVL

TL

REPTILE DISTRIBUTION

This book aimed to collate all distribution data for reptiles in Zambia and Malawi. In a rigorous and lengthy data collection process, more than 16,000 records were scrutinised. Geographic distributions were predicted using computer modelling software. This involved comparing verified occurrences to a suite of environmental variables (including elevation, habitat, and climate variables). For a full overview of the methods used, please visit https://bit.ly/3gAcs8L. As our predicted geographic distributions rely on verified data and a carefully constructed spatial modelling process, they are more accurate than traditional field guide distribution maps that were mostly hand-drawn and relied on the authors' own 'gut feel'. Nevertheless, exercise caution when interpreting these predicted distributions, as they are not the true distribution of a given species, but a likely estimate based on current information.

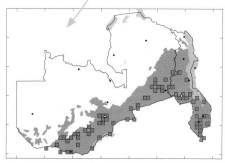

☐ Verified observation   ☐ Predicted distribution

SCALED REPTILES
Order Squamata

SQUAMATA,

or scaled reptiles, is the most diverse order of living reptiles, with 9,400 extant species worldwide. This number is increasing continually as species new to science are discovered and described. These reptiles have a global distribution (excepting Antarctica) and occupy almost all environments, including oceans.

There are two suborders within the scaled reptiles, namely snakes (suborder Serpentes) and lizards (suborder Sauria). Snakes are well known for their elongate shape and lack of external limbs, whereas lizards typically have a long body, four legs and a tail, although some have a serpentine shape and are limbless, giving them a similar appearance to snakes.

Squamates are distinguished from other reptiles by their scaly skin, which is covered by a thin, dry, horny layer. Unlike other reptiles, they periodically shed their skin, exposing a fresh new layer as the old one is sloughed.

Spotted Thick-toed Gecko

Snakes exude a thin layer of moisture between the old skin and the new to promote the removal of the old layer, which is sloughed off in one piece. This gives snakes a light grey or pale blue appearance as the new layer is exposed. Most lizards do not undergo this 'blue' phase, as they shed their skin in pieces. Many lizards eat the skin flakes as they discard them, thereby recycling valuable nutrients.

The squamate skull is diapsid, having both an upper and lower temporal opening, and there is no continuous roof to the mouth. Osteoderms (bony plates) are largely absent, but may be present on the bodies and heads of some lizard species, such as plated lizards.

Most snake and lizard species are oviparous, although several species retain the eggs in the body until after they have hatched. The cloacal aperture is orientated laterally and males have two sex organs called hemipenes. The hemipenes usually bear numerous spines, flounces and sulci. The structure of these organs can play an important role when trying to distinguish between two morphologically similar species. The hemipenes are inverted and stored in sheaths at the base of the tail. During copulation only one hemipenis is used at a time. Owing to the location of the hemipenes, most mature squamates can be sexed during the breeding season by the presence (male) or absence (female) of a pronounced swelling at the base of the tail.

Black-templed Cat Snake ready to strike.

Snakes
Suborder Serpentes

Snakes are specialised elongate squamates that lack external limbs, ear openings and osteoderms. More than 3,500 snake species in more than 450 genera and 18 families have been described worldwide. Of these, 113 species in 13 families have been recorded in the region.

Rhombic Night Adder

The head can be large and distinct from the body, or small and nearly indistinguishable from it. The eyelids are transparent and immovable, and in some species the eyes are reduced and only visible as dark spots beneath the head scales. The tongue is elongate and forked and retracts into a sheath on the floor of the mouth. The left lung is reduced or absent, leaving only the right lung functional. The skeletal system consists of numerous vertebrae (more than 400 in some species) and many articulating ribs. The latter are used to maintain the body's shape and for locomotion. Some primitive species retain vestiges of the pelvic girdle, such as the small spurs present on either side of the cloaca in pythons. In most species the ventral scales are broader than they are long, which further aids locomotion.

Because of the lack of external ear openings (and the loss of tympana and Eustachian tubes), snakes cannot hear airborne sounds, instead detecting low-frequency vibrations with the inner ear. They also sense vibrations that travel through the ground. Snakes rely on their acute sense of 'smell' to detect prey. When the forked tongue is extended, it collects small particles from the air or from surfaces. When retracted, the tongue slides into Jacobson's Organ in the roof of the mouth, where the chemicals trapped on the tongue surface are analysed. By comparing the intensity of odour particles on one fork of the tongue with that on the other, snakes are able to determine the direction of an odour and so 'track' prey items. The same mechanism is used to detect potential mates.

Luke Verburgt

A Snouted Cobra spreads its hood. Like most snakes, its ventral scales are broader than they are long.

Luke Verburgt

The head of the semi-arboreal Eastern Bark Snake is slightly distinct from the neck.

All snakes are carnivorous and adapted to consume large meals infrequently. Prey is swallowed whole and most species are able to dislocate the lower jaw to accommodate the swallowing of large prey. Most species also have the two halves of the lower jaw joined by an elastic ligament, allowing for some lateral movement. The skin of the lower jaw (and neck) is distensible, further facilitating the consumption of large prey, while the individual bones making up the skull are also capable of movement relative to one another (cranial kinesis) when feeding.

Most snake species have numerous teeth, some of which may be enlarged and modified into fangs. Many snake species in the region covered by this field guide are venomous to some degree, but very few have venom that poses a danger to humans. None are poisonous (toxic when ingested).

Snakes, like this Puff Adder, are able to swallow large prey.

Most snakes rely on speed and/or camouflage to escape detection, though some are able to squirt their venom in defence (the so-called spitting cobras of the genus *Naja*). Some species are able to shed their tail, especially sand and whip snakes (*Psammophis*), but once shed the tail cannot be regenerated.

Snakes regularly shed their skin as they grow, usually in a single piece starting from the snout. Prior to shedding, the snake secretes an oily liquid between the new and the old skin, giving it a dull or pale blue appearance. Because the eyes of snakes are covered by a transparent immovable scale, the secreted moisture also covers the eye, thus reducing the snake's vision. Snakes are said to be 'in the blue' during this stage and most remain hidden and inactive until this moisture is reabsorbed and vision is restored. Snakes that are disturbed while 'in the blue' may behave more aggressively and lash out if they detect movement. A snake will loosen the old skin by rubbing its snout against a rock, log or other rough surface. As it slithers along, the loose edges of the skin get snagged on surrounding structures and the snake literally slides out of its old skin, inverting it in the process (like a person removing a sock).

Johan Marais

Snakes shed their skin as a single unit, starting from the head.

Most snakes lay leathery, soft-shelled eggs in a moist, warm location under any suitable cover (logs or rocks, in crevices or holes dug by other species, inside tree hollows, etc.). The females of some species (especially adders of the genus *Bitis*) retain the eggs within their bodies until the embryos complete their development. Certain species show varying degrees of maternal care.

Snakes are amongst the most feared of all reptiles, topped possibly by crocodiles. However, they perform a crucial ecological function, keeping pest numbers (such as many rodent species) in balance. If snakes are removed from the ecosystem, these pests are able to proliferate, with dire consequences for human health and food security.

Snakes occur on every continent except Antarctica and have been introduced into Ireland, New Zealand and various oceanic islands.

HEAD AND VENTRAL BODY SCALES OF AN ADVANCED SNAKE

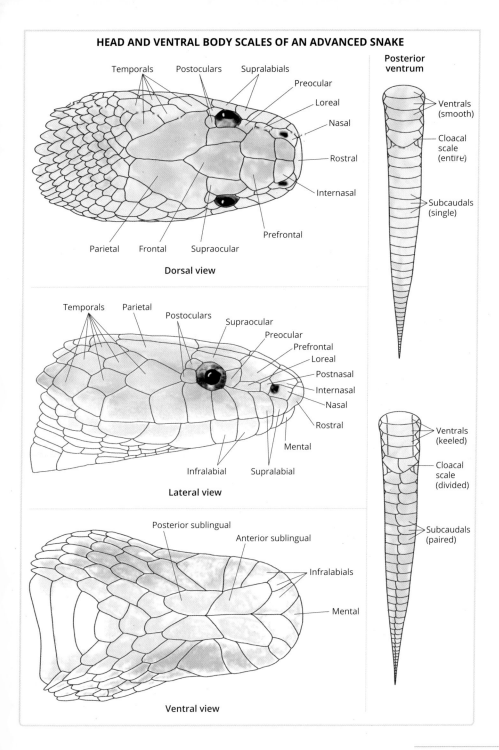

Dorsal view

- Temporals
- Postoculars
- Supralabials
- Preocular
- Loreal
- Nasal
- Rostral
- Internasal
- Prefrontal
- Supraocular
- Frontal
- Parietal

Lateral view

- Temporals
- Parietal
- Postoculars
- Supraocular
- Preocular
- Prefrontal
- Loreal
- Postnasal
- Internasal
- Nasal
- Rostral
- Mental
- Supralabial
- Infralabial

Ventral view

- Posterior sublingual
- Anterior sublingual
- Infralabials
- Mental

Posterior ventrum

- Ventrals (smooth)
- Cloacal scale (entire)
- Subcaudals (single)

- Ventrals (keeled)
- Cloacal scale (divided)
- Subcaudals (paired)

KEY Genera of Serpentes

1a Body worm-like; head not or only slightly distinct from neck; eyes vestigial,
covered by head scales; body covered in small, similar-sized scales **2**

b Body not worm-like; head distinct from body; eyes well developed, moveable
below transparent spectacle; ventrals laterally elongate **5**

2a Ocular borders lip; 14 scale rows at midbody; tail at least 3 times longer than broad **3**

b Ocular does not border lip; 20 or more scale rows at midbody; tail only slightly
longer than broad **4**

3a Cloacal scale broadly crescent-shaped; body reddish brown to flesh pink
above, ventrum white . . . . *Myriopholis* (p. 44)

b Cloacal scale heart-shaped or triangular; body black to dark brown or
chequered silver above and below . . . . *Leptotyphlops* (p. 46)

4a Eyes not visible; ocular smaller than or subequal to preocular; suboculars
present; body unpigmented, appearing pinkish white . . . . *Letheobia* (p. 51)

b Eyes usually visible (rarely not visible); ocular at least twice the size of
preocular; suboculars absent; body pigmented . . . . *Afrotyphlops* (p. 52)

5a >70 midbody scale rows; some supralabials with deep pits; pair of claws
bordering cloaca . . . . *Python* (p. 59)

b <50 midbody scale rows; no deep pits on supralabials; no claws bordering cloaca **6**

6a Head covered in numerous small, keeled scales **7**

b Head covered in large, smooth, symmetrical scales **9**

7a Subcaudals single; tail relatively long, prehensile; body bright green and black . . . . . . *Atheris* (p. 71)

b Subcaudals paired; tail relatively short; body not bright green and black **8**

8a Single, large supraocular; nasals in broad contact with rostral . . . . *Proatheris* (p. 62)

b Supraocular not enlarged; nasals separated from rostral by rows of small scales . . . . *Bitis* (p. 73)

9a Lower flank scales directed obliquely upwards, upper flank scales
directed obliquely downwards . . . . *Causus* (p. 63)

b All flank scales directed posteriorly **10**

10a Rostral dorsoventrally flattened or pointed; rostral projecting **11**

b Rostral normal, not projecting **16**

11a Rostral narrow, pointed; head quill-shaped; body long, slender . . . . *Xenocalamus* (p. 111)

b Head not quill-shaped; body not long and slender **12**

12a Rostral dorsoventrally flattened **13**

b Rostral pointed **14**

13a Internasals fused; tail ends in spine . . . . *Prosymna* (p. 95)

b Internasals discrete . . . . *Hypoptophis* (p. 120)

14a Rostral greatly enlarged, hooked; parietal scales fragmented . . . . *Scaphiophis* (p. 183)

b Parietal scales not fragmented **15**

15a Rostral decurved in lateral view; dorsum uniform or spotted . . . . *Rhamphiophis* (p. 79)

b Rostral straight in lateral view; dorsum with 3 well-defined
dark longitudinal stripes . . . . *Kladirostratus* (p. 82)

16a Tail ends in short spine **17**

b Tail not ending in spine **18**

17a Loreal scale present; enlarged fangs situated in front of eye; internasals
and prefrontals usually wider than long; often arches neck . . . . *Atractaspis* (p. 102)

b Loreal scale absent; enlarged fangs situated below eye; internasals and
prefrontals usually about as long as wide; weakly arches neck . . . . *Polemon* (p. 114)

34a Single, triangular internasal; 6th supralabial in contact with, or narrowly
separated from, parietal . . . . *Limnophis* (p. 156)
  b Internasal paired **35**

35a Body orange with series of large, black vertebral blotches . . . . *Telescopus* (p. 185)
  b Body not predominantly orange with black dorsal markings **36**

36a Predominantly green, sometimes with dark speckles or spots;
vertebral stripe may be present . . . . *Philothamnus* (p. 176)
  b Not predominantly green **37**

37a Nostril pierced in single nasal . . . . *Lycophidion* (p. 125)
  b Nostril pierced in semi-divided or divided nasal **38**

38a Supralabials pale with dark sutures **39**
  b Supralabials uniform, occasionally with dark ventral border
or dark infusions on anterior scales **41**

39a Body robust; usually 2 anterior and 3 posterior temporals . . . . *Grayia* (p. 162)
  b Body not robust; usually 1 anterior and 1–2 posterior temporals **40**

40a Head distinct from neck; pupil vertical; top of head marbled . . . . *Dipsadoboa* (p. 190)
  b Head small, barely distinct from neck; pupil circular;
top of head not marbled . . . . *Natriciteres* (p. 159)

41a No enlarged fangs in upper jaw **42**
  b One or more pairs of fangs present in upper jaw below eye **45**

42a Cloacal scale divided; 2–3 anterior and 2–5 posterior temporals **43**
  b Cloacal scale entire; 1 anterior and 2 posterior temporals **44**

43a Snout pointed; 25–31 midbody scale rows . . . . *Pseudaspis* (p. 100)
  b Snout rounded; 21 midbody scale rows . . . . *Meizodon* (p. 193)

44a 23–35 midbody scale rows; ventrum plain white or dark grey;
pale eye-stripe present . . . . *Boaedon* (p. 129)
  b 19–23 (rarely 25) midbody scale rows; inconspicuous to conspicuous
groove separates supralabials from rest of head scales; ventrum pink,
yellow or orange, often with dark median stripe on subcaudals . . . . *Lycodonomorphus* (p. 133)

45a Nostril pierced in single, semi-divided nasal; head somewhat
depressed; nape usually rusty orange . . . . *Hemirhagerrhis* (p. 80)
  b Nostril pierced between at least 2 scales **46**

46a Pupil vertically elliptical . . . . *Crotaphopeltis* (p. 186)
  b Pupil round **47**

47a Nostril pierced between 2–3 nasals; enlarged fang-like teeth present
below anterior border of eye, separated from true fangs by additional
small teeth (except *P. lineatus*, which lacks anterior enlarged teeth) . . . . *Psammophis* (p. 86)
  b Nostril pierced between 2 nasals and an internasal; no enlarged
fang-like teeth below anterior border of eye . . . . *Psammophylax* (p. 83)

Slender Blind Snakes
Family Leptotyphlopidae

This family contains the smallest and thinnest species of snake. In all species the skull is small and solidly constructed and the mouth is toothless. The body is cylindrical and the tail short to moderate in length, rounded and ending in a small spine. The eyes are small and covered by the head scales, but are usually visible as dark spots. The body scales are small, smooth and shiny, and in 14–16 rows at midbody. The number of middorsal scales is one of the characters used to distinguish between taxa. These scales are counted from the frontal scale to the last scale anterior to the terminal spine.

Peters' Thread Snake

These snakes are fossorial, but they are regularly seen on the soil surface and often take refuge in termitaria and under logs and rocks. They inhabit a wide range of habitats and elevations, from desert and savanna to forest and wetland. They feed frequently, mostly preying on the eggs, larvae and workers of social insects (predominantly ants). If attacked by ants or termites, they will coil into a ball and excrete pheromones to protect themselves. Species in this family are preyed on by large invertebrates (scorpions and spiders) and various other snakes and birds. Females lay clutches of 1–7 small, elongate eggs, which may be strung together.

This family includes 116 described species in 12 genera, although genetic studies suggest that many cryptic species remain to be formally described. They are widespread across Africa, the Americas and the West Indies, with a few species extending into Arabia and south-west Asia. Six species in two genera occur in the region.

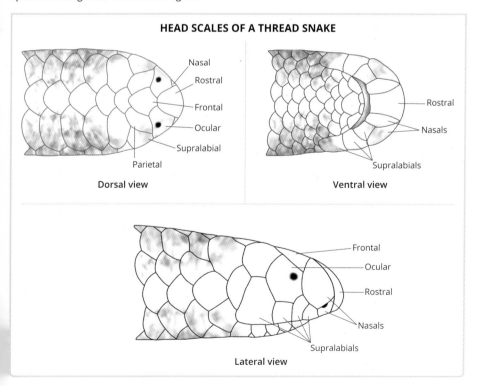

HEAD SCALES OF A THREAD SNAKE

Nasal
Rostral
Frontal
Ocular
Supralabial
Parietal

Dorsal view

Rostral
Nasals
Supralabials

Ventral view

Frontal
Ocular
Rostral
Nasals
Supralabials

Lateral view

Worm and Thread Snakes
Subfamily Leptotyphlopinae

Small, thin snakes with a long tail (4–19% of TL) and 12–58 subcaudals. Species in this subfamily have two or fewer supralabials and fewer than 15 scale rows at midbody. They are dull in colour, usually black, brown or chequered. They occur widely throughout Africa and the associated islands, as well as on the Arabian Peninsula and south-west Asia. A total of 54 species in four genera are recognised, although genetic data suggest that more species await formal description.

WORM SNAKES *Myriopholis*

Small, thin snakes with a small anterior supralabial and single large posterior supralabial (two posterior supralabials in one species). There are 14 scale rows at midbody, 165–558 middorsal scales, 10–12 scale rows at midtail and 25–58 subcaudals. The cloacal scale is broadly crescentic. Worm snakes are usually pale brown to flesh-coloured above and white below.

They are widespread in Africa and also occur on the Arabian Peninsula and south-west Asia and on Socotra Island. A total of 24 species are recognised, two of which occur in the region.

KEY Regional *Myriopholis* species

1a Rostral moderately narrow; anterior supralabial small; 24–38 subcaudals . . . . . . ***M. ionidesi*** (p. 44)
  b Rostral moderately broad; anterior supralabial moderate in size;
      34–58 subcaudals . . . . ***M. longicauda*** (p. 45)

Ionides' Worm Snake *Myriopholis ionidesi*

Max. SVL 135mm
A medium-sized worm snake with a cylindrical body and a head that is slightly narrower than the neck and body. Snout rounded; rostral narrow (but broader than nasals), extending until level with anterior borders of eye. Weak preoral groove present ventrally on rostral. Discrete frontal present. Nostril pierced ventrolaterally in suture between small infranasal and large supranasal. Anterior supralabial small, half the size of infranasal, not reaching level of nostril. Ocular large, in contact with postnasal; eye visible near anterior edge of ocular. Posterior supralabial moderate in size. 14 midbody scale rows; 265–306 middorsal scales. Tail short and thick, abruptly tapering to terminal spine. 10 midtail scale rows; 24–38 subcaudals; cloacal scale small, crescent-shaped. Dorsum light tan; ventrum immaculate creamy

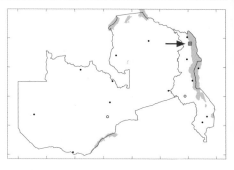

white. **Habitat:** Miombo woodland. **Behaviour:** Presumably similar to Long-tailed Worm Snake (*M. longicauda*). **Prey and Predators:** Probably similar to Long-tailed Worm Snake. **Reproduction:** Female lays 2–3 eggs. **Range:** Northern Malawi, extending to northern Mozambique and south-eastern Tanzania.

Luke Verburgt

The Long-tailed Worm Snake is uniformly pinkish.

Max. SVL 255mm

A large worm snake with a head that is almost indistinct from the body (the head may appear flattened and slightly broader than the body) and a rounded snout. Discrete frontal present; nostril pierced ventrolaterally between 2 nasals. Rostral rounded, fairly broad, separated from supraoculars by frontal. Infranasal diagonally elongate, supralabial small; both situated between rostral and ocular. Ocular large, higher than broad, followed posteriorly by single moderately sized supralabial. 14 midbody scale rows; 266–325 middorsal scales. Tail very long; cloacal scale small, broadly crescent-shaped; terminal spine of tail small. 10 midtail scale rows; 34–58 subcaudals. Dorsum greyish red-brown to fleshy pink; ventrum white. Juveniles uniform fleshy pink. **Habitat:** Mesic savanna. **Behaviour:** Most active on the surface on warm nights after rain. Generally found under logs and rocks at other times. **Prey and Predators:** Feeds mainly on ant and termite larvae. Eaten by Rusty-spotted Genets, various mesocarnivores and birds. **Reproduction:** Female lays 2–3 eggs

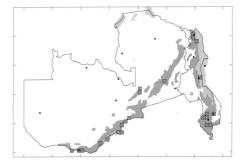

(18–23mm x 3–4mm) in summer. **Range:** Southern and central Zambia and throughout Malawi, but absent from high-elevation areas. Elsewhere from coastal Kenya to South Africa and to eastern Botswana.

The head is nearly indistinct from the body.

THREAD SNAKES   *Leptotyphlops*

Small, slender snakes with a small anterior and large posterior supralabial. In all species the body is cylindrical, the head bluntly rounded and the tail short, usually ending in a small spine. There are 14 scale rows at midbody, 171–322 middorsal scales, 10–12 scale rows at midtail and 18–44 subcaudals. The ventrals and dorsals are the same size and the cloacal scale is heart-shaped or subtriangular. The dorsum and ventrum are usually dark brown to brown (often appearing black). Depending on humidity the skin may dry out and appear chequered. Females grow larger and have shorter tails than males.

Thread snakes prey almost exclusively on various ant and termite castes, which they locate by following pheromone trails. They rely on chemical crypsis to protect themselves from soldier ants and termites, producing a pheromone to disguise their presence. Their smooth, close-fitting scales likely provide additional protection against bites and stings. They may adopt tonic immobility (feign death) if harassed.

This genus contains 22 described species that occur throughout southern and East Africa, four of which occur in the region. Genetic evidence suggests that many species await formal description.

KEY   Regional *Leptotyphlops* species

1a	Discrete prefrontal separates rostral from supraoculars	**2**
b	Rostral fused with prefrontal, in contact with supraoculars	**3**
2a	Cloacal scale triangular; 198–244 middorsal scales; nostril separated from rostral by longer suture	***L. emini*** (p. 46)
b	Cloacal scale heart-shaped; 209–267 middorsal scales; nostril separated from rostral by shorter suture	***L. kafubi*** (p. 48)
3a	Rostral barely extends past posterior border of eye; rostral less than a third of head width at level of eye . . . . ′. . .	***L. incognitus*** (p. 47)
b	Rostral extends well past posterior border of eye; rostral more than a third of head width at level of eye	***L. scutifrons*** (p. 48)

Emin's Thread Snake   *Leptotyphlops emini*

Max. SVL 152mm

A medium-sized thread snake with a cylindrical body and a broadened and flattened head and neck. Rostral moderately broad (much broader than nasals), truncated posteriorly, extending to level of eye. Preoral groove present ventrally. Rostral bordered posteriorly by narrow, vertical infranasal and small supralabial; latter reaches level of nostril. Prefrontal discrete, separates rostral from supraoculars; latter pentagonal. Ocular large, eye visible in centre of upper half, bordered posteriorly by large supralabial. Body scales smooth, imbricate, in 14 rows at midbody. 198–244 middorsal scales. Tail short, slightly tapering to small spine or blunt tail cone. 10 midtail scale rows; cloacal scale triangular; 20–32 subcaudals. Body uniform dark brown to black; supralabials, chin and cloacal scale white. **Habitat:** Mesic

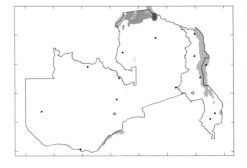

savanna. **Behaviour:** Fossorial, usually found under logs and rocks. Occasionally active on the surface, especially after rain. **Prey and Predators:** Probably similar to other thread snakes. **Reproduction:** Female lays 2–5 eggs. **Range:** Northern Zambia, through East Africa to southern Sudan.

Incognito Thread Snake   *Leptotyphlops incognitus*

Darren Pietersen

The Incognito Thread Snake closely resembles the other thread snake species.

Max. SVL 175mm

A medium-sized thread snake with a rounded snout and relatively narrow rostral. Rostral fused with prefrontal, in contact with supraoculars. Upper nasal usually ends well before posterior border of rostral. Single large supralabial posterior to ocular; latter reaches level of eye. 14 midbody scale rows; 223–292 middorsal scales. Tail long, tapers to small terminal spine; 23–35 subcaudals; 10 midtail scale rows; cloacal scale triangular. Body uniform black above and below, occasionally with white patch on cloacal scale. **Habitat:** Mesic savanna. **Behaviour:** Often found under logs and rocks, in termitaria or in leaf litter, although occasionally active on the surface. **Prey and Predators:** Feeds on termites and ants as well as their eggs, pupae and larvae. Swallows smaller termites whole and attacks larger termites from behind, puncturing their abdomens and ingesting only the abdominal

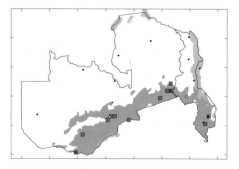

contents. Preyed on by Southern Black Flycatchers, and probably Helmeted and Crested Guineafowl, and various other bird species. **Reproduction:** Female lays 3–4 very small eggs (9–12mm x 2–3mm) in summer. Hatchlings emerge in late summer and measure 51–68mm in TL. **Range:** Southern Zambia and southern Malawi, through Mozambique and Zimbabwe to eastern South Africa.

Shaba Thread Snake *Leptotyphlops kafubi*

Max. SVL 165mm
A medium-sized thread snake with a rounded snout and a short terminal tail spine. Rostral fairly narrow; prefrontal discrete, separating rostral from supraoculars. Upper nasals very large, often extending to level of, or beyond, posterior border of rostral. Upper nasals not in contact behind rostral. Ocular large, reaching upper lip; followed posteriorly by moderate to large supralabial; latter only slightly smaller than ocular, often extending to level of eye. 14 midbody scale rows; 209–267 middorsal scales. 19–27 subcaudals; cloacal scale heart-shaped. Body uniform dark brown to blackish, rarely with white chin and throat. **Habitat:** Moist savanna and woodland. **Behaviour:** Usually encountered under logs and rocks or in termitaria. Seen on the surface after rains.

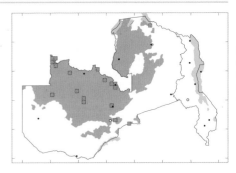

Ecology probably similar to other thread snakes. **Prey:** Probably feeds on ant pupae and larvae. **Reproduction:** Females were recorded to contain up to three eggs. **Range:** Northern, central and southern Zambia. Widespread in the south-eastern DRC and enters eastern Angola.

In the region, the Shaba Thread Snake occurs mainly in northern and central Zambia.

Peters' Thread Snake *Leptotyphlops scutifrons*

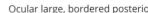

Max. SVL 260mm
A large thread snake with a rounded snout and fairly broad rostral. Rostral fused with prefrontal, in contact with supraoculars, extends well beyond posterior border of eye.

Ocular large, bordered posteriorly by single posterior supralabial that may just reach level of eye, but usually ends below it. 14 midbody scale rows; 225–309 middorsal scales. Tail usually ends abruptly in small terminal spine; 10–12 midtail scale rows; 18–30 subcaudals; cloacal scale triangular. Body uniform black above and below; if dried out, scales have chequered silver appearance. Lower lip and chin (and rarely throat) may have some irregular white patches. **Subspecies:** Four subspecies are recognised. One is confirmed to enter the region and one is likely to occur. *L. s. scutifrons* occurs in southern Zambia and Malawi, as well as through Mozambique, Zimbabwe and eastern Botswana to northern South Africa. It has 225–309 middorsal scale rows, 10 midtail scale rows, and a fairly broad rostral. *L. s. merkeri* occurs in Kenya and Tanzania, with a record on the Tanzanian–Malawian border. It therefore likely occurs in extreme northern Malawi as well. It is smaller, has 201–304 middorsal scales and 12 midtail scale rows, and has a narrower, wedge-shaped rostral. **Habitat:** Savanna. **Behaviour:** Often found sheltering under logs and rocks, in termitaria or in grass roots adjacent to rocks and termitaria. **Prey and Predators:** Preys almost exclusively on the larvae and pupae of small ants. Feeds gluttonously but infrequently. Preyed on by Southern Black Flycatchers,

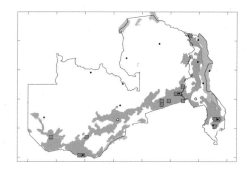

burrowing asps (*Atractaspis*) and various small carnivores, such as Bat-eared Fox, Black-backed Jackal, Rusty-spotted Genet, Small-spotted Genet, Selous' Mongoose, Slender Mongoose and White-tailed Mongoose. **Reproduction:** Female lays clutches of 1–3 eggs (13–25mm x 2–4mm), which are linked together with small 'strings' and hatch in late summer to early autumn. Hatchlings measure 52–58mm in TL. **Range:** Southern Zambia and Malawi. Elsewhere it occurs from southern Tanzania through Mozambique and Zimbabwe to South Africa and westwards to Namibia and southern Angola.

Luke Verburgt

Peters' Thread Snake, like other thread snakes, becomes spotty as it loses moisture.

Blind Snakes
Family Typhlopidae

This family is one of the most ancient groups of snakes. In all species the body is cylindrical and the head and tail are not easily distinguished from it. The tail is very short (typically only 1–3% of TL) and ends in a short spine. The lower jaw is

Schlegel's Giant Blind Snake

toothless. The head scales are greatly reduced in number and typically only the rostral, nasal, preocular, ocular, postoculars and supralabials are present. The body scales are small, close-fitting and smooth. The eyes are covered by the head scales. The number of middorsal scales is one of the characters used to distinguish between taxa. These are counted from the first scale posterior to the rostral to the last scale anterior to the terminal tail spine.

These snakes are predominantly fossorial and are often found in termitaria. Juveniles may be found under logs and rocks. Large adults are rarely seen on the surface but may be active above ground after heavy rains. Owing to their burrowing lifestyle, most species have a similar external morphology, which has greatly hampered species delineations in the past. They prey predominantly on termites, but occasionally feed on other invertebrates. They appear to locate ants and termites by following the scent trails laid down by foraging workers, or by detecting scent particles in the air. Both oviparous and ovoviviparous species are known. When mating, the male tightly coils around the posterior portion of the female's body. The female lays clutches of 4–25 eggs in late summer. Unlike most other snake species, the skin is shed in compact rings.

Blind snakes occur on every continent except Antarctica, but are most diverse in the tropics. At present 238 species in 16 genera have been described in tropical regions around the world. Seven species in two genera have been recorded in the region.

African Blind Snakes
Subfamily Afrotyphlopinae

An almost exclusively African subfamily containing the genera *Afrotyphlops*, *Rhinotyphlops* and *Letheobia*. These medium- to large-sized blind snakes have a robust, round body and a rounded or beaked snout. The tail is very short and ends in a sharp spine. The eyes are covered by the head scales and may be distinct or indistinct. The nasal is completely or incompletely divided and the nasal suture originates at the 1st or 2nd supralabial (rarely at the rostral or suture between the supralabials). There are 2–6 postoculars, and the preocular is usually in contact with the 2nd and/or 3rd supralabial. The body scales are small, smooth, close-fitting, and in 18–45 rows at midbody. There are 216–737 middorsal scales and 4–15 caudal scales.

A total of 67 species are recognised, all but two of which are restricted to sub-Saharan Africa.

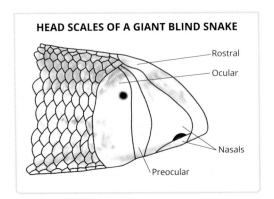

HEAD SCALES OF A GIANT BLIND SNAKE

Rostral

Ocular

Nasals

Preocular

GRACILE BLIND SNAKES   *Letheobia*

Small to medium-sized blind snakes with a slender to moderate body. The snout is bluntly rounded or angular in profile with a keratinised horizontal edge. The mouth and nostrils are situated on the underside of the head. The eyes, which are covered by the head scales, are only rarely visible. The rostral is moderate in breadth to broad and usually extends past the level of the eye dorsally. The ocular is reduced in size and the lower border of the nasal is in contact with the 1st or 2nd supralabial. The nasal is completely or incompletely divided, the nasal suture usually originating on the 1st or 2nd supralabial (rarely the rostral). The supralabials do not overlap any superior head scales, or the 2nd supralabial overlaps the subocular. The preocular is in contact with the 2nd, or 2nd and 3rd, supralabial. Suboculars are usually present (occasionally absent) and there are 2–6 postoculars. There are 18–30 midbody scale rows, 336–737 middorsal scales and 5–17 caudal scales. The tail is short to moderate in length and lacks a terminal spine. The body lacks pigmentation.

Snakes in this genus are fossorial, and individuals are seen above ground only after heavy rains have flooded their burrows. Juveniles are occasionally found sheltering under rocks or logs. They prey on the adults and larvae of social insects (ants and termites).

A total of 29 species are recognised, most of which occur widely in sub-Saharan Africa. One species occurs in the region.

Slender Gracile Blind Snake   *Letheobia gracilis*

The Slender Gracile Blind Snake has a very slender, pinkish body.

Max. SVL 536mm

A medium-sized, slender blind snake with a bluntly rounded snout that has an angular, keratinised horizontal edge. Rostral very broad, with relatively flat posterior border. Frontal narrow, trapezoidal, usually separated from nasals by supraoculars. Supraoculars oblique, laterally elongate, the lateral point inserted between nasal and ocular. Ocular smaller than preocular and subocular, with 1 (rarely 2) temporal separating ocular and subocular. Eye not visible. Nasal suture arises from 2nd supralabial; nasals usually in contact with first 2 supralabials. Supralabials do not overlap any head scales (3rd supralabial rarely overlaps subocular). 22 midbody scale rows; 608–737 middorsal scales; 8–14 subcaudals. Body usually lacks pigmentation, rarely uniform pale brown. **Habitat:** Savanna, miombo woodland and thickets. **Behaviour:** Fossorial. **Prey and Predators:** Presumably similar to other blind snakes, feeding on ants and termites. Preyed on by Bibron's Burrowing Asp (*Atractaspis hibronii*).

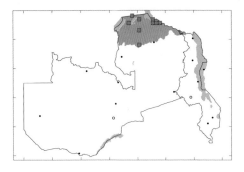

Reproduction: Unknown. Probably lays eggs.
Range: North-eastern Zambia, the southern DRC and south-western Tanzania.

GIANT BLIND SNAKES   *Afrotyphlops*

Endemic African blind snakes that are small to large in size with a slender to robust body and a short to moderate tail. The snout is rounded to sharply angular in profile, with a sharp, horizontal, keratinised edge. The rostral is large (40–75% of the interocular distance dorsally), and the nasals are incompletely divided and lack a posterior concavity. The mouth is small and located ventrally, together with the nostrils. The lower nasal suture is in contact with the 1st supralabial (rarely the rostral). Either the supralabials do not overlap any superior head scales, or the 2nd supralabial overlaps the preocular or presubocular. The preocular is in contact with the 2nd, 2nd and 3rd, or 3rd supralabial. The eyes are moderate in size. The pupil is distinctly visible and covered by the preocular and/or ocular. There are 2–7 postoculars, 18–44 midbody scale rows, 232–624 middorsal scale rows and 5–16 caudal scale rows. The dorsum is pigmented while the ventrum may be pigmented or lack pigmentation.

Snakes in this genus are predominantly fossorial, spending almost all of their life below ground. They occasionally venture onto the soil surface, particularly after heavy rains. Juveniles and sub-adults are more frequently found above ground, mainly in moribund termitaria or under logs and rocks. Giant blind snakes prey almost exclusively on ants and termites and their larvae. Large adults may become obese. Evidence suggests they gain access to active termitaria by producing glandular secretions from their head, which softens the termite mound. They then burrow inside using the spatulate rostral. The female lays large clutches of 12–40 eggs, often in termitaria.

Currently, 29 species are recognised, all of which occur in sub-Saharan Africa. Four species have been recorded in the region while a further two have been recorded near the borders and are expected to occur in the region as well.

KEY Regional *Afrotyphlops* species

1a Snout sharply angular in profile, with keratinised horizontal edge (reduced or absent in juveniles); ventral border of rostral more than half of internarial distance **2**

b Snout rounded in profile, without keratinised horizontal edge; ventral border of rostral less than half of internarial distance **3**

2a Rostral oval in dorsal view and convex in profile; 30–40 midbody scale rows; body with fine longitudinal stripes or dark blotches, large adults sometimes uniform grey-brown . . . . *A. mucruso* (p. 55)

b Rostral posteriorly elongate; 34–44 midbody scale rows; dorsum with black mottling or uniform black; restricted to south-western Zambia . . . . *A. schlegelii* (p. 57)

Angolan Giant Blind Snake   *Afrotyphlops angolensis*

Max. SVL 653mm
A large blind snake with a prominent, rounded snout. Rostral broadly rounded above, narrower below. Frontal subhexagonal. Supraocular transverse, its lateral point inserted between preocular and ocular. Preocular not in contact with 1st supralabial; 2nd supralabial usually overlaps preocular. Eye visible below, or anterior to, preocular–ocular suture. Nasal sulcus arises from 1st supralabial. 24–36 midbody scale rows; 234–578 middorsal scales; 8–13 subcaudals. Body uniform dark brown, or with each scale paler basally and laterally. Individuals from savanna habitat pigmented below; those from forest habitat lack ventral pigmentation. **Habitat:** Forest, woodland and savanna. **Behaviour:** Poorly known. Predominantly

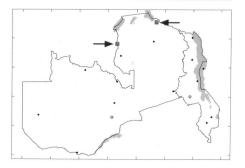

fossorial. **Prey:** Presumably termites. **Reproduction:** Probably lays eggs. **Range:** From central Kenya and northern Tanzania, through Uganda, Rwanda, Burundu, the DRC and north-eastern Zambia to Cameroon and Angola.

Laurent Chirio

In the region, the Angolan Giant Blind Snake occurs only in extreme north-eastern Zambia.

Stephen Spawls

The Lineolate Giant Blind Snake is expected to occur around Lake Mweru Wantipa, but there are no confirmed records from the region as yet.

Max. SVL 634mm

A large blind snake with a prominent, rounded snout. Rostral very broad (three-quarters the width of the head), truncated posteriorly. Frontal broader than long, roughly 4-sided, much broader anteriorly than posteriorly. Supraocular oblique, its lateral apex positioned between nasal and preocular (rarely between preocular and ocular). Eye usually positioned behind preocular–ocular suture; nasal sulcus arising from 1st supralabial. Supralabials usually do not overlap any superior head scales, although 2nd supralabial may overlap ocular. 24–30 midbody scale rows; 295–505 middorsal scales; 6–14 subcaudals. Body dark with two pale yellow spots on each scale (at base and apex, respectively), forming a finely speckled appearance. This pigmentation gradually fades on flanks; middle of ventrum unpigmented. **Habitat:** Savanna, woodland and forest. **Behaviour:** Fossorial. Poorly known, its behaviour is presumably similar to other giant

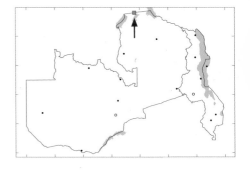

blind snakes. Appears to be more common above ground after rain. Has been found sheltering under rocks and logs. **Prey:** Probably eats termites. **Reproduction:** Presumably lays eggs. **Range:** From West Africa to Ethiopia, southwards to Angola, the southern DRC and northern Tanzania. Has been recorded on the Zambia–DRC border and is expected to occur in extreme northern Zambia in the vicinity of Solwezi and Lake Mweru Wantipa.

Luke Verburgt

The Zambezi Giant Blind Snake is usually blotched (seen above) or uniformly brown above.

Max. SVL 940mm

A very large blind snake with a prominent, angular, keratinised edge to the snout (absent in juveniles). Rostral very large and oval. Frontal crescent-shaped. Supraocular transverse, its lateral point inserted between preocular and ocular. Eye visible near front border of ocular. Nasal suture arising from 1st supralabial; nasal in contact with 1st and 2nd supralabials. Supralabials do not overlap any superior head scales, or 2nd supralabial overlaps preocular. 30–40 midbody scale rows; 307–518 middorsal scale rows; 6–10 subcaudals. Two colour phases occur. In blotched phase, juveniles have faint dark longitudinal stripes, overlaid with large dark blotches. Adults lose longitudinal stripes and are blotched, with yellowish-white ventrum. In striped phase, juveniles are blue-grey with dark longitudinal lines. This dark coloration may extend over entire dorsum in large adults. In this phase the ventrum is usually white to pale yellow, although this may be restricted to narrow medial stripe. **Habitat:** Savanna, woodland and forest-savanna mosaics. **Behaviour:** Fossorial. Juveniles occasionally found sheltering under stones, while adults usually occur deeper in soils and are most often seen after heavy rains. They may also spend large amounts

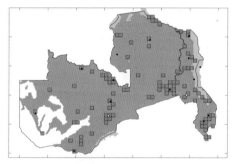

Some individuals have a finely spotted appearance.

of time in termitaria. **Prey and Predators:** Feeds predominantly on ant larvae and pupae; often eats termites as well. Preyed on by purple-glossed snakes (*Amblyodipsas*) and probably small carnivores and birds of prey. **Reproduction:** Female lays 15–40 eggs (17–20mm x 9–11mm) in late spring or early summer. Incubation takes 35–42 days. **Range:** From East Africa through Zambia and Malawi to the southern DRC and eastern Angola, and southwards to northern South Africa.

Slender Giant Blind Snake   *Afrotyphlops obtusus*

The Slender Giant Blind Snake is more slender than the other giant blind snake species.

Max. SVL 370mm

A medium-sized, very slender blind snake with a prominent, rounded snout. Rostral very broad, blunt posteriorly; frontal laterally elongate, roughly 6-sided. Supraocular transversely elongate, its lateral point inserted between preocular and ocular. Eye situated below preocular, usually not visible (occasionally visible as dark spot in subadults). Nasal suture arises from 1st supralabial; nasal in contact with first 2 supralabials. 2nd supralabial overlaps preocular, which is half the size of ocular. 22–26 midbody scale rows; 406–507 middorsal scales; 6–10 subcaudals. Dark brown to black above, each scale with pale base; pale brown to white below. Subadults lighter in colour. **Habitat:** Miombo woodland and forests. **Behaviour:** Predominantly subterranean, preferring

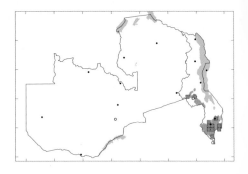

loose, humic soils. Found under logs and rocks in damp locations. **Prey:** Termite larvae. **Reproduction:** Probably similar to other giant blind snakes, i.e. lays eggs. **Range:** Central and southern Malawi, northern Mozambique and into extreme eastern Zimbabwe.

Darren Pietersen

In the region, Schlegel's Giant Blind Snake occurs only in extreme south-western Zambia.

Max. SVL 795mm

A large blind snake with a prominent horizontal, keratinised edge to the snout (reduced or absent in juveniles). Rostral very large, posteriorly elongate, rounded. Frontal fairly small, crescent-shaped. Supraocular transverse, its lateral point inserted between preocular and ocular. Eye distinct, located beneath or just posterior to suture of preocular and ocular. Nasal in contact with 1st and 2nd supralabial; nasal suture arising from 1st supralabial. 2nd supralabial overlaps preocular. 32–45 midbody scale rows; 332–624 middorsal scale rows; 7–10 subcaudals. Body white to yellow, marbled or speckled with black above; occasionally uniform black or with scattered white scales. Ventrum usually plain white to yellowish, rarely with irregular black speckling or dark mid-ventral stripe. **Habitat:** Savanna and woodlands. **Behaviour:** Fossorial. Adults are rarely seen on the surface, spending most of their time below ground where they gorge themselves on termites and lay down massive fat stores, often becoming obese. Juveniles and subadults are seen on the surface more often, especially after rains. Juveniles are occasionally found sheltering under logs and rocks. This species is believed

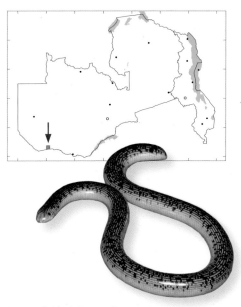

Some individuals have a chequered pattern.

to produce glandular secretions that assist it in penetrating the hard exterior of termite mounds for protection and to access prey. **Prey:** Feeds extensively on ant larvae and pupae, as well as on termites. May spend large amounts of time in or near termitaria. **Reproduction:** Female lays 12–40 eggs (20–22mm x 10–12mm) in late spring or early summer. Incubation takes 35–42 days. **Range:** Southern Angola and northern Namibia, through northern Botswana to South Africa and southern Mozambique. Has been recorded at Katima Mulilo on the Zambian–Namibian border as well as in southern Angola. Likely to occur elsewhere in south-western Zambia.

Schmidt's Giant Blind Snake *Afrotyphlops schmidti*

Schmidt's Giant Blind Snake closely resembles the Zambezi Giant Blind Snake.

Max. SVL 599mm

A large blind snake with a prominent, rounded snout. Rostral very broad (three-quarters of head width), truncated posteriorly. Frontal broader than long, roughly 4-sided, much broader anteriorly than posteriorly. Supraocular oblique, its lateral apex positioned between nasal and preocular. Eye positioned behind suture between preocular and ocular; nasal sulcus arises from 1st supralabial. Supralabials usually do not overlap any superior head scales

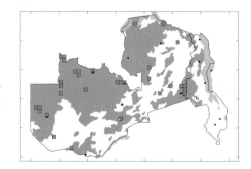

(2nd supralabial rarely overlaps preocular). 22–26 midbody scale rows; 317–374 middorsal scales; 7–11 subcaudals. Body dark brown to black, each scale with yellow tip, occasionally giving rise to a lineolate pattern. Ventrum immaculate or with dorsal coloration extending onto ventrum. A rare blotched morph occurs, in which individuals have a yellowish ground colour with scattered large, dark blotches. **Subspecies:** Two subspecies are recognised, both of which occur in the region. The typical form (*A. s. schmidti*) lacks pigmentation on the belly and occurs across most of the range. In *A. s. laurenti* the dorsal coloration extends onto the ventrum as well. This form is restricted to eastern Zambia. **Habitat:** Savanna, woodland and forest. **Behaviour:** A poorly known, fossorial

Some individuals develop a blotched pattern.

snake. **Prey and Predators:** Probably similar to other giant blind snakes. **Reproduction:** Unknown. Probably similar to other giant blind snakes, i.e. lays eggs. **Range:** Widespread throughout Zambia. Elsewhere it occurs in eastern Angola and the south-eastern DRC.

Pythons
Family Pythonidae

Hatchling Southern African Python

Pythons are Africa's largest snakes. The body is stocky and extremely muscular, and the head is distinct. The body is covered in numerous small scales. The ventrals are enlarged but are not as wide as the body. The head scales are small to moderate in size and are arranged asymmetrically. Heat-sensitive pits are visible as indentations along the upper lip, and these are used to detect warm-blooded prey at night or in burrows. Unlike most snakes, pythons have two functional lungs. Vestiges of the pelvic girdle are expressed externally as a spur on either side of the cloaca. Males have larger spurs than females, which are used to stimulate the female during copulation.

These large snakes constrict their prey before swallowing it whole. Although not venomous, they possess numerous large, recurved teeth that are capable of inflicting nasty, often gashing bites. Although large pythons have been reported to constrict and consume people in Africa, most of these tales are folklore. Nonetheless, large pythons should be treated with caution.

The female lays clutches of numerous large eggs. In some species the female curls around her clutch to protect and incubate them, and provides maternal care to the hatchlings for up to two weeks.

This family is one of the most primitive snake groups. A total of 40 species in eight genera occur widely in Africa, Asia and Australasia. There are four species in a single genus in Africa.

PYTHONS *Python*

Small to large snakes with a heavy, muscular body and partially prehensile tail. The head is covered in numerous small to moderately sized scales, and a series of heat-sensitive pits are present on the upper lip. The body is covered in numerous small scales. Although the ventrals are enlarged, they are not as wide as the body. Small claw-like spurs are present on either side of the cloaca. These are larger in males than in females.

Pythons occur in a wide range of habitats and are particularly fond of riparian vegetation and rocky outcrops where large-bodied prey congregate. Large adults may spend vast amounts of time waiting in ambush in water. They prey on a wide variety of mammals, birds, reptiles and fish.

This genus is widespread in sub-Saharan Africa and south-east Asia. There are 10 species in the genus, one of which occurs in the region.

Southern African Python   *Python natalensis*

Max. SVL ♂ 4,250mm ♀ 5,000mm

A very large, robust snake (weighing up to 60kg) with a cylindrical body and triangular head that is distinct from the neck. Head scales small, numerous. 2 heat-sensitive pits present on supralabials; 4–6 present on infralabials. 10–16 supralabials; 17–24 infralabials. Body scales very small, smooth, in 71–99 rows at midbody. 260–291 ventrals; 63–84 paired subcaudals; cloacal scale entire. Claw-like spur present on either side of cloaca, larger in males. Light to dark brown or grey-green above with sinuous black-edged darker crossbars or blotches. Darker stripe usually present on either side of backbone. Flanks have series of large, often pale-centred dark spots; flanks finely spotted with black. Large spearhead-shaped mark present on top of head, bordered on either side by yellowish to light brown stripe extending

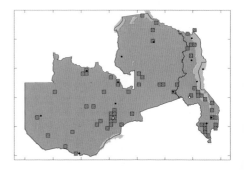

from tip of snout through top of eye to back of head, where it merges with pale lateral blotches. Tail has pale median stripe above, bordered by black-edged brown stripe. Sides of tail mottled with dark and pale bars. Ventrum white to yellowish white, with scattered dark spots and

The Southern African Python is the largest snake species in the region.

Juveniles are more vividly patterned than adults.

Luke Verburgt

flecks. Juveniles more brightly coloured. **Habitat:** A variety of savanna and woodland habitats. Particularly fond of waterside vegetation and rocky outcrops. **Behaviour:** Fond of basking. Regularly enters water, from where it may also ambush prey. Takes refuge in earthen burrows, caves, rock outcrops and hollow trees. Active at any time of the day or night, although most active at night. May fast for more than two years in captivity and has been recorded to live for 27 years. **Prey and Predators:** Feeds on a variety of small and medium-sized mammals (mostly antelope, but also small carnivores such as Honey Badgers), birds, monitor lizards (*Varanus*), Nile Crocodiles (*Crocodylus niloticus*) and fish (mostly Sharp-toothed Catfish), which are ambushed and constricted in its muscular coils. It also eats bird eggs, including those of Yellow-billed Ducks and Egyptian Geese, and possibly those of other large ground-nesting birds. Rarely, very large individuals have been reported to kill humans. It is preyed on by Leopard, Honey Badger, Snouted Cobra (*Naja annulifera*) and Caracal. African Wild Dog, Spotted Hyena and Black-backed Jackal may also attack it after it has consumed a large meal or during drought periods. Warthogs sometimes attack and kill it. **Reproduction:** Mating occurs in winter, males often trailing a female for up to two months beforehand. A receptive female is typically attended by 2–3 (up to 13) males. Males are usually found in close proximity to the female and may even lie within her coils. The female lays 15–74 (up to 100 in very large females) large, leathery eggs (measuring 80–100mm x 60–80mm and weighing 130–160g) in an abandoned earthen burrow, termite mound or cave. The female darkens in colour while breeding to facilitate heat absorption and regularly basks near the burrow entrance. She then enters the burrow and curls around her eggs to protect them and to transfer some of the absorbed heat, aiding incubation. Incubation takes 65–80 days and the female remains with the hatchlings for about two weeks, alternately basking and coiling around the young. Hatchlings measure 450–750mm in TL and often bask together near the mouth of the burrow, returning to the female's coils to sleep at night. They leave the nesting burrow when 1–3 weeks old, usually in a single dispersal event. The female loses about 40% of her mass while breeding, and as a result breeds only once every few years. Sexual maturity is reached in 3–5 years at a TL of about 2–3m for males, and about four metres (and 30kg) for females. **Range:** Widespread throughout Zambia and Malawi. Elsewhere in East Africa and southwards to South Africa.

* This species is not venomous, but is known to have killed people. Its numerous large teeth inflict ripping wounds that may become septic if left untreated.

Adders and Vipers
Family Viperidae

The members of this family are characterised by large, erectile fangs in protective membranous sheaths, situated in the front of the mouth. The fangs are swung forward and locked into position when the snake strikes or eats and folded back against the roof of the mouth when not in use.

Puff Adder

These snakes generally have a squat body and most species have a large, triangular head that is distinct from the body (it is fairly narrow and only slightly distinct in night adders [*Causus*]). The head is covered in numerous small, non-overlapping and asymmetrically arranged scales (in night adders, there are usually nine large scales). The body scales are relatively small and strongly keeled in most species, but smooth and appearing velvety in night adders.

Most species are terrestrial, although some species are arboreal while others are semi-aquatic and a single species is fossorial. They are predominantly nocturnal or crepuscular, but also display a fair amount of diurnal activity. They prey on a wide variety of vertebrates, mainly small mammals, amphibians and lizards, which are killed by envenomation. Hunting is mostly done from ambush, relying on superb camouflage to escape detection. Females either lay eggs which develop outside of their bodies, or retain the eggs within their bodies until the embryos complete their development.

The family consists of two well-defined radiations, namely pit vipers (Crotalinae), which mainly occur in the Americas and Asia, and Old World adders (Viperinae), which largely occur in Western Europe and Africa. There are 331 species in 35 genera which occur near-globally (they are absent from Australia, Antarctica and many oceanic islands). A total of 11 species in four genera occur in the region (with one species that is claimed to occur but lacks supporting evidence).

FLOODPLAIN VIPERS   *Proatheris*

Small adders with a moderately robust body. The dorsal head scales are small and keeled, except for a pair of large, rugose supraoculars. The nasals are in broad contact with the rostral. There is no duplication of transverse dorsal scale rows. The subcaudals are paired. This genus contains a single species.

Floodplain Viper   *Proatheris superciliaris*

Max. SVL ♂ 513mm ♀ 600mm

A small, moderately robust snake with an elongate and depressed head that is distinct from the neck. Snout short, rounded. Head covered in small keeled scales, except for supraoculars, which are large, rugose. Nostrils large, directed dorsolaterally. 1–3 internasals; 5–7 interorbitals; 8–14 circumorbitals. 8–11 supralabials; 10–13 infralabials, first 4 in contact with single pair of sublinguals. Dorsals strongly keeled, imbricate, in 27–29 (rarely 26 or 30) rows at midbody; no duplication of transverse dorsal scale rows. Outermost dorsal scale row enlarged, feebly keeled to smooth. 131–156 ventrals; 32–45 paired subcaudals; cloacal

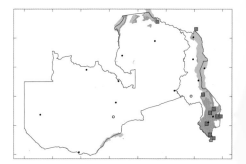

scale entire. Body pale grey-brown to brown, with numerous dark spots or blotches along back. These correspond with dark spots or

The Floodplain Viper is usually found in moist locations.

Gary Brown

blotches on flanks, but are separated from them by pale yellowish bars, the latter forming an interrupted pale dorsolateral stripe. Tip of snout usually dark; dark bar extends from top of head, through eye, to upper lip; 3rd dark bar extends from crown of head over temporals to angle of jaw. Ventrum dirty white with numerous dark blotches, which may be arranged in irregular rows. Underside of tail pale yellow to bright orange, particularly in juveniles. **Habitat:** Floodplains and grassland adjoining floodplains. **Behaviour:** Terrestrial and nocturnal; may shelter in a disused rodent burrow and bask at its entrance. When threatened, the body is withdrawn into loose C-shaped coils. Adjoining sections are rubbed against each other to produce a 'hissing' sound. Can strike with speed. **Venom:** Cytotoxic and results in immediate localised pain, swelling and blistering. No antivenom is known to be effective. In the event of a bite, reassure the patient and elevate the affected limb. Do not apply a tourniquet nor a pressure bandage as this will localise the venom, greatly increasing the tissue damage. No recorded fatalities. **Prey:** Feeds predominantly on frogs (particularly reed frogs and toads) but also eats small rodents and lizards. **Reproduction:** Males engage in combat during the breeding season (June–July) to win the right to mate. The female gives birth to 3–16 young in mid-summer after a gestation period of 177–184 days. Hatchlings measure 135–208mm in TL and may wave their brightly coloured tail in the air to lure prey within striking distance. Male reaches sexual maturity after 18–20 months; female takes 2–3 years. **Range:** From Malawi to northern and central Mozambique. Extends into Tanzania at the northern tip of Lake Malawi. Also in north-east Zambia at Lake Chila.

NIGHT ADDERS *Causus*

Relatively small adders that rarely exceed a metre in length. The body is cylindrical to slightly depressed and the tail is short. The fangs are relatively short but hinged. The head is short and blunt and only marginally distinct from the neck. Unlike other adders, the top of the head is covered in large scales, more typical of colubrid snakes. The pupils are round. The body scales are smooth or slightly keeled and have a velvety appearance. There are a number of enlarged oblique scale rows covering the flanks at midbody, the number of which is a good character to distinguish between taxa. Lower oblique scale rows are characterised by the lower free edge being much longer than the upper free edge. These rows are counted by moving up the flanks until a non-oblique transitional row of scales – characterised by the upper and lower free edges being of approximately equal length – is found. Above the transition row, the scales usually become obliquely downward-pointing.

Night adders are predominantly terrestrial and inhabit forest and moist savanna. They may occasionally climb into low bushes, especially when pursuing prey. Despite their vernacular name they are active both by day and at night, and are fond of basking. When threatened, they will inflate the body while hissing and puffing. The head is usually drawn back into a striking position, often lifted off the ground. They occasionally raise the forepart of the body, flatten the neck and extend the tongue while moving forward, resembling a cobra to some degree. These snakes prey almost exclusively on frogs and toads, which are subdued with venom. The venom glands and venom yields are large, but the venom usually has a weak effect on humans. It is mildly cytotoxic, resulting in localised pain and swelling, usually accompanied by a fever. Symptoms usually resolve within three days without the need for antivenom, and necrosis is rare. The female lays clutches of 3–26 eggs in summer.

Night adders are endemic to, and occur widely in, sub-Saharan Africa. Seven species are recognised, five of which occur in the region. Two additional species, the Spotted Night Adder (*C. maculatus*) and Velvety-green Night Adder (*C. resimus*) may occur in extreme north-eastern Zambia, but there are no confirmed records from the region as yet.

KEY Regional *Causus* species

1a Subcaudals single; 15 (rarely 13) midbody scale rows; dorsum green (brown in juveniles) with distinct white chevron on neck . . . . *C. lichtensteinii* (p. 67)
b Subcaudals paired; usually >15 midbody scale rows; no white chevron on neck **2**

2a Rostral upturned (may be weakly so in juveniles); body brown to pinkish brown, rarely greenish . . . . *C. defilippii* (p. 66)
b Rostral not upturned **3**

3a Head narrow; pale dorsolateral stripes usually present; 27–42 close-set dark crossbands on body; dark chevron on head, usually extending more than half the length of frontal . . . . *C. bilineatus* (p. 64)
b Head broad; no pale dorsolateral stripes; 19–30 widely spaced dark rhomboidal blotches along back; dark chevron on head extends up to half the length of frontal **4**

4a Solid black chevron on head, extending halfway down frontal; body pale grey with 19–24 widely spaced, rhomboidal, black vertebral blotches that are not pale-edged; dark lateral bars usually absent, sometimes indistinct . . . . *C. rasmusseni* (p. 68)
b Dark chevron on head often brown with black border, usually extends less than half the length of frontal; body light grey to brown, reddish brown or olive-green with 20–30 light-edged, dark, rhomboidal blotches along back (occasionally uniform); narrow dark bars or blotches usually present on flanks; dark interorbital bar often present . . . . *C. rhombeatus* (p. 69)

Two-striped Night Adder *Causus bilineatus*

Max. SVL ♂ 576mm ♀ 555mm
A small adder with a narrow head that is slightly distinct from the neck. Head slightly elongate, snout tapers to narrow but rounded point. Body more slender and head narrower than that of Rhombic Night Adder (*C. rhombeatus*). 4–6 circumorbitals; 2 (rarely 1) anterior and 3 (rarely 2 or 4) posterior temporals. 6 supralabials; 8–10 infralabials, first 3–4 in contact with anterior sublingual scales. Body scales weakly keeled dorsally, becoming smooth laterally, in 15–19 (usually 17) rows at midbody. 3–4 lower oblique scale rows on flanks. 119–149 ventrals; 18–35 paired subcaudals; cloacal scale entire. Body

The Two-striped Night Adder usually has a pale stripe along either side of the back.

brown; pinkish brown to grey-brown above. Broad, dark vertebral stripe flanked on each side by narrow pale stripe (latter absent in some individuals), in turn flanked by dark stripe of about same width. Series of dark rhomboidal blotches enclosed by dark vertebral line. Series of 27–42 dark crossbars arise on flanks, extending over dorsum. Scattered dark scales present on flanks. Dark, forward-pointing chevron on head, extending for more than half the length of frontal. Dark stripe often extends from the eye to the temporals; posterior supralabials may be edged with black. Pale ventrolateral stripe may be present, as may a pale stripe along outer margins of ventrals. Ventrum pale grey to black, often with darker stippling; chin and neck pale. **Habitat:** Favours marshy habitats, moist savanna and forest–savanna mosaics. **Behaviour:** Presumably similar to other night adders. **Venom:** Has not been studied. Probably cytotoxic and potentially dangerous to humans. **Prey:** Recorded to prey on African Clawed Frogs, possibly suggesting a more aquatic lifestyle than other members of this genus. **Reproduction:** Female lays up to eight eggs. Hatchlings measure about 130mm in TL. **Range:** From Angola through north-western and north-eastern Zambia to the southern DRC and extreme western Tanzania and Rwanda.

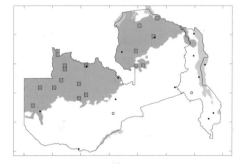

Unlike the Snouted Night Adder, the rostral is not noticeably upturned.

Snouted Night Adder *Causus defilippii*

Max. SVL ♂ 392mm ♀ 387mm

A small, stocky snake with a narrow head that is not, or only marginally, broader than the neck. Rostral upturned. 1–2 preoculars; 1–2 postoculars; 1–2 suboculars; 2 anterior and 3 posterior temporals. 6 (rarely 7) supralabials; 7–10 infralabials, first 3–4 in contact with anterior sublinguals. Body scales weakly keeled, in 17 (rarely 16 or 18) rows at midbody, with 4–6 lower oblique scale rows. 108–130 ventrals (usually 108–117 in males, 118–130 in females); 10–19 paired subcaudals (14–19 in males, 10–15 in females); cloacal scale entire. Velvety grey to pinkish brown or brown (rarely greenish), sometimes with broad darker vertebral band. Series of 20–30 large, white-edged dark blotches or chevrons extends down back and onto tail. Narrow, oblique dark bars often present on

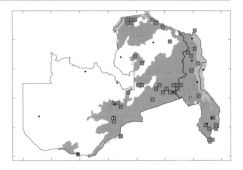

flanks, becoming horizontal towards tail. Large, dark, forward-pointing chevron present on head. Narrow dark stripe often extends from eye to angle of jaw. Supralabials usually dark-edged. Ventrum yellowish white to pinkish grey, uniform or with scattered darker spots. Ventrum may be grey to glossy black in juveniles. **Habitat:** Arid and mesic savannas. **Behaviour:** Terrestrial and active during the day; some crepuscular and nocturnal activity also recorded. When inactive, it shelters in holes and under logs, rocks, piles of debris and

The Snouted Night Adder is usually pinkish in colour. INSERT It has a distinctly upturned rostral.

other suitable cover. Fairly irascible; it will hiss and jerk its body violently if harassed. The body is often flattened during this display. **Venom:** Mildly cytotoxic. Some bites result in intense localised pain and severe swelling, usually accompanied by fever. These symptoms were observed to dissipate after 2–3 days without any necrosis. Antivenom is not required and is not effective. **Prey:** Predominantly toads and frogs; occasionally small rodents.

Reproduction: Males engage in combat, rearing up and attempting to force their opponent's head onto the ground. The female lays 3–9 eggs (20–30mm x 10–16mm) in summer. Incubation takes 90–105 days (one report of a 58-day incubation period). Hatchlings measure about 100mm in TL. **Range:** Southern, central and eastern Zambia, extending through Malawi to southern Kenya and southwards to eastern South Africa.

Forest Night Adder *Causus lichtensteinii*

In the region, the Forest Night Adder occurs only in the Ikelenge Pedicle.

Max. SVL ♂ 605mm ♀ 625mm
A medium-sized night adder with a slightly elongate head that is distinct from the neck. Snout bluntly rounded. 2 preoculars; 2 postoculars; 2 suboculars; 2 anterior and 2–4 posterior temporals. 6 (rarely 7) supralabials; 8–11 infralabials, first 4 in contact with anterior sublinguals. Body scales feebly keeled, soft and velvety, in 13–15 rows at midbody. Transitionary scale row lies at dorsal midline, thus all flank scales are directed obliquely inwards. 132–156 ventrals; 14–23 single subcaudals; cloacal scale entire. Dorsum usually bright green to olive-green with forward-pointing white chevron on nape and some

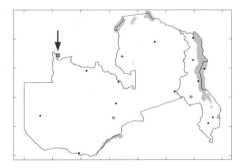

indistinct black vertebral blotches that may break up to form vague chevrons. Ventrum cream to yellow with 2–3 black crossbars on neck. Juveniles usually brown, although some individuals have 2–3 orange crossbands on tail. **Habitat:** Predominantly forests. Sometimes enters swamps, *mushitu* (swamp forests) or degraded habitats. **Behaviour:** Terrestrial, secretive and fairly sluggish, though it can strike quite fast. Predominantly diurnal, but some nocturnal activity has been recorded. Swims well. When inactive, it shelters in holes, piles of debris, tree roots or any suitable refuge. When harassed it inflates the body, hisses and puffs. **Venom:** Probably similar to other night adders, i.e. mildly cytotoxic. No recorded bites. **Prey:** Toads and frogs. **Reproduction:** Female lays 4–8 eggs. **Range:** In the region it has only been recorded from the Ikelenge Pedicle in Zambia. Widespread in West and Central Africa, extending eastwards to western Kenya.

Rasmussen's Night Adder *Causus rasmusseni*

The chevron on the head of Rasmussen's Night Adder is darker than in the Rhombic Night Adder.

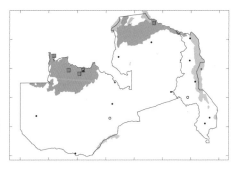

This diurnal adder was first described in 2014.

Max. SVL ♂ 470mm ♀ 620mm
A medium-sized snake with a bluntly rounded snout and a head that is distinct from the neck. 2–3 preoculars; 1–2 postoculars; 1 subocular; 2 anterior and 3 posterior temporals. 6 supralabials; 9–10 infralabials, first 3 in contact with anterior sublinguals. Body scales smooth to feebly keeled, in 16–18 rows at midbody; 4 lower oblique scale rows. 130–139 ventrals; 24–33 paired subcaudals; cloacal scale entire. Body pale grey with 19–24 widely spaced vague to distinct dark rhomboid markings that fade out on, or do not extend onto, tail. Dark lateral bars usually absent, usually indistinct if present. Solid black chevron present on back of head, its apex usually extending halfway down frontal scale. Posterior labials often with black sutures. Ventrum greyish white; dark median band may be present anteriorly. **Habitat:** Moist miombo woodland, possibly also other broad-leaved woodland and savanna. **Behaviour:** Diurnal. Ecology probably similar to other night adders. **Venom:** Unknown, probably very similar to Rhombic Night Adder (*C. rhombeatus*). **Prey:** An individual was photographed feeding on a Southern Flat-backed Toad. **Reproduction:** Unknown. **Range:** Only recorded from northern Zambia, but probably present in the southern DRC along the Zambezi–Congo Watershed.

Rhombic Night Adder *Causus rhombeatus*

Max. SVL ♂ 830mm ♀ 680mm
A medium-sized, fairly stout snake with a rounded snout and a head that is distinct from the neck. 2–3 preoculars; 1–2 postoculars; 1–2 suboculars; 2 (rarely 1) anterior and 3 posterior temporals. 6 (rarely 7) supralabials; 7–13 (usually 9–10) infralabials, first 3–4 in contact with anterior sublinguals. Body scales velvety, weakly keeled dorsally, becoming smooth laterally, in 17–19 (rarely 15 or 21) rows at midbody; 3–4 lower oblique scale rows on flanks. 130–166 ventrals; 20–35 paired subcaudals; cloacal scale entire. Brown to light or dark grey-brown above. Characteristic dark chevron on head uniform or black-edged with paler brown filling. Dark interorbital bar common, as is dark postorbital stripe. Broad darker brown vertebral stripe sometimes present. 20–30 distinct to vague white-edged dark rhomboidal patches extend down dorsal midline onto tail, may fade

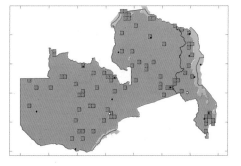

posteriorly (especially in large individuals). Narrow dark bars and blotches usually present on flanks, usually also white-edged. Ventrum dirty white to yellowish pink or grey; scales sometimes dark-edged, giving rise to finely barred appearance or dark median stripe. Occasional individuals uniform brown or dull to bright green. **Habitat:** Marshes and other damp localities in mesic savanna, woodland and grassland. May enter forests. **Behaviour:** Diurnal. Takes refuge in moribund termitaria and holes and under rocks and logs, piles of debris and other suitable cover. Fairly slow moving and docile, but can strike with speed. If threatened, it inflates the body while hissing and puffing profusely, often withdrawing the

The Rhombic Night Adder usually has a series of dark marks down the back.

Some individuals lack the dark dorsal markings.

The body may be red, grey, brown or olive.

head into a striking position and lifting it off the ground at the same time. **Venom:** Mildly cytotoxic, resulting in severe localised pain and swelling. Some blistering of the bite site and swelling of the glands may also occur. These symptoms usually resolve in 2–3 days without the need for antivenom (which is ineffective), although medical attention should be sought and patients treated symptomatically. **Prey and Predators:** Preys almost exclusively on toads and frogs, which are often swallowed alive. Rarely eats small mammals and fledgling birds. Juveniles also eat tadpoles. Preyed on by Water Monitors (*Varanus niloticus*), and various small carnivores and raptors. **Reproduction:** Males may engage in combat. The female lays 7–26 eggs (25–30mm x 13–18mm) in summer and may lay clutches at two-month intervals, apparently without the need to mate between laying clutches. Incubation takes 70–85 days. Hatchlings measure 130–160mm in TL. **Range:** Widespread throughout the region. Occurs widely in East Africa, southwards to South Africa and westwards to Nigeria.

BUSH VIPERS *Atheris*

Slender, laterally compressed snakes with a long, prehensile tail. The head is short and broad and the pupils vertical. The dorsal head scales are small to medium-sized and usually keeled. A series of almost square gular scales are typically present. The rostral is elongate and narrow with 2–9 suprarostrals above it. The suprarostrals are bordered above by the nasals and internasals. There are 9–20 circumorbitals and 5–14 interorbitals. The temporals are keeled. The dorsals are strongly keeled and imbricate, with frequent duplications or fusions and are arranged in 15–36 rows at midbody. The subcaudals are single and the cloacal scale is entire.

Bush vipers inhabit forests where they frequent trees and shrubs. Though their biology is poorly known, all are believed to be nocturnal. They prey on a variety of rodents, arboreal frogs and lizards. When threatened, they form a tight coil and rub their coarse scales together to produce a hissing sound. They are venomous, but their bites are rarely fatal. Females retain their eggs within their bodies until the embryos have completed their development, and thus appear to give birth to live young.

A total of 16 species occur across tropical Africa, two of which enter the region.

KEY Regional *Atheris* species

1a Gular scales strongly keeled; lateral scale rows weakly serrated; dorsum yellow-brown to purple-brown, sometimes with dark-centred and dark-edged rhomboidal yellowish vertebral markings . . . . ***A. katangensis*** (p. 71)
 b Gular scales smooth or feebly keeled; lateral scale rows strongly serrated; dorsum green with irregular darker markings or green to blackish with symmetrical yellow markings. . . . . ***A. rungweensis*** (p. 72)

Katanga Bush Viper *Atheris katangensis*

Max. SVL ♂ 335mm ♀ 310mm
A medium-sized viper with a fairly stout body and a large, flat, triangular head. Tail fairly long and prehensile. 3–6 suprarostrals; 5–6 internasals; 9–11 interorbitals; 14–17 circumorbitals, separated from supralabials by single (sometimes 2) row of scales. 9–12 supralabials; 11 infralabials. Dorsal and gular scales strongly keeled and mucronate; dorsals in 23–31 rows at midbody; ventrolateral rows feebly serrated. 133–144 ventrals; 38–49 single

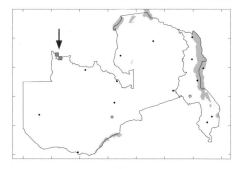

The Katanga Bush Viper was recently recorded in extreme north-western Zambia for the first time.

subcaudals; cloacal scale entire. Yellowish brown to olive or purple-brown above with series of hollow yellow rhomboid markings extending down dorsal midline and onto flanks. Ventrum yellow to yellowish brown anteriorly, occasionally becoming grey-green posteriorly; intermittent yellow lateral spots and short dark transverse bars may be present on ventrals. Tail tip yellow. Juveniles yellow to dirty yellow-brown with white tail tip, plain or with darker crossbands, which may be rhomboidal in shape, extending along dorsal midline and onto flanks. **Habitat:** Gallery forest, sometimes extending into adjacent woodland. **Behaviour:** Poorly known. Generally docile. Usually found on the ground or in low bushes, especially at the forest edge, and recorded up to 60cm above the ground. **Venom:** Assumed to have cytotoxic venom and should be considered dangerous to humans, although no details are known. Antivenom is probably not effective. **Prey:** Believed to prey on frogs. A captive individual readily ate reed and clawed frogs. **Reproduction:** Unknown. Female probably gives birth to live young. **Range:** Recorded only from Upemba National Park in the south-eastern DRC and the Katanga Pedicle in north-western Zambia, although it probably occurs in the intervening areas as well.

Rungwe Bush Viper   *Atheris rungweensis*

Max. SVL ♂ 370mm ♀ 550mm
A medium-sized viper with a fairly stout body and large, flat, triangular head. Tail fairly long, prehensile. 3–7 suprarostrals; 5–6 internasals; 9–13 interorbitals; 15–18 circumorbitals, separated from supralabials by single row of scales. 9–12 supralabials; 11–13 infralabials. Body scales strongly keeled, in 22–33 rows at midbody; lateral rows serrated; gular scales smooth or feebly keeled. 150–165 ventrals; 46–59 single subcaudals; cloacal scale entire.

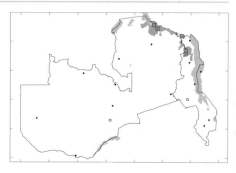

Body bright green to green and black above, often with yellow markings on back of head. Paired yellow dorsolateral lines often present, forming zig-zag pattern; row of yellow spots occasionally extends along flanks. Ventrum uniform yellow to grey-green. Hatchlings dark brown to grey with bright yellow tail tip. **Habitat:** Montane forest. Usually found in bushes or on the ground, especially at the forest edge, and recorded to climb up to three metres into shrubs. Appears to be more common along streams. **Behaviour:** Generally docile. **Venom:** Cytotoxic and should be considered dangerous to humans. Details unknown. Antivenom is probably not effective. **Prey:** Frogs, including puddle frogs. **Reproduction:** Female gives birth to live young, but further details unknown. Neonates measure 150–170mm in TL. **Range:** Restricted to extreme north-eastern Zambia, northern Malawi and western Tanzania.

Colin Tilbury

The stout, brightly coloured Rungwe Bush Viper occurs in extreme north-eastern Zambia and northern Malawi.

TYPICAL AFRICAN ADDERS *Bitis*

Stout-bodied adders with short tails. This group contains both the largest and smallest adder species, although only the large species occurs in the region. In all species the head is very large, triangular and dorsoventrally flattened and very distinct from the neck. The body is covered in numerous small, keeled scales. The head is covered in numerous small, imbricate, keeled scales. Some species also possess keratinous horns. The fangs are very long, recurved and hinged, and are protected by a membranous sheath. A well-developed supranasal sac is present behind the nostrils. This organ is believed to be comparable to the pit organs of rattlesnakes (*Crotalus*) and other pit vipers and enables these snakes to target warm-blooded prey in the dark. All species found in the region can attain a large size and may become very obese.

These adders are common and widespread and are often encountered. They are predominantly nocturnal, but also display some diurnal activity, particularly during the mating season.

They are ambush predators and may remain in the same ambush site for weeks at a time, relying on their superb visual and chemical camouflage to escape detection. They prey on a variety of small mammals, although some of the larger species also prey on small antelope. Prey is usually bitten, envenomated and released, and the snake follows the scent trail to its (by then dead) prey. Small prey may be seized and held in the mouth.

Adders are quite sluggish, but can strike extremely quickly and over a remarkably large distance. When approached, they rarely give way. If a person or animal gets too close, these snakes will usually make their presence known with loud hissing or puffing, effected by rapidly inhaling and expelling air. The head and neck are often retracted into an S-shaped coil, poised to strike. They possess a potent cytotoxic venom considered potentially lethal to humans, and fatalities have been recorded. Most bites result in immediate excruciating pain at the bite site, followed by severe swelling and tissue necrosis. Females retain the eggs within their bodies until the embryos have completed their development. Females typically give birth to clutches of 20–50 young, but up to 156 in exceptional cases.

Adders occur throughout Africa and the Arabian Peninsula. Of the 17 species, two occur in the region. A third species, the Nose-horned Viper (*B. nasicornis*), has been claimed, but as the voucher specimens have been lost, its presence requires confirmation.

KEY Regional *Bitis* species

1a Nasals not modified into horns; pale interorbital bar present; back covered in dark chevrons or blotches. . . . . **B. arietans** (p. 74)

b Nasals modified into one or more horn-like structures; no pale interorbital bar; series of pale vertebral rectangles present **2**

2a Single pair of horns; head pale white to tan with dark median stripe . . . . **B. gabonica** (p. 76)

b 2–3 pairs of horns; head green, turquoise or blue; forward-pointing dark arrowhead present on top of head. . . . . **B. nasicornis** (p. 77)

Puff Adder *Bitis arietans*

The Puff Adder has a distinctive large, triangular head.

Max. SVL ♂ 1,090mm ♀ 1,200mm

A large, thickset snake with a relatively narrow neck and large, flat triangular head. Nostrils large, point vertically upwards. Scales on head small, keeled, overlapping. 2 (rarely 3) rows of scales between nostrils and rostral; 7–11 interorbitals; 11–16 circumorbitals, separated from supralabials by 3 (rarely 2 or 4) rows of scales. 12–17 supralabials; 13–19 infralabials, first 2–5 in contact with anterior sublinguals.

Body scales small, strongly keeled and imbricate, in 27–41 rows at midbody. Tail short. 121–148 ventrals; 13–39 paired subcaudals (usually 25–39 in males and 13–24 in females); cloacal scale entire. Coloration varies considerably depending on geographic location and substrate colour. Base colour various shades of brown with yellow, grey and red tones common. Large, pale-edged, dark chevrons form irregular bars along back. Dark triangular pattern present on top of head between nostrils and eyes, bordered behind by pale interorbital bar. Ventrum yellow to white, usually with scattered darker flecks and blotches. Males slightly smaller and usually more brightly coloured. **Subspecies:** Two races are recognised. Only the typical form (*B. a. arietans*) enters the region. **Habitat:** Common in most habitats; absent only from true forest and desert. **Behaviour:** Almost exclusively terrestrial; spends long periods lying in ambush in a single position, relying on its excellent camouflage to escape detection. May climb into low bushes to bask (especially gravid females and juveniles) and has been recorded up to five metres above the ground. Skilled swimmer. Shelters under logs and rocks and in dense vegetation and uses other suitable cover. Although mainly nocturnal, it is often seen moving around during the day, 'walking' on its ventrals and ribs in a characteristic rectilinear motion. When trying to escape, it may use body undulations to propel itself in a serpentine motion. When disturbed, it will warn the harasser with a loud hiss, effected by inflating the body and then expelling this air, and will try to escape whenever possible. Even when stepped on it will attempt to escape, striking out only as a last resort. If harassed and unable to escape, the head is drawn back into a characteristic S-shaped striking posture with the head raised off the ground. It strikes incredibly fast and accurately, the hinged fangs being erected and fixed in place during the strike. Its fangs are long, measuring up to 18mm. **Venom:** It has a potent cytotoxic venom with some haemotoxic properties, and large venom yields. Owing to its sluggish nature and reliance on camouflage, this species accounts for a large proportion of venomous snake bites in Africa. Bites result in immediate excruciating localised pain followed

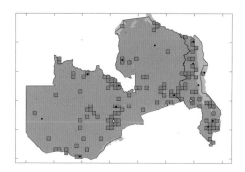

by severe swelling, blistering and tissue necrosis at the bite site. Fatalities are uncommon and usually result from anaphylaxis, kidney failure and other complications due to the extensive swelling. The affected limb occasionally has to be amputated owing to the necrosis. If bitten, the victim should be immobilised and the affected limb elevated, but a tourniquet or pressure bandage should not be applied as this concentrates the venom, often resulting in increased localised tissue damage. Polyvalent antivenom may be required in extreme cases and should be administered by a trained medical professional as soon as possible. **Prey and Predators:** Preys predominantly on rodents, favouring those that have fixed runs. Large individuals in East Africa have been recorded preying on hares and even small antelope. Also feeds on toads, ground-nesting birds, lizards, other snakes and, in exceptional cases, Leopard Tortoises (*Stigmochelys pardalis*). Young have been recorded feeding on termite alates leaving their ports. Prey is bitten and released, and approached once the venom has taken effect. May attract some prey items, especially toads, to within striking distance by using the tongue

Coloration varies between localities.

and occasionally the tail as a lure. Scavenges on occasion. It is a favourite prey of Snouted Cobra (*Naja annulifera*) and is also eaten by White-throated Monitor (*Varanus albigularis*), various diurnal raptors (Southern Banded Snake-Eagle, Martial Eagle, Kori Bustard and Black-headed Heron) and small carnivores (Caracal, Serval and Honey Badger). **Reproduction:** The receptive female produces a scent trail to attract potential mates. Often several males will follow it and vie to breed with her. Males engage in combat from late autumn to early spring, intertwining their bodies and trying to force their opponent's head to the ground. The female retains her eggs within her body until the embryos are fully developed, and gives birth to 20–50 (but up to 156) live young in late summer. Hatchlings measure 150–200mm in TL. They become sexually mature at about three years and can live for more than 14 years. **Range:** Widespread throughout Africa, entering Saudi Arabia and Oman.

Gaboon Adder *Bitis gabonica*

The Gaboon Adder is well camouflaged, resembling a pile of fallen leaves.

Max. SVL ♂ 1,230mm ♀ 1,270mm

A large, heavy snake with a narrow neck and large, flattened, triangular head. Nostrils large; modified scales form short horns. Head covered in small, faintly keeled scales. 13–17 interorbitals; 15–20 circumorbitals, separated from supralabials by 3–5 scale rows. 12–17 supralabials; 16–21 infralabials, first 4–6 in contact with anterior sublinguals. Body scales small, strongly keeled, in 28–46 rows at midbody. Tail short. 124–147 ventrals; 17–33 paired subcaudals; cloacal scale entire. Body covered in geometric patterns of tan, purple, brown and various pastel colours. Series of pale rectangles extends along dorsal midline. Head buffy to light tan with dark median line above and two dark triangles extending from eye to upper lip. Ventrum yellowish to buff with scattered dark flecks and blotches. **Habitat:** Predominantly forest. Prefers forest edges but also enters dense woodlands. Enters more open areas while foraging at night. Recorded in thornveld in Kafue National Park. **Behaviour:** Predominantly nocturnal. It is an ambush predator, remaining in the same location for days or even weeks at a time. Superbly camouflaged; coloration closely matches the leaf litter in which it usually takes refuge or lies in ambush. Very docile and reluctant to bite, even if stepped on. If disturbed it usually makes its presence known with loud hissing, sometimes lifting the forebody simultaneously. Its fangs are large, measuring up to 55mm. **Venom:** Potently cytotoxic and haemotoxic. Venom is produced in large quantities and is potentially lethal. Bites are rare and result in immediate intense pain at the bite site, followed by severe swelling, bleeding, blistering and extensive necrosis. Fatalities have been recorded. Polyvalent antivenom is essential and should be administered intravenously in large doses by a trained medical professional. The affected limb should be elevated but a tourniquet or pressure bandage should not be applied as this will localise the venom, resulting in increased tissue damage. **Prey:** Feeds on rodents, hares and ground-nesting birds and rarely eats frogs, toads, lizards and even Vervet Monkeys and duiker species. Larger prey is bitten and released, the snake following the scent trail to its dead victim. May seize and hold on to small prey. Subadults may hunt more actively and often raid rodent nests. **Reproduction:** Males engage in combat to earn the right to mate. Mating occurs in late summer and autumn. The gestation period is about 12 months. The female retains the eggs within her body until the embryos are fully developed, and gives birth to 8–43 neonates in late summer. Young measure

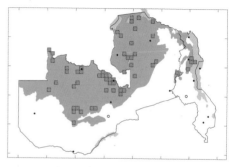

There is no dark triangle on the head.

240–370mm in TL. The female reproduces only every 2–3 years. The species rarely hybridises with the Puff Adder (*B. a. arietans*) and Rhinoceros Viper (*B. rhinoceros*). **Range:** Central and northern Zambia and Malawi and throughout East, Central and West Africa.

Nose-horned Viper   *Bitis nasicornis*

Max. SVL ♂ 1,330mm ♀ 1,388mm
A large, thick-bodied snake with a short tail, narrow neck and large, triangular, flat head. Nostrils large; cluster of 2–3 modified scales form large 'horns' on snout. 13–16 interorbitals; 15–20 circumorbitals, separated from supralabials by 3–4 rows of scales. 15–20 supralabials; 15–20 infralabials, first 4–6 in contact with anterior sublinguals. Body scales strongly keeled, in 39–43 rows at midbody. 117–140 ventrals; 22–34 paired subcaudals; cloacal scale entire. Body covered in geometric patterns of various shades of brown, red, tan and pastels; hues may include blue, pink, green, ochre and black. Series of pale, blue-green or green rectangles extends down back, may have longitudinal orange line down centre. Pale blotches bordered in front

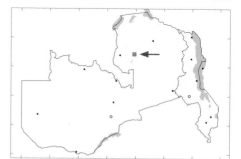

and behind by black blotches. Top of head blue or green, with diagnostic dark forward-pointing arrow-shaped marking on top. Two dark triangles often extend from eye to mouth. Ventrum dirty white to dull green with extensive

The Nose-horned Viper has 2–3 pairs of horns on the nose, and a dark triangle on the head.

Colour varies geographically and between individuals.

dark mottling and blotching. **Taxonomic note:** *B. nasicornis* is traditionally referred to as 'Rhinoceros Viper' and *B. rhinoceros* as 'West African Gaboon Viper'. However, in light of their respective scientific names, the authors prefer to use the more intuitive common names of 'Nose-horned Viper' for *B. nasicornis* and 'Rhinoceros Viper' for *B. rhinoceros*. **Habitat:** A forest specialist; it does not enter woodland, though it is rarely found in human-altered habitats in close proximity to forests. **Behaviour:** Nocturnal and predominantly terrestrial. Shelters in leaf litter, around fallen trees, under shrubs and root tangles or in holes during the day. May climb into low shrubs and small trees, aided by the partially prehensile tail. Sluggish when moving, but can strike extremely quickly. As it strikes, the large and recurved fangs are thrust forward and snap into position. It is an ambush hunter, spending most of its time stationary in a single location waiting for prey to pass. Fairly docile by nature, but if disturbed it makes its presence known with loud hissing and puffing. A skilled swimmer; it may lie in pools in swamp forests. **Venom:** Suspected to be potently cytotoxic, possibly with some haemotoxic and/or neurotoxic properties. Venom is produced in large quantities. Bites are rare. If bitten, the victim should be reassured and the affected limb elevated. A tourniquet or pressure bandage should not be applied as this will concentrate the venom, resulting in greater tissue damage. **Prey:** Juveniles actively hunt and prey on small rodents (often raiding nests), frogs and toads. Adults feed almost exclusively on mice and other rodents. **Reproduction:** The female retains her eggs within her body until the embryos are fully developed and gives birth to 6–42 neonates at the start of the rainy season. Neonates measure 180–250mm in TL. **Range:** Its presence in the region is under debate. Four specimens were collected near Lake Bangweulu, but these were destroyed in a museum fire. Elsewhere it occurs in Central and West Africa, entering Uganda, western Kenya and northern Tanzania.

Sand Snakes and relatives
Family Psammophiidae

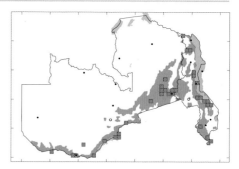

This family is characterised by the presence of large fangs below the posterior border of the eye and the lack of hypapophyses on the posterior vertebrae. Males possess vestigial, tube-like hemipenes.

Dwarf Sand Snake

These snakes inhabit a number of diverse habitats, including desert, grassland, savanna and woodland. Most species are terrestrial and diurnal, although one species, the Eastern Bark Snake (*Hemirhagerrhis nototaenia*), is predominantly arboreal. They are active hunters, preying on a variety of small vertebrates, including small mammals, amphibians and other reptiles. Only one species, the Olive Sand Snake (*Psammophis mossambicus*), possesses venom that could pose a danger to humans in exceptional circumstances. All species are oviparous.

This family is widespread throughout Africa, Madagascar, the Middle East, southern Europe and south-central Asia. A total of eight genera and 52 species are recognised, of which four genera and 12 species occur in the region.

BEAKED SNAKES   *Rhamphiophis*

Medium-sized to large snakes with a hooked snout and stout, muscular body. In all species the skull is short and the rostral bones are braced by the nasals, reinforcing them. The rostral is enlarged, pointed and projecting. Adults are shades of grey or brown, while juveniles may be blotched or spotted.

Beaked snakes are most often found on sandy soils, but are not restricted to it. They are diurnal and terrestrial and will often enter rodent and other burrows while hunting. They may also dig their own holes, an activity facilitated by the enlarged rostral and short, reinforced head. Adults prey on amphibians, small rodents, reptiles and other snakes, while juveniles sometimes include insects in their diet. The female lays clutches of 4–18 eggs.

This genus is widespread in Africa. It contains three recognised species, only one of which occurs in the region.

Rufous Beaked Snake   *Rhamphiophis rostratus*

Max. SVL ♂ 1,105mm ♀ 1,070mm
A large, stout-bodied snake with a prominently hooked snout. 3 (rarely 2) preoculars; 2 (rarely 3 or 4) postoculars; usually 2 anterior and 3 posterior temporals. 8–9 supralabials, 5th entering orbit; 10–12 infralabials, first 5 in contact with anterior sublinguals. Dorsals smooth, in 17 (rarely 19) rows at midbody. 148–194 ventrals; 87–118 paired subcaudals; cloacal scale divided. Yellowish to brown above, usually with darker scale margins, occasionally with scattered small reddish-brown dots. Dark facial mask usually present. Ventrals cream to yellowish white, occasionally with dark posterior borders. Juveniles have darker speckling on body. **Habitat:** Most common on sandy soils in mesic savanna, but occurs on heavy clay soils as well. **Behaviour:** Diurnal. Usually shelters in rodent burrows and old termitaria. Often moves with the head raised

The Rufous Beaked Snake has a coarse spotted appearance.

and swaying from side to side. Relatively slow moving while hunting and has a small gape. If threatened, it puts up a fierce display with much hissing, but rarely bites. It digs holes

Juveniles have a speckled appearance.

using the pointed snout to break the ground and the side of the head to scoop sand out. **Venom:** Rear-fanged and mildly venomous. Venom does not usually have any effect on humans but may occasionally cause mild headaches. **Prey:** Mainly amphibians, including Müller's Clawed Frogs, small rodents, shrews, lizards (including Ornate Scrub Lizards [*Nucras ornata*]), other snakes, fledgling birds and beetles. **Reproduction:** Female lays 8–17 eggs (34–40mm x 20–22mm) over the course of a few days in summer. **Range:** Southern and eastern Zambia, and throughout Malawi. Elsewhere it occurs from South Sudan and Ethiopia to eastern South Africa.

BARK SNAKES   *Hemirhagerrhis*

Snakes in this genus have a short, relatively flattened and narrow head that is distinct from the neck. Two weakly enlarged fangs are present below the posterior border of the eye. The nasal is elongate and partially divided by an oblique cleft extending from the nostril backwards and downwards to the margin of the scale. The tail is moderate to long.

Bark snakes are mildly venomous, although the venom has no effect on humans. They have a small gape and almost never attempt to bite. These diurnal snakes are predominantly arboreal, but one species occurring in Namibia is rupicolous. They prey on small geckos and lizards, with some species occasionally taking their eggs as well. The female lays clutches of 2–8 eggs.

This sub-Saharan genus contains four species, one of which occurs in the region.

Max. SVL ♂ 300mm ♀ 335mm

A medium-sized, slender snake with a moderately depressed head that is slightly distinct from the neck. 1 preocular; 2 (rarely 1) postoculars; 1 (rarely 2) anterior and 2 (rarely 1 or 3) posterior temporals. 8 (rarely 7 or 9) supralabials, 4th and 5th entering orbit; 9 (rarely 8, 10 or 11) infralabials, first 4–5 in contact with anterior sublinguals. Dorsals smooth, in 17 rows at midbody. 151–179 ventrals; 66–90 paired subcaudals; cloacal scale divided. Back grey to grey-brown with dark vertebral stripe and numerous short black crossbands that may break up into two rows of black spots parallel to dark vertebral stripe. Dark stripe passes through lower portion of eye and fades out on neck, often being replaced by row of grey lateral spots down body. Nape usually rusty orange; top of head dark. Flanks mottled grey and black. Ventrum dirty white, mottled with grey. Posterior portion of tail often orange

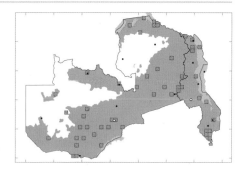

The bright orange tail is used for luring prey.

The Eastern Bark Snake closely resembles a tree branch.

Darren Pietersen

to salmon-pink. **Habitat:** Mesic savanna and woodlands. **Behaviour:** Semi-arboreal and fairly common. Shelters under loose bark or in tree cavities, where its coloration renders it nearly undetectable. **Prey:** Preys on small lizards and geckos, especially Dwarf Geckos (*Lygodactylus*), luring them closer by waving its brightly coloured tail to resemble a caterpillar. Usually hangs its head while prey is consumed. Occasionally feeds on small frogs and gecko eggs. **Reproduction:** Female lays 2–10 eggs (about 24mm x 6mm) in spring. **Range:** Widespread throughout the region. Elsewhere it occurs from South Africa through East Africa to Sudan and westwards to the southern DRC, with scattered records from Central and West Africa.

BRANCH'S BEAKED SNAKES   *Kladirostratus*

Medium-sized snakes with a relatively short, broad head. The rostral bones are weakly braced by the nasal and the rostral is short, acutely pointed and projecting. The nostril is pierced between two nasals and the internasal. Species in this genus have 9–13 subequal maxillary teeth, which are separated from the two enlarged fangs situated below the posterior border of the eye by a diastema, and 21–24 dentary teeth. The body is cylindrical and covered in smooth scales. The tail is of moderate length, with paired subcaudals.

These active diurnal snakes hunt for amphibians, lizards and small rodents, often entering burrows to do so. They are mildly venomous, although the venom is not known to affect humans. Females are oviparous and lay clutches of 10–15 eggs in summer.

They are widespread in the woodland and savanna of Central and West Africa. Two species and two subspecies are recognised, of which one species and two subspecies occur in the region.

Sharp-nosed Beaked Snake   *Kladirostratus acutus*

The snout is sharply pointed.

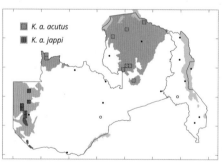

Max. SVL ♂ 875mm ♀ 895mm

A medium-sized snake with a short head and sharp, pointed snout. 1 (occasionally 2) preocular; 2 (occasionally 3) postoculars; 2 (rarely 1 or 3) anterior and 3 (occasionally 2 or 4) posterior temporals. 8 (rarely 9) supralabials, 4th and 5th entering orbit; 9–11 infralabials, first 4–5 in contact with anterior sublinguals. Dorsals smooth, in 17 rows at midbody. 155–201 ventrals; 53–80 paired subcaudals; cloacal scale divided. Back light grey-brown to yellowish brown with dark vertebral band 2 scale rows wide (occasionally faint, rarely absent); narrow pale line may be present along dorsal midline. Dark vertebral line forks on top of head; 3rd dark, central stripe usually present between bifurcation. Broad, dark stripe extends along flanks, originating on snout and passing through eye. Supralabials, lower flanks and ventrum cream to white; narrow pale brown stripe sometimes present on outermost scale row. **Subspecies:** Two subspecies are recognised, both of which enter the region. The typical form (*K. a. acutus*) has fewer ventrals (168–190 in males, 155–184 in females) and subcaudals (58–67 in males, 53–65 in females) and occurs in northern and eastern Zambia. *K. a. jappi* has more ventrals

(186–201 in males, 181–188 in females) and subcaudals (71–80 in males, 66–71 in females) and is restricted to western Zambia. **Habitat:** Shows a preference for miombo woodland; also found in moist savanna, open woodland and around marshes. **Behaviour:** A fast, active, diurnal snake. Appears to spend the majority of its time in burrows, where it presumably hunts. It is rear-fanged and mildly venomous.

Prey: Actively hunts for rodents, worm lizards and probably other small lizards during the day. Also hunts in burrows for rodents (especially neonates), sheltering lizards and (rarely) frogs. **Reproduction:** Female lays 10–15 eggs (about 19mm x 14mm) in summer. **Range:** From Angola through western and northern Zambia and the southern DRC to Tanzania and Rwanda. May occur in northern Malawi.

Luke Verburgt

The Sharp-nosed Beaked Snake resembles the Striped Grass Snake in general coloration.

GRASS SNAKES OR SKAAPSTEKERS   *Psammophylax*

Medium-sized snakes with a head distinct from the neck and a nostril pierced between two nasals and the internasal. The maxilla bears 10–12 subequal teeth, which are separated by a diastema from the two enlarged fangs situated below the posterior border of the eye. The body is cylindrical, the tail is of moderate length with paired subcaudals, and the body scales are smooth.

These active, diurnal snakes are terrestrial and widespread in grassland, savanna and woodland. They actively hunt for lizards, amphibians and small rodents, and are mildly venomous. The venom is relatively viscous and oozes from the venom glands through a hole in the upper jaw into the membranous sheath that encloses the fangs. These snakes strike and grip their prey, holding onto it until it is subdued by the venom. The venom is not known to have major effects on humans, although slight swelling and itching can occur around the site of the bite.

Species in this genus are oviparous and the female either lays eggs or retains the eggs within her body until after they hatch, appearing to give birth to live young. The female lays clutches of 5–30 eggs or gives birth to up to four neonates. Some species curl around their egg clutches to protect them.

Grass snakes occur over much of sub-Saharan Africa, with the greatest diversity in East and southern Africa. Six species are currently recognised, two of which occur in the region.

KEY Regional *Psammophylax* species

1a Usually 2 anterior temporals; ventrum white to yellowish . . . . *P. tritaeniatus* (p. 84)
 b Usually a single anterior temporal; ventrum dark grey . . . . *P. variabilis* (p. 85)

Gary Nicolau

The Striped Grass Snake usually has an orange stripe on the flanks.

Paul Lloyd

Northern individuals are more plainly coloured.

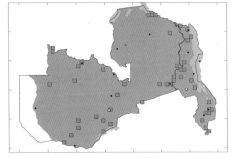

Max. SVL ♂ 734mm ♀ 680mm

A small to medium-sized snake with a head that is slightly broader than the neck and a moderately pointed snout. 1 (rarely 2) preocular; 2 postoculars; 2 anterior and 3 posterior temporals. 8 supralabials, 4th and 5th entering orbit; 9–11 infralabials, first 4–5 in contact with anterior sublinguals. Body scales smooth, in 17 rows at midbody. 139–176 ventrals; 46–69 paired subcaudals; cloacal scale divided. Pale olive-grey to brown above with dark, narrow dorsal stripe, usually pale-centred, originating just behind head. Broad, dark lateral stripe originates just behind nostril and passes through eye. Lower flanks and ventrum yellowish to white. Red stippling or faint red stripe may be present on outermost scale row from side of neck to cloaca. Individuals from northern regions may have very faint lateral stripes or be uniform grey above, may lack vertebral stripe or have it restricted to nape only. **Habitat:** Mesic savanna and grassland. **Behaviour:** Diurnal. When disturbed it escapes into the nearest cover at great speed and then freezes, relying on its coloration to escape detection. When harassed, it may adopt tonic immobility (feign death). May also take refuge under rocks, in logs and in moribund termitaria. It is rear-fanged and mildly venomous, although the venom does not usually affect humans. **Prey:** Hunts for small mammals and lizards, although juveniles will also eat frogs. **Reproduction:** Female lays 5–18 eggs (20–28mm x 10–16mm) under suitable cover, including rocks or in holes, in summer. Embryonic development starts prior to egg deposition and incubation is consequently fairly short (43–45 days). Hatchlings measure 130–220mm in TL. **Range:** Widespread throughout the region. Range extends into Angola, the DRC and Tanzania and southwards to north-eastern South Africa

Grey-bellied Grass Snake *Psammophylax variabilis*

The dark temporal patch is characteristic of the Grey-bellied Grass Snake.

Max. SVL ♂ 835mm ♀ 620mm

A medium-sized snake with a small head and rounded snout. 1 preocular; 2 (rarely 1 or 3) postoculars; 1 anterior and 2–3 posterior temporals. 8 supralabials, 4th and 5th entering orbit; 10–11 infralabials, first 5 in contact with anterior sublinguals. Dorsals smooth, in 17 rows at midbody. 149–167 ventrals; 49–61 paired subcaudals; cloacal scale divided. Grey to olive-brown above, usually with three faint ragged, darker longitudinal stripes (one dorsal and two dorsolateral stripes) running length of body. Dark vertebral stripe usually divided by very narrow pale median stripe. White ventrolateral stripe often present. Supralabials

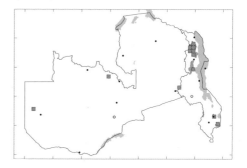

and chin whitish, usually suffused with dark grey; ventrum uniform dark grey. **Habitat:** Montane and floodplain grasslands, showing a preference for moist areas. **Behaviour:** Diurnal. Shelters in rotting logs, vegetation clumps, surface debris and holes. May be locally common. **Venom:** Rear-fanged and mildly venomous, although the venom is not considered dangerous to humans, causing only mild headache. **Prey:** Small mammals, fledgling birds, lizards, frogs and fish. **Reproduction:** The female retains the eggs within her body until the embryos complete their development and gives birth to up to four fully developed young (151–155mm in TL) in mid-summer. **Range:** In the region it is most common on the Nyika Plateau and the Zomba and Mulanje mountains, with scattered records elsewhere. Outside the region it is found from extreme northern Botswana, through Central and East Africa, to Ethiopia.

SAND AND WHIP SNAKES   *Psammophis*

Snakes in this genus are sometimes referred to as grass snakes. In all species the body is slim and elongate, the tail is long, the head is distinct from the neck. The nostril is pierced between 2–3 nasals. There are 10–16 maxillary teeth with 1–2 enlarged, fang-like teeth that are usually present below the anterior border of the eye. These teeth are preceded and followed by a diastema. The Lined Sand Snake (*P. lineatus*) lacks the two enlarged teeth and instead has a single row of mandibular teeth of roughly equal size. The body scales are smooth and the subcaudals are paired. Most species have longitudinal stripes on the dorsum.

Members of this genus are terrestrial to partially arboreal, often climbing into low shrubs to hunt, bask or sleep. They occupy a range of habitats including desert, grassland, savanna and woodland. If grasped by the tail, these snakes will often struggle so violently, including deliberate rotational spinning, that the tail is shed. The tail itself cannot be regrown, but if only the tip is lost, the tail cone can grow back. This can result in erroneously low subcaudal counts. All species in this genus are mildly venomous. They prey on various small vertebrates, including lizards, amphibians and small rodents, although some species also eat other snakes. Prey is struck and grasped until subdued by the venom. Only the venom of the Olive Sand Snake (*P. mossambicus*) poses a danger to humans under extreme circumstances. Envenomation may lead to mild symptoms such as headaches, nausea, and pain and itching at the site of the bite. A bite from a large individual may be life threatening to very young and very old people, the immunocompromised and those that show an unusual sensitivity to the venom. All species are oviparous, the female laying clutches of 3–30 eggs.

This genus is widespread in Africa and also occurs in the Middle East and Asia. To date 34 species are recognised, although the taxonomy of some species groups remains unresolved and more (or fewer) species may be recognised in future. Seven species occur in the region.

KEY Regional *Psammophis* species

1a 11 (very rarely 9) midbody scale rows . . . . *P. angolensis* (p. 87)
  b 15–17 midbody scale rows. 2

2a Usually 2 posterior nasals; upper posterior nasal with posterior projection; usually 7 supralabials, 3rd and 4th entering orbit; 15 scale rows at midbody . . . . *P. jallae* (p. 88)
  b Single posterior nasal, or if 2 then no posterior projection in upper posterior nasal; usually 8–9 supralabials, 4th and 5th or 4th–6th entering orbit; 17 (rarely 15) scale rows at midbody. 3

3a Single (rarely 2) anterior temporals; no enlarged fang-like teeth below eye . . . . *P. lineatus* (p. 89)
  b 2 (rarely 1) anterior temporals; enlarged fang-like teeth present below eye. 4

4a Body usually uniform dark above, sometimes with dark middorsal stripe; body robust. . . . . *P. mossambicus* (p. 89)
  b Pale longitudinal stripes usually present on body; body slender. 5

Dwarf Sand Snake   *Psammophis angolensis*

The Dwarf Sand Snake has a broad, dark vertebral stripe.

Max. SVL ♂ 320mm ♀ 352mm

A small sand snake with a single anterior and posterior nasal. 1 (rarely 2) preocular, usually separated from frontal (rarely in contact); 2 postoculars; usually 1 anterior and 2 posterior temporals. 8 (6–9) supralabials, 4th and 5th (rarely 3rd and 4th, 4th only, or 5th and 6th) entering orbit; 8 (rarely 7 or 9) infralabials, first 4 (rarely 3 or 5) in contact with anterior sublinguals. Dorsals smooth, in 11 (rarely 9) rows at midbody. 133–157 ventrals; 57–82 subcaudals; cloacal scale divided. Body grey to pale or dark olive-brown with dark vertebral stripe edged with narrow black stripe that may break up into spots. Head dark brown to black with three narrow white to yellow crossbands. Supralabials and lower portions of head white. Neck dark brown with 1–2 pale crossbands that are narrowest medially and broaden laterally. Flanks yellow to grey; lower flanks and ventrum white to yellow. Orange mid-ventral band occasionally present.

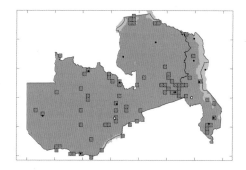

Habitat: Savanna. **Behaviour:** A secretive diurnal snake. If harassed, it takes shelter under rocks and logs, and may also adopt tonic immobility (feign death). **Prey:** Small skinks, lizards and frogs. **Reproduction:** Female lays 3–5 small eggs (15–24mm x 5–8mm). **Range:** Widespread throughout the region. Elsewhere it occurs from South Africa northwards to the DRC and Tanzania.

Jalla's Sand Snake *Psammophis jallae*

Stephen Spawls

Jalla's Sand Snake is a poorly known and rarely seen species.

Max. SVL ♂ 820mm ♀ 650mm
A fairly large, active snake. 1 anterior and 2 (rarely 1) posterior nasals; upper posterior nasal with posterior projection. 1 preocular, in broad contact with frontal; 2 (rarely 1) postoculars; 2 (rarely 1) anterior and 2 (rarely 3) posterior temporals. 7 (rarely 6 or 8) supralabials, 3rd and 4th (rarely 4th and 5th) entering orbit; 9 (rarely 8 or 10) infralabials, first 4 (rarely 3 or 5) in contact with anterior sublinguals. Dorsals smooth, in 15 rows at midbody. 154–175 ventrals; 84–112 subcaudals; cloacal scale divided. Back dark brown to light grey-brown, occasionally with pair of pale dorsolateral stripes. Series of pale spots may be present along dorsal midline. Flanks usually red-brown to chestnut-brown. Supralabials, ventrum and lower flanks white to pale yellow. Lower jaw usually has blue-grey tinge at centre, becoming brick-red at centre of throat. **Habitat:** Grassland and open woodland, especially on

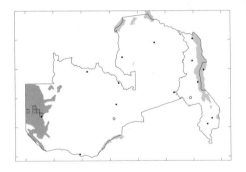

Kalahari sands. **Behaviour:** A rare, diurnal snake. It will climb into low shrubs to bask and search for prey, or when escaping predators. **Prey:** Diet consists mostly of skinks and lizards (including agamas), but otherwise poorly known. **Reproduction:** Unknown. **Range:** South-eastern Angola into Namibia, Botswana, Zimbabwe and extreme northern South Africa, entering the region in western Zambia.

Lined Sand Snake   *Psammophis lineatus*

The Lined Sand Snake is often confused with the Olive Sand Snake.

Max. SVL ♂ 880mm ♀ 768mm

A medium-sized, slender snake with a single anterior and posterior nasal. 1 preocular, usually well separated from frontal; 1–2 (rarely 3) postoculars; 1 (rarely 2) anterior and 2 (rarely 3 or 4) posterior temporals. 8 supralabials, 4th and 5th entering orbit; 9 (rarely 10) infralabials, first 3–4 in contact with anterior sublinguals. Dorsals smooth, in 17 (rarely 15) rows at midbody. 138–159 ventrals; 75–107 paired subcaudals; cloacal scale divided. Head and body light to dark brown or olive-green; individual scales sometimes black-edged. Narrow, pale transverse bar usually present in temporal region and another on nape, these rarely extending over top of head. Supralabials often dark-edged posteriorly; infralabials, chin and throat usually unspotted. Flanks pale yellow, with black lateral edges to each scale, particularly in neck region. Ventrum pale green to greenish yellow, or white. Pre- and postoculars yellow or white, contrasting with

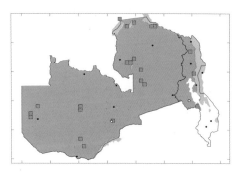

rest of head. Three narrow longitudinal yellow-green stripes may be present on body. **Habitat:** Rivers and swamps in savanna and bushveld. **Behaviour:** Poorly known. An active, diurnal snake. **Prey:** Lizards, frogs and small mammals. **Reproduction:** Female lays 6–9 eggs (23–27mm x 12–18mm) in summer. **Range:** Widespread throughout the region and tropical Africa, from northern Botswana and north-western Zimbabwe to Sudan and West Africa.

Olive Sand Snake   *Psammophis mossambicus*

Max. SVL ♂ 1,415mm ♀ 1,285mm

A large, robust sand snake. 1 anterior and 1 (rarely 2) posterior nasal. 1 preocular, usually well separated from frontal; 2 postoculars; 1–2 anterior and 2–3 posterior temporals. 8 (rarely 6–9) supralabials, 4th and 5th (rarely 3rd and 4th or 5th and 6th) entering orbit; 10 (rarely 9 or 11) infralabials, first 4 (rarely 5) in contact with anterior sublinguals. Dorsals smooth, in 17 rows at midbody. 150–180 ventrals; 82–121 subcaudals; cloacal scale divided. Back olive-brown to yellowish, with scales often

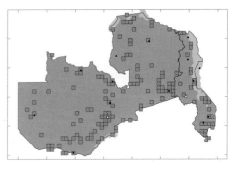

Luke Verburgt

The dark-spotted labials are a good identifying feature.

black-edged, giving slight chequered or striped effect; scattered dark scales (sometimes large dark patches) may be present on body. All-dark individuals and intergrades occur. Series of pale vertebral spots may be present. Head may be unpatterned or have symmetrical chestnut-brown pattern or faint transverse lines. Supralabials and infralabials each have dark spot, often extending onto sides of neck. Ventrum white to yellowish (occasionally bright yellow), immaculate or with scattered dark spots and streaks. **Habitat:** Moist savanna and grassland. Shows a preference for riparian vegetation and the edges of swamps and reedbeds. **Behaviour:** A common, active, diurnal snake. Often seen crossing roads, and regularly forages around human dwellings. **Venom:** Rear-fanged and bites readily. Venom may cause localised pain and swelling, headaches and nausea, but antivenom is ineffective and in most cases not necessary. Repeated exposure to its venom has resulted in anaphylactic shock. **Prey:** A variety of vertebrates, including frogs, lizards (including Ornate Scrub Lizards [*Nucras ornata*]), geckos, other snakes (including young Black Mambas [*Dendroaspis polylepis*]), small mammals and birds. **Reproduction:** Female lays 10–30 eggs (28–40mm x 10–20mm) in sheltered locations in mid-summer. Incubation takes about 65 days. Hatchlings measure 270–300mm in TL. **Range:** Widespread from South Africa to Angola and central Sudan.

The Olive Sand Snake is usually plain brown, but some individuals have darker patches on the body (seen above).

Eastern Stripe-bellied Sand Snake   *Psammophis orientalis*

The Eastern Stripe-bellied Sand Snake closely resembles the Western Stripe-bellied Sand Snake.

Max. SVL ♂ 830mm ♀ 725mm

A medium-sized, slender sand snake with a single anterior and posterior nasal. 1 (rarely 2) preocular in narrow contact with, or separated from, frontal; 2 postoculars; usually 2 anterior and 2 posterior temporals, but fusions common. 8 (rarely 7 or 9) supralabials, 4th and 5th (rarely 3rd and 4th, 4th–6th or 5th and 6th) entering orbit; 10 (rarely 9 or 11) infralabials, first 4 (rarely 3 or 5) in contact with anterior sublinguals. Dorsals smooth, in 17 rows at midbody. 146–170 ventrals; 91–118 paired subcaudals; cloacal scale divided. Back olive-grey to dark brown; flanks paler grey-brown. Scales along vertebral midline have pale bases, giving rise to narrow pale

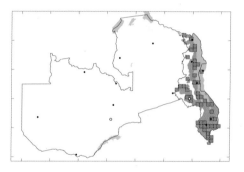

The ventrum is bright yellow, flanked by black lines.

vertebral stripe. Faint pale dorsolateral stripes may be present. Labials and lower scale rows on flanks white to light yellow, separated from grey-brown flanks by narrow black stripe. Second dark stripe separates white-yellow flanks from yellow mid-ventrum. Top of head unpatterned; anterior supralabials may have dark speckling. **Habitat:** Mesic savanna. **Behaviour:** An active, diurnal snake that is predominantly terrestrial but will often climb into low bushes when foraging or basking, or to escape when pursued. Often sleeps curled up in low bushes and the lower branches of trees. Very fast and readily disappears into the nearest cover when pursued. Often found foraging around human habitation. **Venom:** Mildly venomous. Venom not considered dangerous to humans, although bites have resulted in mild localised swelling and slight pain. **Prey:** Actively forages for frogs, lizards, skinks, rodents, small birds and occasionally other snakes (including Speckled Green Snakes [*Philothamnus punctatus*]). Frequently killed by a variety of raptors such as Tawny Eagles, as well as Southern Ground Hornbills. **Reproduction:** Female lays 4–10 eggs (32mm x 12mm) in summer. **Range:** From southern Kenya through Malawi to central Mozambique and eastern Zimbabwe.

Western Stripe-bellied Sand Snake   *Psammophis subtaeniatus*

Max. SVL ♂ 900mm ♀ 885mm

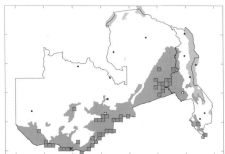

A medium-sized, slender snake with 1 anterior and 1 (rarely 2) posterior nasal. 1 (rarely 2) preocular in narrow contact with, or separated from, frontal; 2 postoculars; usually 2 anterior and 2 (rarely 3) posterior temporals, but fusions common. 9 (rarely 8 or 10) supralabials, 4th–6th (rarely 4th and 5th, 3rd–5th, 5th and 6th, 5th–7th or 4th–7th) entering orbit. 10 (rarely 9 or 11) infralabials, first 4 (rarely 5) in contact with anterior sublinguals.

The Western Stripe-bellied Sand Snake typically has two pale stripes running down its body, but it is sometimes plain brown. INSERT It usually has a series of pale to grey transverse bands on the neck.

Dorsals smooth, in 17 rows at midbody. 155–181 ventrals; 106–132 subcaudals; cloacal scale divided. Back grey-olive to dark brown, sometimes with each scale black-edged. Pair of dorsolateral stripes, pale, edged in black above and below, bordered below by broad chestnut-brown to brown lateral stripe. Lower flanks and outer edges of ventrals white and separated from bright yellow mid-ventrum by pair of narrow black stripes (rarely absent). Head brown, sometimes plain, but usually with series of pale to grey transverse bands that continue onto the neck as faint crossbars. Supralabials, chin and throat white to yellow (sometimes bright orange), usually heavily speckled with black. Some individuals in the middle Zambezi Valley have vestigial or entirely absent dorsal and ventral stripes and appear uniform in colour. **Habitat:** Dry savanna, especially mopane woodland and thornveld. Also commonly encountered on rock outcrops and in riverine vegetation. **Behaviour:** This fast, diurnal snake is predominantly terrestrial but will climb into low shrubs to look for food, bask or escape predators. Often sleeps curled up in low bushes and the lower branches of trees. Very fast and will rapidly disappear into the nearest cover when disturbed. It 'polishes' itself with a nasal gland secretion, thought to reduce moisture loss. The venom is not known to have any effect on humans. **Prey and Predators:** Preys on lizards, skinks, frogs and rodents, which are killed by envenomation. Very rarely eats small birds. Frequently preyed on by a variety of raptors as well as Southern Ground Hornbills. **Reproduction:** Female lays 4–10 eggs (about 32mm x 12mm) in summer. Hatchlings measure about 200mm in TL. **Range:** From southern Angola and northern Namibia, through southern and eastern Zambia to Zimbabwe, parts of western Mozambique and eastern South Africa. Also occurs in extreme southern and western Malawi.

Zambian Sand Snake *Psammophis zambiensis*

The Zambian Sand Snake usually has a coarse reticulate dorsal pattern.

Max. SVL ♂ 711mm ♀ 767mm

A medium-sized snake with undivided anterior and posterior nasals. 1 preocular, usually narrowly separated from frontal; 2 postoculars; usually 2 anterior and 2 posterior temporals, although fusions common. Cuneate scales rarely present. 8 supralabials, 4th and 5th entering orbit (rarely 7 supralabials with 3rd and 4th entering orbit); 10 (rarely 7–9) infralabials, first 4 in contact with anterior sublinguals. Dorsals smooth, in 17 rows at midbody. 148–165 ventrals; 75–90 paired subcaudals; cloacal scale divided. Three pale transverse bars present on head behind eyes. Back greenish to olive-brown, scales often dark-edged and giving rise to reticulate pattern. Narrow pale vertebral stripe usually present, often with pale stripe on either side that may be 'linked' with narrow crossbands, which may result in large brown spots surrounded by pale network. Pale dorsolateral stripes narrowly edged in black; reticulate pattern often present on neck. Uniformly coloured individuals sometimes occur; younger individuals more distinctly marked. Ventrum white, each scale often

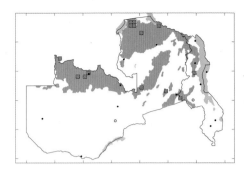

has narrow black posterior border, which is more pronounced in juveniles. **Habitat:** Frequents marshes, dambos and moist miombo woodland. **Behaviour:** Diurnal and terrestrial. **Venom:** Probably similar to Olive Sand Snake (*P. mossambicus*), but milder, and does not pose a threat to humans. **Prey:** Skinks, such as Anchieta's Skink (*Eumecia anchietae*), and frogs. **Reproduction:** Female lays 11–14 eggs (16–19mm x 10–12mm) in summer. **Range:** Northern and eastern Zambia, central Malawi and the southern DRC. Possibly more widespread than currently known.

Juvenile Zambian Sand Snakes are more boldly marked than adults.

Shovel-snouts
Family Prosymnidae

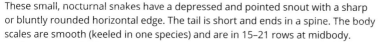

East African
Shovel-snout

These small, nocturnal snakes have a depressed and pointed snout with a sharp or bluntly rounded horizontal edge. The tail is short and ends in a spine. The body scales are smooth (keeled in one species) and are in 15–21 rows at midbody.

They are usually found in leaf litter or buried in loose sand, with one species inhabiting rock crevices. They prey almost exclusively on soft-shelled reptile eggs, but some species also eat gecko eggs. The anterior teeth are absent or very small, with tooth size increasing posteriorly. The last 2–3 teeth are enlarged and lancet-shaped and are used to slit open the eggs as they are being swallowed. The contents are forced out once the eggs are in the gut. Hard-shelled gecko eggs are swallowed whole and the digestive enzymes break down the eggshell to release the contents. These snakes may not be able to determine how fresh an egg is before swallowing it, as well-developed embryos with eggshells still attached to them have been found in the stomachs of some individuals. Some species employ a 'watch-spring' defence, during which the snake forms a tight, flat coil with the head in the centre while it rapidly coils and uncoils the body. Females lay small clutches of 3–6 eggs.

This small family contains a single genus, which is endemic to Africa.

SHOVEL-SNOUTS   *Prosymna*

Small snakes with a short, cylindrical body and a head that is not distinct from the neck. The rostral is very large. The internasals may be discrete or fused into a single band-like scale (fused in all species occurring in the region). A horizontal suture usually extends from the nostril to the loreal. This genus is restricted to sub-Saharan Africa. It contains 16 species, four of which occur in the region.

KEY Regional *Prosymna* species

1a 19–21 midbody scale rows . . . . *P. pitmani* (p. 97)
 b 15–17 midbody scale rows **2**

2a Dorsum light brown with dark blotches . . . . *P. angolensis* (p. 96)
 b Dorsum dark brown, blue-grey or black **3**

3a Rostral acutely angular in profile; dorsum olive to blue-grey, uniform or
   with each scale dark-edged; each ventral with crescent-shaped dark
   mark proximally and pale along free edge . . . . *P. ambigua* (p. 95)
 b Rostral bluntly pointed in profile; dorsum brown, blue-grey or black, often
   with paravertebral series of white spots; ventrum uniform white with
   irregular dark blotches or infusions, or uniform grey to black . . . . *P. stuhlmanni* (p. 98)

Bocage's Shovel-snout   *Prosymna ambigua*

Max. SVL ♂ 254mm ♀ 320mm

A small snake with a sharp snout and fused internasals. 1 preocular; 2 (rarely 1 or 3) postoculars; 1 (rarely 2) anterior and 2 (rarely 3) posterior temporals. 4–8 (usually 6) supralabials, 3rd and 4th (rarely 2nd and 3rd or 2nd–4th) entering orbit; 8 (7–9) infralabials, first 3 (rarely 2 or 4)

in contact with sublinguals. Dorsals smooth, in 17 (rarely 15) rows at midbody. 122–157 ventrals (122–141 in males, 138–157 in females); 15–34 paired subcaudals (25–34 in males, 15–21 in females); cloacal scale entire. Blue-grey to purple-brown above and white below; each ventral and subcaudal scale dark at base.

Subspecies: Two poorly defined subspecies are recognised, with only the typical form (*P. a. ambigua*) entering the region. **Habitat:** Moist savanna, miombo woodland and forest–savanna mosaic. **Behaviour:** A fossorial, predominantly nocturnal snake. If threatened, it may employ a 'watch-spring' coiling defence. **Prey:** Preys almost exclusively on the eggs of other reptiles. **Reproduction:** Female lays 3–6 eggs (about 25mm x 7mm). **Range:** From East Africa through southern Sudan to Cameroon, just entering northern Zambia.

The snout is distinctly upturned.

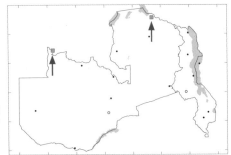

Bocage's Shovel-snout, a small, predominantly nocturnal snake, is rarely recorded in Zambia.

Angola Shovel-snout   *Prosymna angolensis*

Max. SVL ♂ 225mm ♀ 300mm
A small snake with a pointed snout, fused internasals and sharp horizontal edge to the rostral. 1 preocular; 1 (rarely 2) postocular; 1 (rarely 2) anterior and 2 (rarely 3) posterior temporals. 6 (rarely 5 or 7) supralabials, 3rd and 4th entering orbit; 7–8 (rarely 6) infralabials, first 3 (rarely 4) in contact with sublinguals. Dorsals

smooth, in 15 rows at midbody. 121–163 ventrals; 16–26 paired subcaudals; cloacal scale entire. Back light yellow-brown, usually with series of paired black spots. Some individuals finely speckled or with large black blotches along back. Ventrum and lower flanks white. **Habitat:** Favours Kalahari sands in arid and mesic savanna. **Behaviour:** A semi-fossorial, predominantly nocturnal snake. Usually found burrowing under logs and rocks or in leaf litter. Employs a 'watch-spring' coiling defence. **Prey:** Feeds exclusively on reptile eggs. Punctures soft eggs with blade-like rear maxillary teeth. **Reproduction:** Unknown. Presumably similar to other shovel-snouts. **Range:** Western

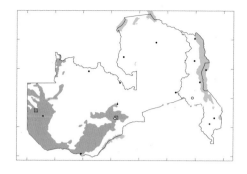

and southern Zambia and adjacent Angola, northern Namibia, northern Botswana and north-western Zimbabwe.

The Angola Shovel-snout occurs in central and western Zambia, and varies in colour.

Pitman's Shovel-snout   *Prosymna pitmani*

Max. SVL ♂ 245mm ♀ 285mm
A small snake with a sharp, shovel-like snout and short tail. Internasals fused. 1–2 preoculars; 2 postoculars; 1–2 anterior and 2 posterior temporals. 6 supralabials, 3rd and 4th entering orbit; 8 infralabials, first 3 in contact with sublinguals. Dorsals smooth, in 19–21 rows at midbody. 139–163 ventrals (139–149 in males, 155–163 in females); 17–28 paired subcaudals (21–28 in males, 17–22 in females); cloacal scale entire. Dark purple-brown above with

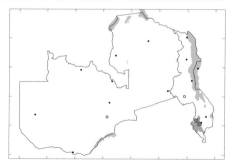

pale spot near centre of each scale. Ventrum white. **Habitat:** Mesic savanna and miombo woodland. **Behaviour:** Nocturnal and partially fossorial. Usually takes refuge amongst dead leaves in rock fissures. **Prey:** Feeds exclusively on reptile eggs. **Reproduction:** A female was documented laying four eggs (20–23mm x 8mm) in June. **Range:** Southern Malawi and adjacent Mozambique, eastwards to northern Mozambique and south-eastern Tanzania.

Pitman's Shovel-snout, a small snake with a short tail, occurs only in southern Malawi.

East African Shovel-snout   *Prosymna stuhlmanni*

Max. SVL ♂ 225mm ♀ 263mm
A small snake with a pointed, shovel-like snout and single band-like internasal. 1 (rarely 0 or 2) preocular; 2 (occasionally 1, rarely 0 or 3) postoculars; 1 (rarely 2) anterior and 2 (rarely 1 or 3) posterior temporals. 4–7 (usually 6) supralabials, 3rd and 4th (rarely 2nd and 3rd or 2nd–4th) entering orbit; 8 (rarely 7 or 9) infralabials, first 3 (rarely 4) in contact with sublinguals. Dorsals smooth, in 15–17 rows at midbody. 122–164 ventrals (122–153 in males, 138–164 in females); 17–39 paired subcaudals (27–39 in males, 17–30 in females); cloacal scale entire. Back dark brown to metallic blue-black, usually uniform but occasionally with paired rows of small white spots or with each scale pale-centred. Head dark, becoming lighter towards tip of snout, latter often straw-yellow. Ventrum

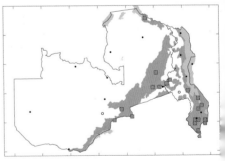

white, occasionally with dark blotches, rarely uniform black or grey. Dark median stripe often present on subcaudals. **Habitat:** Mesic savanna and montane grassland. **Behaviour:** Usually found sheltering under logs and rocks or in dense leaf litter, but active on the surface after rainstorms. It is not known to employ the 'watch-spring' defence, but may lift the anterior part of the body and partially flatten the neck. **Prey:** Feeds almost exclusively on reptile eggs, predominantly gecko eggs. Opportunistically feeds on termite alates. **Reproduction:** Female lays 3–4 eggs (19–30mm x 6–8mm). **Range:** Southern and eastern Zambia, through Malawi to East Africa, northwards to southern Somalia and southwards to eastern South Africa.

Darren Pietersen

The East African Shovel-snout usually has a row of pale spots down each side of the back.

Luke Verburgt

The tip of the snout is typically pale to bright yellow.

Mole Snakes and relatives
Family Pseudaspididae

This small family consists of morphologically different snakes that all have 42 chromosomes, a condition that is unknown in other advanced snakes (i.e. all snakes to the exclusion of worm snakes, thread snakes, blind snakes, and pythons).

Snakes in this family are non-venomous, and feed on a variety of vertebrates.

Two monotypic genera occur in Africa and two species in one genus occur in Asia. The close relatedness of these three genera, despite their disjunct distribution, was recently confirmed genetically. A single species occurs in the region.

Mole Snake

MOLE SNAKES   *Pseudaspis*

This genus contains a single species, which is widespread in southern and East Africa. It is unusual in that the female gives birth to live young.

Mole Snake   *Pseudaspis cana*

Max. SVL ♂ 1,265mm ♀ 1,820mm
A large, stout snake with a cylindrical body and slightly hooked snout. Head small, not distinct from neck or body. Tail thick, usually bluntly rounded. 1 preocular; 3 postoculars; 2–3 anterior and 3–5 posterior temporals. 7 supralabials, 4th entering orbit; 10–13 infralabials, first 4–7 in contact with anterior sublinguals. Body scales smooth, overlapping, in 25–31 (usually 27) rows at midbody. 175–218 ventrals (usually 175–196 in males, 197–218 in females); 43–70 paired subcaudals (55–70 in males, 43–57 in females); cloacal scale divided. Coloration varies regionally and with age. Adults usually uniform light grey to brown above; ventrum yellowish, sometimes with darker infusions. Juveniles light grey to reddish brown or brown, usually with numerous dark cross-bands or blotches; 1–2 rows of pale lateral and ventrolateral spots may be present; ventrum yellowish, sometimes with darker spotting or

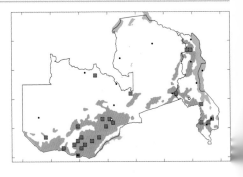

blotching. Subadults greyish white to light brown above, with dark blotches or continuous zig-zag pattern along dorsal midline; series of pale dorsolateral spots often present; series of dark blotches on flanks; lower flanks and ventrum pale. Some adults retain juvenile coloration. **Habitat:** Sandy environments and montane grassland. **Behaviour:** A secretive, diurnal snake. Spends most of its time underground in rodent

The adult Mole Snake is usually uniformly brown in colour.

burrows. Displays ferociously if threatened, resembling a venomous cobra (*Naja*). Truculent and bites readily. Its large, blade-like teeth have sharp posterior cutting edges and often leave deep wounds. When inactive, it takes refuge in burrows, although it sometimes submerges itself in soft sand with just the head exposed. **Prey:** Mainly rodents, particularly those that live in burrows, where they can be captured and constricted with minimal effort. Some individuals ambush molerats by inserting the forepart of the body into a mole mound and waiting for an unwary victim to pass by. It eats birds and their eggs as well. Juveniles also prey on lizards. **Reproduction:** Males engage in combat, crawling over each other while trying to press their opponent's body down. Their teeth are razor-sharp and males bite at each other's tails in what is believed to be an attempt to damage their opponent's reproductive organs. Mating occurs in late spring. Viviparous, the female gives birth to 25–50 (up to 95 in very large females) young in late summer. Hatchlings measure 200–310mm in TL. **Range:** Recorded throughout the region, but largely absent from northern and eastern Zambia. Elsewhere it occurs from Kenya southwards to South Africa and westwards to Angola.

Juveniles look very different to the adults, and have darker markings on the back.

African Burrowing Snakes
Family Atractaspididae

This predominantly African family consists of robust to extremely slender snakes, many of which are fossorial. Members of the subfamily Atractaspidinae have cytotoxic venom and are considered dangerous to humans, while species in the subfamily Aparallactinae are mildly venomous or harmless and are not considered a threat to humans.

There are 69 species in 11 genera recognised at present, of which 13 species in seven genera have been recorded in the region.

Bibron's Burrowing Asp

Burrowing Adders and relatives
Subfamily Atractaspidinae

Snakes in this subfamily are small and have a relatively slender body and a small head that is not distinct from the neck. The eyes are small, the tail is short and the loreal is absent. The body is cylindrical and the snout is rounded. They have long, hollow fangs near the front of the mouth that are extruded out of the side of the mouth and typically employed in a stabbing motion. The body scales are smooth, shiny and lack apical pits. Most species are uniformly grey to black, sometimes with pale lower flanks and ventrums. The hypapophyses of the middle and posterior vertebrae are reduced to flat platforms that barely project.

These snakes are fossorial and predominantly nocturnal. They make use of existing insect or mammal burrows or simply push their way through loose sand or leaf litter. Burrowing asps (*Atractaspis*) have venom that poses a danger to humans and caution should be exercised before handling a snake that in any way resembles any of these species. Many species in this group have specialised diets. All species are oviparous.

This subfamily occurs widely in Africa, with two species entering the Middle East. A total of 23 species in two genera are known, with two species from a single genus occurring in the region.

BURROWING ASPS   *Atractaspis*

Snakes in this genus have a small head that is not distinct from the neck. The head is rounded (pointed in the Beaked Burrowing Asp [*A. duerdeni*]) and the eyes are very small. One to two long, hollow, erectile fangs are present on either side in the front of the mouth. The nostril is pierced between two nasals and the loreal is absent. The body is cylindrical and covered in smooth, shiny scales. The tail is short and ends in a short, sharp spine. The dorsum is usually uniformly grey or purple-brown to black. The ventrum may be white, grey or the same colour as the dorsum. In some individuals, this coloration extends onto the lower flanks.

These snakes are fossorial and nocturnal, typically making use of existing small mammal and insect burrows. They also push their way through loose sand and leaf litter or use their head to excavate hollows under stones. They are frequently found on the surface following good rains.

Species in this genus prey on a variety of reptiles (especially other snakes, legless skinks and sleeping lizards), amphibians and small mammals (especially nestlings). They can 'stab' prey in the confines of a burrow, typically flicking a single fang out of the side of the mouth in a downward and sideways motion without opening their mouth. Usually, only a single fang is exposed at a time.

Their venom is cytotoxic and poses a danger to humans. Many bites result from amateur (and occasionally professional) herpetologists handling these snakes and mistaking them for one of the similar-looking harmless snake species, especially purple-glossed snakes (*Amblyodipsas*), snake-eaters (*Polemon*) and wolf snakes (*Lycophidion*). When disturbed, they have the peculiar habit of arching the neck with the head pointing downwards, which is a characteristic identification feature. Burrowing asps cannot strike forward and will not strike out, even when approached closely. Owing to their small head and the action of their fangs these snakes cannot be safely secured behind the head. Although some bites do not result in any symptoms, many cause intense pain, swelling and localised necrosis, sometimes resulting in the affected digit or part thereof having to be amputated. Three West and North African species have caused human fatalities. Polyvalent antivenom is ineffective in the treatment of bites.

Females are oviparous and lay clutches of 3–11 elongate eggs.

The genus occurs throughout sub-Saharan Africa, with one species also occurring in the Middle East and on the Arabian Peninsula. Recent studies suggest that numerous cryptic species await formal description. Of the 21 recognised species, two occur in the region.

KEY Regional *Atractaspis* species

1a Usually 21–23 midbody scale rows; cloacal scale entire; subcaudals all single ... **A. bibronii** (p. 103)

b Usually 19 midbody scale rows; cloacal scale entire or divided; first 9 subcaudals single or paired, posterior subcaudals all paired .... **A. congica** (p. 105)

Bibron's Burrowing Asp   *Atractaspis bibronii*

Bibron's Burrowing Asp often arches the neck.

Max. SVL ♂ 650mm ♀ 645mm
A moderately stocky snake with a small, flattened head that is slightly broader than the neck. Eyes small. Tail fairly short, slightly tapered, ends in short spine. Preocular small; 1 postocular; 1 supraocular; 1 anterior and 2 posterior temporals. 5 (rarely 6) supralabials, 3rd and 4th entering orbit; 5 (rarely 6) infralabials, first 3 (rarely 4) in contact with anterior sublinguals. Dorsals smooth, close-fitting, in 17–25 (usually 21–23) rows at midbody. 196–262 ventrals; 18–28 single subcaudals; cloacal scale entire. Back uniform purple-brown to black. Ventrum may be same colour as back, brown, white or dirty white (this coloration often extending onto lower 2–3 scale rows on flanks),

sometimes with large dark patches. **Habitat:** Moist savanna, woodland and floodplains, regardless of soil structure. **Behaviour:** Fossorial. Often found on the surface at night after rain. During the day it shelters in moribund termitaria, under logs and rocks, or in loose soil. It is an irascible little snake that will bite at the least provocation and is best left alone. When harassed, it arches its neck while keeping its head on the ground and rapidly jerking it from side to side. If picked up by the tail, this snake will poke the handler with the spike on its tail, often giving the impression of a bite. The large, erectile front fangs are directed backwards, allowing it to 'stab' sideways and backwards without opening its mouth. As such, it cannot be safely held behind the head. It is frequently mistaken for harmless species that look similar, resulting in bites. **Venom:** Cytotoxic. Bites cause intense localised pain and swelling that may lead to necrosis, especially if treated incorrectly. This may be accompanied by neurotoxic symptoms such as nausea, vertigo, a dry throat, headaches, difficulty in swallowing, and painful eye movements. The tissue surrounding the bite site often becomes discoloured and blistering may follow. Polyvalent antivenom is ineffective in the treatment of bites. This species appears to regularly give dry bites as not all bite victims display symptoms. Nonetheless, many handlers have lost digits after being bitten. No fatalities have been recorded. In the event of a bite,

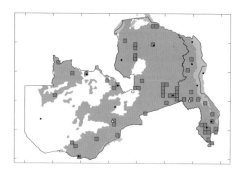

the limb should be continuously moved for at least 15–20 minutes and massaged to help spread the venom, thus reducing localised tissue damage. Bites should be treated symptomatically. **Prey:** Feeds predominantly on other burrowing reptiles (Slender Gracile Blind Snake [*Letheobia gracilis*] and Anchieta's Worm Lizard [*Monopeltis anchietae*]), sleeping lizards (such as Ornate Scrub Lizard [*Nucras ornata*]) and nestling rodents, but will eat terrestrial reptiles (including snakes), reptile eggs, adult rodents and frogs as well. Prey is most often captured while asleep in burrows, where this snake's rapid sideways stabbing motion is most effective. **Reproduction:** Female lays 3–7 eggs (27–36mm x 10–12mm) in summer. Hatchlings measure about 150mm in TL. **Range:** Widespread throughout the region. Elsewhere it occurs from Somalia through East Africa to Angola and South Africa.

Some individuals are dark above with pale flanks and ventrums.

Congo Burrowing Asp *Atractaspis congica*

Luis Ceríaco

The Congo Burrowing Asp looks very similar to Bibron's Burrowing Asp.

Max. SVL ♂ 481mm ♀ 506mm
A moderately stocky snake with a flattened head that is slightly broader than the neck. Tail short, non-tapering, ends in sharp, hard spine. 1 preocular; 1 postocular; 1 anterior and 2 posterior temporals. 5 supralabials, 3rd and 4th entering orbit; 5 infralabials, first 3 in contact with anterior sublinguals. Body scales smooth, close-fitting, in 18–21 (usually 19) rows at midbody. 190–225 ventrals; 18–25 subcaudals; cloacal scale and first 9 subcaudals may be divided or entire; remaining subcaudals paired. Body uniform purple-brown to black. **Habitat:** Moist savanna and forests. **Behaviour:** A fossorial snake; usually active on the surface only after heavy rains. During the day it takes shelter under logs and rocks, in leaf litter or in burrows under the soil. When harassed it arches its neck while keeping its head on the ground and jerking it back and forth. The large, erectile front fangs are directed backwards, allowing it to 'stab' sideways and backwards at its prey or tormentor. **Venom:** Cytotoxic. Bites result in intense localised pain, moderate

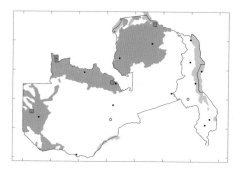

swelling of the bite site and surrounding areas, hypersensitivity in the region of the bite, localised discoloration, profuse sweating, and a mild headache. Swelling may persist for a week and blistering at the bite site persists for up to three weeks. There is no antivenom and treatment should be symptomatic. In the event of a bite, the limb should be moved and massaged continuously for at least 15–20 minutes to help spread the venom and reduce localised tissue damage. **Prey:** Nestling rodents. Probably feeds on other snakes and lizards as well. **Reproduction:** Female lays 3–6 elongate eggs (62mm x 12mm) in summer. **Range:** Northern and western Zambia. Elsewhere from Cameroon through the DRC and northern Angola to extreme northern Namibia.

Centipede-eaters and relatives
Subfamily Aparallactinae

Snakes in this subfamily are small to medium-sized with body shapes that range from long and slender to relatively stout. The head is not distinct from the neck and the tail is either pointed or bluntly rounded. The eyes are small and the loreal is absent. The snout is usually rounded, but in quill-snouted snakes (*Xenocalamus*) distinctly pointed with an enlarged, projecting rostral. The body scales are smooth and often shiny, and lack apical pits.

These snakes are fossorial and predominantly nocturnal and make use of burrows or simply push their way through loose sand or leaf litter. Some species also inhabit rock crevices. Many species have specialised diets and are rear-fanged, but none has venom considered dangerous to humans. All species are oviparous.

This subfamily occurs widely in Africa. It contains eight genera and approximately 44 species, of which 12 species in six genera occur in the region. An additional species, the Congo Centipede-eater (*Aparallactus moeruensis*), has been recorded on the Zambia–DRC border and is assumed to occur in the region as well.

PURPLE-GLOSSED SNAKES   *Amblyodipsas*

Medium- to large-sized snakes with an elongate or fairly robust body. The head is fairly small and not distinct from the neck, with a very small to minute eye. Loreals, preoculars and anterior temporals are absent. The snout is usually bluntly rounded but may be pointed in some species. Two large, grooved fangs are present below the posterior border of the eye. The tail is short, sometimes feebly tapering, and bluntly rounded. The dorsals are smooth and in 15–23 rows at midbody. The subcaudals are paired and the cloacal scale is divided.

These species are found in a myriad habitats, from forests to deserts. They are specialised fossorial, nocturnal snakes and are encountered above ground only after heavy rains. They spend most of their time burrowing in loose sand or leaf litter, sometimes making use of small mammal burrows. They prey predominantly on fossorial reptiles, including worm lizards and skinks, but will also eat amphibians and small mammals. Prey is bitten and held until the venom takes effect and may be enveloped by body coils during this process (which may take up to four hours). They are docile and rarely bite. Their venom is mild and not considered dangerous to humans.

The female lays clutches of 2–11 eggs, although a female Natal Purple-glossed Snake (*A. concolor*) was once recorded giving birth to 12 young.

This genus is restricted to sub-Saharan Africa, with the greatest diversity in southern and East Africa. Nine species are recognised at present, of which three occur in the region.

KEY Regional *Amblyodipsas* species

1a Internasals fused with prefrontals . . . . *A. katangensis* (p. 107)
 b Internasals not fused with prefrontals **2**

2a 6 supralabials, 3rd and 4th entering orbit; 19–23 midbody scale rows;
 body uniformly dark . . . . *A. polylepis* (p. 108)
 b 5 supralabials, 2nd and 3rd entering orbit; 15 midbody scale rows; dorsum
 yellow to white with broad, dark middorsal stripe; ventrum white . . . . . . *A. ventrimaculata* (p. 109)

Katanga Purple-glossed Snake   *Amblyodipsas katangensis*

The Katanga Purple-glossed Snake has a characteristic golden sheen.

Max. SVL ♂ 340mm ♀ 345mm

A small snake with a prominent, rounded snout. Tail flattened on sides, does not taper, bluntly rounded. Nasal undivided; internasals fused with prefrontals. Preocular absent; postocular may be present or absent; 1 temporal. 5 supralabials, 2nd and 3rd entering orbit; 5 infralabials, first 3 in contact with sublinguals. Dorsals smooth, in 15 rows at midbody. 178–181 ventrals and 25–27 subcaudals in males; 196–201 ventrals and 18–21 subcaudals in females; subcaudals paired; cloacal scale divided. Body uniform black above and below, with golden sheen. **Subspecies:** Two subspecies are recognised. Only the typical form (*A. k. katangensis*) occurs in the region. **Habitat:** Woodland and savanna. **Behaviour:** Poorly known. Probably similar to other purple-glossed snakes. **Prey:** Worm lizards and other fossorial reptiles. **Reproduction:** Female believed to lay 2–3 eggs. **Range:** Extreme southern DRC and adjacent Zambia (Copperbelt Province).

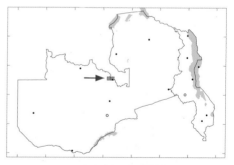

The internasals are fused with the prefrontals.

Common Purple-glossed Snake   *Amblyodipsas polylepis*

Max. SVL ♂ 495mm ♀ 1,050mm

A large snake with a flattened head, rounded snout and blunt tail. Eyes small. Nasal entire in juveniles, semi-divided in adults; internasals not fused with prefrontals. Preocular absent; 1 postocular; 1 temporal. 6 supralabials, 3rd and 4th entering orbit; 7 infralabials, first 4 in contact with sublinguals. Body scales smooth, overlapping, in 19–21 (rarely 23) rows at midbody. 154–180 ventrals in males; 176–215 ventrals in females. 24–31 subcaudals in males, 15–24 in females. Subcaudals paired (first few rows may be single); cloacal scale divided. Body uniform glossy purple-brown to black with purple sheen, may become pale milky grey when extremely stressed. Often confused with burrowing asps (*Atractaspis*), from which it can be distinguished by the absence of

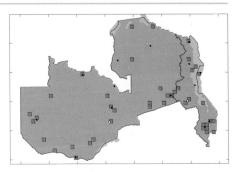

a preocular, a bluntly rounded tail without terminal spine, and not displaying habit of arching its neck when threatened. **Taxonomic note:** Two subspecies have been recognised. As there is overlap in all of the purportedly diagnostic scale characters, the authors do not recognise any subspecies here. **Habitat:** Woodlands and mesic savanna. **Behaviour:** A fossorial snake that may be locally common, although it is usually seen above ground only after heavy rains. When threatened, it buries its head in its coils and raises and waves its tail to draw attention away from its head. It may also flatten its body and slither backwards while

The Common Purple-glossed Snake is a uniform glossy purple-brown to black with a purple sheen.
INSERT It closely resembles a burrowing asp, but lacks a preocular.

waving its tail, further deceiving a predator into mistaking the tail for the head. **Prey:** Preys almost exclusively on other fossorial reptiles, such as giant blind snakes (*Afrotyphlops*), thread snakes (*Leptotyphlops*), legless skinks (*Acontias*), worm lizards, including Anchieta's Worm Lizard (*Monopeltis anchietae*), and dwarf worm lizards (*Zygaspis*). Also eats other snakes and lizards (including Ornate Scrub Lizards [*Nucras ornata*]). Prey items are usually seized by the anterior portion of the body and wrapped in a few coils until they succumb to envenomation, which may take several hours. **Reproduction:** Female lays up to seven eggs (about 30mm x 15mm). **Range:** Widespread throughout Zambia and Malawi. Elsewhere it occurs in the southern DRC, Tanzania and Somalia, as well as from northern Namibia eastwards through northern Botswana, Zimbabwe and central and southern Mozambique to South Africa.

Kalahari Purple-glossed Snake *Amblyodipsas ventrimaculata*

The Kalahari Purple-glossed Snake occurs in deep Kalahari sands in western Zambia.

Max. SVL ♂ 305mm ♀ 445mm
A medium-sized snake with a flattened head and rounded snout. Tail feebly tapered, bluntly rounded. Nasal not divided; internasals not fused with prefrontals. Preocular absent; 1 postocular; 1 temporal. 5 supralabials, 2nd and 3rd entering orbit; 5 infralabials, first 3 in contact with anterior sublinguals. Body scales smooth, in 15 rows at midbody. 172–191 ventrals and 22–29 subcaudals in males; 180–205 ventrals and 18–24 subcaudals in females. Subcaudals paired, although several anterior subcaudals may be entire; cloacal scale divided. Dorsal midline has medium to broad (3–11 scale rows wide) purple-brown to black band, with scales sometimes pale-edged. Flanks and subcaudals bright yellow, ventrum uniform white (rarely with scattered dark blotches). **Habitat:** Kalahari sands in

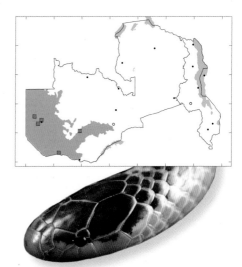

Internasals are not fused with the prefrontals.

moist savanna. **Behaviour:** A rare, fossorial snake. **Prey and Predators:** Preys on a variety of fossorial reptiles, including Kalahari Dwarf Worm Lizard (*Zygaspis quadrifrons*), Roux's Dart Skink (*Typhlacontias gracilis*) and other reptiles. Preyed on by genets and probably other small carnivores. **Reproduction:** Poorly known. One female was found to contain three eggs. **Range:** Western Zambia and adjacent Angola, extending southwards into eastern Zimbabwe, Botswana and Namibia, and just entering South Africa.

STRIPED BURROWING SNAKES   *Chilorhinophis*

These fairly small, slender snakes are rarely seen owing to their fossorial and nocturnal habits. The head is small and not distinct from the neck and the eyes are small. A pair of large, grooved fangs are present below the anterior border of the eye. There is a single nasal, which entirely contains the nostril. There are no internasals or loreals and a preocular may be present or absent. The prefrontals are very large and cover the snout. The body is slender and cylindrical and the scales smooth and in 15 rows at midbody. The cloacal scale is divided and the tail is short, with paired subcaudals.

Coloration consists of vivid longitudinal black and yellow lines, with the tail tip being either blue or black. The tail tip closely resembles the head and probably has an anti-predatory function. When threatened, these snakes will cover the head with loose body coils and raise the tail, which is slowly waved in the air to attract attention away from the head. All species are oviparous.

The genus occurs in Central and East Africa, reaching its southern limit in eastern Zimbabwe. Three species are recognised, with some authors also recognising two subspecies. Only one species occurs in the region.

Gerard's Striped Burrowing Snake   *Chilorhinophis gerardi*

The head and tail of Gerard's Striped Burrowing Snake resemble each other.

Max. SVL ♂ 460mm ♀ 545mm
A fairly small snake with a slender body and a short head that is not distinct from the neck.

Tail short, does not taper, resembles head. Snout rounded. Eyes small with rounded pupils. Nasal undivided, not fused with 1ˢᵗ supralabial.

1 preocular; 1 postocular. 4 supralabials, 3rd entering orbit; 5 infralabials, 1st pair in broad contact behind mental, first 3 pairs in contact with anterior sublinguals. Body scales smooth, in 15 rows at midbody. 254–375 ventrals; 19–31 paired subcaudals; cloacal scale divided. Back yellow, with three longitudinal black stripes extending length of body to tip of tail. Head black; broad black nape collar present; nape collar and black head may be continuous. Tail black, sometimes with blue tip. Both head and tail tip have yellow blotches. Ventrum bright yellow or orange; throat and chin white. Underside of tail normally light blue. **Taxonomic note:** Two subspecies are recognised, separated on ventral counts. However, owing to the extensive overlap in ventral counts and no additional morphological differences the authors recognise no subspecies here. **Habitat:** Sandy areas in dry savanna. **Behaviour:** Rarely seen owing to its fossorial and predominantly nocturnal habits. Spends most of its time below the surface. Occasionally emerges after heavy rains, including during the day. When threatened, this snake rests its head on the ground and waves its brightly coloured tail, which resembles the head, in

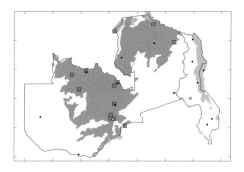

the air to draw attention away from its head. This habit has given rise to its other colloquial name of 'two-headed snake'. **Venom:** Rear-fanged and mildly venomous, although the venom has no effect on humans. **Prey and Predators:** Feeds on other snakes, including Common Wolf Snakes (*Lycophidion c. capense*) and worm lizards, and is also cannibalistic. Preyed on by Dark Chanting Goshawks and probably other raptors. **Reproduction:** Female lays up to six eggs (30mm x 6mm) in summer. **Range:** Occurs widely in central and northern Zambia. Elsewhere it occurs in the southern DRC, eastwards to Tanzania and southwards to northern Zimbabwe.

QUILL-SNOUTED SNAKES *Xenocalamus*

A group of elongate, slender snakes with a small, pointed head that is not distinct from the neck. The head is flattened with a greatly enlarged, sharp, projecting rostral. The eyes are minute and the mouth is underslung. The mental is narrowed and forms a postrostral cavity, which is believed to assist in subterranean breathing. The frontal is elongate and in broad contact with the internasals, displacing the prefrontals laterally (the latter appearing as pseudo preoculars). The dorsals are smooth and in 17 (rarely 21) rows at midbody. The subcaudals are paired and the cloacal scale is divided. Two fangs are present below the eye. The tail is short and not (or only feebly) tapered, with a bluntly rounded tip. The colour patterns of this genus are too variable to aid in species identification.

These specialised fossorial snakes are encountered above ground during the rainy season, especially after rains. They are most common on sandy soils. They prey almost exclusively on worm lizards, which are captured in their subterranean tunnels. Females are oviparous and lay clutches of 2–4 small eggs.

There are five species in the genus, which occur throughout southern and Central Africa. Two species are found in the region.

KEY Regional *Xenocalamus* species

1a Supraocular usually separates frontal from orbit; occurs in southern Zambia . . . . . **X. bicolor** (p. 112)

b Frontal borders orbit; restricted to western Zambia . . . . **X. mechowii** (p. 113)

Bicoloured Quill-snouted Snake   *Xenocalamus bicolor*

The Bicoloured Quill-snouted Snake has various colour phases, and coloration is not a good identifying feature.

Max. SVL ♂ 530mm ♀ 674mm

A long, slender snake with a small, pointed head that is not distinct from the neck. Lower jaw underslung, appearing shark-like. Eyes small. Tail slightly tapered with bluntly rounded tip. Nasal divided. Supraocular in contact with orbit; 1 postocular; 1 temporal. 6 supralabials, 3rd and 4th entering orbit; 5 infralabials, first 3 in contact with sublinguals. Dorsals smooth, in 17 rows at midbody. 198–234 ventrals and 28–36 subcaudals in males; 216–256 ventrals and 20–29 subcaudals in females. Subcaudals paired; cloacal scale divided. Coloration variable. Usually uniformly dark above with lowest 1–3 rows of flank scales white, occasionally with dark blotches or infusions. Scales may be pale-edged; poorly defined pale blotches or transverse bars may also be present. **Subspecies:** Four subspecies are recognised, with only the typical form (*X. b. bicolor*) entering the region. In this subspecies the supraocular separates the frontal from the

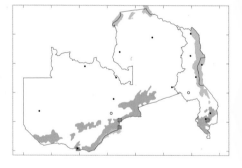

orbit and the head is not more than twice as long as it is broad. It occurs widely from Namibia to Mozambique and south to central South Africa, just entering southern Zambia. **Habitat:** Deep Kalahari sands or alluvium in savanna and woodland. **Behaviour:** Fossorial; sometimes active on the surface at night. **Prey and Predators:** It is a specialist predator of worm lizards, which may be captured either above or below ground. It is preyed on by

Small-spotted Genets and Black-backed Jackals. Other mesocarnivores are also likely predators. **Reproduction:** Female lays 3–4 eggs (40–47mm x 15mm) in summer. Hatchlings measure about 200mm in TL. **Range:** In the region it has been recorded only on the northern shores of Lake Kariba and at Livingstone, with a historical record from Blantyre. Occurs widely from the southern DRC through Angola and Zambia to South Africa and Mozambique.

Elongate Quill-snouted Snake   *Xenocalamus mechowii*

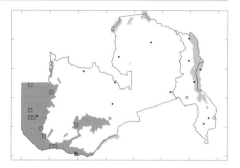

Max. SVL ♂ 580mm ♀ 795mm
A long, slender snake with a small, pointed head that is not distinct from the neck. Tail slightly tapered with bluntly rounded tip. Lower jaw underslung, appearing shark-like. Eyes small. Nasal divided. Frontal forms long suture with orbit, displacing supraocular; latter resembles upper of two minute postoculars. 1 minute postocular (sometimes absent); single temporal. 6 supralabials, 3rd and 4th entering orbit; 5 infralabials, first 3 in contact with sublinguals. Dorsals smooth, in 17 rows at midbody. 237–263 ventrals and 27–32 subcaudals in males; 253–296 ventrals and 21–27 subcaudals in females. Subcaudals paired; cloacal scale divided. Coloration varies; two main colour phases. Bicolor pattern: broad dark dorsal stripe; lowest 2–4 flank scales yellow; ventrum uniform white. Maculate pattern: dorsum yellow, with 2 rows of more or less confluent dark markings; ventrum pale; dark blotches occasionally present below tail. Reticulate pattern in some individuals: back grey-brown with each scale pale-edged; lower flanks and ventrum white. Intergrades (see Taxonomic note) black or brown above with irregular white transverse bands or blotches and pale ventrums. Melanistic individuals sometimes occur. **Taxonomic note:** Two subspecies have been recognised in the past. However, individuals from northern Zambia appear to be intergrades between these two subspecies and in light thereof the authors do

The Elongate Quill-snouted Snake occurs predominantly in western Zambia.

Luke Verburg

The head is long, narrow and pointed.

not recognise subspecies here. **Habitat:** Kalahari sands in woodland and savanna. **Behaviour:** A fossorial snake; only occasionally found on the soil surface on warm summer nights. **Prey and Predators:** Appears to eat only worm lizards, which are captured below ground. Little is known of its predators, although a specimen was recovered from the stomach of a Bat-eared Fox. **Reproduction:** Female lays up to four eggs. **Range:** Western Zambia. Range extends into adjacent Angola and southwards into Namibia, Botswana and eastern Zimbabwe.

SNAKE-EATERS *Polemon*

Small to medium-sized snakes with a short, stubby tail that ends in a short, sharp spine. The loreal is absent and the internasals and prefrontals are usually about as long as they are wide. There are large fangs situated below the small eyes. The scales are smooth and arranged in 15 rows at midbody. The subcaudals are paired and the cloacal scale is divided. Coloration is usually uniform dark brown or black, although some extralimital species may have pale nape bands. They bear a close resemblance to venomous burrowing asps (*Atractaspis*) and extreme caution should be exercised when distinguishing between these species.

Snake-eaters are scarce and nocturnal and as a result are poorly known. They are predominantly subterranean, usually living in burrows or in leaf litter. Most species occur in forests, although some also enter dense woodlands and moist miombo woodland. As their common name suggests, they prey on other snakes and often eat snakes that are the same size as themselves. Their venom has no effect on humans. Females are oviparous.

The genus occurs fairly widely in tropical Africa. Their taxonomy remains unresolved, with the validity of several species and subspecies being questioned. Of the 12 species currently recognised, only one occurs in the region.

Black Snake-eater *Polemon ater*

Max. SVL ♂ 254mm ♀ 640mm
A medium-sized snake with a stout, cylindrical body and a head that is slightly broader than the neck. Tail very short, stubby, rapidly tapering to short spine. Eyes small, pupils round. Nasals squarish. 1 sub-quadrangular preocular; 1–2 postoculars (upper postocular noticeably larger than lower postocular); 1 anterior and 1–2 posterior temporals. 7 (rarely 6) supralabials, 3rd and 4th entering orbit; 7 infralabials, first pair in contact with each other behind mental and first 3–4 in contact with anterior sublinguals. Enlarged fangs present anterior to eye. Scales smooth, in 15 rows at midbody. 202–242 ventrals; 15–24 paired subcaudals; cloacal scale divided. Body uniform shiny blue-black to plumbeus, rarely pale blue-grey. Pale posterior

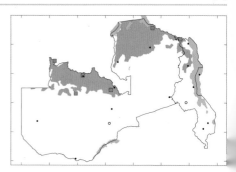

borders to ventrals and subcaudals. Juveniles grey-brown above and whitish below, sometimes with pale collar. **Habitat:** Forest, woodland (mostly moist miombo woodland, sometimes in the vicinity of relict gallery forest), moist

Colin Tilbury

The Black Snake-eater looks very similar to purple-glossed snakes and burrowing asps.

savanna and grassland. **Behaviour:** Nocturnal and fossorial; spends most of its time in holes, in leaf litter or under suitable cover (logs and rocks) on the surface, emerging after rains. A slow-moving and inoffensive snake that bears a striking resemblance to venomous burrowing asps (*Atractaspis*). Extreme care should be taken when handling what is assumed to be this species. When threatened, it may flatten its body while jerking the anterior portion to and fro. It may weakly arch its neck, similar to burrowing asps. **Venom:** The venom has not been studied but is not believed to be dangerous to humans. **Prey:** Other snakes, including Schmidt's Giant Blind Snake (*Afrotyphlops schmidti*), thread snakes (*Leptotyphlops*) and Black-templed Cat Snake (*Crotaphopeltis hotamboeia*). **Reproduction:** Unknown. Probably similar to other snake-eaters, i.e. oviparous. **Range:** Northern Zambia and northern Malawi. Elsewhere it occurs in the south-eastern DRC, central-western Tanzania and possibly in Burundi.

CENTIPEDE-EATERS *Aparallactus*

These small snakes can be quite common in suitable habitats. They have a slender body and a small head that is not, or only slightly, distinct from the neck. The head is slightly depressed and the eyes are small. Relatively large fangs are situated below the eye. The loreal is absent. The scales are smooth and arranged in 15 rows at midbody. The subcaudals are single and the cloacal scale is entire.

Predominantly nocturnal, they are often found in moribund termitaria or under logs and rocks. They may also be found sheltering in leaf litter or in loose sand. These snakes prey predominantly on centipedes, although other small invertebrates are also eaten. Prey is seized and chewed and quickly succumbs to the venom. The venom has no effect on humans. Most species lay clutches of 3–4 eggs.

The genus occurs widely in sub-Saharan Africa. Of the 11 recognised species, three have been recorded in the region, with a fourth, the Congo Centipede-eater (*A. moeruensis*), likely to occur.

KEY Regional *Aparallactus* species

1a Single temporal; 5th and 6th supralabials in contact with parietal; nasal
partially divided . . . . **A. moeruensis** (p. 119)
b 2 temporals; 0–1 supralabials in contact with parietal; nasal entire
or completely divided **2**

Common Centipede-eater   *Aparallactus capensis*

Max. SVL ♂ **270mm** ♀ **324mm**

A fairly small and slender snake with a head that is not distinct from the neck. Nasal undivided. 1 preocular; 1 postocular; 1 anterior and 1 posterior temporal. 5–6 supralabials, 2nd and 3rd or 3rd and 4th entering orbit; 5 (rarely 4 or 6) infralabials, first 3 in contact with anterior sublinguals, 1st pair separated from each other by mental. Body scales smooth and imbricate, in 15 rows at midbody. 126–191 (usually 140–178) ventrals; 29–63 (usually 39–53) single subcaudals; cloacal scale entire. Head and nape black (rarely same colour as back), may be divided by narrow pale band. Back red to grey-brown or buffy, usually uniform, fine darker vertebral line occasionally present. Ventrum

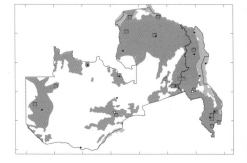

white to dirty white. **Taxonomic note:** Three poorly defined subspecies are recognised by some authors, but owing to extensive overlap in morphological characters, these are not

The Common Centipede-eater has a characteristic black head.

recognised here. Recent studies, however, suggest that *A. capensis* consists of several cryptic species. **Habitat:** Occurs in almost any habitat type, including savanna and woodland. **Behaviour:** A common terrestrial, nocturnal snake. Takes refuge in moribund termitaria (where numerous individuals may be found in the same termitarium, often alongside other reptile species), in leaf litter, and under logs, rocks and other suitable cover, including building rubble. It is mildly venomous. Its venom has no effect on humans. **Prey and Predators:** Feeds almost exclusively on centipedes, which can be as broad as, or even broader than, the snake. The smooth scales provide protection against centipede forcipules, which are unable to grip onto the snake. This species is preyed upon by burrowing asps (*Atractaspis*) and garter

The head is not distinct from the neck.

snakes (*Elapsoidea*). **Reproduction:** Female lays 2–6 slender eggs (23–32mm x 4–5mm) in mid-summer. Hatchlings measure about 85–120mm in TL. **Range:** Widespread throughout the region and extending to Tanzania, South Africa, the DRC and Angola.

Black Centipede-eater   *Aparallactus guentheri*

The adult Black Centipede-eater is uniformly dark above with a paler ventrum.

The head is fairly robust.

Luke Verburgt

Max. SVL ♂ 345mm ♀ 380mm
A small, slender snake with a head that is not distinct from the neck. Nasal divided. 1 preocular; 1 postocular; 2 temporals. 6 (rarely 5 or 7) supralabials, 3rd and 4th (rarely 2nd and 3rd) entering orbit; 5 (rarely 6) infralabials, 1st pair separated from each other by mental, first 3 (rarely 4) in contact with anterior sublinguals. Body scales smooth and overlapping, in 15 rows at midbody. 137–173 ventrals; 42–60 single subcaudals; cloacal scale entire. Adults uniform blue-grey or black above and paler below. Juveniles have two narrow yellow bands on nape and neck. Chin and ventrum dirty white. **Habitat:** Evergreen forest and miombo woodland in areas of high rainfall. **Behaviour:** Poorly known, but believed to be similar to Reticulated Centipede-eater (*A. lunulatus*). **Prey:** In addition to centipedes, one individual consumed a snail. **Reproduction:** Unknown. **Range:** From southern Kenya through Malawi to northern and eastern Zimbabwe.

Reticulated Centipede-eater   *Aparallactus lunulatus*

As the name suggests, the Reticulated Centipede-eater has a distinct reticulated pattern.

Max. SVL ♂ 390mm ♀ 430mm
A small snake with a slightly robust body and a marginally flattened head that is not distinct from the neck. Nasal divided. 1 preocular; 1 postocular; 2 (rarely 1) temporals. 6 (rarely 7) supralabials, 3rd and 4th entering orbit; 6 (rarely 5 or 7) infralabials, 1st pair in contact with each other behind mental; first 4 in contact with anterior sublinguals. Body scales smooth and imbricate, in 15 rows at midbody. 140–176 ventrals; 41–67 single subcaudals; cloacal scale entire. Body light olive-grey to

Some individuals are uniformly dark.

Juveniles are much more boldly patterned.

dark brown, each scale usually dark-edged, giving reticulated appearance. Dark collar on neck and series of dark crossbars (most distinct anteriorly and fading posteriorly) in juveniles. Ventrum white to greenish white, sometimes with darker infusions. Ventrum uniform dark in some individuals, sometimes with paler chin and throat. Melanistic individuals rarely occur. **Subspecies:** Four subspecies are recognised, with only the typical form entering the region. **Habitat:** Savanna and woodland, occurring on sandy, loose soils as well as heavy clay and rocky soils. **Behaviour:** A rare, predominantly fossorial snake that is usually encountered at night. During the day, it takes refuge under logs and rocks and in leaf litter. Mildly venomous. The venom has no apparent effect on humans. **Prey:** Preys mainly on centipedes (including the genus *Scolopendromorpha*, which contains the largest

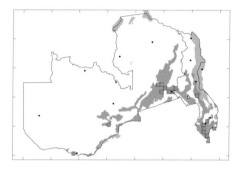

predatory species). Occasionally eats scorpions. **Reproduction:** Female lays 2–4 elongate (30mm x 7–10mm) eggs in summer. **Range:** Widespread, occurring from Sudan through East Africa and the DRC to South Africa and west to Ghana. Found in southern and eastern Zambia and central and southern Malawi.

Congo Centipede-eater   *Aparallactus moeruensis*

Max. SVL ♂ 302mm ♀ 310mm
A relatively small, slender snake with a flattened head that is barely distinct from the neck. Nasal partially divided. 1 preocular; 1 postocular; anterior temporal fused with 6th supralabial, resulting in 5th and 6th supralabials being in contact with parietal; posterior temporal present. 6 supralabials, 3rd and 4th entering orbit; 5 infralabials, 1st pair separated from each other by mental; first 3 in contact with anterior sublinguals. Body scales smooth, in 15 rows at midbody. 155–182 ventrals; 57–67 subcaudals. Head dark brown-black; pale patch usually present between eye and snout. Pale collar present just

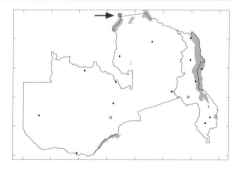

behind head, followed by dark collar (about four scales wide) on neck and second pale collar about 1–2 scales wide. Remainder of back olive-grey. Ventrum pale yellowish. **Habitat:** All specimens were collected at 700–1,000m a.s.l. in woodland. **Behaviour:** Probably similar to other centipede-eaters. **Prey and Predators:** Unknown. Probably similar to other centipede-eaters. **Reproduction:** Unknown. **Range:** Believed to be endemic to the southern DRC but as the type specimen was collected at Pweto on Lake Mweru, it is likely to occur in extreme north-eastern Zambia.

WEDGE-SNOUTED BURROWING SNAKES   *Hypoptophis*

Fairly small snakes with a head that is not distinct from the neck. The body is cylindrical and the tail short, with single subcaudals. The snout is depressed and pointed, with a prominent horizontal edge that extends far beyond the lower mandible. The eyes are very small, with vertically elliptical pupils. The nasal is semi-divided. These snakes are rear-fanged, but the venom is not believed to be dangerous to humans. They are fossorial, spending the majority of their time underground. There is a single described species, which is restricted to the DRC and Zambia.

Wedge-snouted Burrowing Snake   *Hypoptophis wilsonii*

Max. SVL ♂ 423mm ♀ 507mm
A fairly small snake with a cylindrical body and head not distinct from the neck. Tail short. Snout very flattened, pointed, with sharp horizontal edge that extends far beyond lower jaw. Head and eyes small. Nasal partially divided. 1 preocular; 1–2 postoculars; loreal absent; 1 anterior and 1 posterior temporal. 7 supralabials, 3rd and 4th entering orbit; 7 infralabials, 1st pair in contact with each other behind mental, first 4 in contact with anterior sublinguals. Anterior body scales smooth, sometimes becoming slightly keeled posteriorly and on tail; in 15 rows at midbody. 101–118 ventrals; 32–45 single subcaudals; cloacal scale entire. Body uniform blackish brown above and below. **Habitat:** Prefers sandy soils in moist savanna. **Behaviour:** Fossorial, but otherwise

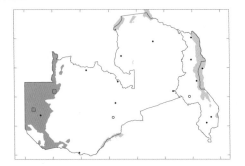

poorly known. **Venom:** Rear-fanged. Little is known of its venom, although it is not believed to be dangerous to humans. **Prey:** Probably other fossorial reptiles and possibly fossorial rodents. **Reproduction:** Unknown. **Range:** The DRC, western Zambia and probably adjacent Angola.

The Wedge-snouted Burrowing Snake occurs in western Zambia, but is rarely observed.

Old World Snakes
Family Lamprophiidae

This family contains many of the characteristic and common African snake species. They lack fangs, although large teeth may be present in the front of the mouth and are used to capture and manipulate prey. They have hypapophyses on all the vertebrae and are further characterised by various hemipenial features. Most species are terrestrial, with some species being arboreal, rupicolous, semi-aquatic or aquatic. They prey predominantly on rodents and lizards, with many species constricting their prey. None are venomous. All are oviparous.

Common Wolf Snake

There are 15 genera and about 72 species in the family, of which five genera and 11 species occur in the region.

BEAUTIFUL FILE SNAKES   *Limaformosa*

Large snakes with a body that is characteristically triangular in cross-section. The head is broad and depressed and noticeably distinct from the neck. The nostrils are very large and the eyes are moderate in size with vertically elliptic pupils. The 7–10 anterior maxillary teeth increase in size posteriorly and are separated from the 13–19 very small posterior teeth by a gap. The dorsals are strongly keeled, lack apical pits and are arranged in 15–21 rows at midbody. The vertebral scale row is enlarged and bicarinate or quadricarinate, and the ventrals have a lateral keel. The subcaudals are paired and the cloacal scale is entire. The interstitial skin is prominent.

These snakes feed predominantly on other reptiles, although frogs and toads are also occasionally eaten. They lack venom and fangs, but have numerous teeth and a crushing bite which, together with constriction, is used to subdue prey. Docile by nature, they rarely attempt to bite and are harmless to humans. They are nocturnal, secretive and move slowly. As such, they are not frequently seen. Females are oviparous, laying 5–13 eggs per clutch.

Beautiful file snakes occur throughout sub-Saharan Africa, with six species recognised at present, although genetic studies suggest that additional species await formal description. One species occurs in the region.

Common File Snake   *Limaformosa capensis*

Max. SVL ♂ 1,311mm ♀ 1,612mm
This medium-sized to large snake has a characteristic triangular body in cross-section (hence the common name, which refers to a triangular metal file). Head broad, flat, often rugose, distinct from neck. Nostrils large. 1–2 preoculars; 1–2 (rarely 3) postoculars (rarely absent); 1 (rarely 2) anterior and 2 (rarely 1 or 3) posterior temporals. 7 (rarely 6 or 8) supralabials, 3rd and 4th (rarely 3rd–5th, 4th–6th, 2nd and 3rd, 4th and 5th or 3rd only) entering orbit; 8 (rarely 7 or 9) infralabials, first 5 (rarely 3 or 4) in contact with anterior sublinguals. Body scales keeled, widely spaced, in 15–21 rows at midbody,

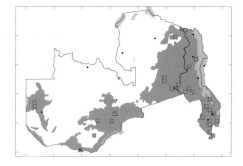

with bare interstitial skin prominent. Enlarged vertebral scales each have two keels. 193–268 ventrals; 38–69 paired subcaudals; cloacal scale entire. Grey, olive-brown, purple-brown or blackish brown above with distinct pale dorsal stripe. Interstitial skin pale pink to pale purple. Ventrum white to yellowish white. Females much larger and heavier than males. **Habitat:** Savanna and woodland. **Behaviour:** This nocturnal, slow-moving snake is rarely seen, but may be locally common. Predominantly terrestrial, but occasionally climbs into trees and reedbeds after prey. Takes refuge under logs and rocks and in hollow stumps and termitaria. When handled it usually does not attempt to bite, but often secretes a foul-smelling liquid from glands in the cloaca. It is immune to the venom of other snake species. **Prey:** Feeds exclusively on other reptiles and amphibians. Agamas and plated lizards feature prominently in its diet and are probably caught at night while they are asleep. Prey is usually seized on the body and constricted while the snake works its way up to the head. Uses its blunt teeth and the crushing force of its powerful jaws to subdue its prey. **Reproduction:** Female lays 5–13 eggs (47–55mm x 20–31mm) in summer and may lay two clutches per season. Incubation takes 90–100 days (in captivity). Hatchlings measure 390–420mm in TL. **Range:** Widespread in Zambia and Malawi, although apparently absent from northern Zambia. Elsewhere it occurs from southern Ethiopia and Somalia southwards to South Africa and westwards to Cameroon.

The interstitial skin of the Common File Snake is visible between the small scales.

SLENDER FILE SNAKES   *Gracililima*

Fairly small, slender snakes with a triangular body. The head is moderately broad, depressed and distinct from the neck. The nostrils are large and the eyes moderate in size with vertically elliptic pupils. There are 7–8 anterior maxillary teeth which increase in size posteriorly and are separated by a gap from the posterior 16–18 very small teeth. The dorsals are keeled, lack apical pits and are arranged in 15 rows at midbody. The vertebral scale row is enlarged and bicarinate, and the ventrals have a lateral keel. The cloacal scale is entire and the subcaudals are paired.

Slender file snakes feed predominantly on other reptiles (occasionally also eating frogs), which are constricted before being ingested. They are nocturnal and secretive and are rarely seen. Docile by nature, they rarely attempt to bite and are harmless to humans. The female lays 2–6 eggs per clutch.

This monotypic genus is restricted to southern and East Africa.

Darren Pietersen

The Black File Snake is uniformly dark, or dark above with pale flanks.

Max. SVL ♂ 458mm ♀ 520mm

A small snake with a characteristic triangular body shape and flattened head. 1–2 preoculars; 1 (rarely 2) postocular; 1 anterior and 2 posterior temporals. 7 supralabials, 3rd and 4th (rarely 2nd and 3rd) entering orbit; 7–8 infralabials, first 5 in contact with anterior sublinguals. Body scales keeled, close-fitting, in 15 rows at midbody; scales along dorsal midline enlarged with 2 distinct keels. 165–184 ventrals with lateral keels; 43–79 paired subcaudals; cloacal scale entire. Uniform dark brown to black above, with pink to grey interstitial skin. Ventrum usually dark brown to black; ventrals sometimes pale-edged, or white with or without scattered dark blotches. **Habitat:** Savanna and woodland. **Behaviour:** Uncommon and nocturnal. Shelters in holes, under rocks and logs, and in moribund termitaria. When threatened it may hide its head under the coils of the body. When handled it often secretes a pungent fluid from glands situated in the cloaca. **Prey:** Feeds predominantly on lizards, especially African writhing skinks (*Mochlus*) and typical skinks (*Trachylepis*) but also

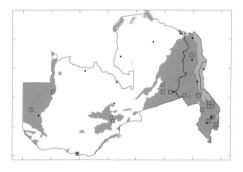

legless skinks (*Acontias*). It rarely eats snakes such as thread snakes (*Leptotyphlops*) and East African Shovel-snouts (*Prosymna stuhlmanni*), as well as frogs. **Reproduction:** Female lays 2–6 eggs (10–18mm x 4–6mm) in summer and may lay two clutches per season. Hatchlings measure 200–220mm in TL. **Range:** Western, central, southern and eastern Zambia, and throughout Malawi. Elsewhere it occurs from southern Somalia through East Africa to South Africa, with apparently isolated populations in Botswana and Namibia.

TRUE FILE SNAKES   *Mehelya*

Snakes whose bodies are subtriangular or cylindrical in cross-section. The head is elongate and rectangular, dorsoventrally flattened and distinct from the neck. The eyes are moderate to small with vertically elliptical pupils and the nostrils are very large. The eight anterior maxillary teeth increase in size posteriorly and are separated from the 15–26 very small posterior teeth by a gap. The dorsals are moderately to very feebly keeled, lack apical pits and are arranged in 13–19 rows at midbody. The vertebral scale row is enlarged and more or less bicarinate, while the ventrals may have a distinct or indistinct lateral keel. The tail ranges from very short to long. The subcaudals are paired and the cloacal scale is entire.

True file snakes feed predominantly on agamas and skinks, although they will also eat other snakes and rodents, and probably amphibians as well. They do not have fangs and are not venomous, but have numerous teeth and subdue prey using constriction. They are nocturnal, slow-moving and secretive and are not seen often. Docile by nature, they rarely attempt to bite. Females are oviparous and lay 8–10 eggs per clutch.

This genus occurs widely in the Congo–Guinean forest and associated savanna, with five species recognised at present, although genetic studies suggest that additional species await formal description. A single species occurs in the region.

Western Forest File Snake   *Mehelya poensis*

The Western Forest File Snake has a long, rectangular head.

Max. SVL ♂ 691mm ♀ 1,050mm

A large, slender file snake with a subtriangular body (not as triangular as in other file snake species). Tail long (about 20–25% of TL). Head rectangular, flat. Snout short, appears quite pointed in profile. Nostrils relatively large. 1 (rarely 2) preoculars; 2 (very rarely 3) postoculars; 1 (rarely 2) anterior and 2 (rarely 3) posterior temporals. 7 (rarely 6 or 8) supralabials, 3rd and 4th usually entering orbit; 8 infralabials, first 5 (rarely 4) in contact with

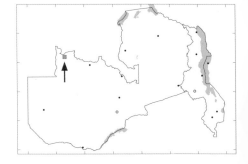

anterior sublinguals. Body scales strongly keeled, in 15 rows at midbody; enlarged vertebral scales each have two keels. 227–262 ventrals; 85–147 paired subcaudals; cloacal scale entire. Body uniform olive-grey to dark grey; exposed skin appearing light grey or blue-grey. Ventrum light grey to yellowish or white; each scale having a dark posterior border. **Habitat:** Lowland, high-elevation and riverine forests. **Behaviour:** A slow-moving, nocturnal and secretive snake that hides in holes in the ground, in leaf litter and in dense foliage in the tree canopy during the day. Although sometimes seen on the ground, it is believed to be predominantly arboreal, which is corroborated by its slender build and long tail. It will rapidly ascend into a tree to escape terrestrial threats. **Prey:** Preys largely on reptiles including agamas, skinks (including Speckle-Lipped Skinks [*Trachylepis maculilabris*]) and snakes, but also eats mice and probably frogs. **Reproduction:** Female lays 8–10 eggs (20–25mm x 8–10mm) in early summer. **Range:** Widespread in the Congolese and Upper Guinean forests from Guinea east to Uganda, and south to northern Angola and the southern DRC. In the region it has been recorded in the Ikelenge Pedicle in north-western Zambia.

WOLF SNAKES *Lycophidion*

Small snakes with a cylindrical to slightly depressed body and a broad, flattened head that is barely distinct from the neck. The eyes are small, with vertical pupils. The nostril is pierced in a single nasal and the preocular is large and extends onto the top of the head, replacing the supraocular anteriorly. The front teeth in both the upper and lower jaws are long and recurved, giving rise to the common name. The dorsals are smooth and arranged in 15–19 (usually 17) rows at midbody. The tail is short, the subcaudals are paired and the cloacal scale is entire.

Wolf snakes are terrestrial and nocturnal, foraging for sleeping lizards which they grasp in their retreats and pull out before constricting and consuming them. Docile, they rarely bite. They are not venomous. The female lays 3–9 eggs.

The genus contains 20 species that occur widely across sub-Saharan Africa. Four species are found in the region.

KEY Regional *Lycophidion* species

1a	Postnasal absent; snout pointed in profile	*L. acutirostre* (p. 125)
b	Postnasal present	2
2a	Postnasal not in contact with 1st supralabial	*L. variegatum* (p. 128)
b	Postnasal in contact with 1st supralabial	3
3a	Reddish brown to grey-blue above; western populations have paired dark blotches that usually fuse to form crossbands; eastern populations have dorsals stippled with white	*L. multimaculatum* (p. 127)
b	Dorsals dark brown to black; white restricted to scale margins (rarely absent); no dark blotches or crossbands	*L. capense* (p. 126)

Mozambique Wolf Snake *Lycophidion acutirostre*

Max. SVL ♂ 260mm ♀ 280mm
A small snake with a broad, depressed, spatulate head that has sharp sides. Snout appears somewhat pointed when viewed in profile. Nostril pierced in centre of divided or semi-divided nasal; no postnasal. 2 postoculars; 1–2 anterior and 2–3 posterior temporals. 8 supralabials, 3rd–5th entering orbit; 7–8 infralabials, first 4–5 in contact with anterior sublinguals. Body scales smooth, in 17 rows at midbody. 132–161 ventrals; 18–31 paired subcaudals (28–31 in males, 18–25 in females); cloacal scale entire. Head and body dark brown to black, usually with dorsals lightly

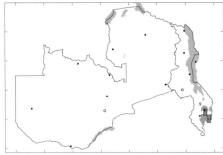

The Mozambique Wolf Snake has a spatulate head.

stippled with white. Ventrolateral scales more distinctly white-tipped; posterior edges of ventrals edged with white. White dorsolateral stripe (sometimes with darker spots) present on head, breaking up behind eyes. Sides of head yellowish, marbled with black. **Habitat:** Woodlands. Will also enter plantations. **Behaviour:** Nocturnal and terrestrial, it shelters in holes in the ground and under logs, rocks and other suitable cover. **Prey:** Small skinks. **Reproduction:** Female lays up to four eggs. **Range:** Southern Malawi. Elsewhere it occurs in central and northern Mozambique and southern Tanzania.

Common Wolf Snake   *Lycophidion capense*

The Common Wolf Snake is dark above, usually with pale spots.

Max. SVL ♂ 440mm ♀ 558mm

A small snake with a broad, flattened, spatulate head. Nostril pierced at posterior edge of nasal; postnasal in contact with 1st supralabial. 1 preocular; 2 postoculars; 1 anterior and 2 posterior temporals. 8 supralabials, 1st in contact with postnasal, 3rd–5th entering orbit; 8 (rarely 7 or 9) infralabials, first 4–5 in contact with anterior sublinguals. Dorsals smooth, in 17 rows at midbody. 159–221 ventrals; 24–58 paired subcaudals; cloacal scale entire. Body dark brown to black above, usually with each scale white-tipped, giving a fine to fairly extensive mottled appearance; rarely reddish brown or uniformly black. White vermiculation on head. Ventrum ranges from white to black, with varying degrees of darker blotching and infusions. **Subspecies:** Three subspecies are recognised, with only the typical form (*L. c. capense*) entering the region. 159–205 ventrals. 24–52 subcaudals. Body dark brown to black, usually with each scale pale-tipped. Head has fine white stippling or vermiculation. Ventrum may be immaculate or uniformly black, or blotched and infused to varying degrees. **Habitat:** Moist savanna. **Behaviour:** Nocturnal and terrestrial. When inactive, it shelters in moribund termitaria and under logs, rocks, piles of debris and other suitable shelter. The rear teeth are hinged, enabling them to be folded back when consuming prey. It is not venomous. **Prey and Predators:** It preys predominantly on skinks, although geckos, including Button-scaled Geckos (*Chondrodactylus laevigatus*), lizards such as Ornate Scrub Lizards (*Nucras ornata*) and snakes such as green snakes (*Philothamnus*) are also eaten. Captures prey in their retreats while they are sleeping, then drags them out and constricts them. This species is preyed upon by sand snakes (*Psammophis*) and Gerard's Striped Burrowing Snake (*Chilorhinophis g. gerardi*). **Reproduction:** Female lays 3–9 eggs (20–32mm x 8–15mm) in early summer. Incubation takes

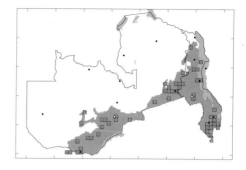

50–65 days. Hatchlings measure 65–120mm in TL. **Range:** Occurs throughout most of the region, largely replaced by the Spotted Wolf Snake (*L. multimaculatum*) in northern and western Zambia. Elsewhere it occurs from southern Tanzania south to South Africa and west to Angola.

Spotted Wolf Snake *Lycophidion multimaculatum*

Spotted Wolf Snake populations in western Zambia are stouter than those in the east.

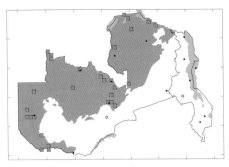

Northern populations have pale-centered scales.

Max. SVL ♂ 286mm ♀ 475mm

A small snake with a broad, depressed, spatulate head. Populations in western Zambia are relatively short and stocky. 1 preocular; 2 postoculars; 1 anterior and 2 posterior temporals. Nostril pierced towards posterior border of undivided nasal; postnasal in contact with 1st supralabial. 8 supralabials, 3rd–5th entering orbit; 8 infralabials, first 4–5 in contact with anterior sublinguals. Dorsals smooth, in 17 rows at midbody. 153–188 ventrals; 22–38 paired subcaudals (26–38 in males, 22–33 in females); cloacal scale entire. Coloration varies geographically. Individuals from western Zambia grey to red-brown with white stippling and paired darker markings that may fuse into dark crossbands; ventrum predominantly white, although chin may be dark; thin, dark median stripe or blotches may be present. Individuals from north-western Zambia pale blue-grey above with paired darker markings that may fuse to form dark crossbands; top of head vermiculated; ventrum blue-grey, although chin, throat and posterior borders of ventrals white. Individuals from east of the Zambezi River plain blue-grey above with white stippling covering scales to varying extents. **Habitat:** Moist savanna. **Behaviour:** Nocturnal. Shelters under logs and other suitable cover during the day. **Prey:** Preys predominantly on sleeping lizards, including skinks, which are dragged from their burrows and constricted. **Reproduction:** Female lays up to seven eggs in summer. **Range:** Occurs over most of Zambia, absent only from the extreme south and east. Found northwards to southern Gabon and eastwards to western Tanzania; just enters the Zambezi Region of Namibia.

Variegated Wolf Snake *Lycophidion variegatum*

Max. SVL ♂ 323mm ♀ 389mm

A small snake with a broad, flattened, spatulate head and a more slender body than other wolf snakes. Nostril pierced near posterior border of undivided nasal; postnasal not in contact with 1st supralabial. 1 preocular; 2 postoculars; 1 anterior and 2 posterior temporals. 8 supralabials, 3rd–5th entering orbit; 8 (rarely 7) infralabials, first 4–5 in contact with anterior sublinguals. Dorsals smooth, in 17 rows at midbody. 183–204 ventrals; 28–40 paired subcaudals (33–40 in males, 28–33 in females); cloacal scale entire. Body dark brown to black, each scale with white tip. White markings usually more extensive than those of Common Wolf Snake (*L. c. capense*), especially on flanks,

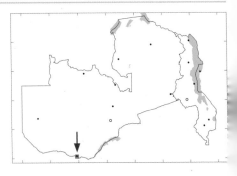

often form irregular white patterns. Ventrum usually uniform dark brown to black, although irregular pale patches may be present. Head finely speckled with white. **Habitat:** Rocky

In the region, the Variegated Wolf Snake has been recorded only in south-western Zambia.

outcrops in moist savanna. **Behaviour:** Non-venomous and nocturnal. Shelters under logs, rocks and other plant debris when inactive. **Prey:** Catches sleeping skinks where they are sheltering in rock cracks and kills them by constriction. **Reproduction:** A female was found to contain three eggs. **Range:** A single record from Livingstone in southern Zambia. Elsewhere it occurs in three apparently isolated populations in western Zimbabwe, the Eastern Highlands of Zimbabwe and north-eastern South Africa.

HOUSE SNAKES   *Boaedon*

Medium-sized snakes with a moderately elongate body and a short to moderate tail. The head is of moderate size, slightly flattened above and distinct from the neck. The eyes are moderately large with vertically elliptical pupils. The body scales are smooth, overlapping, and in 23–35 rows at midbody. Subcaudals are paired (single in one species) and the cloacal scale is entire.

These snakes are terrestrial and shelter under rocks, in holes or in moribund termitaria. They lack fangs and venom and are completely harmless to humans. They prey on various small vertebrates, mostly lizards (including geckos) and small rodents. Prey is grasped and constricted until it succumbs. They are often found in and around houses, drawn by the large numbers of rodents, lizards and geckos that are often attracted to dwellings, as well as the prevalence of rubble under which they can shelter. All species are oviparous, and males have a prominent hemipenial bulge.

This genus is widespread in Africa, extending onto the Arabian Peninsula and the Seychelles. A total of 20 species are currently recognised. Additional extralimital species currently assigned to *Lamprophis* possibly also belong to this genus and several cryptic species likely await formal description. Three species occur in the region.

Brown House Snake *Boaedon capensis*

The Brown House Snake has a broad, pale stripe above the eye.

Max. SVL ♂ 735mm ♀ 1,185mm

A medium-sized to large snake with a relatively long head that is distinct from the neck. 1–2 preoculars; 2 postoculars; 1 anterior and 2 posterior temporals. 8 supralabials, 4th and 5th entering orbit; 9 infralabials, first 3–4 in contact with anterior sublinguals. Parietals slightly longer than distance between posterior border of frontal and tip of snout. Dorsals smooth, overlapping, in 23–35 rows at midbody. 181–232 ventrals; 37–66 paired subcaudals;

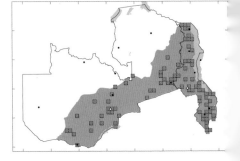

cloacal scale entire. Body usually light to dark brown or reddish brown; xanthic individuals rarely occur. Juveniles often have large darker blotches on neck and flanks, which may persist in some adults. Broad pale stripe extends from tip of snout, through top of eye to back of head; second pale stripe often extends from snout over lower margin of eye to angle of jaw. Ventrum immaculate to creamy white, rarely yellowish, may be slate-grey in juveniles. **Taxonomic note:** Molecular studies suggest that *B. capensis* is a species complex, with several cryptic species awaiting formal description. **Habitat:** Savanna and woodland. Often found around human habitations. **Behaviour:** A common terrestrial, nocturnal constrictor. During the day it shelters in moribund termitaria and under logs, bark,

rocks, rubble and any other suitable debris. Juveniles may adopt tonic immobility (feign death). **Prey:** Predominantly small rodents such as Striped Mice, shrews, fat mice and Pygmy Mice, lizards such as Blue-headed Tree Agamas (*Acanthocercus atricollis*) and skinks (*Trachylepis*) as well as geckos, although other snakes, frogs, bats (including Cape Serotine Bats) and birds (including Speckled Mousebirds) are also eaten. **Reproduction:** Female lays 8–18 oval eggs (24–50mm x 12–24mm) in spring or summer. Incubation takes 60–90 days. Hatchlings measure 190–260mm in TL. The female may produce multiple clutches per season. **Range:** Across Malawi and the south-eastern half of Zambia. Elsewhere it occurs from East Africa to South Africa.

Frade's Brown House Snake   *Boaedon fradei*

Frade's Brown House Snake is olive-green in colour, with narrow, pale eye stripes.

Max. SVL ♂ 608mm ♀ 738mm

A medium-sized snake with a fairly short head that is slightly distinct from the neck. 1–2 preoculars; 1–2 postoculars; 1 anterior and 2 posterior temporals. 8–9 supralabials, 4th and 5th or 5th and 6th entering orbit; 9 infralabials, first 3–4 in contact with anterior sublinguals. Parietal longer than length between posterior border of frontal and tip of snout. Loreal up

to twice as long as it is high. Dorsals smooth, overlapping, in 25–29 rows at midbody. 195–221 ventrals and 63–69 paired subcaudals in males; 213–223 ventrals and 50–52 paired subcaudals in females; cloacal scale entire. Body light to dark olive-green; ventrum pale yellow to cream with scattered yellow blotches. Narrow, pale stripe extends from snout through top of eye to back of head; second pale stripe extends from lower posterior border of eye to posterior angle of jaw. **Habitat:** Open woodland, often on sandy soils. **Behaviour:** A common, nocturnal snake that shelters under any suitable cover, including logs, rocks and rubble. **Prey:** Small rodents, lizards, skinks and geckos; probably also frogs, birds and possibly bats. **Reproduction:** Unknown, presumably similar to Brown House Snake (*B. capensis*). **Range:** From eastern Angola to the eastern DRC, south through Zambia to northern Namibia and Botswana.

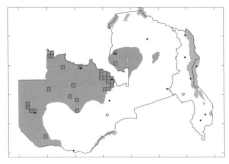

Sooty House Snake   *Boaedon fuliginosus*

Max. SVL ♂ 550mm ♀ 705mm
A medium-sized to large snake with a fairly long head that is distinct from the neck. 1–2 preoculars; 2 postoculars; 1 anterior and 2 posterior temporals. 8 supralabials, 4th and 5th entering orbit; 9 infralabials, first 3–4 in contact with anterior sublinguals. Parietal as long as distance between posterior border of frontal and tip of snout. Loreal more than twice as long as it is high. Dorsals smooth, overlapping, in 25–33 rows at midbody. 197–249 ventrals; 43–88 paired subcaudals; cloacal scale entire. Body uniform dark grey to black, usually with narrow, pale stripe extending from snout, above eye to back of the head. Ventrum pale grey to white.

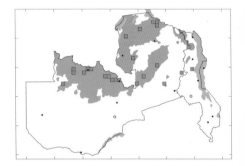

Habitat: Savanna and woodlands. Often found near human habitations. **Behaviour:** This common, terrestrial, nocturnal constrictor

The Sooty House Snake is dark overall, with a narrow pale eye stripe that may be absent.

shelters in moribund termitaria and under logs, bark, rocks, rubble and other suitable debris. **Prey:** Feeds predominantly on small rodents, lizards and geckos. Occasionally eats frogs, bats and birds. **Reproduction:** A female was found to contain 11 eggs (24mm x 14mm). **Range:** Northern Zambia and northern Malawi. Records from southern Malawi may represent misidentifications, or human-assisted translocations. Elsewhere it occurs from East Africa through the DRC and northern Angola to West Africa.

WATER SNAKES   *Lycodonomorphus*

Medium-sized snakes with a cylindrical body and a short to moderate tail. The head is slightly broader than the neck and barely distinct from it. The eyes are of moderate size and the pupil is vertically elliptical to round. The nostrils are directed upwards and are situated in a semi-divided or divided nasal. An inconspicuous to conspicuous groove separates the supralabials from the remainder of the head scales. The body scales are smooth and overlapping, in 19–23 (rarely 25) rows at midbody. The subcaudals are paired and the cloacal scale is entire (rarely divided). Males have an obvious hemipenial bulge.

These semi-aquatic snakes are usually found in or near waterbodies, often under logs and rocks near water. One species endemic to South Africa is terrestrial and preys on rodents, lizards and even other snakes. They may be very common in suitable habitat. They are predominantly nocturnal, although some species may forage during the day. The prey consists mainly of frogs and tadpoles, although fish are also occasionally eaten. Water snakes are not venomous. Large prey may be constricted, while smaller prey is grasped and immediately swallowed. Females are oviparous, laying clutches of 4–23 eggs.

This genus occurs widely in Central, East and southern Africa. Nine species are recognised, four of which occur in the region.

KEY   Regional *Lycodonomorphus* species

1a 23–25 midbody scale rows; usually 7 supralabials, 4th entering orbit; endemic to Lake Tanganyika . . . . ***L. bicolor*** (p. 133)
b 19–21 midbody scale rows; usually 8 supralabials, 4th and 5th entering orbit **2**

2a 21 midbody scale rows; 1st supralabial with posterior projection; throat usually immaculate white . . . . ***L. mlanjensis*** (p. 134)
b 19 midbody scale rows; 1st supralabial without posterior projection; throat with dark flecking or coloured **3**

3a Ventrum orange-yellow, uniform or with scattered dark infusions; 37–52 subcaudals; restricted to southern Malawi . . . . ***L. obscuriventris*** (p. 135)
b Ventrum pinkish to yellowish white, uniform or with dark median band that may break up into discrete narrow stripes; 47–62 subcaudals; restricted to northern Malawi . . . . ***L. whytii*** (p. 136)

Lake Tanganyika Water Snake   *Lycodonomorphus bicolor*

Max. SVL ♂ 420mm ♀ 615mm
A medium-sized aquatic snake with a fairly short head and round pupils. Nasal partially or completely divided (rarely undivided). 0–2 preoculars; 2 postoculars; 1 anterior and posterior temporals. 7 (rarely 8) supralabials, th (rarely 4th and 5th) entering orbit, or narrowly separated from orbit by 1–2 small suboculars or an anterior extension of postocular; 8 infralabials, first 4–5 in contact with anterior sublinguals, latter much larger than posterior sublinguals. Body scales smooth, in 23 (rarely 24 or 25) rows at midbody. 152–166 ventrals; 52–71 paired subcaudals; cloacal

scale entire. Back grey to olive-brown or brown; supralabials often tinged with yellow. Ventrum and lower 2–3 scale rows on flanks yellow or yellowish white. Tail often has dark median stripe below. **Habitat:** Shoreline and shallow waters in Lake Tanganyika. **Behaviour:** Predominantly nocturnal; it can be seen swimming in the lake at night. During the day it shelters under stones, logs and other suitable cover on the lake shore. It has also been found sheltering in disused gerbil burrows. It also shelters under stones in shallow water, occasionally raising its head to breathe. Activity appears to peak during moonless nights and individuals are less active during the full moon period. **Prey and Predators:** Feeds exclusively on fish (mainly cichlids), which are constricted in open water. Many individuals have severed

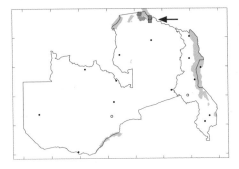

tails, presumably due to predation attempts by freshwater crabs or terrapins. **Reproduction:** Breeding appears to occur throughout the year. The female lays clutches of 4–8 eggs near the water's edge. **Range:** Endemic to Lake Tanganyika.

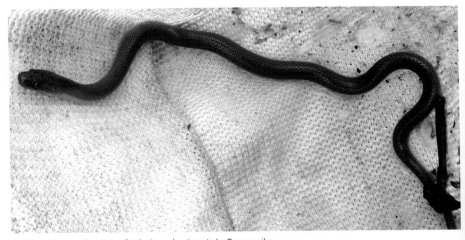

The Lake Tanganyika Water Snake is endemic to Lake Tanganyika.

Mulanje Water Snake   *Lycodonomorphus mlanjensis*

Max. SVL ♂ 580mm ♀ 750mm
A medium-sized water snake. Nasals divided; nostril pierced between 2 nasals. 1 preocular; 2 postoculars; 1 anterior and 2 posterior temporals. 8 supralabials, 4th and 5th entering orbit; 8 infralabials, first 4 in contact with anterior sublinguals. 1st supralabial has posterior projection. Anterior sublinguals only slightly larger than posterior sublinguals. Body scales smooth, in 21 rows at midbody. 163–169 ventrals; 51–76 paired subcaudals;

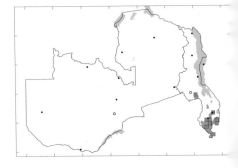

cloacal scale entire. Glossy olive-black above with lowermost 1–2 scale rows pale with darker infusions. Infralabials white with darker infusions anteriorly. Ventrum immaculate pinkish white to dull orange, occasionally with scattered darker flecks. Dark median stripe present on subcaudals. **Habitat:** Streams, pans and marshes. **Behaviour:** Nocturnal. Shelters under stones at waterside or in shallows. **Prey:** Preys predominantly on amphibians, which it constricts. **Reproduction:** Female lays up to nine eggs (25mm x 13mm) in summer. **Range:** High-elevation areas of southern and central Malawi. Elsewhere there is an unconfirmed record from southern Tanzania, while an isolated population occurs in the Eastern Highlands of Zimbabwe.

The Mulanje Water Snake is a glossy olive-black above.

Floodplain Water Snake *Lycodonomorphus obscuriventris*

Max. SVL ♂ 440mm ♀ 575mm

A small to medium-sized snake with a short tail. Head flattened, moderately distinct from the neck. Pupil vertically elliptical. Nasals divided; nostril pierced on posterior border of anterior nasal. 1 preocular, separated from frontal by suture between prefrontal and supraocular; 2 postoculars; 1 anterior and 2 posterior temporals. 8 (rarely 9) supralabials, 4th and 5th (rarely 5th and 6th) entering orbit; 8 infralabials, first 4–5 in contact with anterior sublinguals. Scales smooth, in 19 rows at midbody. 164–176 ventrals; 37–52 paired subcaudals (51–52 in males, 37–42 in females). Dark olive-brown to blackish above; supralabials yellow with dark longitudinal stripe. Ventrum uniform orange-yellow or with scattered dark spots, especially on chin; tail yellow below with dark median stripe. **Habitat:** Reedbeds, lowland floodplains,

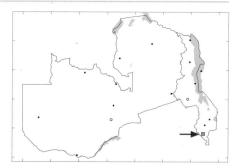

marshes and edges of dambos. **Behaviour:** Poorly known. Individuals have been observed in the late afternoon and evening. **Prey:** Frogs. **Reproduction:** Unknown. **Range:** In the region only recorded from Elephant Marsh in southern Malawi. Elsewhere it occurs through Mozambique and extreme eastern Zimbabwe to eastern South Africa.

Whyte's Water Snake   *Lycodonomorphus whytii*   ☠

In the region, Whyte's Water Snake occurs only in extreme northern Malawi, favouring high-elevation streams.

Max. SVL ♂ 268mm ♀ 605mm

A medium-sized water snake with a fairly short tail. Nasals divided; nostril pierced between 2 nasals. 1 (rarely 2) preocular; 2 (rarely 1) postoculars; 1 anterior and 2 posterior temporals. 8 supralabials, 4th and 5th entering orbit (rarely 9 supralabials, 5th and 6th or 3rd–5th entering orbit); 7 infralabials, first 4 in contact with anterior sublinguals; latter about same size as posterior pair. Body scales smooth, in 19 rows at midbody. 159–169 ventrals; 47–62 paired subcaudals; cloacal scale entire. Dark brown, olive or slate-grey above, sometimes with outermost scale row pinkish or yellowish white. Ventrum pinkish to yellowish white, may be plain, or with broad, dark median band extending across width of ventrum; band may break up into narrow discrete median dark patches. Supralabials white in adults, pigmented anteriorly in juveniles; in some adults pigmentation may extend along lower border of supralabials to form dark lower border to pale supralabial stripe. Anterior infralabials and mental dark. **Habitat:** High-

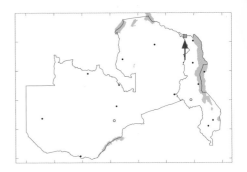

elevation montane streams. **Behaviour:** A rare, semi-aquatic snake known from only a few specimens. No documented details regarding behaviour. **Prey:** Has been recorded preying on frogs and tadpoles. **Reproduction:** Unknown. **Range:** The only record from the region originates from the Chipata area of northern Malawi. However, some authorities believe that this specimen was likely collected in the Misuku Mountains as it is a forest-dwelling species. This assumption is accepted here. Elsewhere it has been recorded in southern Tanzania.

Malagasy Snakes and relatives
Family Pseudoxyrhophiidae

This family consists of a number of morphologically divergent genera, which are characterised by various vertebral and hemipenial features in addition to genetic traits. They display a diverse array of life history traits and may be diurnal or nocturnal and terrestrial or arboreal. Although most species are oviparous, several retain the eggs within their body until they hatch. Most are harmless, although bites from some species have resulted in mild envenomation. There are 22 genera and 89 species in the family, most of which are restricted to Madagascar. Two genera and five species occur on the African mainland, with a single genus and species found in the region.

Shire Slug-eater

SLUG-EATERS *Duberria*

Small, stout-bodied snakes with a small, blunt head that is not or hardly distinct from the neck. The eyes are relatively small, with round pupils, and the nostril is situated in a single nasal. The loreal is absent or greatly reduced in size. The scales are smooth and arranged in 15 rows at midbody. The cloacal scale is entire and the tail is short, with paired subcaudals.

These snakes can be quite common in suitable habitat. They forage amongst leaf litter, rotting logs, grass roots and in other damp locations for slugs and land snails, which they eat exclusively. They track prey by following their slime trails. Slugs are swallowed whole, and to extract snails, the snake inserts its head into the shell opening. Females retain the eggs inside their body until they hatch, giving birth to a few live neonates.

Four species are currently recognised, although several subspecies and isolated populations of the widespread South African Slug-eater (*D. lutrix*) likely represent valid species. The genus occurs widely in southern and eastern Africa, with one species found in the region.

Shire Slug-eater *Duberria shirana* ☠

The Shire Slug-eater, a small, stout snake, occurs across the higher elevations of Malawi.

Max. SVL ♂ 316mm ♀ 272mm
A small, stout snake with a short head that is not distinct from the body. Loreal absent. 1 preocular; 1 (rarely 2) postocular; 1 anterior and 2 posterior temporals. 6 supralabials, 3rd and 4th entering orbit; 6–7 infralabials, first 3 in contact with anterior sublinguals. Dorsals smooth, in 15 rows at midbody. 124–148 ventrals; 24–48 paired subcaudals; cloacal scale entire. Uniform olive-brown above, occasionally with darker vertebral line. Ventrum yellowish medially, becoming grey laterally, may be uniformly dark. **Habitat:** Montane grassland, swamp verges and other damp localities. **Behaviour:** A common snake that shelters in grass tussocks, under logs and rocks, and in accumulated leaf litter. Never attempts to bite when handled. **Prey:** Feeds almost exclusively on slugs, which it locates by

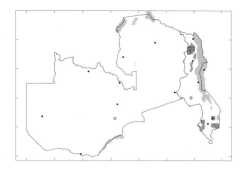

following the slime trail. **Reproduction:** Female gives birth to 4–13 neonates (100–120mm in TL) in late summer. **Range:** High-elevation regions of Malawi, just entering north-eastern Zambia on the Nyika Plateau. Elsewhere it occurs in the southern DRC, Tanzania, Burundi and northern Mozambique.

Mambas, Cobras and relatives
Family Elapidae

Anchieta's Cobra

This family contains some of the most venomous snake species in the world. Snakes in this group are easily distinguishable by the presence of a pair (rarely two pairs) of short, immovable and hollow fangs at the front of the upper jaw, and the absence of a loreal.

Most species are medium-sized to large and have round pupils. Many are capable of spreading a narrow to broad hood, but only cobras (*Naja*) regularly do so. The body scales are shiny, unpitted and usually smooth (keeled in one species from southern Africa). The juveniles of many species are banded and this coloration may persist into adulthood.

These snakes have a diverse array of life history traits and may be terrestrial, semi-fossorial, arboreal or aquatic. Most species are venomous, possessing cytotoxic or neurotoxic venom, or a combination thereof. The so-called 'spitting cobras' can squirt their venom. Many species pose a danger to humans owing to their venom potency and several species have caused human fatalities. Many of the larger species are confident and will stand their ground if harassed. The majority of species are oviparous.

This family occurs widely in tropical and subtropical regions and has a near-global distribution, being absent only from Madagascar and Europe. There are 55 genera and 358 recognised species, of which three genera and 12 species occur in the region.

Mambas, Cobras and Garter Snakes
Subfamily Elapinae

Genetic evidence indicates that the family Elapidae should be partitioned into two subfamilies: Elapinae, containing the terrestrial species from Africa, Asia and the Americas; and Hydrophiinae, which includes sea snakes (*Hydrophis*), sea kraits (*Laticauda*) and the terrestrial Australasian Elapidae species.

MAMBAS *Dendroaspis*

A group of large, slender snakes with a narrow, coffin-shaped head. A pair of large fangs is situated in the front of the upper jaw. The loreal is absent. The pupil is round. The anterior ribs are slightly elongate, allowing these snakes to spread a narrow hood. The body scales are smooth, narrow, lack apical pits and are arranged in 13–25 very oblique rows at midbody. The tail is long, the cloacal scale is divided and the subcaudals are paired.

Most species are arboreal, with the Black Mamba (*D. polylepis*) being equally at home in trees as on the ground. The arboreal species are restricted to forests or thickets, and the Black Mamba is widespread in savannas. They are predominantly diurnal, although nocturnal activity has been reported for the Black Mamba.

Mambas are the most feared African snakes, attributable to their agility, size, potent venom and reputed aggressiveness, but also to certain myths that persist. Their venom is potently neurotoxic, causing general paralysis and respiratory failure. Only the Black Mamba is known to bite humans with any regularity. The arboreal species rarely come into contact with humans and are generally very reluctant to bite. Mambas prey on small mammals, birds and chameleons which are actively pursued (Black Mamba) or ambushed (arboreal species). Prey is struck rapidly and often repeatedly until it succumbs to the venom. All species are oviparous, the female laying clutches of 6–17 eggs.

These snakes occur widely in tropical Africa, from Somalia in East Africa to Senegal in West Africa and south to South Africa. Three of the four recognised species occur in the region.

KEY Regional *Dendroaspis* species

1a Light grey, olive or dark brown above, uniform or with faint to distinct diagonal
bands; interior mouth lining dark; 23–25 (rarely 21) midbody scale rows . . . . . . *D. polylepis* (p. 142)
 b Dull or bright green to bluish green, uniform or with each scale dark-edged;
interior mouth lining pale; 15–19 (rarely 21) midbody scale rows 2

2a Uniform bright green to bluish green; supralabials immaculate; usually
19 (rarely 17–21) midbody scale rows; occurs in Malawi . . . . *D. angusticeps* (p. 139)
 b Dull green, uniform or with each scale dark-edged; head scales (including
supralabials) dark-edged; 15–17 (rarely 19) midbody scale rows;
occurs in Zambia . . . . *D. jamesoni* (p. 141)

Green Mamba *Dendroaspis angusticeps*

Max. SVL ♂ 1,453mm ♀ 1,480mm
A large, fairly slender snake with a narrow, coffin-shaped head. 3 (rarely 4) preoculars; 2–5 (usually 3 or 4) postoculars; 2 (rarely 1) anterior and 3 (rarely 2 or 4) posterior temporals. Lower anterior temporal occasionally reaches lip, or fuses with supralabials. 7–10 supralabials, 4th

(rarely 3rd and 4th) entering orbit; 10–14 (usually 11–13) infralabials, first 4–5 in contact with anterior sublinguals. Body scales smooth, arranged in 19 (rarely 17 or 21) rows at midbody. 201–232 ventrals; 99–126 paired subcaudals; cloacal scale divided. Body uniform bright green to bluish green; neonates typically bluish green. Ventrum pale yellow-green; interior mouth lining pale. **Habitat:** Montane and lowland forests, occasionally entering dense thickets. **Behaviour:** Secretive, arboreal and diurnal, but will descend to the ground to cross open ground or to chase prey. Spends most of its time in ambush and is not aggressive, preferring to quickly slither away into cover or up a tree to escape. Rarely attempts to bite. It sleeps curled up on branches at night. **Venom:** Neurotoxic, with some cytotoxic properties. Bites are rare, and result in pain and swelling around the bite site, rapid onset of dizziness and nausea,

and difficulty in breathing and swallowing. If untreated, bites may be fatal. Polyvalent antivenom is effective in treating bites from this species and should be administered by a trained medical professional. In the event of a bite, the affected limb should be splinted, a pressure bandage applied and the limb elevated. Medical assistance should be sought immediately. Artificial respiration may be required if paralysis occurs before medical assistance is reached. **Prey:** Birds and nestlings form the bulk of its diet, but it also eats rodents (including terrestrial species), bats and chameleons. **Reproduction:** Males

Coloration varies from bright to dull green.

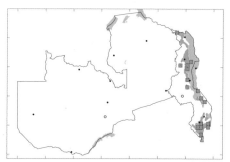

Tyrone Ping

The Green Mamba has a distinctive coffin-shaped head.

engage in combat during the breeding season, intertwining their bodies and trying to force their opponent's head to the ground. The female lays 6–17 eggs (47–65mm x 25–35mm) in leaf litter or hollow logs in summer.

Incubation takes 70–80 days. Neonates measure 350–450mm in TL. **Range:** Widespread in Malawi and East Africa, extending along the East Coast from Kenya to northern South Africa and extreme eastern Zimbabwe.

Jameson's Mamba *Dendroaspis jamesoni*

The head scales are black-edged in Jameson's Mamba. This snake's presence in the region is under debate.

Bill Branch

Max. SVL ♂ 1,980mm ♀ 1,835mm
A large, slender snake with an elongate coffin-shaped head and a relatively small eye. 3 preoculars; 2–4 (usually 3) postoculars; 1 subocular. 1 (rarely 2) anterior and 2 posterior temporals. 7–9 (usually 8) supralabials, 4th entering orbit; 8–10 infralabials, first 4 in contact with anterior sublinguals. Body scales smooth, in 15–17 (rarely 19) rows at midbody. 202–236 ventrals; 91–122 paired subcaudals; cloacal scale divided. Dull green above, paler below; neck and throat yellowish. Scales on head (and occasionally those on body) narrowly black-edged. Tail yellow; its scales black-bordered. Interior mouth lining pale. **Subspecies:** Two races are recognised. Only the typical form (*D. j. jamesoni*) enters the region. **Habitat:** Rainforests and dense woodland, although it is

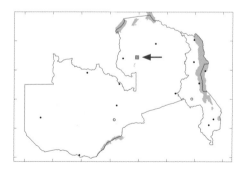

able to persist in disturbed areas. **Behaviour:** A fast-moving, predominantly diurnal snake (some nocturnal activity has been recorded). It may ascend 30m or more into the canopies of tall trees. Owing to its shy and secretive nature, it is rarely seen. It is not aggressive and will attempt to escape if threatened. It may spread a narrow hood. It descends to the ground to cross open spaces, including large open tracts, to access isolated thickets. If disturbed on the surface, it usually escapes along the ground rather than seeking shelter in a tree. **Venom:** Possesses a potent neurotoxic venom, but rarely bites. **Prey:** Its diet includes birds, fruit bats, squirrels and other arboreal rodents, which are captured from ambush. Terrestrial rodents are rarely eaten. Juveniles also prey on chameleons, agamas and (rarely) toads. **Reproduction:** Male combat and mating takes place in winter. The female lays clutches of 7–16 eggs in summer, usually in moribund termitaria. **Range:** Its presence in the region is under debate. It has been recorded only in the vicinity of the Bangweulu Swamps, but these specimens were later destroyed in a museum fire. It may occur in the Ikelenge Pedicle in Zambia. Elsewhere it is found from Sudan and East Africa through the Congo basin to Angola and West Africa.

Black Mamba *Dendroaspis polylepis*

Max. SVL ♂ 2,330mm ♀ 2,530mm
Max. TL 4,500mm

A very long, slender snake with a narrow, coffin-shaped head. 3 (rarely 4) preoculars; 2–5 (usually 3–4) postoculars; 2 (rarely 3) anterior and 3–4 posterior temporals. 7–12 supralabials, 4th (rarely 3rd and 4th, or 5th) entering orbit; 11–13 (rarely 10 or 14) infralabials, first 4–5 in contact with anterior sublinguals. Body scales smooth and overlapping, in 23–25 (rarely 21) rows at midbody. 242–282 ventrals; 104–132 paired subcaudals; cloacal scale divided. Uniform grey to olive-brown above, often with faint to distinct lighter diagonal bands on flanks. Some individuals near-uniform black. Ventrum mottled grey to greenish grey; chin, throat and labials white. Interior mouth lining black. **Habitat:** Occurs widely in savanna and woodland, showing a preference for rocky hillsides and rock outcrops. **Behaviour:** A predominantly terrestrial snake, but equally at home in trees. Although generally diurnal, it is reported to occasionally be active at night in some parts of its range. When inactive, it will shelter in caves, rock piles, moribund termitaria, old earthen burrows, hollow logs, in tree hollows and on branches. It is territorial and a favoured retreat will often be used for long periods, sometimes many years. It is a fast-moving, agile and competent climber. Its fearsome reputation is largely unfounded and it is shy and retiring by nature, preferring to escape when confronted. However, it will stand its ground if cornered, raising up to half of the body and spreading a narrow hood, often with

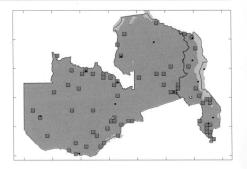

the mouth agape to display the dark mouth lining. The snake may also hiss and emit a pungent curry-like smell. It is best to retreat from this situation if outside striking distance (or not to make any sudden movements if within striking distance), as the snake will also back off if left unmolested. If harassment continues, however, it will bite readily and repeatedly. **Venom:** This is the largest venomous snake in the region. The venom is potently neurotoxic and cardiotoxic and is produced in large quantities. Although dry bites sometimes occur, all bites should be treated as life threatening and medical assistance must be sought immediately. The onset of symptoms is rapid and usually signified by a sensation of pins and needles around the mouth and in the hands and feet, as well as nausea, excessive salivation, and sweating. This progresses to difficulty with speech and swallowing, weakness of the legs, drooping eyelids, and chest and muscle pain. Frothing at the mouth, paralysis and respiratory failure usually follow. During paralysis, victims are

The Black Mamba is the largest venomous snake in the region.

often fully conscious yet unable to speak or move. In the event of a bite, the victim should be immobilised and a pressure bandage and splint immediately applied to the affected limb, which should also be elevated. In cases where paralysis started long before arrival at the hospital, the victim's life has been saved by applying artificial respiration. Polyvalent antivenom is effective and should be administered by a trained medical professional as soon as possible. Large quantities (often up to 10 vials) may be required. Patients usually respond rapidly to treatment. If untreated, death as a result of respiratory failure usually occurs within 7–15 hours (but within 20 minutes in very rare occasions). **Prey:** Feeds predominantly on squirrels, other rodents, birds and hyraxes, but also eats bushbabies and bats. Will opportunistically eat termite alates. **Reproduction:** Males engage in combat during the breeding season, intertwining their bodies while trying to force their opponent's head to the ground. The female lays 6–20 eggs (60–91mm x 30–45mm) in summer. Incubation takes 80–90 days and neonates measure 300–600mm in TL. Initial growth is rapid and young may reach two metres in TL in the first 12 months. **Range:** Widespread throughout the region and from South Africa to East, Central and West Africa.

It is usually grey to olive-brown in colour.

This species is named for its black mouth lining.

COBRAS *Naja*

Large snakes with an average to stout body and a moderately long tail. The head is fairly short and broad and moderately distinct to indistinct from the neck. The loreal is absent and the pupil is round. A pair of large, strong, grooved fangs are situated in the front of the mouth. The body scales are smooth, lack apical pits and are arranged in 15–27 rows at midbody. The subcaudals are usually paired.

Species in this genus can be either diurnal and nocturnal. They are terrestrial, but often climb into low shrubs to bask or forage. When threatened, they lift the anterior portion of the body off the ground and spread a narrow to broad hood. All species possess neurotoxic or cytotoxic venom, or some combination thereof. Any bite from a cobra should be treated as a medical emergency. Some species are able to 'spit' their venom up to three metres. This is achieved through the contraction of the muscles around the venom glands, forcing the dilute venom into the hollow fangs and then out of a small, forward-facing opening near the base of the fang. Cobras prey on a variety of small mammals and amphibians, although bird eggs and other reptiles are also eaten. All species are oviparous, the female laying clutches of 8–33 eggs.

This genus is widespread in Africa and Asia, with 28 recognised species. Additional cryptic species may await description. Six species occur in the region.

KEY Regional *Naja* species

1a   Dorsals not arranged obliquely; body brown or grey; tail black;
     largely aquatic . . . . *N. annulata* (p. 146)
  b   Dorsals arranged obliquely; terrestrial 2

2a   Rostral prominent; suboculars usually separate supralabials from orbit 3
  b   Rostral not prominent; 1 or 2 supralabials usually entering orbit 4

3a   Usually 17 (15–19) midbody scale rows; dorsals on neck enlarged . . . . *N. anchietae* (p. 144)
  b   Usually 19 (17–21) midbody scale rows; dorsals on neck not enlarged . . . . . . *N. annulifera* (p. 147)

4a   6th supralabial largest, in contact with postoculars; 1 preocular; dorsals shiny . . . *N. subfulva* (p. 151)
  b   6th supralabial not largest, not in contact with postoculars; 2 preoculars;
     dorsals matt 5

5a   23–27 midbody scale rows; light grey to olive-brown above, dorsals often
     dark-edged, giving rise to chequered effect; throat and ventrum salmon-
     pink; series of irregular black bands or blotches on throat . . . . *N. mossambica* (p. 148)
  b   17–21 midbody scale rows; dark olive-brown, grey or black above, paler
     below; single broad black band on throat . . . . *N. nigricollis* (p. 150)

Anchieta's Cobra *Naja anchietae*

Max. SVL ♂ 1,990mm ♀ 1,870mm
A medium- to large-sized snake with a robust body and broad head. Tail fairly short, tapers to bluntly rounded point. Nostril pierced in very large nasal; internasals in contact (rarely separated by rostral). Snout pointed; rostral very large, prominent. 1 (rarely 2) preocular; 2–3 postoculars; 1–3 suboculars, usually separating supralabials from orbit. 7 (rarely 6 or 8) supralabials; 7–10 (usually 9) infralabials, first 4 (rarely 3 or 5) in contact with anterior sublinguals. Body scales smooth,
imbricate, in 17 (rarely 15 or 19) rows at midbody. 171–200 ventrals; 49–66 paired subcaudals; cloacal scale entire. Coloration variable. Juveniles mustard-yellow to yellowish above and below, often mottled with darker brown-grey that may form dark crossbands; distinct broad black band on throat. Adults uniform grey-brown or orange-brown above, often with darker mottling; yellow-brown to orange-brown below, usually with darker blotching; broad, dark band present on throat. Some individuals develop banded pattern with

Anchieta's Cobra may spread a broad hood.

6–9 pale bands on body and 2–3 on tail; pale bands as wide as, or wider than, dark bands. **Habitat:** Relatively arid to moist savanna or woodland, especially along riverbanks and wetlands. **Behaviour:** Common; active both by day and by night. It shelters in termite mounds, holes in the ground and hollow logs, as well as on rocky outcrops, and may use the same refuge for many years. It is fairly confident in its defence and will stand its ground if cornered, spreading a broad hood and hissing loudly. It may adopt tonic immobility (feign death) when threatened. **Venom:** Neurotoxic, with some cytotoxic properties. It has large venom yields. It cannot 'spit' its venom. Bites result in burning and swelling at the bite site, often accompanied by some blistering. This progresses to breathing difficulties which, if left untreated, leads to respiratory failure and death. In the event of a bite, the affected limb should be splinted, a pressure bandage applied and the limb elevated. Medical assistance should be sought immediately. Artificial respiration may be required in the event of respiratory failure. Polyvalent antivenom is effective and should be administered by a trained medical professional. **Prey:** The diet is varied and includes other reptiles, such as Puff Adders (*Bitis a. arietans*) and lizards, birds, amphibians, small mammals and bird eggs. **Reproduction:** Female lays 8–33 eggs (47–

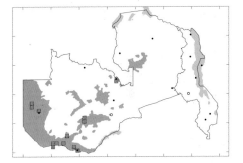

60mm x 25–35mm) in early summer. Incubation takes 60–90 days. Neonates measure 240–340mm in TL. **Range:** Western Zambia, with an isolated population around the Katanga Pedicle in the DRC. Elsewhere it occurs in southern Angola, northern and central Namibia, northern Botswana and north-western Zimbabwe.

The large scales on the back of the neck are diagnostic.

Banded Water Cobra   *Naja annulata*

The Banded Water Cobra has 2–4 narrow dark stripes on the back of the neck.

Max. SVL 2,000mm

A large, heavy-bodied cobra with a broad head that is distinct from the neck. Tail long. 1 preocular; 1–3 postoculars; subocular absent; 1 anterior and 2 posterior temporals. 7 (rarely 8) supralabials, 3rd and 4th entering orbit; 7–10 infralabials, first 4 in contact with anterior sublinguals. Body scales smooth and glossy, in 21–23 (rarely 25) rows at midbody. 193–226 ventrals; 67–77 paired subcaudals; cloacal scale entire. Dark olive-brown to grey-brown above, darkening towards tail; latter glossy black.

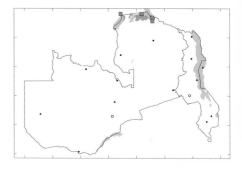

2–4 narrow dark stripes on back of neck, may extend onto ventrum to form continuous rings; sometimes followed posteriorly by five irregular dark spots. Ventrum dirty white to yellow. Head scales sometimes black-edged; black blotch may be present on side of neck. **Subspecies:** Two subspecies are recognised, one of which enters the region. Storm's Water Cobra (*N. a. stormsi*) is endemic to Lake Tanganyika and Lake Mweru. **Habitat:** Large waterbodies in forest and well- wooded savanna. **Behaviour:** This common snake prefers regions with dense waterside vegetation in which it can hide, although it occasionally ventures onto open beaches and small sand bars. It is aquatic, spending most of its time in the water, and is active both by day and by night. Although sluggish on land, it is a skilled swimmer and may remain submerged for up to 10 minutes and dive to depths of 25m. When not hunting, it floats below the water surface with just its nostrils exposed, or takes refuge amongst rocks and vegetation along the shoreline. It shelters under jetties, stone bridges, boats and huts near the water's edge. Shy and retiring by nature, it will escape beneath the water if approached or attempt to enter water if encountered on land. If cornered, it will rear up and spread a narrow hood, but will not rush forward. **Venom:** Neurotoxic. Although no bites have been recorded, the venom is believed to be capable of causing human fatalities. In the event of a bite, the limb should be splinted, a pressure bandage applied and the limb elevated. Medical assistance should be sought immediately. **Prey:** Feeds almost exclusively on fish. **Reproduction:** Female lays 22–24 eggs in early spring. **Range:** In the region, it has been recorded only in Lake Tanganyika and Lake Mweru. Elsewhere it occurs from northern Angola northwards to Cameroon, and eastwards to the DRC.

Snouted Cobra   *Naja annulifera*

Max. SVL ♂ 2,125mm ♀ 1,975mm

A medium to very large snake with a robust body and broad head. Snout pointed; rostral large, extending posteriorly up snout, sometimes separating internasals. Tail fairly short, tapers to bluntly rounded point. Nostril pierced in very large nasal; internasals usually in contact. 1 (rarely 2) preocular; 2–3 (rarely 1) postoculars; 1–3 suboculars, latter usually excluding supralabials from orbit. 7 (rarely 6 or 8) supralabials; 7–10 infralabials, first 4 (rarely 3 or 5) in contact with anterior sublinguals. Body scales smooth, imbricate, in 19 (rarely 17 or 21) rows at midbody. 169–208 ventrals; 48–69 paired subcaudals; cloacal scale entire.

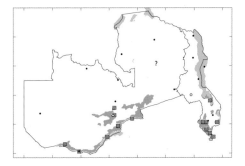

Coloration highly variable. Juveniles mustard-yellow to yellow dorsally and ventrally, often mottled with darker brown-grey that may

The Snouted Cobra has a single, broad dark band on the throat.

form dark crossbands; distinct broad black band present on throat. Adults orange-brown with grey-black mottling (rarely uniform yellow-orange), becoming grey-black with age. Coloration usually darkens posteriorly; tail of adults often uniform dark brown-black. Some individuals develop 6–9 alternating dark and pale bands on body and 2–3 on tail (colloquially called a 'banded cobra'); pale bands (which may be divided by thin black transverse line) usually half the width of dark bands. Ventrum yellow-brown to orange-brown, occasionally with darker mottling. Broad, dark band usually present on throat, but rarely absent and often not distinct in dark individuals. **Habitat:** Moist savanna and woodland. **Behaviour:** This common snake is active both by day and by night. It generally takes refuge in moribund termitaria, holes in the ground or hollow logs, as well as on rocky outcrops. It may use the same refuge for many years if not disturbed. It is one of the largest venomous snakes in the region, with individuals reaching up to 2.4m in TL. Generally shy and docile by nature, it flees at the first sign of danger. It will stand its ground if harassed, however, raising the forepart of the body, spreading an impressive hood and hissing loudly. It may even rush forward in short bursts and occasionally adopt tonic immobility (feign death). **Venom:** It has a potent neurotoxic venom with some cytotoxic properties. The venom yields are large. This snake cannot 'spit' its venom. Bites result in a burning sensation, some localised swelling at the bite site, occasionally accompanied by blistering, and respiratory difficulties. If left untreated, it can lead to respiratory failure and even death. In the event of a bite, medical assistance should be sought immediately. The affected limb should be splinted, a pressure bandage applied, and the limb elevated. The onset of paralysis may result in respiratory failure, in which event artificial respiration should be administered. Polyvalent antivenom is effective and should be administered by a trained medical professional as required. **Prey:** A wide variety of vertebrates, including monitor lizards (*Varanus*) and Puff Adders (*Bitis a. arietans*). It also preys on Southern African Pythons (*Python natalensis*) and, exceptionally, Leopard Tortoises (*Stigmochelys pardalis*). Birds, amphibians (including toads and African Bullfrogs), small mammals and bird eggs are also eaten. **Reproduction:** Female lays 8–33 eggs (47–60mm x 25–35mm) in early summer. Incubation takes 60–90 days and neonates measure 220–340mm in TL. **Range:** Southern Zambia and Malawi, and southwards through Mozambique, Zimbabwe and eastern Botswana to eastern South Africa. A juvenile collected at Mpika in north-eastern Zambia is believed to be a stowaway.

Mozambique Spitting Cobra *Naja mossambica*

Max. SVL ♂ 1,285mm ♀ 1,620mm

A medium-sized, stout-bodied cobra with a blunt head that is slightly broader than the neck. Nostril pierced in suture between 2 nasals; internasals in broad contact. 2 (rarely 1) preoculars; 3 (rarely 2) postoculars; subocular absent; 11–14 scales bordering parietals. 6–7 supralabials, 3rd entering orbit; 8–11 (usually 9) infralabials, first 4 in contact with anterior sublinguals. Body scales smooth and overlapping, in 23–27 rows at midbody. 177–205 ventrals; 52–71 paired subcaudals; cloacal scale entire. Grey to olive-brown above; scales black-edged, giving rise to chequered effect. Interstitial skin black. Ventrum salmon-pink to yellowish; each scale dark-edged, may

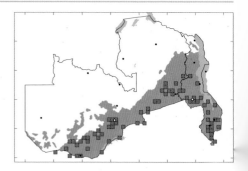

be predominantly black with pinkish edges. Irregular dark bands on throat. **Habitat:** Inhabits a variety of habitats, but most common in mesic savanna and bushveld. Particularly

The Mozambique Spitting Cobra has irregular dark bands on the throat.

Luke Verburgt

common on well-wooded rocky hillsides and are frequently found in and around houses. **Behaviour:** Active both by day and by night. Although predominantly terrestrial, it will climb into low trees and shrubs. Shelters in any suitable cover, such as old termitaria, holes in the ground, hollow logs and rock crevices, as well as amongst building rubble and in quiet outbuildings. This irascible snake is quick to 'spit' its venom, which it can do from any position: it does not have to spread a hood or raise its head first. 'Spitting' is achieved by contracting the muscles surrounding the venom glands, forcing the venom out through the forward-facing fang openings. It can accurately 'spit' to distances of two metres, often hitting the victim in the eyes, but can reach well over three metres and can 'spit' numerous times in quick succession. 'Spitting' is often prompted by movement – if a hand or object is waved off to the side, it will typically aim at this movement instead of the eyes. Despite being irascible, it will rarely stand its ground and will quickly move off if afforded the opportunity. It rarely adopts tonic immobility (feigns death). It may spread a hood that is quite broad. **Venom:** Fairly dilute and predominantly cytotoxic. When sprayed in the eyes, it results in an immediate burning sensation and, if left untreated, permanent tissue damage. The victim's eyes should be immediately and thoroughly rinsed with running water (or any other inert liquid in the absence of water) and medical advice sought. Owing to its irascible nature and tendency to enter houses, this species is responsible for numerous bites. Bites are characterised by intense localised pain, swelling and tissue damage. Necrosis and blistering usually occur at the bite site within a few days. Fatalities have been recorded but are extremely rare. Victims are usually bitten multiple times, often while sleeping. In the event of a bite, the limb should be elevated but a pressure bandage or tourniquet should not be applied, as these measures will localise the venom and increase tissue damage. Medical assistance should be sought immediately. The early administration of polyvalent antivenom by a trained medical professional may limit the extent of tissue damage. **Prey and Predators:** The diet is varied. Amphibians are the main prey, but any small mammals (such as Southern Multimammate Mice), birds and other reptiles (including Schlegel's Giant Blind Snake [*Afrotyphlops* *schlegelii*], Puff Adders [*Bitis a. arietans*], Black-templed Cat Snakes [*Crotaphopeltis hotamboeia*]) and even smaller conspecifics are also eaten. It will also opportunistically scavenge, and occasionally eats bird eggs. It is preyed on by a variety of other snakes and birds, including Saddle-billed Storks. **Reproduction:** Female lays 10–22 eggs (37–51mm x 18–21mm) in summer. Neonates measure 230–250mm in TL. **Range:** Widespread in southern and south-eastern Zambia and central and southern Malawi. Elsewhere it occurs from south-eastern Tanzania southwards to South Africa and westwards to southern Angola.

Black-necked Spitting Cobra   *Naja nigricollis*

The Black-necked Spitting Cobra is the most common cobra species in the region.

Max. SVL ♂ 1,470mm ♀ 2,000mm
A large cobra with a robust body, rounded snout and a broad head that is distinct from the neck. 2 preoculars; 3 (rarely 2) postoculars; subocular absent; 2 anterior and 3–4 posterior temporals; 7–10 scales bordering parietals. 6 (rarely 7 or 8) supralabials, 3rd entering orbit; 8–11 (usually 9) infralabials, first 4 in contact with anterior sublinguals. Body scales smooth, in 17–21 (rarely 23) rows at midbody. 174–226 ventrals; 52–72 paired subcaudals; cloacal scale entire. Back uniform olive-brown or dark grey, becoming black in large individuals; ventrum pale grey. Throat and neck uniformly black in some individuals, with 2–3 pale bands; ventrum grey-white, yellow, pink or orange with some dark mottling. Dark band right around neck and throat often present in juveniles. **Taxonomic note:** Some authors refer to populations in northern Zambia and northern Malawi as the Zambian Spitting Cobra (*N. crawshayi*). It has 17–21 midbody scale rows and 174–201 ventrals and ranges from Angola through Zambia, the southern DRC and northern Malawi to Tanzania and south-western Uganda. **Habitat:** Mesic savanna and woodlands. **Behaviour:** A common snake that is largely terrestrial, but will often enter marshes. Predominantly nocturnal, although juveniles may be active during the day. Shelters in moribund termitaria, hollow tree trunks, holes in the ground and under rocks. It is fiercely defensive, often spreading a broad hood and 'spitting' its venom by contracting the muscles surrounding the venom glands and forcing the venom out of forward-facing openings near the tip of the fangs. If cornered, it will stand its ground and may make short rushes at its harasser. It does not have to spread a hood before 'spitting', nor does it have to raise its head. It can 'spit' its venom well over of three metres (although only accurately to about two metres) and can 'spit' numerous

times in quick succession. Juveniles adopt tonic immobility (feign death) on rare occasions. It can be common around human habitations and is responsible for numerous bites. **Venom:** Fairly dilute, but yields are large and the venom has both cytotoxic and neurotoxic properties. Bites usually result in severe localised swelling and necrosis, blistering, scarring and loss of digits or even limbs. Some bites result in excessive salivation, drooping eyelids and breathing difficulties. Fatalities have been recorded. In the event of a bite, the limb should be elevated but should not be bandaged nor should a tourniquet be applied, as this localises the venom and increases the swelling and resultant tissue damage. Medical assistance should be sought immediately. Polyvalent antivenom should be administered by a trained medical professional in the case of a severe bite. The venom causes immediate intense pain when it comes into contact with the eyes and can cause permanent blindness if not treated. The eyes should be thoroughly rinsed with running water (or other inert liquid in the absence of water) and medical advice sought. **Prey:** The diet is varied and includes amphibians, small mammals, lizards (including monitor lizards [*Varanus*]) and other reptiles such as house snakes (*Boaedon*), birds and their eggs. **Reproduction:** Female lays 8–22 eggs (35–40mm x 20–25mm) in summer. Neonates measure about 360mm in TL. **Range:** Widespread throughout Zambia and central

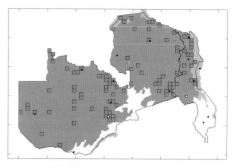

Northern populations are sometimes referred to as Zambian Spitting Cobras.

and northern Malawi, although less common in the south where it is largely replaced by the Mozambique Spitting Cobra (*N. mossambica*). Elsewhere it occurs throughout much of sub-Saharan Africa, although absent from the extreme south.

Brown Forest Cobra   *Naja subfulva*

Max. SVL ♂ 2,050mm ♀ 1,564mm

A large cobra with a fairly slender body and broad, blunt head that is distinct from the neck. Nostril pierced in suture between 2 nasals; internasals in broad contact. 1 preocular; 3 postoculars; subocular absent; 1 anterior and 2–3 posterior temporals. 7 supralabials (very rarely 5 or 6), 3rd and 4th entering orbit; 8 (rarely 7) infralabials, first 4 (rarely 3) in contact with anterior sublinguals. Scales glossy and smooth, in 19 (rarely 17 or 21) rows at midbody. 196–226 ventrals; 55–71 paired subcaudals; cloacal scale entire. Adults brown to blackish brown anteriorly, becoming glossy black posteriorly. Ventrum yellow, heavily flecked with black, with

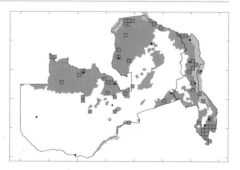

two dark bands on neck. Labials have alternating vertical yellow and black bands. Juveniles typically have uniformly dark dorsum with white-tipped scales, resulting in a stippled effect, or may be golden-brown with darker speckling. **Habitat:** Forests and dense woodlands. **Behaviour:** The largest of the African cobras, it is equally at home in trees as on the ground and frequently enters marshes and pans. Active both by day and night. Takes refuge in any suitable cover, including holes in the ground, hollow logs, termite mounds and exposed root tangles. When threatened, it raises a substantial portion of the forebody and spreads a long, narrow hood, but cannot 'spit' its venom. Accounts of its temperament range from it being reluctant to bite to it being one of the most irascible cobras – this behaviour probably varies between regions and individuals. **Venom:** Potently neurotoxic, with some cytotoxic properties. Bites are rare, but fatalities have been recorded. In the event of a bite, the affected limb should be splinted, a pressure bandage applied and the limb elevated. Medical assistance should be sought immediately. Polyvalent antivenom is effective and should be administered by a trained medical professional. Artificial respiration may be required in the event of respiratory failure. **Prey:** The diet is varied and includes other reptiles (such as White-throated Monitor [*Varanus albigularis*] and Water Monitor [*V. niloticus*]), amphibians, small mammals and fish. **Reproduction:** Males engage in combat, twisting around each other and trying to force their opponent's head to the ground. The female lays 11–26 eggs (46–61mm x 24–32mm) in summer. Incubation takes 75–91 days. Neonates measure 250–400mm in TL. **Range:** Northern, central and eastern Zambia, and throughout Malawi. Widespread in the forest–savanna mosaics of East and Central Africa, ranging from western Cameroon and Chad eastwards to South Sudan and southwards to Angola and eastern South Africa.

It can lift a large part of the body off the ground.

The Brown Forest Cobra always has two distinct dark bands on the throat, and sometimes more on the ventrum.

GARTER SNAKES *Elapsoidea*

Small to medium sized snakes with a moderate to robust body and a very short tail. The head is medium-sized to small, slightly distinct or indistinct from the neck, and the eyes are small with round pupils. There are two fixed front fangs. The snout is bluntly rounded to obtusely pointed. The nasal is divided, the loreal is absent, and there is a single preocular and two postoculars. There are 7 supralabials (3rd and 4th entering orbit) and 7 (rarely 6) infralabials, the first 3–4 of which are in contact with the anterior sublinguals. There is 1 anterior and 2 posterior temporals. The dorsals are smooth, without apical pits, and arranged in 13 rows at midbody. The cloacal scale is entire, while the subcaudals are paired. This genus shows very little morphological variation, which often complicates accurate identification. Species can, however, be separated on habitat choice, variations in colour pattern (especially in juveniles) and sometimes on differences in scale counts.

They are predominantly fossorial, spending most of their time in burrows or burrowing in sandy or humic soils. They usually emerge at night, but occasionally also during the day. Their diet consists predominantly of other fossorial reptiles, with amphibians and small mammals also occasionally eaten. They are venomous but docile and reluctant to bite, and the venom is not known to be life threatening to humans. The few recorded bites resulted in localised swelling, pain and tingling, vertigo, nausea and nasal congestion. These symptoms resolved within four days without the need for antivenom. The female lays clutches of 2–10 eggs.

This genus occurs throughout sub-Saharan Africa, with three of the 10 species occurring in the region. The taxonomic validity of some species is being questioned.

KEY Regional *Elapsoidea* species

1a Pale bands often indistinct (even in juveniles), about twice as wide as dark bands (sometimes as wide); ventrum grey; usually 4 infralabials in contact with anterior sublinguals; occurs east of the Zambezi River . . . . ***E. guentheri*** (p. 154)

b If visible, pale bands or paired white rings much narrower than dark bands; pale bands well developed in juveniles; usually 3 infralabials bordering anterior sublinguals (4th infralabial occasionally in short contact) **2**

2a Pale bands or paired white rings a quarter to half the width of dark bands; adults usually uniformly dark; ventrum dark grey to black; occurs east of Zambezi River . . . . ***E. boulengeri*** (p. 153)

b Pale bands about half as wide as dark bands; adults with paired white rings (occasionally absent in very large individuals); ventrum white; occurs west of Zambezi River . . . . ***E. semiannulata*** (p. 155)

Boulenger's Garter Snake *Elapsoidea boulengeri*

Max. SVL ♂ 710mm ♀ 603mm
A medium-sized snake with a moderately rounded snout and fairly robust body. 140–163 ventrals and 18–27 subcaudals in males; 138–158 ventrals and 14–22 subcaudals in females. Usually 3 infralabials in contact with anterior sublinguals. Juveniles black, with 8–17 narrow white or yellow bands on body and 0–3 on tail that are at most half as wide as dark bands and often narrower on flanks; head white, with dark longitudinal band extending from nape onto top of head; chin and throat white; rest of ventrum usually dark grey or brown (occasionally greyish white); pale ventrolateral stripe occasionally present. Pale bands begin to darken from centre, leaving paired pale rings that usually disappear in large individuals; adults usually uniform brown-black, although faint paired white rings or scattered pale scales may persist. **Habitat:** Favours moist savanna, often being found on open floodplains or in mopane woodland. **Behaviour:** Fossorial and predominantly nocturnal, although occasionally diurnal after heavy rains. **Venom:** Has not been studied. One bite caused immediate localised pain and

transient nasal congestion. This was followed by the entire hand swelling and becoming painful to the touch, and the lymph glands in the armpit swelling. Symptoms resolved themselves after three days without treatment, although some swelling reappeared three days later, accompanied by minor blistering. **Prey:** Predominantly amphibians and skinks, although small snakes are also eaten. It is prone to cannibalism. **Reproduction:** Female lays 4–8 large eggs (about 40mm x 16mm), in summer. **Range:** Throughout Zambia (east of the Zambezi River) and central and southern Malawi. Possibly present in northern Malawi as well. Elsewhere it occurs from Tanzania westwards to the eastern DRC, and southwards through Mozambique, Zimbabwe, Botswana and northern Namibia to South Africa.

TOP Juvenile Boulenger's Garter Snakes have a distinct banded pattern. ABOVE Adults are uniformly dark, sometimes with a pale ventrum.

Luke Kemp

Günther's Garter Snake   *Elapsoidea guentheri*

Max. SVL ♂ 570mm ♀ 500mm

A medium-sized snake with a stout body and rounded snout. 7 supralabials, 3rd and 4th entering orbit; 7 infralabials, first 3–4 in contact with anterior sublinguals. 135–156 ventrals and 19–26 subcaudals in males; 131–148 ventrals and 15–19 subcaudals in females. Juveniles dark, with 14–24 grey or brown bands on body, 2–4 pale bands on tail, white head with broad black longitudinal median band. Pale bands on body usually twice the width of dark bands, sometimes of similar width. Pale bands often barely discernible from dark bands; coloration virtually uniform once SVL of 200mm has been attained; faint paired white dotted lines may persist in some adults. Adults usually uniform grey-black above, with grey ventrum. **Habitat:** Miombo woodland. **Behaviour:** A fossorial, nocturnal snake. **Venom:** Has not been studied. Only a single bite has been recorded. It resulted in immediate tingling and slight pain at the bite site. This was followed by the entire arm becoming sore, the lymph glands swelling and the bitten digit becoming tender and stiff. Symptoms resolved after a day without treatment. **Prey:** Juveniles may prey on insects, while adults prey on reptiles and amphibians (and occasionally

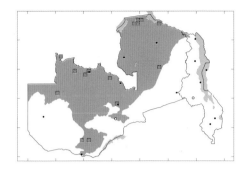

large scorpions). **Reproduction:** Female lays up to 10 large eggs in summer. **Range:** From the DRC through Angola and Zambia to Zimbabwe.

The adult Günther's Garter Snake is dark above, with a grey ventrum.

Angolan Garter Snake *Elapsoidea semiannulata*

Max. SVL ♂ 532mm ♀ 495mm
A medium-sized snake with a moderately rounded snout. 3–4 infralabials, in contact with anterior sublinguals. 137–161 ventrals and 20–28 subcaudals in males; 136–152 ventrals and 13–19 subcaudals in females. Juveniles dark above, with pale ventrums; 12–19 pale bands on body, 2–3 on the tail; pale bands usually about half as wide (sometimes almost equal in width) as dark bands, although widening on flanks; head predominantly white, with narrow

black median line. Transverse bands fade into prominent paired white lines in individuals with SVL of 200–450mm, these bands fading in very large individuals; ventrum uniform white in adults, this coloration sometimes extending onto lower half of outer scale rows. **Subspecies:** Two subspecies are recognised, with only the typical form (*E. s. semiannulata*) entering the region. It has fewer than 150 ventrals. **Habitat:** Relatively dry savanna, usually on sandy soils. **Behaviour:** A rare, fossorial snake that is mainly nocturnal, although it is occasionally spotted during the day after heavy rains. **Venom:** The venom has not been studied, but is likely similar to other garter snakes and should be considered dangerous to humans. **Prey:** Mainly skinks, amphibians and small snakes. **Reproduction:** Believed to be similar to the other garter snakes. **Range:** The typical form ranges from Zambia west of the Zambezi River into adjacent Angola, the south-western DRC and northern Namibia.

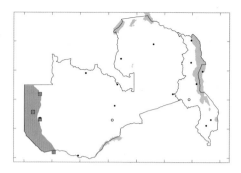

Old World Water Snakes
Family Natricidae

An iridescent Olive Marsh Snake

Old World Water Snakes are small to medium-sized aquatic or semi-aquatic snakes. The scales may be smooth or keeled (always smooth in the region). They are both diurnal and nocturnal and frequent damp locations such as marshes and moist forests. Most species are harmless, although some Asian species have potent venom that may prove fatal. Their diet consists of amphibians, tadpoles and fish. They are oviparous.

This family occurs widely in Central and North America, Eurasia, northern Australia and Africa. At present 39 genera and more than 220 species are recognised, but the African members remain poorly studied. Two genera and five species occur in the region.

SWAMP SNAKES   *Limnophis*

Small snakes with a moderately stout, cylindrical body. The head is small and barely distinct from the neck. The eyes are of moderate size and the pupils are round. There is a single, triangular internasal. The scales are smooth and arranged in 19 rows at midbody. The tail is short, with paired subcaudals, and the cloacal scale is entire.

These aquatic snakes frequent slow-flowing rivers and marshes. They feed on amphibians, tadpoles and fish, including eels. Females are oviparous, laying 5–18 eggs.

This genus is restricted to south-central Africa. There are three species in the genus, two of which occur in the region.

KEY Regional *Limnophis* species

1a Snout pointed; posterior supralabials without dark sutures; dark horizontal stripe along lower border of supralabials; flanks with thin, dark stripes; gular region with dark patterning . . . . **L. bangweolicus** (p. 157)

  b Snout rounded; posterior supralabials with dark sutures; no dark stripe along lower border of supralabials; gular region immaculate . . . . **L. bicolor** (p. 158)

Eastern Striped Swamp Snake   *Limnophis bangweolicus*

The Eastern Striped Swamp Snake has a dark stripe on the supralabials.

Max. SVL ♂ 495mm ♀ 558mm
A medium-sized, slender snake with a small head that is barely distinct from the neck. Snout moderately pointed; eyes fairly large; pupils round. Single triangular internasal. 1 preocular; 2–3 postoculars; 1 anterior and 2 posterior temporals. 8–9 (rarely 7) supralabials, 3rd and 4th (occasionally 5th as well) entering orbit, 6th supralabial very large, often in contact with parietal; 8–10 infralabials, first 5 (rarely 4) in contact with anterior sublinguals. Dorsals smooth, in 19 rows at midbody. 132–150 ventrals; 32–68 paired subcaudals; cloacal scale divided. Back dark olive-brown, often with paler dorsolateral stripes; flanks even paler, each scale row edged with black above and below, forming continuous or interrupted black lines that span length of body. Ventrum yellow to brick-red, with black median stripe on tail. Supralabials white, bordered below by black stripe; labial sutures may be slightly darker. Dark patterning usually present on gular region. **Habitat:** Rivers, streams and other waterbodies, including reedbeds. **Behaviour:** Poorly known. Non-venomous and

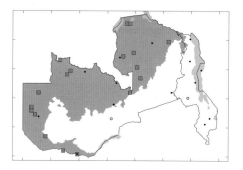

aquatic; it probably shelters in waterside rock crevices and flood debris. Emerges onto sand bars and riverbanks at night to hunt. **Prey:** Fish (including spiny eels), amphibians and tadpoles. **Reproduction:** Female lays 5–6 eggs (21–28mm x 11–15mm) in January. **Range:** Widespread in the major drainage basins of northern and western Zambia, including the Zambezi and Okavango river drainage basins, as well as Lake Bangweulu and Lake Mweru Wantipa, and southwards to the Chobe and Linyanti rivers and the Okavango Delta.

Angolan Swamp Snake   *Limnophis bicolor*

The labials of the Angolan Swamp Snake have dark sutures.

Max. SVL ♂ 405mm ♀ 553mm

A small aquatic snake with a large, blunt head that is barely distinct from the neck. Body cylindrical; eyes fairly large; pupils round. Single triangular internasal. 1 (rarely 2) preocular; 2 postoculars; 1 anterior and 2 (rarely 3) posterior temporals. 8 (rarely 7 or 9) supralabials, 3rd and 4th or 3rd–5th (rarely 2nd and 3rd or 4th and 5th) entering orbit; 6th largest, usually in contact with (occasionally narrowly separated from) parietal. 10 (rarely 9) infralabials, first 4–5 in contact with anterior sublinguals. Dorsals smooth, in 19 rows at midbody. 127–143 ventrals; 37–61 paired subcaudals; cloacal scale divided. Body uniform dark olive-green to black above, usually with pale dorsolateral stripe; gular and ventrum uniformly yellow to brick-red; gular region immaculate. Subcaudals uniform cream-yellow. Labials have dark sutures, especially

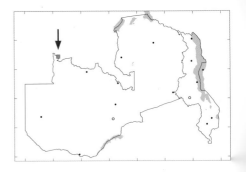

posteriorly. **Habitat:** Permanent waterbodies, including rivers, streams and reedbeds. **Behaviour:** Poorly known. Aquatic and non-venomous. **Prey:** Feeds on tadpoles and fish, including Banded Tilapia and suckermouth catlets. **Reproduction:** Female lays 6–18 eggs. **Range:** Widespread on the Angolan Highlands, eastwards to extreme north-western Zambia.

MARSH SNAKES *Natriciteres*

Small snakes with a cylindrical body and a small head that is barely distinct from the neck. The eyes are moderate in size, with round pupils. There are two internasals. The nostril is pierced between two nasals, or separated from the posterior nasal by a narrow rim. The scales are smooth and in 15–19 rows at midbody. The cloacal scale is divided or entire, and the tail moderately long with paired subcaudals.

These semi-aquatic snakes frequent marshes and other damp locations, and are active both by day and by night. They prey on fish and amphibians. If grasped by the tail they often struggle violently until it breaks off, which may be a defence strategy for avoiding predators. The tail does not grow back. They lack fangs and venom and are harmless. Females are oviparous, laying 4–11 eggs.

The genus occurs widely in tropical sub-Saharan Africa. Three of the six species occur in the region.

KEY Regional *Natriciteres* species

1a Dorsals in 19 anterior and 17 posterior rows; usually 9–10 infralabials,
    first 5 in contact with anterior sublinguals . . . . *N. olivacea* (p. 159)
  b Dorsals in 13–17 anterior and 13–15 posterior rows; usually 8 infralabials,
    first 4 in contact with anterior sublinguals **2**

2a 2 (rarely 3) postoculars; 15–17 midbody scale rows . . . . *N. bipostocularis* (p. 159)
  b 3 postoculars; 13–15 midbody scale rows . . . . *N. sylvatica* (p. 160)

South-western Forest Marsh Snake *Natriciteres bipostocularis*

Max. SVL ♂ 255mm ♀ 202mm

A small, fairly slender snake with a cylindrical body, small head and round pupil. 1 (rarely 2) preocular; 2 (rarely 3) postoculars; 1 anterior and 2 posterior temporals. 8 (rarely 7 or 9) supralabials, 4th and 5th (rarely 3rd and 4th or 5th and 6th) entering orbit; 8 (rarely 9) infralabials, first 4 in contact with anterior sublinguals. Dorsals smooth, in 15–17 rows at midbody (with 17 rows anteriorly and 15 rows posteriorly). 124–143 ventrals; 60–78 paired subcaudals; cloacal scale divided. Brown to black above, with broad dark to maroon vertebral stripe, latter usually flanked by paler dorsolateral stripe or row of small white spots. Brown to blackish-brown dorsolateral stripes usually present. Supralabials yellow, with dark sutures. Ventrum yellow or orange, grey laterally. **Habitat:** Swamps bordering evergreen

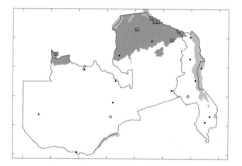

forests. **Behaviour:** Probably similar to Olive Marsh Snake (*N. olivacea*). The tail tip is often shed if grasped. **Prey:** Preys on tadpoles, but probably also feeds on frogs, and perhaps on small fish. **Reproduction:** Female lays 5–6 eggs. **Range:** Northern Zambia and adjacent central Angola and the southern DRC.

Olive Marsh Snake *Natriciteres olivacea*

Max. SVL ♂ 380mm ♀ 460mm

A small, fairly slender snake with a small head and round pupil. 1 (rarely 2) preocular; 3 (rarely 2) postoculars; 1 anterior and 2 (very rarely 3) posterior temporals. 8 (very rarely 7 or 9) supralabials, 4th and 5th (rarely 4th or 4th–6th) entering orbit; 9–11 infralabials (very rarely 8), first 5 (rarely 4 or 6) in contact with anterior sublinguals. Dorsals smooth, in 19 (rarely 17 or 18) rows at midbody, 19 rows anteriorly and

17 rows posteriorly. 128–160 ventrals; 51–95 paired subcaudals; cloacal scale divided. Body usually grey, blue-black, olive or chestnut. Broad vertebral band extends length of body, may be darker than rest of body, a shade of maroon, or dull green; sometimes bordered by series of small white spots. Some individuals uniform bluish black. Ventrals yellow medially and usually pale blue, olive, grey, red or mauve laterally. Chin and throat white. Supralabials yellow with dark borders. Melanistic individuals rarely recorded. **Habitat:** Streams and marshlands in woodlands and savanna. **Behaviour:** Semi-aquatic, but may be found away from water during the rainy season. **Prey and Predators:** Feeds predominantly on frogs, tadpoles and small fish, but may exceptionally eat termite alates. It

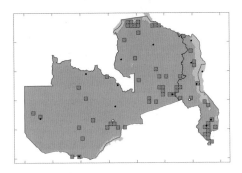

is often preyed on by Hamerkop and shows a high frequency of tail autotomy. **Reproduction:** Female lays 3–11 eggs (20–25mm x 7–15mm) in early summer. **Range:** Widespread in the savanna of sub-Saharan Africa.

The small, fairly slender Olive Marsh Snake is widely distributed across the region.

Forest Marsh Snake   *Natriciteres sylvatica*   ☠

Max. SVL ♂ 276mm ♀ 330mm

A small, fairly slender snake with a small head and round pupil. 1–2 preoculars; 3 (rarely 2) postoculars; 1 anterior and 2 posterior temporals. 8 (rarely 7) supralabials, 4th and 5th (rarely 3rd and 4th or 3rd–5th) entering orbit; usually 8 (rarely 9 or 10) infralabials, first 4 (rarely 5) in contact with anterior sublinguals. 125–143 ventrals; 60–84 paired subcaudals; cloacal scale divided. Body scales smooth, in 13–15 rows at midbody, usually 17 rows anteriorly and 13–15 rows posteriorly. Body dark olive to grey-black or chestnut, usually with broad dark brown, black or maroon vertebral stripe; latter may be edged with white spots. Faint pale collar may be present on nape. Supralabials yellow with distinct dark sutures. Ventrum yellow to cream with grey lateral edges. **Habitat:** Edges of montane and lowland evergreen forests. **Behaviour:** Poorly known. It is active at any time during the day and night, foraging in leaf litter and shallow water. Many individuals have truncated tails. **Prey:** Frogs, tadpoles and fish-eating spiders. **Reproduction:** Female lays 5–6 eggs. **Range:** Recorded from extreme north-eastern Zambia and throughout the Malawi lowlands. Elsewhere it occurs from southern Tanzania through Mozambique and the Eastern Highlands of Zimbabwe to extreme eastern South Africa.

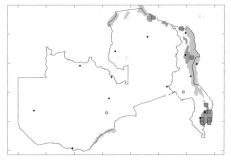

The Forest Marsh Snake looks very similar to the Olive Marsh Snake.

Typical Snakes
Family Colubridae

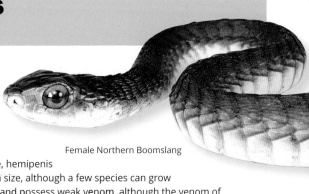

This large family contains numerous genera and species, although the precise taxonomy is still under debate and varies between authorities. No obvious morphological characters unifying this group. Genera are largely assigned to this family based on genetic studies and, to a lesser degree, hemipenis

Female Northern Boomslang

morphology. Most species are medium in size, although a few species can grow quite large. The majority are rear-fanged and possess weak venom, although the venom of boomslangs (*Dispholidus*) and vine snakes (*Thelotornis*) is potent and poses a danger to humans. Some lack fangs and venom, such as the green snakes (*Philothamnus*), Semiornate Snake (*Meizodon semiornatus*) and egg-eaters (*Dasypeltis*).

These snakes occupy a vast array of habitat types, ranging from rocky areas in arid environments through arid and mesic savannas to moist coastal forest. They may be fossorial, terrestrial, arboreal or semi-aquatic, and diurnal or nocturnal. The prey consists predominantly of small vertebrates, although some species are bird egg specialists. All species are oviparous.

The family is highly successful and has a near-global distribution, with the greatest diversity in the Palaearctic. A total of 29 species in 13 genera occur in the region.

Large Water Snakes
Subfamily Grayiinae

This subfamily contains four species of large water snakes belonging to the genus *Grayia*. They are fairly large snakes with a robust body and large head. All species are aquatic and occur widely in West, Central and East Africa. None are venomous.

LARGE WATER SNAKES   *Grayia*

Medium- to large-sized snakes with a robust body and a large head that is usually distinct from the neck. They lack fangs. The body scales are smooth and arranged in 15–20 rows at midbody. The body is grey to brown or black, often with lighter bands or blotches that may be restricted to the flanks. The tail is often a uniform black, as are the supralabial sutures. The tail is often truncated, probably owing to attempted predation events.

These snakes are almost entirely aquatic, but will shelter in dense waterside vegetation and even man-made structures such as jetties. They prey predominantly on fish, but will also eat frogs and occasionally tadpoles. They are harmless to humans. The female lays clutches of 9–20 eggs.

There are four species, which occur widely in West, Central and East Africa. Two species are found in the region.

KEY Regional *Grayia* species

1a Dorsals in 17 (rarely 19 or 20) rows at midbody; 65–87 subcaudals . . . . **G. ornata** (p. 162)
 b Dorsals in 15 rows at midbody; 110–133 subcaudals . . . . **G. tholloni** (p. 163)

Ornate Water Snake   *Grayia ornata*

The body of the Ornate Water Snake is darker posteriorly, the tail being entirely black.

Max. SVL ♂ 760mm ♀ 984mm
A fairly large snake with a robust body
and a head that is broader than the neck.
Nasal divided or semi-divided. 1 preocular;
2 postoculars; 2 anterior and 3 posterior
temporals. 8 supralabials, 4th entering orbit
(rarely 9 supralabials with 3rd and 4th entering
orbit); 10–12 infralabials, first 4–5 in contact with
anterior sublinguals. Dorsals smooth and glossy,
in 17 (rarely 19 or 20) rows at midbody. 142–161
ventrals, 65–88 paired subcaudals; cloacal scale
divided. Body grey-brown above, with 21–25
narrow dark crossbands that fork on flanks. Body

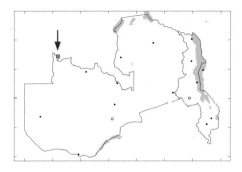

darker posteriorly; tail entirely black. Supralabials
pale with dark sutures and dark labial stripe;
latter broadens posteriorly and extends onto
side of head. Chin and throat dark; infralabials
with pale longitudinal streaks and spots.
Ventrum cream-coloured, each scale black-edged
posteriorly. Subcaudals heavily infused with
black, becoming entirely black towards tip of
tail. Juveniles black, with 15–32 pale crossbands
that fork on flanks; pale crossbands gradually

darken from centre with age; background colour
fades until adult coloration attained. **Habitat:**
Lowland tropical forests, occasionally along
rivers in savanna. **Behaviour:** Poorly known.
An aquatic snake that, despite its appearance,
is not venomous. **Prey and Predators:** Feeds
on frogs and fish (including catfish). Eaten by
Eastern Slender-snouted Crocodiles (*Mecistops
leptorhynchus*). **Reproduction:** Unknown. **Range:**
Extreme north-western Zambia and adjacent
Angola, through the DRC to Cameroon.

Thollon's Water Snake   *Grayia tholloni*

Thollon's Water Snake occurs in large rivers and lakes in northern Zambia.

Harald Hinkel

Max. SVL 720mm
A fairly large, robust snake with a broad head
and round pupil. Tail very long, nearly 40%
of TL, truncated in many individuals. Nasal
divided or semi-divided. 1 preocular; 2 (rarely

3) postoculars; 2 anterior and 3 posterior
temporals. 8 (rarely 7) supralabials, 4th and
5th, or only 4th, entering orbit; 9–10 (rarely 11)
infralabials, first 4–6 in contact with anterior
sublinguals. Dorsals smooth, glossy, in 15 rows

at midbody. 130–150 ventrals; 100–135 paired subcaudals; cloacal scale divided. Brown to dark grey-brown above, pale orange-white bars on flanks giving rise to blotched appearance. Dark blotches often black-edged, especially laterally; series of black spots may be present on lower flanks. Supralabials pale, sutures dark. Ventrum yellow to cream with dark spots laterally. Juveniles blackish above with narrow white bars; latter pronounced on anterior half of body, fading posteriorly. **Habitat:** Rivers and lakes in moist savanna and woodlands. **Behaviour:** An aquatic, diurnal snake that likely shelters in waterside vegetation. It is not venomous. **Prey and Predators:** Preys on fish, frogs and tadpoles. Many individuals have truncated tails,

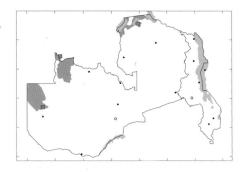

probably as a result of predation attempts by water birds. **Reproduction:** Female lays up to three eggs. **Range:** Northern Zambia through Angola, Central and East Africa to West Africa.

Typical Snakes
Subfamily Colubrinae

This large subfamily contains predominantly northern hemisphere species and is poorly represented in Africa. The snakes are distinguished by asymmetrical hemipenes, which have a simple sulcus. Some genera have developed rear fangs, whilst one genus has greatly reduced teeth. Some species have potent venom that poses a danger to humans.

This subfamily has a global distribution, with more than 700 species in nearly 100 genera. A total of 27 species in 12 genera occur in the region.

BLACK TREE SNAKES *Thrasops*

These large, slender snakes have a short head and large eyes. The tail is about a third of the total length. The dorsals are smooth or keeled and are arranged in 13–21 rows at midbody. There are three enlarged maxillary teeth, which are separated from the small anterior teeth by a gap.

These snakes are diurnal and arboreal, preferring forests and other dense vegetation. When angry, they inflate their neck and anterior portion of the body, move the head from side-to-side and often strike out at the harasser. If confronted in a tree and unable to escape, they may launch themselves to the ground and rapidly slither away. Their diet is varied and includes various small vertebrates, including birds, lizards, frogs and rodents. Females are oviparous, laying clutches of 7–12 eggs. Whether these snakes possess fangs and venom still remains unresolved, but they should be treated as potentially dangerous to humans.

The genus is endemic to tropical sub-Saharan Africa. Of the four recognised species, one occurs in the region.

Jackson's Tree Snake *Thrasops jacksonii*

Max. SVL ♂ 1,320mm ♀ 1,550mm
This large snake has a fairly blunt snout and large eyes with circular pupils. 1–2 (rarely 3) preoculars; 3 (very rarely 2 or 4) postoculars; 1 anterior and 1 (very rarely 2) posterior temporal. 8 (rarely 7 or 9) supralabials, 4th and 5th (rarely 5th and 6th) entering orbit; 9–13 infralabials, first 4–6 in contact with anterior sublinguals. Dorsals strongly overlapping, in 19 (rarely 17 or 21) rows at midbody; vertebral

Jackson's Tree Snake inflates its throat when harassed.

It closely resembles a boomslang.

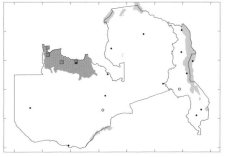

and paravertebral scale rows keeled; remaining scale rows usually smooth (occasionally keeled). 178–214 keeled ventrals; 125–155 paired subcaudals; cloacal scale divided. Adults uniformly glossy black above and below, except for yellowish-white chin and throat. Some scattered grey markings may be present on head. Iris dark. Juveniles mottled with black and yellow or orange above and below, head may be olive-green to brown. Subadults may be uniform black with broad variegated vertebral band consisting of brown and black mottling; may have greenish ventrals with black edges. Emits a strong liquorice-like smell, especially if it sloughed recently. **Habitat:** Primary and riparian forest. **Behaviour:** Diurnal and arboreal. If cornered, it will rapidly climb higher into the tree. If this is not possible, it may drop to the ground and slither off at great speed. When threatened, it will inflate its neck in a threat display and strike out. **Venom:** This species appears to be rear-fanged, although it apparently lacks fangs in some regions. The potency of the venom is also under debate, with some authorities regarding it as harmless to humans while others consider this species to be venomous. Of the few reported bites, most did not result in any symptoms, but when the snake was able to chew the victim for a while, considerable pain, swelling and excessive bleeding resulted. It is best to treat this species as having potentially dangerous venom. **Prey:** Varied. Arboreal lizards, chameleons, birds (including nestlings and eggs), rodents, bats and frogs comprise the bulk of the diet. **Reproduction:** Female lays 7–12 eggs (about 30mm x 10–15mm) in mid-summer. **Range:** In the region it has been recorded only in north-western Zambia. Elsewhere it occurs in the southern DRC east to Kenya and Tanzania.

BOOMSLANGS   *Dispholidus*

Large, slender-bodied snakes with a short, blunt head that is distinct from the neck. The eyes are very large with round or horizontally pear-shaped pupils. The nostril is pierced in a single nasal. Three very large fangs are situated below the posterior border of the eye. The scales are very narrow, keeled and arranged in 19–21 oblique rows at midbody.

These snakes are diurnal and arboreal, coming to ground only to cross open spaces between trees. They are able to remain motionless in ambush for extended periods of time, their coloration rendering them difficult to detect. When angry, they inflate the neck, and occasionally the anterior portion of the body as well, displaying bright interstitial skin. They are docile and will attempt to flee, but will stand their ground if cornered. They have potent haemotoxic venom that poses a danger to humans and has caused fatalities. Despite being rear-fanged, they have a very large gape and it is often not necessary for them to chew in order to envenomate a victim. They prey predominantly on chameleons and birds, but will also eat other small vertebrates, such as rodents and frogs. Females are oviparous, laying clutches of 8–27 eggs in summer.

The genus occurs widely in sub-Saharan Africa. In the past, only a single widespread species (Boomslang [*Dispholidus typus*]), containing between two and four subspecies, was recognised. Recent genetic data suggest that four described and two undescribed taxa exist. As the taxa are diagnosable on coloration, are genetically distinct and are for the most part geographically separated, the authors treat each taxon as a separate species, but concede that they may be subspecies of a widespread *D. typus*.

KEY   Regional *Dispholidus* species

1a Males black above with orange and/or yellow spots, ventrals cream, yellow or violet with dark margins; females reddish brown dorsally (occasionally uniform olive-grey) and paler below, often with a white chin and throat; occurs in north-western Zambia and the Luapula Province of Zambia . . . . *D. punctatus* (p. 167)

b Males green; females grey, brown or blackish brown; does not occur in north-western Zambia **2**

2a 94–110 subcaudals (99–110 in males, 94–104 in females); occurs in extreme north-eastern Zambia . . . . *D. kivuensis* (p. 166)

b 104–142 subcaudals (110–142 in males, 104–127 in females); occurs in central and southern Zambia, and Malawi . . . . *D. viridis* (p. 168)

Kivu Boomslang   *Dispholidus kivuensis*

Max. SVL ♂ 1,290mm ♀ 1,260mm
A medium-sized to large snake with a short, bluntly rounded head and a very large eye. 1 preocular; usually 3 postoculars; usually 1 anterior and 2 posterior temporals. Usually 7 supralabials (rarely 8), 3rd and 4th entering orbit; 8–13 infralabials, first 3–6 in contact with anterior sublinguals. Usually 19 (rarely 17 or 21) rows of strongly keeled and overlapping scales at midbody, arranged in oblique rows. 164–201 ventrals; 89–110 paired subcaudals (99–110 in males, 89–104 in females); cloacal scale divided. Males green dorsally, often with each scale black-edged, with green ventrum; females grey or brown. Juveniles grey-brown, often with blue

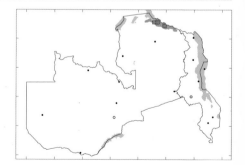

spots (especially along the vertebral line). Flanks light grey to pinkish with darker speckling. Head grey to olive-brown; chin and throat white.

Habitat: Savanna and woodland, but absent from forest and grassland. **Behaviour:** Arboreal and diurnal. Will descend to the ground to cross between trees or to lay eggs. It is fast-moving and alert, but may spend hours inactive in one position in a tree or shrub. It is not aggressive and will usually move off if approached. If cornered, it will typically inflate the neck to display the bright interstitial skin. **Venom:** It is rear-fanged and has potent haemotoxic venom that is deadly to humans, resulting in internal and orificial bleeding. Despite being rear-fanged, this snake has a very large gape and can envenomate a victim without having to chew. Dry bites are fairly common. The venom is slow-acting and it may take 24–48 hours for symptoms to appear. A monovalent antivenom is available only from South African vaccine producers and, if required, should be administered by a trained medical professional. In the event of a bite, the victim should be transported to a medical facility and remain under observation for at least 48 hours. **Prey:** Feeds predominantly on arboreal lizards, with chameleons being a particular favourite. It will also prey on agamas, birds and their eggs, small mammals and arboreal frogs. **Reproduction:** Female lays 8–25 eggs (40mm x 20mm) in a tree hollow or leaf litter in late spring or early summer. Incubation takes 90–120 days. **Range:** North-eastern Zambia, extending into Tanzania and Kenya.

Spotted Boomslang *Dispholidus punctatus*

The male Spotted Boomslang is dark above, with diagnostic pale spotting.

Bill Branch

Max. SVL ♂ 1,110mm ♀ 1,070mm

A large snake with a short, blunt head, rounded snout and a very large eye. 1 preocular; 3 (rarely 2) postoculars; usually 1 anterior and 2 posterior temporals. Usually 7 supralabials, 3rd and 4th entering orbit; 8–13 infralabials, first 3–6 in contact with anterior sublinguals. Dorsals strongly keeled and arranged obliquely, in 19 (rarely 17 or 21) rows at midbody. 164–201 ventrals; 90–117 paired subcaudals (97–117 in males, 90–110 in females); cloacal scale divided. Males black, with each scale having an orange or yellow spot; ventrals cream to violet, with dark margins. Females reddish brown above and paler below with white chin and throat, occasionally uniform olive-grey. In both sexes

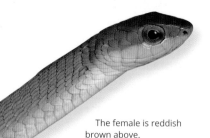

The female is reddish brown above.

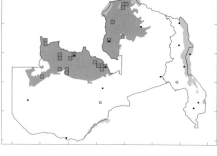

blue spots may become visible when the body is inflated. Juveniles grey to brown above, with blue spots on interstitial skin; head dark brown above and white below; throat bright yellow; iris bright green. Ventrum grey, with darker (often dull red) stippling. **Habitat:** Ocurs in savanna and woodlands, but absent from forests. **Behaviour:** Diurnal and arboreal. Can remain motionless for many hours, thus avoiding detection. Shy and retiring by nature, it will attempt to escape rather than face a harasser. When cornered, it inflates its neck, exposing the bright interstitial skin. **Venom:** It has fixed rear fangs and a potent haemotoxic venom that is extremely dangerous to humans. This snake has a very wide gape and is capable of envenomation with a single bite. The venom is fairly slow-acting and symptoms may appear only after 24–48 hours. In the event of a bite, the victim should be transported to a medical facility and remain under observation for at least 48 hours. If required, antivenom should be administered by a trained medical professional. Monovalent antivenom is available only from South African vaccine producers. **Prey:** Feeds predominantly on chameleons and birds, but will also eat other arboreal lizards, frogs, mice and bird eggs. Prey is usually retained in the mouth while the venom takes effect. Eggs are swallowed whole. **Reproduction:** Mating occurs in spring and the female lays 10–18 eggs (31–32mm x 17–18mm) in a tree hollow or in leaf litter in summer. Incubation takes 60–90 days. Neonates measure 290–330mm. **Range:** Northern Zambia, northern Angola and the southern and eastern DRC.

Northern Boomslang   *Dispholidus viridis*   ☠

Max. SVL ♂ 1,150mm ♀ 1,440mm
A medium to large snake with a blunt, rounded head and a very large eye. Tail long, tapering. 1 preocular; usually 3 postoculars (rarely 2 or 4); usually 1 (rarely 2) anterior and 2 (rarely 1 or 3) posterior temporals. 7 (rarely 6 or 8) supralabials, 3rd and 4th (occasionally 4th and 5th) entering orbit; 8–13 infralabials, first 3–6 in contact with anterior sublinguals. Body scales keeled and overlapping, in 19 (rarely 17 or 21) oblique rows at midbody. 164–201 ventrals; 104–142 paired subcaudals (110–142 in males, 104–127 in females); cloacal scale divided. Males bright green above, paler yellowish green to white below. Females usually uniform grey-brown to blackish brown. Juveniles grey to brown above. Head

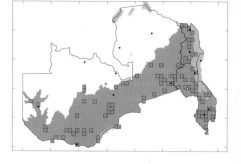

brown above; broad, dark vertebral band usually extends down back. Grey to pinkish or yellowish grey below, with varying degrees of darker speckling. Supralabials white to yellowish. Iris bright green. **Habitat:** Frequents

The male Northern Boomslang is usually green.

The female is uniformly brown.

Juveniles are a mottled grey, with large green eyes.

savanna and woodland but absent from forest. **Behaviour:** A common diurnal, arboreal snake, occasionally seen on the ground when it crosses between trees or while hunting. Frequently lies motionless in a tree or shrub for hours on end to ambush prey, and may remain in the same tree for days or weeks at a time. Usually sleeps coiled up on the outer limbs of dense vegetation or in tree hollows, but occasionally in moribund termitaria. In winter it may be seen basking at the entrance to its favourite refuge. Very inquisitive, it may move through trees to get closer to activity that has attracted its attention. When threatened, it inflates its neck, displaying the bright interstitial skin. It is fairly docile and will try to escape rather than face a harasser. May live for up to 12 years. **Venom:** It has potent haemotoxic venom that is very dangerous to humans, and causes severe bleeding from the mucous membranes and body orifices, in addition to internal bleeding. Fatalities are rare and usually result from untreated bites. Although rear-fanged, this snake has a very large gape and can envenomate a victim without having to chew. Dry bites are fairly common. The venom is slow-acting and symptoms may appear only after 24–48 hours (but fatalities have been recorded within 12 hours in children). In the event of a bite, the victim should immediately be transported to a medical facility and remain under observation for at least 48 hours. A monovalent antivenom is available only from producers in South Africa. If required, it should be administered by a trained medical professional. **Prey and Predators:** Feeds on birds, chameleons (especially Flap-necked Chameleons [*Chamaeleo dilepis*]) and other arboreal lizards, and will also eat small mammals, frogs (including Southern Foam-nest Frogs and African Bullfrogs), and bird eggs and chicks. Various bird species are known to mob this snake: Grey-headed Bush Shrikes, Arrow-marked Babblers and Burchell's Starlings sometimes kill individuals through sustained harassment. It is eaten by various raptors and other snakes. **Reproduction:** Males engage in combat. The female lays 8–27 eggs (27–53mm x 15–37mm) in late spring or early summer in hollow tree trunks, rotting logs or leaf litter. Neonates measure 290–380mm in TL. **Range:** Central and southern Zambia and throughout Malawi. Elsewhere through Botswana, Namibia and Mozambique to northern South Africa.

DAGGER-TOOTH TREE SNAKES   *Rhamnophis*

Relatively large snakes with a slender body and fairly short, bulbous head. The eyes are quite large, with round pupils. There is a single temporal. The dorsals are smooth and arranged in 13–17 (rarely 19) rows at midbody, with the vertebral scale row enlarged. Three distinctive dagger-like teeth are present below the posterior margin of the eye.

Diurnal and arboreal, snakes in this genus prefer lowland and riverine forests where they spend most of their time in trees. The diet consists largely of birds and frogs. When threatened, they inflate the neck to ward off a would-be attacker, but they are harmless to humans. Females are oviparous, laying up to 17 eggs.

The genus is endemic to tropical sub-Saharan Africa. Two species are recognised, one of which occurs in the region.

Splendid Dagger-tooth Tree Snake   *Rhamnophis aethiopissa*   ☠

In the region, the Splendid Dagger-tooth Tree Snake occurs only in the Ikelenge Pedicle.

Max. SVL ♂ 948mm ♀ 950mm

A large, slender snake with a very big, blunt head and a large, prominent eye. Mouth curves markedly upwards; 3 prominent dagger-like teeth in back of upper jaw, below posterior margin of eye. 1 (very rarely 2) preocular; 3 (rarely 2 or 4) postoculars; 1 temporal. Pair of enlarged occipital scales present. 6–9 supralabials, 3rd and 4th, 4th and 5th or 5th and 6th entering orbit; 7–11 infralabials, first 3–6 in contact with anterior sublinguals. Body scales smooth, in 15–17 (rarely 13 or 19) rows at midbody, vertebral scale row enlarged. 154–179 keeled ventrals; 117–159 paired subcaudals; cloacal scale divided. Body bright green, with varying intensities of black and orange or yellow spots. Yellow and orange spots particularly prominent on enlarged vertebral scale row. Each body scale usually black-bordered. Alternating longitudinal orange and black stripes on tail. Head dull blue-green to green, posterior head scales often with broad dark sutures. Chin and throat white. Ventrum pale orange to pinkish white. Dark median stripe present on the subcaudals. Iris gold or green-yellow. Unlike Jackson's Tree Snake (*Thrasops jacksonii*), this species does not emit a liquorice-like smell. **Subspecies:** Three poorly defined subspecies are recognised, although intergrades are

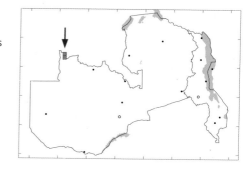

common and the validity of these subspecies needs to be investigated. *R. a. ituriensis* occurs in the eastern DRC south to extreme northern Zambia and adjacent north-eastern Angola. **Habitat:** Gallery and primary forest. **Behaviour:** Diurnal and arboreal, this snake is a fast and graceful climber. It is shy and spends most of its time in thick vegetation. Although harmless, it may inflate its neck in a threat display if harassed. **Prey:** Feeds predominantly on birds, lizards (including chameleons) and small mammals, although frogs are also eaten. **Reproduction:** Female lays 5–17 eggs (35–40mm x 15–17mm). Neonates measure 300–340mm in TL. **Range:** Widespread from West Africa through Central Africa to East Africa, just entering the region in extreme north-western Zambia.

VINE OR TWIG SNAKES *Thelotornis*

Large, extremely slender snakes with a narrow, elongate head that is slightly flattened and distinct from the neck. The tail is long. The eyes are fairly large with horizontal key-hole or dumbbell-shaped pupils. Three large fangs are positioned below the posterior border of the eye. The nostril is pierced in a single nasal. The body scales are narrow and weakly keeled, and in 19 oblique rows at midbody. The body is usually grey with darker spots, blotches and

Eastern Vine
Snake threat display

infusions both above and below, while the top of the head may be a similar colour to the body, or bright green. This coloration, combined with the slender body, results in a motionless snake closely resembling a twig or vine, hence the common name. When agitated, these snakes inflate the neck to make themselves look bigger, which results in the anterior part of the body resembling a bird. They are therefore sometimes referred to as bird snakes.

Vine snakes are diurnal and arboreal, rarely coming to ground, and inhabit forest, woodland and savanna. They are able to spend extended periods lying motionless in ambush, with their thin body and superb coloration rendering them almost undetectable. They prey on arboreal lizards and frogs, occasionally eating birds as well. Terrestrial lizards and snakes are eaten on occasion, these being ambushed from above. The snakes are rear-fanged with potent haemotoxic venom that poses a danger to humans and has caused fatalities. They are docile, however, and rarely bite, and their small gape usually requires them to chew on a victim to ensure envenomation (although this may not be the case if the victim is bitten on a small extremity, such as a finger). Females are oviparous, laying 4–18 eggs.

Vine snakes occur across sub-Saharan Africa. Four species are recognised, three of which occur in the region.

KEY Regional *Thelotornis* species

1a Top of head (including temporal region) uniform bright green; supralabials uniform white; distinct black bands or chevrons on neck; occurs in forests in the Ikelenge Pedicle in Zambia . . . . *T. kirtlandii* (p. 174)

 b Top of head bright green, blue-green or brown, with or without dark spotting; temporal region brown or pink with dark speckling; supralabials white with dark triangle below eye; 1–2 elongate dark blotches on neck 2

2a Top of head blue-green with dark and pink speckling forming Y-shaped pattern; temporals pink, each scale with dark margin . . . . *T. capensis* (p. 172)

 b Top of head bright green to pale brown, uniform or with black speckling; temporals brown with black speckling . . . . *T. mossambicanus* (p. 175)

Savanna Vine Snake   *Thelotornis capensis*

The Savanna Vine Snake closely resembles twigs or vines.

Max. SVL ♂ 1,062mm ♀ 1,050mm

A large, very slender snake with a lance-shaped head and large eyes with horizontal keyhole-shaped pupils. Rostral and nasal barely visible from above. 1 preocular; usually 3 (rarely 1, 2 or 4) postoculars; 1 anterior and 2 (rarely 1 or 3) posterior temporals. 8 (rarely 7 or 9) supralabials, the 4th and 5th (rarely 3rd and 4th, 5th and 6th or 3rd–5th) entering orbit; 9–13 (usually 11) infralabials, first 3–5 in contact with anterior sublinguals. Body scales weakly keeled, in 19 (rarely 17) rows at midbody. 144–177 ventrals; 126–173 paired subcaudals; cloacal scale divided. Crown of head bluish green to brown, with pink and black speckling forming a well-defined Y-pattern; arms of latter extend forwards towards supraoculars. Temporal region pink, with each scale black-edged. Head patterning poorly developed in juveniles. One or two faint dark blotches may be present on side of neck, followed by faint black crossbars. Body pale grey to grey-brown, often tinged with pink, with paler oblique crossbands or scattered blotches and striations. Ventrum greyish with darker stippling and striations that become more pronounced posteriorly. Labials, chin and throat white with darker stippling. Tongue orange-red with black tip. **Subspecies:** Two subspecies are recognised, one of which enters the region. Oates's Savanna Vine Snake (*T. c. oatesii*) has 150–177 (usually more than 160) ventrals and the dark speckling on the head is arranged in a distinct Y-pattern. It occurs from southern Angola and northern Namibia east through Zambia, Malawi and the southern DRC to western Mozambique and south to Botswana and Zimbabwe. The subspecies intergrade, however, and recent genetic results have cast doubt on their validity. **Habitat:** Savanna and woodland. **Behaviour:** A common diurnal and predominantly arboreal snake, although individuals occasionally descend to the ground to cross open spaces or to pursue prey. Some nocturnal hunting has also been recorded. The coloration and slender build recall a small branch or vine, hence the common name, and renders it very well camouflaged. It often lies in the same position for hours on end, but may enter tree hollows if disturbed. When threatened, it inflates its neck and sticks out its brightly coloured tongue. The keyhole-shaped pupils and loreal groove enable acute stereoscopic vision, allowing it to see stationary prey. It ambushes its prey, the attack culminating in either a short dash or a strike from above. It is rear-fanged, chewing larger prey to effect envenomation. It usually hangs with its head downwards while ingesting prey. **Venom:** The venom is potently haemotoxic and life threatening to humans. The blood not being able to clot results in extensive haemorrhaging. Symptoms may appear only 24–48 hours after a bite and human fatalities are extremely rare. There is no antivenom for this snake and treatment relies on blood and

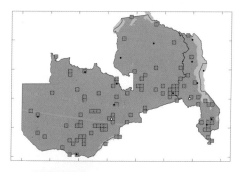

The top of the head has a distinct brown Y-pattern.

plasma transfusions. In the event of a bite, the victim should be transported to a medical facility and remain under observation for at least 48 hours. As the snake is extremely docile, most recorded bites have been on snake handlers or when the snake is accidentally trodden on. **Prey:** Lizards (including chameleons and skinks) and frogs (including Southern Foam-nest Frogs, rain frogs, reed frogs and sand frogs) form the bulk of the diet. Other snakes (especially green snakes [*Philothamnus*]), fledgling birds, bird eggs and small mammals (including bats) are also eaten. **Reproduction:** Males engage in combat in early spring, intertwining their bodies and trying to force their opponent's head down. The victor mates with the female over the course of a few days. The female lays 4–18 eggs (25–44mm x 12–18mm) in mid-summer. Incubation takes 60–90 days. Neonates measure 230–331mm in TL. Females may lay two clutches per season. **Range:** From South Africa to Tanzania, the southern DRC and Angola. Widespread across the region.

In the region, the long, very slender Forest Vine Snake occurs only in the Ikelenge Pedicle.

The top of the head is uniformly green.

Max. SVL ♂ 850mm ♀ 1,050mm

A long, very slender snake with a long tail, large eyes and horizontal keyhole-shaped pupils. Head narrow, elongate. Rostral and nasals curved posteriorly onto upper surface of snout. 1 preocular; 2–4 (usually 3) postoculars; 1 (rarely 2) anterior and 2 (rarely 1) posterior temporals. 8 (rarely 7, 9 or 10) supralabials, 4th and 5th (rarely 5th and 6th or 4th–6th) entering orbit; 7–12 (usually 9) infralabials, first 4–5 (rarely 3) in contact with anterior sublinguals. Dorsals feebly keeled, in 19 (rarely 17 or 21) rows at midbody. 146–206 ventrals; 110–175 paired subcaudals; cloacal scale divided. Crown of head and temporal region uniform bright green. Supralabials uniform white or finely stippled with grey or green. Series of dark crossbars on neck; first narrow, may be interrupted dorsally. Body mottled in brown, green and pale grey, often with faint paler crossbands. Ventrum whitish grey, usually with darker striations and stippling. Tongue bright red, with black tip. **Habitat:** Restricted to forests and forest edges. **Behaviour:** Similar to Savanna Vine Snake (*T. capensis*). Prey is ambushed and may also be attacked from above or pursued along the ground. **Venom:** It has a potent haemotoxic venom that is likely dangerous to humans. Symptoms of envenomation and treatment should follow that outlined for Savanna Vine Snake. **Prey:** Lizards, including chameleons and Western Tree Agamas (*Acanthocercus cyanocephalus*), frogs, small snakes and birds. **Reproduction:** Female lays clutches of 4–12 eggs (30–35mm x 15mm). **Range:** Widespread from West Africa through Central Africa to Somalia and southwards to Tanzania and northern Angola. In the region it has been recorded only in the Ikelenge Pedicle in Zambia.

Eastern Vine Snake   *Thelotornis mossambicanus*

ABOVE The Eastern Vine Snake has brown temporals with darker speckling. BELOW The tongue tip is black.

Max. SVL ♂ 910mm ♀ 920mm

A medium-sized, very slender snake with a long tail and narrow, lance-shaped head. Eyes large; pupils horizontal, keyhole-shaped. Rostral and nasal barely visible from above. 1 preocular; 3 (rarely 2 or 4) postoculars; 1 (rarely 2) anterior and 2 (rarely 1 or 3) posterior temporals. 8 (rarely 6, 7 or 9) supralabials, 4th and 5th (rarely 5th and 6th or 3rd and 4th) entering orbit; 9–13 (usually 11) infralabials, first 4–5 in contact with anterior sublinguals. Body scales weakly keeled, in 19 (very rarely 17, 21 or 23) rows at midbody. 144–172 ventrals; 123–167 paired subcaudals; cloacal scale divided. Top of head uniform bright green, or with a speckled black Y-pattern on the head, the arms of which extend diagonally forward towards the supraoculars. Head may be brownish with extensive black stippling; in that case temporal region is brown with black speckling. Supralabials white, with black speckling and dark triangle on 6th supralabial. Chin and throat greyish

white with black stippling; usually one or two elongate dark blotches on side of neck. Body ashy grey to greyish brown, with diagonal pale blotches; latter usually black-edged anteriorly. Scattered pink and orange patches often present. Ventrum greyish white with brown streaks, usually darker posteriorly. Tongue red, with black tip. **Habitat:** Savanna, woodland and forests, but typically in drier locations than the Forest Vine Snake (*T. kirtlandii*). **Behaviour:** Similar to Savanna Vine Snake (*T. capensis*). Remains motionless low down in a bush until terrestrial prey passes, at which point it quietly descends to the ground and follows, capturing its prey with a final short dash. Prey is repeatedly chewed along the length of its body to inject venom. **Venom:** As with other vine snakes, it has potent haemotoxic venom that has resulted in human fatalities. Symptoms of envenomation and treatment should follow that outlined for Savanna Vine Snake. **Prey:** Lizards, including chameleons and agamas, frogs, fledgling birds and other snakes. **Reproduction:** Female lays 4–13 eggs (about 35mm x 15mm), in mid-summer. **Range:** From central Mozambique and extreme eastern Zimbabwe through Malawi and extreme north-eastern Zambia to East Africa and southern Somalia.

GREEN AND WATER SNAKES   *Philothamnus*

Small to medium-sized snakes with a slender to moderate body. The head is moderate to elongate and is distinct from the neck. The eyes are medium-sized to large, with round pupils. The nasal is divided. A single loreal is present, as is a single preocular (which may be divided). Fangs are absent. The body scales are smooth and arranged in 11–15 rows at midbody. The ventral and subcaudal scales may be smooth to weakly or strongly keeled, and may be faintly to distinctly notched along the keel. The tail is relatively long, with paired subcaudals.

These active, diurnal snakes inhabit a range of vegetation types, including savanna, woodland, forest and damp areas. They may be terrestrial, arboreal or semi-aquatic, and all species swim well. They are harmless, but are often mistaken for venomous species. They prey on amphibians, nestling birds, lizards and fish. The female lays clutches of 3–16 eggs, sometimes in communal sites.

The genus occurs throughout sub-Saharan Africa. A total of 20 species are recognised, six of which are found in the region.

KEY Regional *Philothamnus* species

Note: Species in this genus show a fair degree of variation in the number and shape of head scales (this can be the case on one or both sides of the head). It is therefore advisable to consider other avenues of evidence, e.g. the number and shape of the ventral and subcaudal scales, and in some instances coloration, to confirm the identity of the species.

1a Back emerald- to olive-green, with dark reddish-brown vertebral stripe, bordered by golden-yellow band . . . . *P. ornatus* (p. 180)
  b Uniform green or bluish green, with or without dark spots, speckles or bands **2**

2a 2 anterior and 2 posterior temporals; subcaudals keeled **3**
  b 1 anterior and 1–2 posterior temporals; subcaudals not keeled **4**

3a 9 supralabials, 5th and 6th usually entering orbit; 157–188 ventrals; no concealed pale spots on dorsals; dark speckles never fused into short crossbars . . . . . . *P. punctatus* (p. 181)
  b 9 supralabials, 4th–6th usually entering orbit; 170–209 ventrals; concealed pale blue or white spots present on dorsals; dark spots often fused into short crossbars, especially on neck . . . . *P. semivariegatus* (p. 182)

4a 8 supralabials, 4th and 5th entering orbit; snout tip usually yellowish . . . . *P. hoplogaster* (p. 178)
  b 9 supralabials, 4th–6th entering orbit; snout tip usually not yellowish **5**

5a Body moderately slender; head moderate in size; concealed white spots on dorsals; 143–184 slightly keeled ventrals; 87–134 subcaudals; widespread . . . . *P. angolensis* (p. 177)
  b Body extremely slender; head very small and narrow; no concealed white spots on dorsals; 164–194 smooth ventrals; 101–144 subcaudals; restricted to northern and western Zambia . . . . *P. heterolepidotus* (p. 178)

Western Green Snake *Philothamnus angolensis*

The Western Green Snake has a robust head and a pale throat.

Max. SVL ♂ 790mm ♀ 808mm

A small to medium-sized, slender green snake. 1 preocular; 2 postoculars; 1 (occasionally 2) anterior and 2 (rarely 1) posterior temporals. Supraoculars slightly raised. 9 (rarely 8 or 10) supralabials, 4th–6th usually entering orbit; 8–11 infralabials, first 4–6 (usually 5) in contact with anterior sublinguals. Dorsals smooth, in 15 rows at midbody. 143–184 slightly keeled ventrals; 87–134 smooth, paired subcaudals; cloacal scale divided. Body bright emerald-green to olive-green, with black interstitial skin and often scattered blue-white spots on anterior portion of body. Ventrum pale green to yellowish green, occasionally darkening posteriorly. Melanistic individuals rarely occur. **Habitat:** Rivers, streams, reedbeds and other waterbodies. **Behaviour:** A common waterside snake, often seen in trees overhanging water, reedbeds or other vegetation near water. It is often seen traversing the sandy banks of large rivers and is a skilled, graceful swimmer, sometimes taking refuge in water if disturbed. Aggregations of 80–100 individuals sometimes occur in prime habitat, and communal nesting sites are common. It may inflate the neck as a threat display, revealing the dark interstitial skin, and will readily bite, though it is not venomous. **Prey:** The diet consists mainly of frogs, toads and lizards, although nestling birds are also eaten. **Reproduction:** Female lays 5–17 eggs (25–43mm x 9–18mm) in rotting logs,

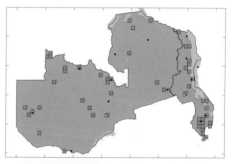

There are usually one anterior and two posterior temporals. Three supralabials enter the orbit.

leaf litter or similar vegetation in mid-summer, often in communal sites. Incubation takes about 60 days. Neonates measure 220–260mm in TL. **Range:** Has a widespread but patchy distribution in the region. Elsewhere it has a patchy occurrence from eastern South Africa through East Africa and Angola, and northwards to Cameroon and South Sudan.

Slender Green Snake *Philothamnus heterolepidotus*

Max. SVL ♂ 492mm ♀ 488mm
A small to medium-sized green snake with a very slender body and narrow head. 1 preocular; 2 postoculars; 1 anterior (rarely absent) and 1 (rarely 2) posterior temporal. 9 (rarely 7, 8 or 10) supralabials, 4th–6th (rarely 3rd and 4th, 4th and 5th or 3rd–5th) entering orbit; 9–11 infralabials, first 5 (rarely 4 or 6) in contact with anterior sublinguals. Dorsals smooth, in 15 rows at midbody. 164–194 smooth ventrals; 101–144 paired, smooth subcaudals; cloacal scale divided. Uniform light green above, without concealed pale spots. Interstitial skin black. Ventrum pale yellow to very pale green. Chin

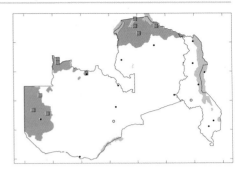

Three supralabials enter the orbit.

and throat white. **Habitat:** Woodlands and mesic savanna, often in association with papyrus swamps or gallery forest. **Behaviour:** An active, non-venomous diurnal snake. **Prey:** Frogs. Possibly lizards, including geckos. **Reproduction:** Female lays 2–8 eggs (21–35mm x 8–12mm) in summer. **Range:** From Sierra Leone eastwards to South Sudan and southwards through East Africa to Zambia and Angola. In the region it occurs in northern and western Zambia.

The Slender Green Snake has a narrow head and a more slender build than other green snakes.

South-eastern Green Snake *Philothamnus hoplogaster*

Max. SVL ♂ 662mm ♀ 685mm
A small, slender green snake with a head that is moderately distinct from the neck and a long,

tapering tail. 1 (rarely 2) preocular, 2 (rarely 3) postoculars; 1 anterior (rarely 2 or absent) and usually 1 (rarely 2 or absent) posterior temporal. 8 (rarely 7 or 9) supralabials, 4th and 5th (rarely 3rd and 4th, 3rd–5th, 4th–6th or 5th and 6th) entering orbit; 8–11 infralabials, first 5 (occasionally first 4 or 6) in contact with anterior sublinguals. Body scales smooth, arranged in 15 (rarely 13) rows at midbody. 138–167 laterally keeled or smooth ventrals; 64–106 paired smooth subcaudals; cloacal scale divided. Body uniform bright green to bluish green or olive-green. Interstitial skin black. Small number of black spots or bars may be present on anterior portion of body. Ventrum pale bluish white to yellowish green. **Habitat:** Usually found close to water or marshes. **Behaviour:** Active and diurnal. It is predominantly arboreal, but is also a skilled swimmer and is occasionally seen on the ground. It may lose its tail if grasped. The tail does not regenerate. It is not known to inflate the neck as a threat display and is usually docile. It is not venomous. **Prey and Predators:** The diet consists mainly of frogs and tadpoles, including Müller's Platanna, which it is able to catch in the water but consumes on dry land. Toads, lizards and even small fish have been recorded in its diet. Grasshoppers have been

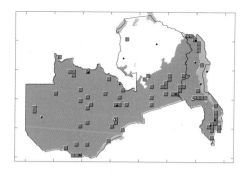

found in the stomachs of some specimens, but these may have been released from ingested frogs during digestion. This species is eaten by Tiger Fish and Woodland and Brown-Hooded kingfishers. **Reproduction:** Males may engage in combat in spring, intertwining their bodies and trying to wrestle their opponent's head to the ground. The female lays 3–8 eggs (25–34mm x 8–12mm) in early summer. Neonates measure 150–200mm in TL and are darker than the adults. **Range:** Widespread throughout the region. Elsewhere it occurs from South Sudan southwards through East Africa to South Africa and westwards to the DRC.

The South-eastern Green Snake usually has a yellow snout. INSERT Two supralabials enter the orbit.

Stephen Spawls

Ornate Green Snake *Philothamnus ornatus*

The Ornate Green Snake has a diagnostic dark middorsal stripe.

Max. SVL ♂ 420mm ♀ 595mm

A small to medium-sized, slender green snake with a rounded head that is slightly broader than the neck. 1 preocular; 2 postoculars; usually 1 anterior and 1 (rarely 2) posterior temporal 8–9 (rarely 10) supralabials, 3rd–5th or 4th–6th (rarely 3rd and 4th or 4th and 5th) usually entering orbit; 8–11 infralabials, first 5 (rarely first 4 or 6) in contact with anterior sublinguals. Dorsals smooth, in 15 rows at midbody. 147–174 smooth or faintly keeled ventrals; 85–111 paired subcaudals; cloacal scale divided. Back emerald- to olive-green with dark reddish-brown vertebral stripe; latter bordered on each side by golden-yellow band extending from head to tail tip. Dark spots may be present on flanks, especially anteriorly. Interstitial skin black. Pale green spots visible when skin stretched. Head heavily blotched with black in some individuals. Ventrum white to cream, occasionally with bronze tint. Juveniles have dark vertebral band bordered by golden-yellow band, prominent black edging to scales and extensive white spotting, especially anteriorly. **Habitat:** Wet open grasslands near swamps, streams, dambos

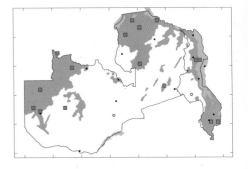

and reedbeds in mesic savanna. **Behaviour:** A harmless diurnal snake that may inflate the neck and strike out as a threat display. **Prey:** Frogs. **Reproduction:** Female lays eggs. No further details are known. **Range:** It has a patchy distribution, occurring in western, northern and eastern Zambia and northern and southern Malawi. Elsewhere it occurs sporadically from southern Angola and the southern DRC to northern Botswana and Zimbabwe, just entering extreme south-western Tanzania. Two apparently isolated populations are found in the north-eastern DRC and central Cameroon.

Stephen Spawls

The dark marks on the forebody of the Speckled Green Snake don't fuse into bars (unlike the Spotted Bush Snake).

Max. SVL ♂ 790mm ♀ 805mm

A large, slender green snake with a blunt, upturned snout and a long tail. Supraoculars raised, forming 'eyebrow'. 1 preocular; 2 postoculars; usually 2 anterior and 2 posterior temporals. Usually 9 supralabials, 5th and 6th entering orbit; 9–11 infralabials, first 4–5 in contact with anterior sublinguals. Scales smooth, in 15 rows at midbody. 157–188 strongly keeled ventrals; 126–170 paired, keeled subcaudals. Bright green to yellow-green, usually with dark speckling. Ventrum ranges from white or cream to pale green or bluish green. **Habitat:** It has a wide habitat tolerance, being found in woodland, thickets and arid and mesic savannas. **Behaviour:** An active, diurnal and predominantly arboreal snake. It does not show a strong affinity for moist locations but may be found near water. If threatened, it may inflate the neck and strike out. **Prey and Predators:** Preys predominantly on lizards, including dwarf geckos (*Lygodactylus*), other geckos and chameleons, but will also eat frogs and are reported to eat nestling birds. It is preyed on by Eastern Stripe-bellied Sand Snakes (*Psammophis orientalis*), Southern Banded Snake-Eagles and

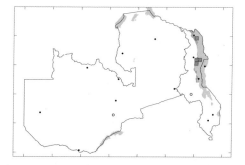

Luke Verburgt

Two supralabials usually enter the orbit.

Saddle-billed Storks. **Reproduction:** Female lays 3–6 eggs (approximately 30mm x 10mm) in summer. Neonates measure 210–240mm in TL. **Range:** In the region it is restricted to northern Malawi, predominantly along Lake Malawi, but it may be more widespread owing to previous confusion with the Spotted Bush Snake (*P. semivariegatus*). It also occurs in East Africa, from Somalia through Kenya and Tanzania to central Mozambique.

Spotted Bush Snake *Philothamnus semivariegatus*

The dark markings on the forebody of the Spotted Bush Snake often fuse into short transverse bars.

Some individuals are plain green in colour.

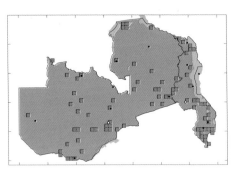

Max. SVL ♂ 825mm ♀ 850mm

A large, slender green snake with a well-developed head that is wider than the neck. Tail very long, slender, tapered. Supraoculars raised, forming 'eyebrow'. 1 preocular; 2 (rarely 3) postoculars; 2 (rarely 1) anterior and 2 (rarely 1 or 3) posterior temporals. 8–12 (usually 9) supralabials, 4th–6th (rarely 4th and 5th, 5th and 6th, 3rd–5th or 5th–7th) entering orbit; 9–12 infralabials, first 4–5 (rarely 6) in contact with anterior sublinguals. Body scales smooth, in 15 rows at midbody. Ventrals and subcaudals strongly keeled, notched laterally. 170–209 ventrals; 122–166 paired subcaudals; cloacal scale divided. Bright green to blue-green or olive anteriorly, usually becoming olive-bronze to grey posteriorly. Anterior two-thirds of body covered with dark spots and crossbars; anterior (covered) edges of scales usually paler. Individuals occasionally uniform green, or with white spot at base of each scale. Ventrum yellowish to greenish white anteriorly, becoming olive to bronze posteriorly. **Taxonomic note:** Recent genetic evidence suggests that *P. semivariegatus* may be a species complex. **Habitat:** Arid and mesic savannas, woodland and riparian vegetation. **Behaviour:** A common diurnal snake that is not strongly reliant on moist locations. A good swimmer, and equally at home in trees as on the ground. Takes refuge in the tops of trees, under bark, in tree hollows, under rocks and in cracks on rock outcrops. If threatened, it will inflate its neck to reveal the bright blue interstitial skin and may strike at the harasser, although it is not venomous. When hunting, the body is often kept still while the head and neck sway from side to side. It actively hunts in trees and bushes and has excellent vision. **Prey and Predators:** The Southern Foam-nest Frog is a favourite prey item, but other frogs and lizards, such as geckos and chameleons, are also frequently eaten. This species is eaten by Savanna Vine Snake (*Thelotornis capensis*) and

Luke Verburgt

In some areas the posterior body is olive to bronze.

Woodland Kingfisher. **Reproduction:** Female lays 3–12 eggs (23–41mm x 8–14mm) in mid-summer. Neonates measure 230–300mm in TL. **Range:** Widespread across the region. Occurs throughout sub-Saharan Africa.

HOOK-NOSED SNAKES   *Scaphiophis*

Fairly large snakes with a robust body and fairly short tail. The rostral is greatly enlarged, pointed and projecting. The parietals are fragmented and the last supralabial is greatly enlarged. The nostrils are narrow and recessed and the lower jaw is underslung. The inside of the upper lip has a flange into which the lower jaw fits, resulting in a nearly airtight seal. The eyes are small, with round pupils. The teeth are minute, there are no fangs, and the mouth lining is black. The dorsals are smooth and arranged in 19–31 rows at midbody.

These harmless snakes spend most of their time in burrows or in soft soil or sand. They occur in a variety of habitats, ranging from forests and thickets to semi-arid regions. They are probably diurnal, but are rarely seen and poorly known. They prey predominantly on rodents which they capture and kill in burrows. It is speculated that they also eat bird eggs. Females are oviparous, laying up to 48 eggs in spring.

The genus occurs widely in West, Central and East Africa. There are two species in the genus, one of which occurs in the region.

Grey Hook-nosed Snake   *Scaphiophis albopunctatus*

Max. SVL ♂ 949mm ♀ 1,302mm

A fairly large, thick-bodied snake with a short tail. Head not distinct from body. Snout sharply pointed; rostral prominent, projecting. Eyes small. 1–4 (usually 2) loreals; 1–2 preoculars; 2–3 postoculars; 2–3 suboculars; 4–6 anterior temporals. 5 (very rarely 6) supralabials, 5th very long; 7–9 infralabials, first 2–5 in contact with sublinguals. Dorsals smooth, in 19–25 rows at midbody. 170–228 ventrals; 49–76 paired subcaudals; cloacal scale divided. Adults light grey-brown to brown or orange, with broad grey vertebral stripe. Dark brown or black spots on head and back usually present, may be confluent. Ventrum ranges from white through cream and pink to orange.

Juveniles grey or bluish grey, heavily speckled with white. **Habitat:** In the region it occurs in moist miombo woodland. It appears to have a wide habitat tolerance, having been recorded in arid and mesic savannas and forest elsewhere. **Behaviour:** A harmless, fossorial snake that lacks fangs. Spends most of its time in underground burrows, but is sometimes seen above ground. Large concentrations have been found in suitable refuges. When threatened, it may tuck its head into its body coils as a defence. It occasionally employs an elaborate threat display: the head is flattened,

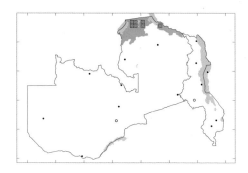

Juveniles are bluish grey with white speckles.

the lips are parted and the tongue is extruded, displaying the blue-black tongue and mouth lining to great effect. If further harassed, it may strike out at the harasser with such force that most of the body leaves the ground, yet always purposefully missing the target. **Prey:** Feeds on rodents, which it kills by crushing them against the burrow wall with its powerful body. **Reproduction:** Female lays 40–48 eggs in early summer. **Range:** North-eastern Zambia. Elsewhere it occurs through East Africa northwards to Ethiopia and Sudan and westwards to West Africa.

The adult Grey Hook-nosed Snake is grey to orange in colour.

TIGER SNAKES   *Telescopus*

Small to medium-sized, slender snakes with relatively large eyes and vertically elliptic pupils. The broad head is dorsoventrally flattened and very distinct from the neck. A pair of enlarged fangs are present below the posterior border of the eye. The body scales are smooth and arranged in 19–25 rows at midbody. The tail is moderately short and the subcaudals are paired.

These snakes are nocturnal and predominantly arboreal. The diet consists of various small vertebrates, including lizards, birds and bats. They are quite aggressive, regularly striking out, and are mildly venomous, although the venom does not have any effect on humans. They occur in open savanna, semi-desert and forest environments. The female lays clutches of 3–20 eggs in summer.

The genus occurs throughout much of Africa and the Middle East to south-eastern Europe and south-western Asia. A total of 14 species are recognised, nine of which occur in Africa. A single species occurs in the region.

Eastern Tiger Snake   *Telescopus semiannulatus*

The orange-and-black banded pattern of the Eastern Tiger Snake is diagnostic.

Max. SVL ♂ 760mm ♀ 880mm

A medium-sized snake with a fairly thin body and a broad head that is distinct from the neck. Eyes large; pupil vertical; iris yellowish to cinnamon-brown. 1 preocular; 2 postoculars; 2 (rarely 1 or 3) anterior and 2 or 3 (rarely 4) posterior temporals. 8–9 (rarely 7 or 10) supralabials, 3rd–5th or 4th–6th (rarely 3rd and 4th or 4th and 5th) entering orbit; 10–13 infralabials, first 3–5 in contact with anterior sublinguals. Body scales smooth, overlapping, in 19 rows

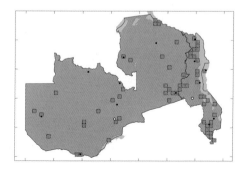

at midbody. 190–244 ventrals; 51–85 paired subcaudals; cloacal scale divided (rarely entire). Bright to dull orange above with 22–52 dark dorsal blotches or crossbands that extend to tail tip. Ventrum uniform yellowish to orange, often with pink tinge. **Subspecies:** Two subspecies are recognised, with only the

Luke Verburgt

The head is flattened when ready to strike.

typical form (*T. s. semiannulatus*) occurring in the region. **Habitat:** Woodland and savanna. **Behaviour:** Uncommon and nocturnal. Shelters under tree bark, rocks, in rock crevices, in tree hollows and occasionally in thatched roofs during the day. It is equally at home on the ground as in trees. It is irascible and rear-fanged, and its venom is harmless to people. **Prey:** Feeds predominantly on geckos, skinks, chameleons, and small and fledgling birds, but rodents and bats are also eaten. It will often hold on to prey until it succumbs to envenomation and may wrap its body around larger prey items. **Reproduction:** Mating occurs in late winter and early spring and eggs are laid in early to mid-summer after a gestation period of 45–95 days. The female lays 3–20 eggs (23–55mm x 10–17mm) per clutch and may lay two clutches per season without the need for a second mating. Incubation takes 71–85 days. Neonates measure 170–230mm in TL. **Range:** From southern Africa through East Africa to Kenya and the DRC. Widespread throughout the region.

CAT SNAKES   *Crotaphopeltis*

Small to medium-sized snakes with a short, flattened head that is distinct from the neck. The eyes are large, with vertical pupils. The nasal is completely divided. Small fangs are present behind the posterior margin of the eye. There are no posterior gular scales – the three pairs of gular scales are immediately followed by the ventrals. The body scales are mostly smooth but may be faintly keeled posteriorly and are arranged in 17–21 rows at midbody.

Terrestrial and nocturnal, these snakes are most common in moist locations such as swamps, pans and dams, but may also be found away from water. They prey almost exclusively on amphibians. They are mildly venomous, but the venom does not have any effect on humans. Despite being harmless, they put up an elaborate display when threatened: they retract the forepart of the body into a loose S-shaped curve, flatten the head and flare the lips, which may be yellow, orange, red or white. They will also hiss and readily strike out at the harasser. The female lays clutches of 5–19 eggs in a moist location in summer.

The genus occurs widely in tropical sub-Saharan Africa. There are six species, three of which occur in the region.

KEY Regional *Crotaphopeltis* species

1a	Usually 2 preoculars; upper preocular often in contact with frontal; ventrum dark (but pale or cream-coloured in juveniles); eyes red or orange . . . . **C. tornieri** (p. 189)
b	Usually 1 preocular, not in contact with frontal; ventrum white or cream, with or without darker stippling; eyes dark **2**
2a	17 midbody scale rows; no dark temporal patch . . . . **C. barotseensis** (p. 187)
b	19 (rarely 21) midbody scale rows; distinct dark temporal patch present . . . **C. hotamboeia** (p. 188)

Barotse Cat Snake   *Crotaphopeltis barotseensis*

The iridescent Barotse Cat Snake occurs in north-western and western Zambia.

Max. SVL ♂ 545mm ♀ 470mm

A small snake with a broad, distinct head and a fairly short tail. 1 preocular; 2 postoculars; 1 (rarely 2) anterior and 2 posterior temporals. Upper postocular may be fused with parietal, which enters orbit. Usually 8 (rarely 9) supralabials, 3rd–5th or 4th and 5th (rarely 4th–6th or 5th and 6th) entering orbit; 9–11 (usually 10) infralabials, first 4–6 in contact with anterior sublinguals. Body scales smooth, glossy, in 17 rows at midbody. 151–164 ventrals; 32–39 paired subcaudals; cloacal scale entire. Iridescent light grey-brown to dark red-brown above, each scale dark-bordered. No dark temporal patches; top of head not darker than body. Ventrum cream, with varying degrees of brown stippling. **Habitat:** Papyrus swamps. **Behaviour:** Fairly docile and aquatic, rarely giving a threat display or biting. It is mildly venomous, but the venom does not have any effect on humans. **Prey:** The diet consists exclusively of frogs and toads. **Reproduction:** Female lays 6–13 eggs (17–21mm x 10–12mm) in mid-summer. **Range:** Upper Zambezi River in western Zambia and southwards to the Okavango Swamps in northern Botswana.

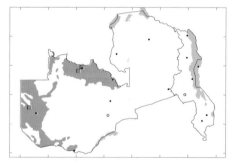

The supralabials are pale orange to yellow.

Darren Pietersen

The Black-templed Cat Snake has diagnostic dark temples.

Luke Verburgt

The lips are flared in defence.

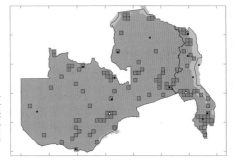

Max. SVL ♂ 751mm ♀ 710mm
A small snake with a broad, fairly flat head that is distinct from the neck and a fairly short tail. 1 (rarely 2) preocular; 2 (rarely 1 or 3) postoculars; 1 anterior and 2 (rarely 1 or 3) posterior temporals. 7–9 (usually 8) supralabials, 3rd–5th entering orbit; 8–11 infralabials, first 4–5 in contact with anterior sublinguals. Body scales dull, smooth anteriorly, may be bluntly keeled posteriorly, in 19 (rarely 17 or 21) rows at midbody. 139–182 ventrals; 24–65 paired subcaudals; cloacal scale entire. Greyish to brown, olive-brown or blackish above, sometimes with small white spots. Head iridescent dark blue-black, with distinct dark patch on sides of head. Lips usually white or blackish, but may be orange or red. Ventrum uniform white to cream. **Habitat:** Mesic savanna and open woodland, especially in moist and swampy locations. **Behaviour:** Common and widespread. Nocturnal, it shelters under any available refuge during the day, especially under rocks or in moribund termitaria. Quite aggressive, it regularly flattens its head, inflates its body and lunges in an elaborate threat display. It occasionally adopts tonic immobility (feigns death) when disturbed. It is mildly venomous, although the venom is not known to have any effect on humans. **Prey and Predators:** The diet consists predominantly of

frogs and toads, which are chewed and held until the venom takes effect. It will exceptionally prey on rodents, lizards (including agamas and geckos) and fish. It is preyed on by bullfrogs.

Reproduction: Female lays 5–19 eggs (21–35mm x 8–15mm) in summer. Incubation takes about 61–64 days. Neonates measure 130–180mm in TL. **Range:** Widespread throughout Africa.

Tornier's Cat Snake   *Crotaphopeltis tornieri*

Max. SVL ♂ 567mm ♀ 522mm

A small snake with a broad, distinct and relatively flattened head and a short tail. 2 (rarely 1) preoculars, often in contact with frontal; 2 (rarely 3) postoculars. Dorsals smooth (but feebly keeled posteriorly), in 17 (rarely 19) rows at midbody. 144–186 ventrals; 35–56 paired subcaudals; cloacal scale entire. Pale grey, plumbeus to almost black above, with varying degrees of brown and blue infusions. Body iridescent blue-black when skin has just been shed. Lips pale yellow, cream or reddish in juveniles, becoming progressively dusky with age. Ventrum cream or white in juveniles, becoming paler shade of dorsal colour in adults. Iris distinctly red or orange. **Habitat:** Moist montane evergreen forests. **Behaviour:** Nocturnal, it seeks refuge under fallen logs and in leaf litter during the day. Fairly placid,

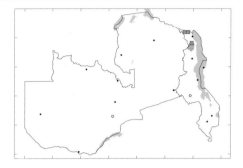

rarely giving a threat display. **Prey:** The diet probably consists exclusively of frogs and toads. **Reproduction:** Female lays 9–12 eggs in late summer, often in a communal laying site. Neonates measure about 130mm in TL. **Range:** Northern Malawi, extending into the Eastern Arc Mountains in Tanzania.

Tornier's Cat Snake has bright orange to red eyes.

Michele Menegon

MARBLED TREE SNAKES   *Dipsadoboa*

Medium-sized, very slender snakes with a broad, flattened head that is distinct from the neck. The eyes are fairly large with vertical pupils, and the tail is moderately long. It has small rear fangs. Posterior gulars are present, separating the three pairs of anterior gulars from the ventrals. The body scales are smooth and arranged in 17–19 rows at midbody.

These interesting snakes are predominantly nocturnal and arboreal, but also frequent reedbeds. Although rarely seen, they may be quite common in suitable habitats. They occur in forests, woodlands and moist savanna. Their diet consists of amphibians, geckos, sleeping chameleons and small birds, which are actively hunted. They are mildly venomous, but the venom does not have any effect on humans. The female lays small clutches of 4–9 eggs in summer.

The genus occurs widely in sub-Saharan Africa, with the greatest diversity in East Africa. It contains 10 species, three of which occur in the region.

KEY   Regional *Dipsadoboa* species

1a 19 midbody scale rows; uniform blue-grey to black . . . . **D. shrevei** (p. 192)
 b 17 midbody scale rows; reddish brown, usually with white or yellow marbling
   or crossbands **2**

2a Dorsum brown to reddish brown, usually with 38–57 pale crossbars;
   167–190 ventrals, 74–97 subcaudals . . . . **D. aulica** (p. 190)
 b Dorsum predominantly yellow, usually with 65–95 red-brown dorsal blotches;
   188–206 ventrals; 93–106 subcaudals . . . . **D. flavida** (p. 191)

Marbled Tree Snake   *Dipsadoboa aulica*

The Marbled Tree Snake is predominantly brown, often with light and dark bands, and has a white to yellow marbled pattern on the head.

Max. SVL ♂ 660mm ♀ 630mm

A small to medium-sized, slender snake with a long tail and a depressed head that is distinct from the neck. 1 (rarely 2) small preocular; loreal enters orbit (rarely excluded) below preocular; 2 (rarely 3) postoculars; 1 anterior and 1 (rarely 2) posterior temporal. 8 (rarely 7 or 9) supralabials, 3rd–5th (rarely 3rd and 4th or 4th and 5th only) entering orbit; 10 (8–11) infralabials, first 5 (rarely first 3, 4 or 6) in contact with anterior sublinguals. Dorsals smooth, in 17 rows at midbody. 167–190 ventrals; 74–97 paired subcaudals; cloacal scale entire. Back brown to light reddish brown, with 38–57 dark-edged whitish crossbars. Tail often flecked with white. Adult coloration tends to fade from behind and may be uniform brown with scattered white spots on neck. Head covered in white to yellow marbled network; supralabials may have dark sutures. Dark band usually extends from nostril, through the eye and onto the side of the head. Ventrum creamy white, may have darker spots posteriorly and laterally. Tongue tip white. **Habitat:** Riparian forest and reedbeds. **Behaviour:** A nocturnal, predominantly arboreal snake that takes refuge

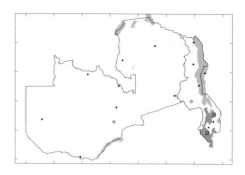

in hollow logs, under tree bark, in piles of grass and even thatched roofs. When disturbed, it adopts a loosely coiled posture, with the head raised off the ground. It strikes readily, but is not venomous. **Prey:** Feeds predominantly on arboreal geckos, reed frogs and Southern Foam-nest Frogs, but will also eat skinks, other frogs and toads and small rodents. **Reproduction:** Female lays 7–8 eggs (23–29mm x 10–14mm) in mid-summer. Neonates measure about 180mm in TL. **Range:** Southern Malawi and central Mozambique to eastern Zimbabwe and South Africa. A single record from Tanzania is probably an incorrect collecting locality.

Cross-barred Tree Snake   *Dipsadoboa flavida*

Max. SVL ♂ 585mm ♀ 481mm

A slender snake with a broad, flattened head that is distinct from the neck. Tail long. Loreal enters orbit below single preocular; 2 postoculars; 1 anterior and 1 posterior temporal. 8 (rarely 7 or 9) supralabials, 3rd–5th (rarely 4th–6th) entering orbit; 10 (rarely 9 or 11) infralabials, first 5 (very rarely first 4 or 6) in contact with anterior sublinguals. Body scales smooth, in 17 rows at midbody. 188–206 ventrals; 93–106 paired subcaudals; cloacal scale entire. Bright saffron-yellow anteriorly, becoming progressively paler posteriorly. Tail uniform red-brown above. 65–95 red-brown blotches dorsally between nape and cloaca and red-brown marbling on flanks, which becomes more pronounced posteriorly, resulting in isolated yellow speckling. Ventrum bright yellow anteriorly, fading gradually posteriorly, with some red-brown blotches postero-laterally; subcaudals often mottled red-brown. Head bright yellow, with

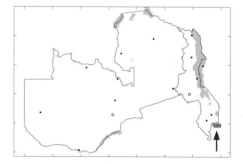

extensive red-brown mottling; dark stripe extends from snout through eye to corner of mouth. Supralabial sutures dark, this coloration restricted anterior to the eye. **Subspecies:** Two subspecies are recognised, with only the typical form (*D. f. flavida*) occurring in the region. It is distinguished by its predominantly yellow coloration with 65–95 red-brown dorsal blotches and the number of ventrals and subcaudals:

Gary Brown

The Cross-barred Tree Snake is bright yellow anteriorly, becoming progressively paler posteriorly.

193–206 ventrals and 97–106 subcaudals in males; 188–197 ventrals and 93–97 subcaudals in females. **Habitat:** Golden Bamboo thickets and other waterside vegetation, also entering tea estates. **Behaviour:** A nocturnal, predominantly arboreal snake. Often takes refuge in bamboo stems. When threatened, it will adopt a loosely coiled posture with the head raised and may vigorously strike at the harasser. **Prey:** Arboreal frogs, including reed frogs and leaf-folding frogs. **Reproduction:** Female lays 7–8 eggs (20–25mm x 10–11mm) in summer. **Range:** The typical form is endemic to Mount Mulanje and its vicinity in southern Malawi.

Shreve's Marbled Tree Snake   *Dipsadoboa shrevei*

Max. SVL ♂ 825mm ♀ 857mm
A medium-sized, fairly slender snake with a very long tail and a broad head that is distinct from the neck. 1 preocular; 2 postoculars; 1 anterior and 1 (rarely 2) posterior temporal. 8 (rarely 9) supralabials, 3rd–5th (rarely 4th and 5th only) entering orbit; 10–11 infralabials, first 5 in contact with anterior sublinguals. Dorsals smooth, in 19 rows at midbody. 199–219 ventrals; 71–91 paired subcaudals; cloacal scale entire. Adults uniform blue-grey to black above and below, sometimes with pale chin and throat. Juveniles grey-brown above, paler below. **Habitat:** Moist miombo woodland and gallery forest. **Behaviour:** Nocturnal and predominantly arboreal. Rear-fanged, although the venom is not dangerous to humans. **Prey:** Sleeping chameleons, including Flap-neck

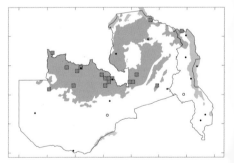

Chameleons (*Chamaeleo dilepis*), small birds, such as Pied Mannikins, and small frogs. **Reproduction:** Female lays eggs in summer, but no details are known. **Range:** From Angola through central and northern Zambia and the southern DRC to northern Malawi.

Shreve's Marbled Tree Snake is uniformly blue-grey to black.

AFRICAN SMOOTH SNAKES *Meizodon*

Small snakes with a small head that is only slightly distinct from the neck and slightly flattened. The body is cylindrical and the scales are smooth and arranged in 19–21 rows at midbody. The cloacal scale is divided and the subcaudals are paired.

These secretive snakes are diurnal and terrestrial, sheltering under logs and rocks. They feed on small frogs and lizards. The female lays small clutches of 2–3 large eggs in spring.

They occur widely in sub-Saharan Africa, with the greatest diversity occurring in East Africa. There are five species, one of which occurs in the region.

Semiornate Snake *Meizodon semiornatus*

Max. SVL ♂ 455mm ♀ 600mm
A small, slender snake with a flattened head that is slightly broader than the neck, a fairly long tail and a round pupil. 1 (rarely 2) preocular; 2 (rarely 1) postoculars; 2 (rarely 1 or 3) anterior and 2–3 posterior temporals. 8 supralabials, 4th and 5th entering orbit; 8–10 infralabials, first 4–5 in contact with anterior sublinguals. Dorsals smooth, in 21 rows at midbody. 159–204 ventrals; 66–91 paired subcaudals; cloacal scale divided. Back grey to olive-brown. Numerous dark crossbars on anterior half of body, more pronounced in juveniles, may disappear in adults. Top of head dark; sides of head barred in dark and pale yellow. Ventrum white to yellowish, occasionally uniform but more often darker towards sides. Ventrum nearly uniformly dark in old individuals, with white chin and throat. **Subspecies:** Two subspecies are recognised. Only the typical form (*M. s. semiornatus*) occurs in the region. **Habitat:** Savanna and woodland. **Behaviour:** A shy, diurnal snake that frequents riparian vegetation, floodplains and other moist environments. Shelters in hollow logs, under bark and under rocks and logs.

2–3 individuals can often be found together in such refuges. Harmless and rarely bites when handled. **Prey:** Diet includes skinks, diurnal geckos, small frogs and (rarely) small rodents. **Reproduction:** Female lays 2–3 eggs (29–40mm x 8–10mm) in early to mid-summer. **Range:** Widespread in southern, central, eastern and north-eastern Zambia, and central and southern Malawi. Elsewhere it occurs from Ethiopia and Somalia through Chad and East Africa to eastern South Africa.

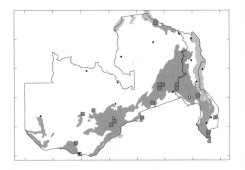

The Semiornate Snake has a slightly flattened head and dark bands anteriorly.

EGG-EATERS *Dasypeltis*

Small to medium-sized snakes with a small, blunt head that is barely distinct from the neck. The nasal is partially divided (undivided in some West African species) and the loreal is absent. There are no gulars and the mentals (usually three pairs) are in direct contact with the ventrals. The teeth are rudimentary and are replaced by thick folds of gum tissue. They have modified vertebral structures (hypapophyses) projecting into the gullet in the neck region. The inside of the mouth is pleated and the scales on the lower jaw are only loosely attached to the underlying bones, allowing the head to expand considerably. The body scales are elongate, strongly keeled and arranged in 19–29 rows at midbody.

Egg-eaters are predominantly nocturnal and equally at home in trees as on the ground. They prey exclusively on bird eggs, which are swallowed whole. The ingested egg comes to rest against and below the hypapophyses, which puncture the egg through rhythmic sideways movements of the head and neck. Once the shell is pierced, the neck muscles are constricted, forcing the contents of the egg into the gullet while the empty shell is compacted into a 'boat-shaped' bundle and subsequently regurgitated. These snakes have a well-developed sense of smell and can usually distinguish between fresh eggs (which are consumed) and those that are old or contain well-developed embryos (which are usually ignored). When threatened, they put up an elaborate display, coiling the body and rubbing the keeled scales together to produce a hissing sound and mimicking adders. The forepart of the body is simultaneously raised and the mouth is flared. They readily strike out, but will intentionally miss the harasser on account of their lack of teeth. They are oviparous, the female laying clutches of 6–28 eggs.

The genus occurs widely across sub-Saharan Africa and the Arabian Peninsula, with 17 species recognised at present. Three species occur in the region.

KEY Regional *Dasypeltis* species

1a Pink to reddish brown (occasionally grey or brown); 3–8 narrow, anteriorly directed
 chevrons on the neck; 71–109 subcaudals . . . . **D. medici** (p. 196)

b Grey to brown, with series of dark rhombic markings along back; dark chevrons
 restricted to head and nape; 38–80 subcaudals **2**

2a Dark dorsal saddles diamond-shaped; dark lateral bars positioned alongside,
 and usually confluent with, dark dorsal saddles . . . . **D. confusa** (p. 195)

b Dark dorsal saddles rhomboid to irregular; dark lateral bars positioned between,
 and usually not linked to, dark dorsal saddles . . . . **D. scabra** (p. 197)

Diamond-back Egg-eater *Dasypeltis confusa*

The Diamond-back Egg-eater has dark dorsal saddles, with dark flank bands situated alongside.

Max. SVL ♂ 551mm ♀ 635mm

A medium-sized, fairly slender snake with a small head that is not distinct from the neck and a bluntly rounded snout. Nasal semi-divided. 1 preocular; 2 (rarely 1) postoculars; 2 (very rarely 1) anterior and 3 (rarely 2 or 4) posterior temporals. 7 (rarely 6 or 8) supralabials, 3rd and 4th (rarely 2nd and 3rd) entering orbit; 7 (rarely 8) infralabials, first 3 in contact with anterior sublinguals. Dorsals elongate and strongly keeled, in 21–27 rows at midbody. 2–4 lateral scale rows reduced in size, with keels strongly serrated. 199–242 ventrals (199–227 in males, 212–242 in females); 48–75

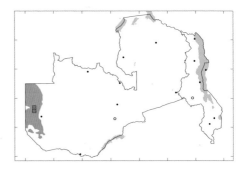

paired subcaudals (51–75 in males, 48–67 in females). Body grey to pale brown, with 50–79

Werner Conradie

oval to diamond-shaped dark vertebral patches; latter usually separated by large pale patches. Dark dorsal markings often bordered by pale margins, emphasising them. Thin to broad dark vertical bars present on flanks, majority positioned alongside, and often confluent with, dark saddles. Ventrum usually pale to cream with darker speckles along edges, and occasionally larger dark blotches laterally. **Habitat:** Savanna and forest–savanna mosaics, but does not enter forests. **Behaviour:** Similar to other egg-eaters. **Prey:** Feeds exclusively on bird eggs. **Reproduction:** Female lays up to nine eggs in summer. **Range:** Western Zambia and Angola, northwards to Senegal and eastward to Kenya and southern Sudan.

Eastern Forest Egg-eater *Dasypeltis medici*

The Eastern Forest Egg-eater usually has a pink to reddish-brown coloration.

Max. SVL ♂ 679mm ♀ 912mm

A relatively slender snake with a bluntly rounded snout and a long tail. Head small, not distinct from neck. 1 (rarely 2) preocular; 2 (rarely 1) postoculars; 2 (rarely 3) anterior and 3 (rarely 4) posterior temporals. 7 (rarely 6) supralabials, 3rd and 4th (rarely 2nd and 3rd or 3rd and 4th) entering orbit; 7 (rarely 8) infralabials, first 3 in contact with anterior sublinguals. Dorsals strongly keeled, in 22–27 rows at midbody. 206–259 ventrals (similar for males and females); 61–109 paired subcaudals (75–109 in males, 61–90 in females); cloacal scale entire. Body usually pink to reddish brown, but may be grey or brown, usually with 57–108 narrow, dark rectangular saddles separated by pale interspaces. Dark saddles may be elongate and closely positioned, giving impression of broad, dark vertebral stripe interrupted by pale interspaces. Dark lateral bars mostly occur adjacent to pale interspaces. 1–8 narrow, anteriorly directed dark chevrons on nape and anterior portion of body. Some individuals uniformly coloured, or show only very vague patterning. Ventrum cream to pink, with brown or grey stippling. Lining of mouth white to pink. **Habitat:** Montane and lowland forests and dense woodland. **Behaviour:** Similar to Rhombic

Egg-eater (*D. scabra*), although the long tail suggests that it may be more arboreal. When disturbed, it adopts an impressive coiled posture and will vigorously strike out at the harasser. Its teeth are minute. **Prey:** Feeds exclusively on bird eggs, which are swallowed whole and cracked in the throat. The egg shell is regurgitated. **Reproduction:** Female lays 6–28 eggs (24–30mm x 8–15mm) in summer. **Range:** From eastern South Africa through Malawi to East Africa and Somalia, with an isolated record from gallery forest near Chirundu in southern Zambia. Considering the lack of appropriate habitat and the prevalence of plain-phase Rhombic Egg-

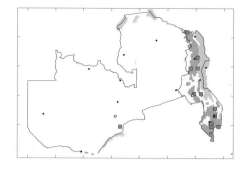

eaters in southern Zambia, the Chirundu record may in fact refer to the latter species.

Rhombic Egg-eater *Dasypeltis scabra*

The dorsal saddles are rhomboid to irregular in the Rhombic Egg-eater.

Luke Verburgt

Max. SVL ♂ 678mm ♀ 964mm
A relatively slender snake with a bluntly rounded snout. Head not distinct from neck. Tail short. 1 (rarely 2) preocular; 2 (rarely 1 or 3) postoculars; usually 2 (rarely 3) anterior and 3 (rarely 4) posterior temporals. Usually 7 supralabials (rarely 5, 6 or 8), the 3rd and 4th (occasionally 2nd and 3rd, very rarely 4th and 5th) entering orbit; 7 (rarely 8 or 9) infralabials, first 3 in contact with anterior sublinguals. Dorsals elongate, strongly keeled, in 21–28 rows at

midbody. Lower 3–4 rows of lateral scales smaller, obliquely orientated, with distinctly serrated keels. 180–249 ventrals (180–226 in males, 202–249 in females); 38–80 paired subcaudals (47–80 in males, 38–67 in females); cloacal scale entire. Usually grey to brown above with series of 46–94 dark blotches along vertebral line, which may be rhombic, rectangular, oval or irregular in shape, and may occasionally join to form a zig-zag pattern. Dark blotches separated by paler interspaces, may be pale-edged or have pale centres. Series of irregular dark vertical bands present on flanks, aligned with pale vertebral interspaces (at least some may be confluent with dark vertebral markings). Usually 1–2 faint, forward-pointing, incomplete chevrons on top of head; another bold chevron present on nape. Ventrum white to light yellow, often with dark flecks. Mouth lining black. Some individuals plain brown to reddish brown (especially on Nyika Plateau, in Luangwa Valley and around Lusaka). **Habitat:** Savanna, woodland and grassland. **Behaviour:** A common, nocturnal snake. It is not venomous and has only minute teeth, but puts up an elaborate display when disturbed by coiling the body in successive semicircles and vigorously rubbing the scales together to produce a hissing sound. The snake simultaneously gapes its mouth, revealing the black mouth lining, and strikes out at the harasser, purposefully missing its target. Its colour pattern closely resembles that of the more venomous Rhombic Night Adder (*Causus rhombeatus*), thus tricking predators into avoiding it. It can be distinguished from the Rhombic Night Adder by that species having a solid, forward-pointing dark chevron on the head, weakly keeled scales and a more robust

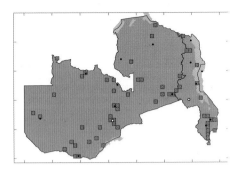

body, while the Rhombic Egg-eater has an incomplete chevron on the head. **Prey:** Feeds exclusively on bird eggs, which are swallowed whole and crushed in the back of the throat by bony structures that project from the neck vertebrae. The egg contents are swallowed, while the shell is regurgitated as a neat, elongate, 'boat-shaped' package. The snake is able to assess the condition of the egg and will not eat rotten ones. **Reproduction:** Female lays 6–25 eggs (27–46mm x 15–21mm) in summer. Incubation takes 70–100 days. Neonates measure 115–260mm in TL. Females may produce multiple clutches per season. **Range:** Widespread throughout the region as well as in Central, East and southern Africa.

BROAD-HEADED TREE SNAKES   *Toxicodryas*

Medium-sized to large snakes that are often robust and have a triangular or laterally compressed body. The head is large and broad, the eyes are large and the pupils are vertical. Enlarged rear fangs are present. The body scales are smooth and may be velvety or rubbery in texture. The vertebral scale row is enlarged.

These snakes are predominantly arboreal and nocturnal, although large-bodied individuals are ponderous climbers. They frequent forests and dense woodland where they ascend up to 30m into tall trees, but will cross open spaces to move between trees. They prey on sleeping birds, bats, lizards, amphibians and rodents. All species are rear-fanged, but the effect of the venom on humans remains largely unknown. Laboratory studies indicate that the venom is toxic and produced in large quantities and it is therefore best to treat these snakes as potentially dangerous. Bites to humans are extremely rare. The female lays 2–14 eggs, usually in summer.

The genus contains two species, both of which are endemic to the African continent. A single species occurs in the region.

Blanding's Tree Snake   *Toxicodryas blandingii*

Max. SVL 2,072mm
A very large, robust snake with a broad, short, flattened head that is distinct from the narrow

neck. Eyes prominent, dark, with vertical pupils; iris yellowish brown. Nostril large. 1–3 preoculars; 2–3 postoculars; usually 2 anterior

In the region, the large, robust Blanding's Tree Snake has been recorded only from the Mporokoso District.

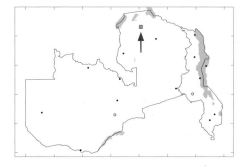

and 2–3 posterior temporals. 8–10 (usually 9) supralabials, 3rd–5th or 4th–6th entering orbit; 12–14 infralabials, first 3–5 or 4–5 in contact with anterior sublinguals. Body triangular in shape; head and body rubbery in texture. Body scales large and velvety, arranged in 21–25 (usually 23) rows at midbody. Vertebral scale row enlarged. 240–289 keeled ventrals; 115–147 paired subcaudals; cloacal scale divided or entire. Males usually glossy black above and yellow below; yellow coloration occasionally extending onto flanks or restricted to narrow mid-ventral stripe; labials yellow with black sutures. Females usually brown, yellow-brown or grey above, with faint to distinct darker crossbars or diamonds on flanks, and a yellowish-brown ventrum; interstitial skin bluish grey; lips yellowish brown. Juveniles brown, with distinct irregular black bars; latter roughly diamond-shaped, may have pale centres or may be pale-edged. **Habitat:** Forests and woodlands. **Behaviour:** A nocturnal, arboreal snake that may ascend to the tops of trees. It is rather sluggish when moving through trees and will descend to the ground to cross open spaces. During the day it shelters in tree hollows, piles of debris and other suitable cover. When harassed, it inflates the body and flattens the head while simultaneously withdrawing it, poised ready to strike. If the disturbance continues, it will open its mouth to display the pink lining and lunge out at the harasser. This is mostly a bluff and rarely on target. It is an active hunter, moving along branches and investigating nests and tree hollows for prey. **Venom:** It has a neurotoxic venom and should be considered dangerous to humans. Although rear-fanged, it has a very wide gape and probably does not have to chew to effect envenomation. **Prey:** Feeds predominantly on birds, but also eats bird eggs, arboreal agamas, chameleons, rodents, bats and frogs. Birds are apparently detected by smell and once located the snake approaches slowly, capturing the bird in the nest. It may take up position in a tree outside bat roosts, catching bats as they emerge. **Reproduction:** Female lays 7–14 eggs (approximately 40mm x 20mm) in summer. **Range:** There is a single Zambian record from the Mporokoso District. Elsewhere it occurs from Sudan south to Tanzania, through the DRC to northern Angola and into West Africa.

Lizards
Suborder Sauria

Rough-scaled Plated Lizard

Lizards are the most abundant reptile group, with more than 6,000 species in over 400 genera occurring globally. These reptiles occupy almost all habitats on Earth, including the Arctic Circle and many small oceanic islands, although they are less common in colder, high-elevation areas.

Most lizards are easily recognised by having four limbs, although some specialised taxa have reduced limbs or entirely lack limbs, resembling snakes. Although limb remnants are not always visible, all lizards retain a pectoral and pelvic girdle. Limbless taxa usually develop a more elongate body, with a corresponding increase in the number of vertebrae. Fossorial limbless taxa are often characterised by a shortening of the tail (which is usually fat and bluntly rounded). When moving backwards in a burrow or tunnel, this blunt tail can act as a guide. In contrast, limbless species or those with reduced limbs that inhabit grassy environments often develop long tails – up to three times the length of the body – and so gain greater surface area to propel themselves forward.

In all lizard species the two halves of the lower jaw are fused (as are the bones in the skull) generally resulting in less movement than in the jaws of snakes. The tongue is usually fleshy and undivided (except in monitor lizards [*Varanus*], which have forked tongues). The body is covered in granules, tubercles or scales that may be close-fitting or overlapping, smooth or keeled. The horny external covering is periodically shed. Unlike snakes, lizards usually shed only sections of their skin at a time (some limbless species may shed the skin in one piece). Worm lizards have soft scales that have the appearance of rings rather than scales. Although soft to the touch, these scales are extremely tough. Some lizard species have underlying bone-like plates (osteoderms) in their skin, affording them extra protection.

Enlarged head shield of a worm lizard.

A reduced, fully formed limb.

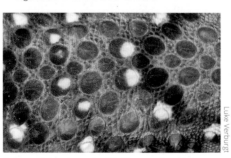

Enlarged tubercles embedded in granular skin.

The vertical pupil in the unblinking eye of a gecko.

ABOVE The Montane Three-striped Skink inhabits high-elevation areas.
RIGHT The curled, prehensile tail of a chameleon.

Some species use the tail to store fat reserves, and in these cases the tail base may become particularly fat. Chameleons often have prehensile tails that act as a fifth limb while climbing, while the monitor lizards use their long, hard tails as a whip for defence, and for swimming. Many lizards can shed their tail as a defence mechanism, it being severed across a vertebra rather than between two vertebrae. Most species can regenerate their tails (chameleons, monitors and agamas cannot). Regeneration usually occurs fairly rapidly, although this varies according to the species and prevailing climate. The lost vertebrae are regenerated from a continuous, unsegmented rod of calcified tissue. In some species the regenerated tail appears abnormal, being shorter and fatter than the original tail (carrot-shaped), sometimes with a different colour or scale pattern. It is not uncommon to see a lizard with a bifurcated (split) tail, which happens when the original tail is only partially severed and remains attached as a new tail is generated.

The eyes of lizards are usually visible in terrestrial and arboreal species and may be covered by a head scale in fossorial species. In species possessing an exposed eye, a fixed upper eyelid and moveable lower eyelid are usually present, although some genera (such as snake-eyed skinks [*Panaspis*]) have immovable eyelids. The lower eyelid may be scaly or transparent, or scaly with a large transparent window, the latter affording the lizard the ability to see movement despite having closed eyelids. Most geckos have fused eyelids with the lower transparent eyelid covering the eye.

The ear opening may be large and distinct, partially covered by scales or flaps of skin, or minute or even absent (especially in fossorial species).

Most lizards are capable of some degree of colour change – usually shifting between light and dark depending on temperature, light intensity and mood. Chameleons are famed for their range of skin colours and ability to change between them rapidly. Males of many lizard species are brightly coloured, particularly during the breeding season. This coloration is believed to ward off rival males rather than to attract females. Males are often aggressive towards each other and will usually defend a territory or harem during the breeding season. Females and juvenile males are tolerated, but other mature males are chased off. The juveniles of many species are often more brightly coloured than the adults and can appear vastly different to the adults.

Lizards are insectivorous, although many species display some degree of herbivory and many of the larger species are carnivorous and may eat anything they are able to overpower. They are preyed on by a large variety of creatures, including birds of prey, small mammalian carnivores, snakes, and also other lizards. There are no venomous or poisonous lizards in the region.

In all lizard species the cloacal opening is transverse, and the male reproductive organs (hemipenes) are paired. Most species are oviparous (lay eggs), although some retain the eggs in their body until the embryos are fully developed, or are viviparous (give birth to live young). Some species may lay eggs and give birth to live young, and the exact factors determining which reproductive strategy is employed remain to be ascertained. The eggs may be hard-shelled (as is the case with geckos) or have soft, leathery shells (most other taxa). Eggs are laid in a secluded location (such as in a rock crevice, termite mound or tree hollow, under a rock or buried underground). There is no parental care after laying.

The presence and number of precloacal and femoral pores is often a useful character to distinguish between different genera and species. Both femoral and precloacal pores excrete pheromones which are used to attract mates and to mark territories. Femoral pores are located on the inside thighs of lizards, while precloacal pores are situated in scales anterior to the cloaca. These pores are usually situated in enlarged, modified scales and are visible as small to large pits or holes in the scales. Depending on the species, femoral and precloacal pores may be present in only males, in both males and females, or entirely absent.

The Water Monitor (here a juvenile) almost always occurs near water.

HEAD SCALES OF A TYPICAL LIZARD

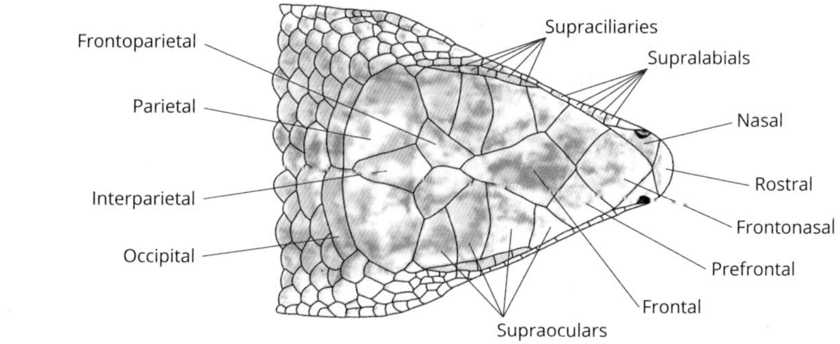

Frontoparietal

Parietal

Interparietal

Occipital

Supraciliaries

Supralabials

Nasal

Rostral

Frontonasal

Prefrontal

Frontal

Supraoculars

Dorsal view

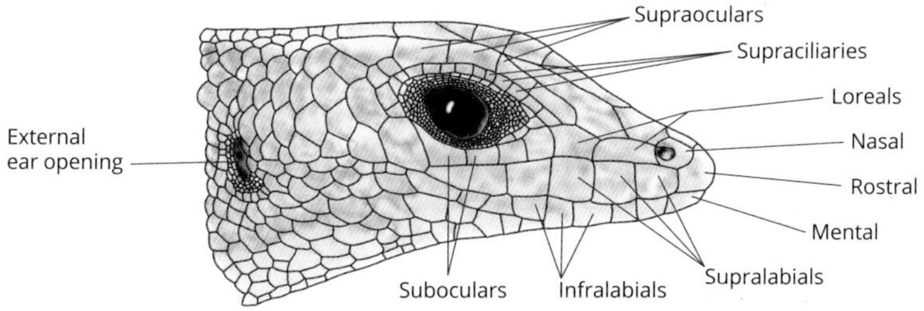

Supraoculars

Supraciliaries

Loreals

Nasal

Rostral

Mental

External
ear opening

Suboculars   Infralabials   Supralabials

Lateral view

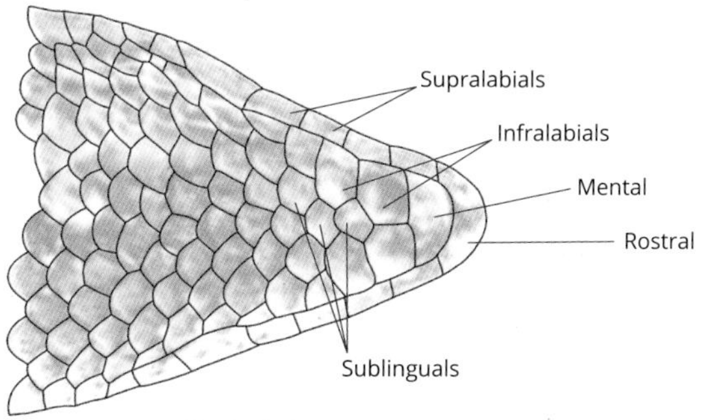

Supralabials

Infralabials

Mental

Rostral

Sublinguals

Ventral view

POSTERIOR VENTRAL FEATURES OF A TYPICAL LIZARD

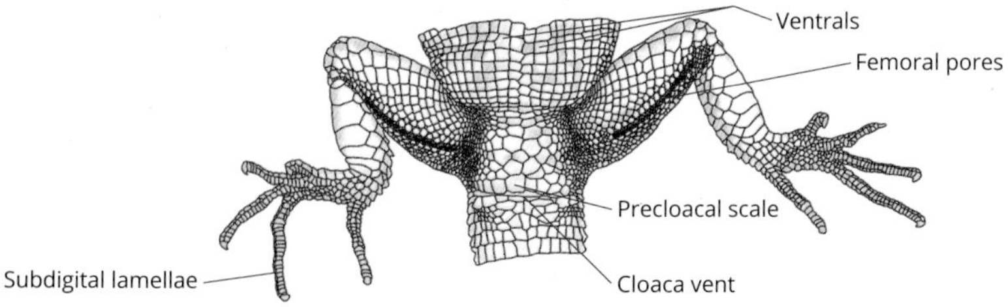

Ventrals

Femoral pores

Precloacal scale

Subdigital lamellae

Cloaca vent

KEY Genera of Sauria

1a Body covered in rings of rectangular, non-overlapping scales; limbs absent;
body pale pink to purple, occasionally with alternating light and dark bands **2**

b Body covered in non-rectangular granules or scales, or, if covered with
rectangular scales, then limbs well developed **4**

2a Snout rounded without cutting edge; pectoral scales not enlarged . . . . *Zygaspis* (p. 282)

b Snout with sharp horizontal cutting edge; pectoral scales enlarged **3**

3a Tail short, bluntly rounded; nasals well separated by rostral . . . . *Monopeltis* (p. 285)

b Tail long, ending abruptly in calloused pad; nasals usually in contact
above rostral . . . . *Dalophia* (p. 289)

4a Top of head covered in small granules or irregular scales **5**

b Top of head covered in large, symmetrical scales **18**

5a Body covered in small, soft scales, granules or tubercles;
eye exposed, lacking eyelids **6**

b Body covered in hard scales, granules or tubercles; eye exposed,
possessing eyelids or covered by head scale **10**

6a Pupil round; subcaudal scansors on tail tip; diurnal . . . . *Lygodactylus* (p. 218)

b Pupil vertical; no subcaudal scansors on tail tip; nocturnal **7**

7a Head large, triangular; snout much shorter than the distance between
eye and ear opening . . . . *Chondrodactylus* (p. 212)

b Head not large and triangular; snout as long as, or longer than, the
distance between eye and ear opening **8**

8a Snout much longer than the distance between eye and ear opening;
toes with large claws . . . . *Hemidactylus* (p. 208)

b Snout about the same length as the distance between eye and ear
opening; toes clawless or with minute, usually retractile claws **9**

9a 8–14 undivided scansors beneath 4th toe; skin fragile, tears easily . . . . . . *Elasmodactylus* (p. 210)

b 2–5 undivided scansors beneath 4th toe . . . . *Pachydactylus* (p. 214)

10a Digits arranged in two opposable clusters for grasping; eyes in revolving
cones, able to move independently; body laterally compressed **11**

b Digits separate in single plane; eyes not in revolving cones; body
dorsoventrally flattened **16**

11a Tail very short, not prehensile **12**

b Tail long, prehensile **13**

12a Interorbital ridge absent; interorbital space deeply concave; slightly
raised skin ridge on flanks . . . . *Rieppeleon* (p. 312)

b Interorbital ridge present; no raised skin ridge on flanks . . . . *Rhampholeon* (p. 314)

13a Casque absent, replaced by cranial crest . . . . *Nadzikambia* (p. 313)

b Casque present **14**

14a Gular and ventral crests present . . . . *Chamaeleo* (p. 318)

b Gular and ventral crests absent **15**

15a Tail about equal to SVL; occipital lobes present . . . . *Trioceros* (p. 321)

b Tail distinctly longer than SVL; occipital lobes absent . . . . *Kinyongia* (p. 311)

16a Head not noticeably wider than neck, slightly elongate; body scales
granular; tail laterally compressed . . . . *Varanus* (p. 306)

b Head noticeably wider than neck, triangular to subtriangular; body scales
keeled, often overlapping; tail cylindrical **17**

17a Scales along dorsal midline enlarged, strongly keeled; scattered enlarged
scales present across dorsum; large black shoulder patch present;
tail covered in whorls of large, strongly keeled scales . . . . *Acanthocercus* (p. 325)
  b Enlarged scales absent, or not concentrated along dorsal midline,
but scattered throughout dorsum or forming distinct longitudinal rows;
if shoulder patch present, not black; tail slender without enlarged spines . . . . *Agama* (p. 330)

18a Dorsals quadrangular or granular and juxtaposed; femoral pores or row
of glandular scales present on posterior surface of thigh **19**
  b Dorsals cycloid, overlapping, smooth or longitudinally keeled; scales
often highly polished; femoral pores absent **31**

19a Ventrolateral skin fold present between front and hind limbs. **20**
  b Ventrolateral skin fold absent **23**

20a Body serpentine; forelimbs absent, hind limbs reduced . . . . *Tetradactylus* (p. 230)
  b Body not serpentine; all limbs well developed **21**

21a Body markedly dorsoventrally flattened; ventrals in 12–20 longitudinal
rows; rupicolous . . . . *Matobosaurus* (p. 228)
  b Body not markedly dorsoventrally flattened; ventrals in 10 or fewer
longitudinal rows; terrestrial **22**

22a Head scales rough; dorsals in 14–21 longitudinal and 31–38
transverse rows . . . . *Broadleysaurus* (p. 227)
  b Head scales smooth or weakly ridged; dorsals in 20–35 longitudinal
and 49–67 transverse rows . . . . *Gerrhosaurus* (p. 231)

23a Dorsals quadrangular, arranged in regular rows; caudal scales often spiny
or keeled, arranged in regular whorls **24**
  b Dorsals granular, juxtaposed; caudal scales non-spinose **25**

24a Body serpentine; limbs vestigial; tail 3–4 times SVL . . . . *Chamaesaura* (p. 241)
  b Body not serpentine; limbs well developed; tail about equal to SVL . . . . *Cordylus* (p. 242)

25a Tail flattened, with enlarged dorsal and lateral plates; arboreal . . . . *Holaspis* (p. 303)
  b Tail cylindrical, without enlarged dorsal or lateral plates **26**

26a Scales along dorsal midline distinctly larger than those on flanks;
body scales large, rhomboid; <26 midbody scale rows; inhabits forest . . . . *Adolfus* (p. 304)
  b Scales along dorsal midline not distinctly larger than those on flanks; >26 midbody scale rows . . . **27**

27a Body extremely dorsoventrally flattened; rupicolous; males brightly coloured,
females dark with three pale stripes . . . . *Platysaurus* (p. 237)
  b Body not extremely ventrolaterally flattened; terrestrial; males usually not
brightly coloured **28**

28a Subdigital lamellae smooth . . . . *Nucras* (p. 293)
  8b Subdigital lamellae keeled **29**

29a Frontonasal longitudinally divided; subocular not bordering lip . . . . *Meroles* (p. 302)
  b Frontonasal entire; subocular borders lip **30**

30a Nostril in contact with, or narrowly separated from, 1st supralabial;
tail much longer than SVL . . . . *Latastia* (p. 297)
  b Nostril well separated from 1st supralabial; tail about equal to SVL . . . . *Ichnotropis* (p. 298)

31a Eyes covered by head scales, visible as dark spots . . . . *Acontias* (p. 244)
  b Eyes exposed, not covered by head scales **32**

32a Eyelid immovable . . . . *Panaspis* (p. 255)
  b Eyelid present, functional **33**

33a Nostril pierced in, or bordered by, rostral **34**
  b Nostril well separated from rostral **37**

Geckos
Family Gekkonidae

Chobe Dwarf Gecko

These predominantly nocturnal lizards have a number of adaptations to their mode of life. The head may be covered in numerous small, asymmetrical and often granular scales, or in tubercles. The body is covered in small, smooth scales, often with scattered large tubercles, or may be predominantly covered in tubercles above. Most species have large eyes but lack moveable eyelids, these having fused together. The lower eyelid covers the eye, and has a large, transparent spectacle in it. Geckos use their long, flat tongue to lick it clean. The pupil is usually vertical (although reduced and round in some diurnal species) and contracts to a narrow slit in bright light, often leaving a few 'pin-prick' openings. The tympanum (ear drum) is usually exposed. The head and body are dorsoventrally flattened and the limbs are always well developed and pentadactyle (in some species the innermost digits are rudimentary). The digits are often flared and most species have claws, which may be retractable. Adhesive discs, termed scansors, are present beneath the digits and may be arranged in a single row or as two separate rows. The scansors are covered in microscopic hair-like structures called setae which afford geckos amazing grip by clinging to minute imperfections on surfaces, and allowing them to cling to vertical surfaces and even walk upside down. Some species (such as the dwarf geckos [*Lygodactylus*]) have a scansorial pad on the ventral surface near the tip of the tail, which affords extra grip.

  The tail is usually cylindrical and tapering and may be dorsoventrally flattened at the base or have regular septa along its length. It is easily shed but regenerates, although regenerated tails often differ from the original tail by being smooth and/or carrot-shaped. In the case of partial autotomy, a new tail may grow alongside the partially lost tail, resulting in a gecko with two tails, termed a bifurcated tail. Some species store fat reserves in their tails, which then also become carrot-shaped.

GECKO SCANSORS

Adhesive discs, known as scansors, are visible beneath the digits (fingers and toes) of a **1** Button-scaled Gecko, **2** Katanga Thick-toed Gecko, **3** Kalahari Thick-toed Gecko, **4** Common Tropical House Gecko, **5** Tete Fragile-skinned Gecko and **6** Common Dwarf Gecko.

Geckos are predominantly insectivorous, although some of the larger species may eat small vertebrates, including other geckos – even smaller individuals of their own species. A few species are omnivorous and will eat plant material, especially nectar and flowers. Most species are capable of vocalisations, which usually take the form of rhythmic clicking, but some species may squeal if grasped. Geckos are capable of limited colour change, which usually involves the lightening and darkening of the skin in response to temperature, mood and light intensity.

Most male geckos have a series of precloacal or femoral pores, while many females have similar corresponding enlarged scales that may be pitted. Males also have a small, semicircular post-cloacal bone on either side of the tail, while both males and females have post-cloacal sacs just below the skin on either side of the tail. In addition, females often have neck pouches (endolymphatic sacs) that are used to store calcium prior to egg formation.

Most species are oviparous, laying pairs of eggs (which are often glued together) in rock cracks, tree cavities and other suitable nooks and crannies. The eggs are relatively small and circular to oval. They are soft-shelled and sticky when first laid, but the calcareous shell rapidly hardens after exposure to air. Females often lay several clutches in a season. Some species have communal nesting sites.

Geckos are more tolerant of cold conditions than most other lizards and occupy all habitats from the coast to mountain tops. They are widespread throughout the tropics and temperate regions. There are 55 genera and more than 1,040 species globally, with numerous cryptic taxa awaiting formal description. At present, 17 species in five genera are known to occur in the region.

Tail tip scansors of a Common Dwarf Gecko

HEAD SCALES OF A TYPICAL GECKO

Rostral
Nostril
Supralabials

Dorsal view

Rostral
Infralabials   Supralabials

Lateral view

Infralabials
Sublinguals
Postmental
Mental

Ventral view

TROPICAL HOUSE GECKOS *Hemidactylus*

Medium- to large-bodied nocturnal geckos. In all species the eyes are large with distinct upper eyelids and vertical pupils. The dorsals are uniformly granular or intermixed with scattered, enlarged tubercles. The digits may be unwebbed or partly webbed, and are flared at the tips, with paired scansors. Each digit has a large, retractile claw. Precloacal and/or femoral pores are usually present in males.

These geckos are predominantly arboreal, although some species are terrestrial or rupicolous. They are commonly seen in houses and around outdoor lights and their rhythmic clicking call is a common sound at night. Males will defend their territories vigorously, approaching another male on raised legs and attempting to bite the intruder's tail or legs. These geckos feed on a large array of invertebrates, although large individuals may eat small vertebrates and even smaller individuals of their own species. All species lay two large, hard-shelled eggs.

This diverse genus occurs widely in the tropics. Owing to their synanthropic nature (living in close proximity to humans and benefitting from human-made habitats), many species have increased, and continue to increase, their range through accidental translocations. The genus contains 132 described species, two of which enter the region.

KEY Regional *Hemidactylus* species

1a Medium-sized (SVL up to 70mm); enlarged tubercles on back arranged in 12–18 (rarely 10) longitudinal rows; 22–40 precloaco-femoral pores in males; caudal spines well developed . . . . *H. mabouia* (p. 208)

  b Large (SVL up to 94mm); enlarged tubercles on back arranged in 8–12 (usually 10) longitudinal rows; 45–57 precloaco-femoral pores in males; caudal spines poorly developed . . . . *H. platycephalus* (p. 209)

Common Tropical House Gecko   *Hemidactylus mabouia*

The Common Tropical House Gecko may be a uniform pink-grey, although coloration varies.

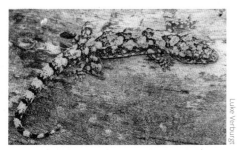
Coloration depends on mood, amongst other factors.

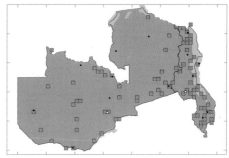

SVL 50–60mm; max. SVL ♂ 66mm ♀ 68mm

A medium-sized gecko with a flattened head and body. Dorsals small, granular, with 12–18 (rarely 10) longitudinal rows of enlarged, weakly keeled tubercles. Single row of 22–40 precloaco-femoral pores on males (fewer in immature males). Strong, recurved claws present on all digits. 6–11 paired scansors beneath 4th toe. Tail cylindrical, segmented, flattened below, with 6 transverse rows of enlarged tubercles. Coloration varies according to mood and light intensity: pale grey to grey-brown or brown, with 4–5 dark or faint, wavy crossbars on the body. Individuals may appear uniform pink-grey or near-black. Ventrum white to translucent. 10–12 dark rings on tail. **Habitat:** A common gecko that adapts to most habitats and situations; widespread in arid and mesic savannas. Predominantly arboreal, often seen on trees and walls of houses. Also found on rock outcrops. **Behaviour:** Nocturnal. Frequently pursues insects attracted to lights. Individuals are very vocal, regularly emitting rapid clicking sounds. Males are territorial, approaching each other slowly while flicking or waving the tail back and forth and vocalising with clicking sounds. **Prey and Predators:** Its diet includes moths, beetles, cockroaches, spiders and a multitude of other invertebrates. Large individuals occasionally eat small lizards and other small geckos, including their own kind. It is preyed on by a variety of reptiles and birds, including kestrels, Brown House Snakes (*Boaedon capensis*), Spotted Bush Snakes (*Philothamnus semivariegatus*), typical skinks (*Trachylepis*), Button-scaled Geckos (*Chondrodactylus laevigatus*) and various large spiders, including Rain Spiders. It is frequently parasitised by Red Mites, which are visible as red speckles. **Reproduction:** Female usually lays eggs (9–13mm x 8–10mm) singly, sometimes in pairs, in summer. Hatchlings measure 30–46mm in TL. **Range:** Patchy distribution in the region may reflect accidental translocations by humans, with subsequent establishment of naturalised populations. Widespread throughout eastern Africa, with a patchy distribution in West Africa. Has been accidentally introduced to South and Central America.

Flat-headed Tropical House Gecko   *Hemidactylus platycephalus*

SVL 75–85mm; max. SVL ♂ 94mm ♀ 90mm

A large, fairly stout gecko with a flattened head and body. Dorsals small, granular, with 8–12 (usually 10) longitudinal rows of enlarged tubercles. Skin quite fragile, tears easily. Single row of 45–57 precloaco-femoral pores on males. Tips of digits flared, with strong, retractile claws. 8–12 paired scansors beneath 4th toe. Tail cylindrical, segmented, flattened below, with 6 rows of enlarged tubercles. Coloration varies according to mood, light intensity and

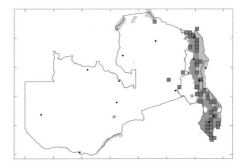

background colour, ranging from uniform pale grey to grey-brown, with or without 4–5 faint, transverse dark bands on body. Ventrum creamy white to pale yellow. 10 faint dark rings on tail. **Habitat:** Mesic savanna. Usually encountered on the trunks of large trees or in houses, and occasionally on rock outcrops. **Behaviour:** Similar to other tropical house geckos. **Prey:** Various invertebrates. Large adults also eat small geckos and other lizards. **Reproduction:** Female lays two eggs (10–13mm), which are glued together, under bark or in a rock crevice. **Range:** From southern Somalia through East Africa to southern Mozambique and westwards to Malawi and eastern Zimbabwe. Records in northern and eastern Zambia may be accidental human translocations. Also occurs on the Comoro Islands.

The coloration of the Flat-headed Tropical House Gecko often has a 'smudged' appearance. INSERT Coloration can closely resemble that of the Common Tropical House Gecko.

FRAGILE-SKINNED GECKOS   *Elasmodactylus*

Large geckos (SVL >75mm) with a robust body and flattened tail. The skin is covered in enlarged tubercles and is fragile, tearing easily. This fragile skin is believed to be an anti-predatory adaptation. The tips of the digits are flared, with 8–14 undivided scansors beneath the 4th toe. Males have a series of precloacal pores.

This genus occurs throughout tropical south-east Africa, from the southern banks of the Zambezi River northwards to Tanzania and the southern DRC. Two species are recognised, both of which occur in the region.

KEY Regional *Elasmodactylus* species

1a Rostral without median cleft; nasal ring greatly swollen; each caudal verticil with pair of slightly enlarged dorsal tubercles; occurs in lower Zambezi Valley . . . . **E. tetensis** (p. 210)

b Rostral with median cleft; nasal ring not swollen; each caudal verticil with row of 6 enlarged dorsal tubercles; occurs in extreme northern Zambia . . . **E. tuberculosus** (p. 211)

Tete Fragile-skinned Gecko   *Elasmodactylus tetensis*

SVL 70–85mm; max. SVL ♂ 100mm ♀ 87mm
A large, robust gecko with a relatively large head and flattened tail. Head somewhat flattened; snout rounded. Top of head covered in small scales; back covered in large, strongly keeled tubercles. Enlarged tubercles often arranged in 8 irregular rows, separated by small, granular scales. Skin fragile, tears easily.

8–14 scansors beneath middle toe. 8–14 precloacal pores on males. Back uniform pale grey. Ventrum white. **Habitat:** Prefers deep, wide cracks on isolated boulders or exfoliating rock flakes on large rock plates. Occasionally occurs communally with Button-scaled Gecko (*Chondrodactylus laevigatus*). Although predominantly nocturnal, it can be seen basking next to a rock crevice retreat during the day. It has also been collected in hollow baobab trees. **Behaviour:** Rupicolous and usually solitary (occasionally forms colonies). **Prey:** Various insects. **Reproduction:** Probably similar to the Tubercled Fragile-skinned Gecko (*E. tuberculosus*). **Range:** Largely restricted to the lower Zambezi Valley, with isolated populations in northern Mozambique and southern Tanzania.

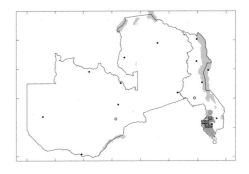

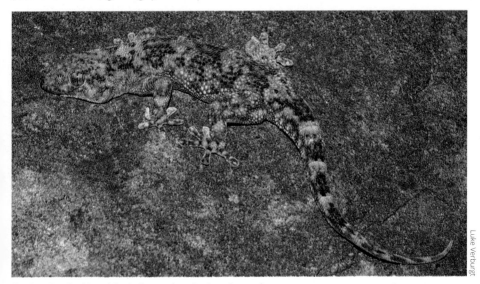

The Tete Fragile-skinned Gecko has a robust body and a rough appearance.

Luke Verburgt

Tubercled Fragile-skinned Gecko   *Elasmodactylus tuberculosus*

SVL 45–70mm; max. SVL ♂ 79mm ♀ 80mm
A large gecko with a robust body and flattened tail. Head moderately depressed; snout rounded. Top of head covered in small granules, intermixed with larger granules on back of head; back covered in enlarged tubercles, interspersed with small granular scales. Dorsal midline covered in uniform small granular scales. Skin fragile, tears easily. 12–13 precloacal pores present in males. Tail about equal to SVL. Dark grey-brown to brown above, with

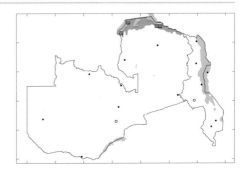

irregular darker crossbars. Dark line sometimes present from nostril, through eye, to ear opening. Ventrum white to cream. Tail covered in irregular dark transverse bands. Juveniles have six pairs of dorsal dark blotches on back, 11 dark crossbars on tail. **Habitat:** Wooded and open savannas. **Behaviour:** Nocturnal and predominantly arboreal. Found on trees and buildings. Also descends to the ground and enters holes. **Prey:** Beetles, mosquitoes, ants, grasshoppers and other insects. **Reproduction:** Female lays clutches of two eggs (9–12mm x 7–8mm). **Range:** Central Tanzania, through extreme northern Zambia and the eastern DRC.

The Tubercled Fragile-skinned Gecko is dark grey-brown to brown above, with a white to cream ventrum.

GIANT GROUND GECKOS   *Chondrodactylus*

Giant ground geckos are characterised by their large body size (SVL >80mm) and robust appearance. The digits are flared and scansors may be present or absent. The dorsal surface is covered in enlarged, usually keeled, tubercles that extend onto the tail and limbs as well. The tail is weakly to moderately depressed. Precloacal pores are absent, as are claws.

Members of this genus are terrestrial, rupicolous and arboreal, and are often found on house walls or in quiet outbuildings. They prey on a wide variety of invertebrates, as well as small geckos of other species. All species are oviparous, with clutches of two large eggs being the norm.

Four species and two subspecies are recognised, which occur from South Africa to Angola and Kenya. Only one species enters the region.

Button-scaled Gecko   *Chondrodactylus laevigatus*

SVL 65–85mm; max. SVL ♂ 102mm ♀ 92mm
A very large, robust gecko with numerous enlarged dorsal tubercles. Rostral does not border nostril; latter directed almost vertically. Dorsals small, granular, interspersed with rows of enlarged, smooth to weakly keeled tubercles. Longitudinal row of smaller enlarged tubercles extends along dorsal midline. Flanks

and limbs covered in enlarged tubercles. Ventrals slightly larger than dorsals. Tail as long as, or slightly shorter than, SVL, fat, slightly flattened, segmented, covered in enlarged, spinose scales dorsally; latter arranged in 6 rows at tail base. Scales beneath tail smooth, subequal in size, arranged irregularly; median row slightly enlarged. Regenerated tails lack enlarged tubercles. Precloacal pores absent. Ear opening large, vertically oval. Tips of digits flared. Scales below toes (above scansors) not, or only slightly, enlarged; 11–13 scansors beneath middle toes. Coloration varies from grey to dark brown; 3–7 wavy dark crossbands usually bordered posteriorly by enlarged white tubercles. Scattered enlarged black and white tubercles usually present. Near-black individuals occasionally found. Ventrum plain white. **Habitat:** Arid and mesic savannas and open woodland. **Behaviour:** A common, predominantly nocturnal gecko that is usually encountered singly, but may form dense colonies. Shelters under bark and in holes in trees as well as in rock outcrops and moribund termitaria. Frequently enters houses and is often seen on thatched roofs and hunting insects around outdoor lights at night. If captured, it will not hesitate to bite, often

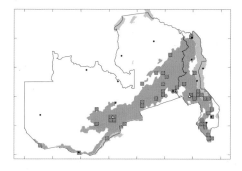

relentlessly hanging on to the victim. **Prey and Predators:** Preys on a wide variety of insects, including moths, termites, ants, crickets and beetles. Preyed on by snakes, including Brown House Snakes (*Boaedon capensis*) and Spotted Bush Snakes (*Philothamnus semivariegatus*), as well as raptors. **Reproduction:** Female lays two large eggs (11–20mm x 10–16mm) between August and December in a hole dug in sand (sometimes under a rock) or in a rock crack. May lay 2–3 clutches per season. Incubation takes 60–80 days. Hatchlings measure 55–65mm in TL. **Range:** Southern, south-central and eastern Zambia; widespread in Malawi. Elsewhere it occurs from northern South Africa northwards to Angola and Kenya.

Luke Verburgt

The Button-scaled Gecko is covered in large tubercles.

THICK-TOED GECKOS *Pachydactylus*

A very diverse group of small-bodied geckos (SVL generally under 65mm, but up to 85mm in one species) that inhabit a range of different habitats. The eyes are large and surrounded by non-functional eyelids that form a distinct ridge around the eye. The body form ranges from short and stout to slender and moderately elongate. The tail is depressed to cylindrical in cross-section. The skin on the back can be smooth or covered in tubercules and is generally not fragile. The scales beneath the toes may be granular or scansorial, and femoral and precloacal pores are generally absent. Males have swollen pouches at the base of the tail, which house the hemipenes.

Most species are terrestrial or rupicolous and all are nocturnal. They prey on a wide variety of invertebrates. All species lay eggs, usually in clutches of two, and females may lay several clutches during a season.

Currently, 69 species are recognised, though many more await formal description. Four species occur in the region.

KEY Regional *Pachydactylus* species

1a 2 narrow, undivided scansors beneath 4ᵗʰ toe . . . . *P. wahlbergii* (p. 217)
 b 3–5 undivided scansors beneath 4ᵗʰ toe **2**

2a Body scales uniformly small, no enlarged tubercles; median row
    of scales beneath 4ᵗʰ toe and above scansors enlarged . . . . *P. punctatus* (p. 216)
 b Body scales small with enlarged tubercles either scattered or in rows;
    median row of scales beneath middle toe and above scansors not enlarged **3**

3a Tubercles on back large and keeled; 6–8 narrow pale crossbands on body;
    8 infralabials; 5 rows of scansors beneath middle toe . . . . *P. katanganus* (p. 214)
 b Tubercles on back enlarged but not keeled; 3–5 broad pale crossbands
    on body; 7 infralabials; 4 rows of scansors beneath middle toe . . . . *P. oshaughnessyi* (p. 215)

Katanga Thick-toed Gecko *Pachydactylus katanganus*

The Katanga Thick-toed Gecko has 6–8 pale bands on the body.

SVL 40–50mm; max. SVL 56mm

A fairly small gecko with a rounded snout, robust body and short limbs. Scales on snout slightly larger than those on head; scales on head granular, keeled, interspersed with smaller granular scales. 8 supralabials; 8 infralabials. Mental slightly smaller than adjacent infralabials; gulars small, juxtaposed. Body covered in small, juxtaposed scales interspersed with large, keeled tubercles (tubercles larger than in O'Shaughnessy's Thick-toed Gecko [*P. oshaughnessyi*]). Ventrals larger than dorsals. Digits short, slightly flared at tip; 5 rows of scansors beneath 4th toe. Middle row of scales beneath toes and above scansors not enlarged. Precloacal and femoral pores absent. Tail fattened at base, tapering to tip, slightly longer than SVL. Regenerated tails carrot-shaped. Light to dark brown or purple-brown above with series of 6–8 narrow, dark-edged, yellowish crossbands on body and 8–13 on tail. First pale crossband forms dark-edged pale crescent on nape. Dark line passes from nostril through eye and encompasses nape. Scattered white tubercles

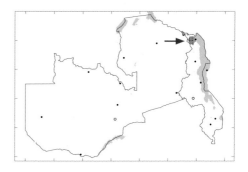

often present on flanks. Ventrum uniform pale white. Original tail pale brown below, spotted with yellow; regenerated tail paler than body with darker flecks below. **Habitat:** Mesic savanna and *Baikiaea–Julbernardia* woodland. **Behaviour:** A terrestrial gecko found sheltering under rocks. **Prey:** Probably small invertebrates. **Reproduction:** Probably similar to other thick-toed geckos. **Range:** Thus far recorded only in extreme northern Malawi and the south-eastern DRC. Probably occurs in extreme north-eastern Zambia as well.

O'Shaughnessy's Thick-toed Gecko *Pachydactylus oshaughnessyi*

O'Shaughnessy's Thick-toed Gecko has 3–5 pale bands on the body.

Juveniles are darker than adults.

SVL 45–55mm; max. SVL 58mm

A fairly small gecko with a rounded snout and robust body. Limbs fairly short. Scales on snout much larger than those on back; rest of head covered in small granules interspersed with larger ones. 8 supralabials; 7 infralabials, 1st as long as and broader than mental. Mental slightly narrowed posteriorly, twice as long as broad. 18–24 rows of enlarged, weakly keeled tubercles on back, interspersed with small granular scales. Outer surfaces of limbs covered with enlarged tubercles. Throat covered in small granules; belly covered in imbricate scales of moderate size. Precloacal and femoral pores absent. Original tail round, as long as, or slightly longer than, SVL, with thick base, tapering to point, covered in large, cycloid scales and lacking enlarged tubercles. 4 rows of scansors beneath middle toe. Middle row of scales beneath toes and above scansors not enlarged. Regenerated tails carrot-shaped. Head paler than body, with dark streak arising at nostrils and encompassing back of head. Body light brown to grey-brown above. Broad, crescent-shaped cream band present on nape, bordered posteriorly by broad black band. 2–4 additional broad cream crossbands present on body, may be truncated or break up laterally. Usually seven broad pale bands on tail. Ventrum uniform cream-white (grey-brown laterally in juveniles). Underside of tail light brown. Juveniles more brightly coloured, with dark markings appearing purple-brown to black. **Habitat:** Moist savanna. **Behaviour:** Terrestrial. Usually found sheltering under rocks, logs and other surface debris. Occasionally enters houses. **Prey:** Small invertebrates. **Reproduction:** Probably similar to other thick-toed geckos. **Range:** South-central regions of Zambia and Malawi, southwards through Mozambique to north-central Zimbabwe.

Speckled Thick-toed Gecko   *Pachydactylus punctatus*

SVL 25–35mm; max. SVL ♂ 39.5mm ♀ 40mm

A small, fairly slender gecko with a short, rounded snout. Body scarcely depressed, covered in small, overlapping scales. No enlarged tubercles. Scales on snout larger than those on back of head. 6–9 supralabials; 5–8 infralabials. Precloacal and femoral pores absent. Tail round, tapering to point, covered in small scales; latter about twice the size of back scales. 3–4 scansors beneath 4th toe. Middle row of scales beneath toes and above scansors enlarged. Body and tail light orange to grey-brown or brown with numerous scattered pale spots; latter often dark-edged. Upper lip white. Dark band passes from nostril,

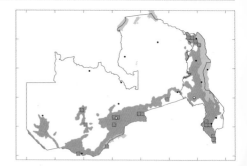

through eye to back of head. Ventrum white. **Taxonomic note:** This species is currently under taxonomic revision and likely comprises several cryptic species. **Habitat:** Sandy or clay soils, rocky ground, rock outcrops and areas with large scattered rocks in semi-arid and mesic savanna. **Behaviour:** A nocturnal, terrestrial gecko that shelters under logs, rocks and other surface debris. Mostly solitary, although sometimes found in pairs. **Prey:** Small invertebrates. **Reproduction:** Female lays clutches of two eggs in summer (8–10mm x 6–7mm). Hatchlings measure 30–40mm in TL. **Range:** Southern Zambia and southern and northern Malawi. Possibly occurs in the intervening regions as well. Elsewhere it occurs westwards to Angola and southwards to South Africa, with an isolated population in the southern DRC.

Luke Verburgt

The Speckled Thick-toed Gecko lacks enlarged tubercles.

Kalahari Thick-toed Gecko   *Pachydactylus wahlbergii*

SVL 45–55mm; max. SVL ♂ 52mm ♀ 61mm
A fairly small, gracile gecko with a moderately elongate body and rounded snout. Small ridge present above and in front of eye. Scales on body small, imbricate. No claws on fingers; small claws on toes in females; large, flat, nail-like scales present on digits in both sexes. Palms covered in irregular, smooth granules; underside of digits covered by blunt granules. Two undivided, transverse scansors at tip of each digit. Tips of digits bent upwards, exposing enlarged scales under first interphalangeal joints, used for digging and walking (protecting scansors). Precloacal and femoral pores absent. Tail cylindrical, unsegmented, tapering, slightly shorter than SVL. Back pale brown to pinkish brown, with dark-edged pale transverse patches extending from neck to tail tip. Pale patches may fuse along dorsal midline, resulting in broad, pale

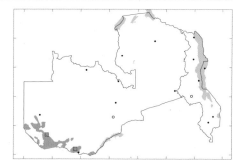

vertebral streak with irregular dark margins. Dark band usually extends from posterior margin of eye to shoulder, sometimes up to cloaca. Pale line extends from tip of snout to between eyes. Fringe above eyes white. Ventrum chalky white. Limbs light brown, sometimes with darker stippling. Regenerated tails brown with irregular darker markings.

Subspecies: Two subspecies are recognised, with only the typical form entering the region. **Habitat:** Restricted to Kalahari soils in arid and mesic savanna. **Behaviour:** Terrestrial and nocturnal, particularly active after rain storms. Shelters in holes dug by other animals or under suitable surface debris. **Prey and Predators:** Preys on small insects, including termites, grasshoppers and antlions. Preyed on by giant ground geckos (*Chondrodactylus*), Brown House Snakes (*Boaedon capensis*) and other snakes. **Reproduction:** Female lays two hard-shelled eggs. **Range:** From north-western South Africa through Botswana, Namibia and extreme north-western Zimbabwe and southern Angola, just entering western and south-western Zambia.

Luke Verburgt

The Kalahari Thick-toed Gecko has a velvety appearance.

DWARF GECKOS   *Lygodactylus*

A diverse group of generally small-bodied geckos with short, rounded snouts. The eyes are surrounded by distinctly raised, immobile eyelids, and the pupils are round. The scales on the back are small and soft, while those on the ventrum are overlapping. The digits are slender and unequal in length. The innermost digit is rudimentary with a vestigial claw. All the other digits have a minute claw that is retractile into a sheath between the anterior pair of scansors. There are two rows of oblique scansors beneath each digit, separated by a median groove. The tail is cylindrical, with a series of scansors near the tip that provide additional grip. Males have precloacal pores, while femoral pores are absent.

These diurnal geckos are quite common in suitable habitat and are frequently seen on houses. Most species are arboreal, with a few rupicolous species. Males dominate a plant or rock and will share it with a number of females and juveniles, but rival males are not tolerated. If threatened, they may run and freeze, relying on their camouflage to escape detection. They may also run around the far side of the tree branch or boulder, keeping it between them and danger, or may quickly run into a narrow crevice or tree cavity. They feed predominantly on ants and are often seen perched next to an ant column from where they lick up passing victims. The female lays two hard-shelled eggs in a tree cavity, rock crevice or similar small fissure, with some species using communal egg sites.

This genus occurs widely throughout continental Africa as well as on Madagascar, with two species occurring in South America. There are 62 species, eight of which enter the region.

Angola Dwarf Gecko   *Lygodactylus angolensis*

SVL 25–30mm; max. SVL 36mm
A small gecko with an elongate snout and
lateral clefts in the mental. No soft spines
above eyes. Rostral enters nostril (rarely
excluded from it); latter situated behind
suture between rostral and 1st supralabial.
2–3 postmentals. Tips of digits slightly flared,
with retractile claws and paired, oblique
scansors; 4–5 pairs of scansors beneath 4th toe.
7–10 precloacal pores in males. Subcaudals
irregular in size; median row not, or only feebly,
enlarged. Tail about equal to SVL. Coloration
varies from grey through olive to brown; dark
stripe extends from nostril through eye to
shoulder. Head and back finely vermiculated.
Series of pale lateral spots, often bordered
anteriorly and/or above by large dark blotches,
may be present or broken up into scattered
flecks. Tail uniform, or with darker flecks or

The Angola Dwarf Gecko has spotted flanks.

Darren Pietersen

lighter crossbands. Ventrum creamy white, occasionally with scattered darker flecks or streaks on throat. Belly, hind limbs and base of tail light yellow in males. **Habitat:** Prefers dry deciduous woodland, savanna and grassland. **Behaviour:** An arboreal, diurnal gecko that is usually found on tree trunks or hiding under loose bark. Sometimes descends to the ground, taking refuge under piles of leaves or in rotting logs. **Prey and Predators:** Preys on ants and termites. Preyed on by Eastern Bark Snakes (*Hemirhagerrhis nototaenia*). **Reproduction:** Female lays two eggs (6mm). **Range:** Occurs widely across Zambia and Malawi, south to

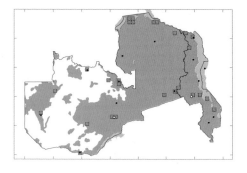

northern Zimbabwe, northwards to southern Kenya and westwards to Angola.

Angulate Dwarf Gecko   *Lygodactylus angularis*

SVL 35–40mm; max. SVL ♂ 42mm ♀ 46mm
A small gecko with a broad snout and no lateral clefts in the mental. Rostral enters nostril; latter situated above suture between rostral and 1st supralabial. 1–2 small postmentals. Tips of digits slightly flared with paired, diagonal scansors and a large, retractile claw on each toe; 5–6 pairs of scansors beneath 4th toe. 5–8 precloacal pores in males. Median row of subcaudals transversely enlarged. Olive, grey-brown or fawn above, usually marbled with darker and lighter flecks. Pale dorsal midline may be present, as may dark stripe from nostril, through eye to above ear opening (both often indistinct). Series of light and dark spots, occasionally a pale band, extends from behind ear to base of tail. 3–5 large, dark spots usually present on flanks. Tail blotched in brown and fawn, often with dark streaks and spots. Series of dark lines extend over throat from infralabials and converge at base of throat, forming two chevrons on the throat with a single median line extending posteriorly. Males have a yellow throat in addition to the two chevrons,

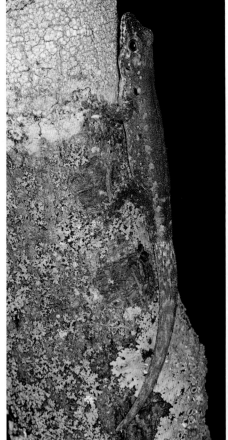

Some individuals are boldly patterned.

Angulate Dwarf Geckos can be uniformly olive above.

but occasionally have a uniform dark throat and light pink to orange belly and subcaudals; females uniform yellow below. **Habitat:** Inhabits medium- and high-elevation woodland and forest. **Behaviour:** Diurnal, but may also be active around houses at night where it is sometimes attracted to insects around lights. **Prey and Predators:** Preys on a variety of invertebrates and their larvae, including beetles, flies, weevils, caterpillars, ants, bugs and spiders. Preyed on by African Pygmy Kingfishers and parasitised by Red Mites, which are visible as red speckles. **Reproduction:** Female lays two eggs (6–8mm x 5–6mm) in summer, occasionally in communal egg sites. A number of females may use the same communal laying site for

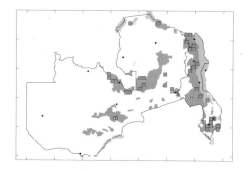

consecutive seasons. Hatchlings measure 20–25mm in TL. **Range:** Widespread in Malawi and central and eastern Zambia, north-east to Tanzania and extreme south-eastern Kenya.

Mulanje Dwarf Gecko   *Lygodactylus bonsi*   Endemic

Colin Tilbury

The Mulanje Dwarf Gecko is a high-elevation endemic.

SVL 33–37mm; max. SVL ♂ 39mm ♀ 40mm
A robust dwarf gecko with a pair of lateral clefts in the mental. 4–7 soft spines above each eye. 7–10 precloacal pores in males. Body olive-brown with scattered pale spots that may be black-bordered. Pale dorsal and dorsolateral line may be present. Flanks light to dark brown with dark-edged white spots. Throat pale blue-white to yellow; rest of ventrum yellowish white. Infralabials usually dark, bordered by broad yellow band; latter bordered by dark line, forming dark chevron parallel to jawline. Tail paler with alternating pale and darker bands and scattered pale spots dorsally, sometimes orange to orange-brown below.

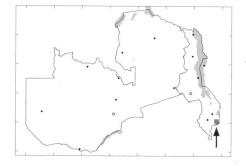

Habitat: Rupicolous, inhabiting rock outcrops in high-elevation montane grassland and boulder-fields with scrub-heathland. Usually

present above 2,000m a.s.l., becoming very common above 2,500m a.s.l. **Behaviour:** Similar to other dwarf geckos. **Prey and Predators:** Similar to other dwarf geckos. **Reproduction:**

Female lays two small eggs (7–8mm x 6–7mm) in a rock crack. Communal egg sites have been recorded. **Range:** Endemic to Mulanje Mountain in Malawi.

Common Dwarf Gecko   *Lygodactylus capensis*

The Common Dwarf Gecko usually has a pale dorsolateral stripe.

SVL 30–35mm; max. SVL ♂ 39mm ♀ 43mm
A small gecko with a broad, rounded snout and a pair of lateral clefts in the mental. No soft spines above eyes. Rostral enters nostril (rarely excluded from it); latter situated behind suture between rostral and 1st supralabial (rarely above it). 3 small postmentals. Digits clawed, flared at tip; 4–5 pairs of scansors beneath 4th toe. 3–7 precloacal pores in males. Tail slightly longer than SVL, easily shed. Subcaudals irregular in size; median row not, or only feebly, enlarged. Coloration varies greatly depending on mood, light intensity and background. Back usually grey, olive or brown, may be very dark in cold weather. Dark line extends from nostril, through eye to shoulder, sometimes extending along flanks. Fine black stippling on head and back. Pale dorsolateral stripe arises on snout, extends through eye and continues along back, where it may fade out or continue to base of tail. Series of pale spots occasionally present along flanks, may extend onto base of tail. Tail mottled with grey and white, often with scattered pale spots. Ventrum dirty white

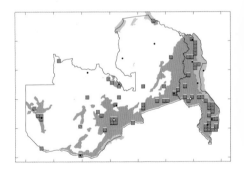

to yellowish; fine grey or brown-black flecks sometimes present on throat. Breeding males develop a yellow throat and become orange-brown below the tail. Tail reddish brown in hatchlings. **Habitat:** Savanna and woodland. Usually seen on trees, large bushes, walls, piles of debris, rock piles and any other suitable surface. **Behaviour:** A common, widespread, diurnal gecko. Short-lived, with a lifespan of only 15–18 months, although some live for more than 30 months. Quite social and rarely shows any territoriality. **Prey and Predators:** Shows a distinct preference for ants and termites, but will feed on small beetles, flies and their larvae, small grasshoppers, spiders, bugs and most other invertebrates that are small enough. Often infested with Red Mites, which are visible as irregular red speckles. It is a favourite prey item of African Pygmy Kingfishers and Eastern Bark Snakes (*Hemirhagerrhis nototaenia*) and is also eaten by Common Slit-faced Bats.

Reproduction: Reproduction occurs throughout the year, the female laying two eggs (7–12mm x 5–11mm) glued together (rarely separate) beneath rocks, under bark or under any other suitable cover. Incubation takes 2–5 months. Hatchlings measure 25mm in TL. Sexual maturity is reached after eight months. **Range:** Widespread from South Africa northwards to Kenya, Angola and the southern DRC.

Chobe Dwarf Gecko   *Lygodactylus chobiensis*

Luke Kemp

The Chobe Dwarf Gecko often has a dark spot in front of the shoulder.

Darren Pietersen

The breeding male has a dark throat and yellow belly.

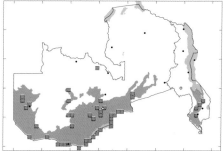

SVL 30–35mm; max. SVL ♂ 44mm ♀ 40mm
A small gecko with a rounded snout and no lateral clefts in the mental. No soft spines above eye. Rostral usually separated from nostril; latter situated behind suture between rostral and 1st supralabial. 3 small postmentals. Digits clawed, flared at tip; 5 pairs of scansors beneath 4th toe. 7–11 precloacal pores in males. Median subcaudal row strongly enlarged transversely. Dull grey-brown to brown above, irregularly mottled with dark-edged pale spots and blotches. Dark stripe extends from nostril, through eye, to shoulder. Tail slate-grey, sometimes with faint darker medial line. Throat

white, with two dark chevrons running parallel to jawline (occasionally uniform black), these markings being paler or absent in females. **Belly** yellow. **Habitat:** Moist savanna and woodland. **Behaviour:** Usually forages high up in trees, occasionally found lower down and on buildings. Short-lived, most living for only about 18 months. **Prey:** Predominantly ants and termites, but it also eats flies and small grasshoppers. **Reproduction:** Males reach sexual maturity after 9–10 months and females after 8–9 months.

Breeding occurs throughout the year, the female laying two hard-shelled eggs (6–7mm x 4–5mm) under bark, in disused termitaria, and in tree hollows at 7–8-week intervals. Incubation takes about 125 days. Hatchlings measure 30–32mm in TL. **Range:** Most common along the Zambezi Valley and its tributaries, the Okavango Basin and the Zimbabwe Plateau. In the region it occurs in western and southern Zambia and southern Malawi, with an apparently isolated population in the Copperbelt Province.

Chevron-throated Dwarf Gecko   *Lygodactylus gutturalis*

The Chevron-throated Dwarf Gecko enters Zambia at Lake Mweru.

SVL 30–35mm; max. SVL ♂ 42mm ♀ 38mm
A small gecko with a broad snout, no lateral clefts in the mental and no soft spines above the eyes. Rostral usually separated from nostril; latter situated behind (rarely above) suture between rostral and 1st supralabial. 1–3 (usually 2) small postmentals. Digits clawed, slightly flared at tips, with paired, oblique scansors; 5–6 scansors beneath 4th toe. 6–9 precloacal pores in males. Tail about equal to SVL. Median row of subcaudals strongly enlarged. Body grey-brown, mottled with light and dark streaks and spots. 2–3 dark chevrons on throat in both sexes, 3rd sometimes taking form of dark arrow-head or spot, may be indistinct in females. Belly yellow.

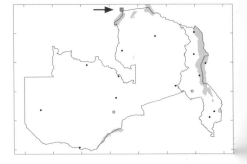

Subcaudals yellow or orange, with median series of dusky spots. **Habitat:** Prefers forest, woodland and moist savanna. **Behaviour:** An active, diurnal gecko usually encountered on tree trunks. Also found In piles of vegetable debris. **Prey and Predators:** Preys on ants, termites, flies, wasps, beetles and their larvae, spiders, and any other invertebrate that is small enough. Preyed on by Spotted Bush Snakes (*Philothamnus semivariegatus*). **Reproduction:** Breeding occurs throughout the year. The female lays two eggs (8mm x 6mm). **Range:** From Tanzania and Kenya through the DRC to Senegal. Enters the region in north-eastern Zambia at Lake Mweru.

Heenen's Dwarf Gecko *Lygodactylus heeneni*

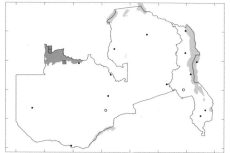

SVL 27–32mm; max. SVL ♂ 34mm ♀ 38mm
A small gecko with a broad snout and no lateral clefts in the mental. Rostral enters nostril, latter situated above suture between rostral and 1st supralabial. 2–3 postmentals. Tips of digits slightly flared, with paired, diagonal scansors and a large, retractile claw on each digit; 5 pairs of scansors beneath 4th toe. Median row of subcaudals transversely enlarged. 7–10 precloacal pores in males. Back olive, grey-brown or fawn, usually marbled with darker and lighter flecks; snout often paler. Pale dorsal midline may be present, as may a dark stripe from nostril through eye to above ear opening (both often indistinct). Series of light and dark spots and occasionally a pale band extends from behind ear to base of tail. Tail blotched in brown and fawn, often with dark streaks and spots. Series of dark lines extends over throat from infralabials, converging at base of throat and forming two chevrons with single median line extending posteriorly. Gular markings faint or absent in females. Ventrum white. **Habitat:** Forest. **Behaviour:** Diurnal and arboreal. **Prey:** A variety of small invertebrates, including small beetles and grasshoppers. **Reproduction:** Female probably lays two eggs. **Range:** Restricted to extreme north-western Zambia and the south-western DRC.

Heenen's Dwarf Gecko occurs in north-western Zambia.

Frank Willems

King Dwarf Gecko *Lygodactylus rex*

SVL 40–50mm; max. SVL ♂ 55mm ♀ 46mm
A very large dwarf gecko with a long, broad snout and lateral clefts in the mental. 2–3 (usually 2) large postmentals. 8–11 precloacal pores; 2 rows of 7–8 large, glandular scales on ventral surface of thighs in males. Subcaudals unequal in size; median row not enlarged. Tail longer than SVL. Back dark red-brown, often with wavy darker crossbands. Flanks with series of large orange patches that may be surrounded by thin, dark line; series of smaller orange dots form broken dorsolateral band. Conspicuous white eyespot present above shoulder, sequentially surrounded by black and orange. Tail with series of lateral orange dots with alternating broad dark bands and narrower pale bands dorsally. Throat and chest white in both sexes, with four pairs of dark chevrons extending from infralabials. Two anterior pairs of dark chevrons merge along gular midline in adults (anterior-most pair of chevrons absent in juveniles). 3rd pair of chevrons does not merge medially, running parallel to jawline, while posterior-most pair extends along side of neck to forearm insertion. Belly and subcaudals pale green-yellow to bright yellow in males, grey-white in females and juveniles. Juveniles lack orange flank spots. **Habitat:** Mid-elevation montane forest, occasionally entering houses. **Behaviour:** Diurnal and arboreal. **Prey and Predators:** Probably preys on a variety of small invertebrates. Preyed on by various snakes and birds. **Reproduction:** Female lays two eggs (7.5–8.5mm x 6.5–7.5mm) under bark, in a tree hole or in a rock crevice. Eggs have been found in an exfoliating rock crack in forest. Hatchlings measure 34–36mm in TL. **Range:** Mount Mulanje in Malawi and adjacent inselbergs in Mozambique. The population in Lichenya Hut on Mount Mulanje is likely introduced.

The King Dwarf Gecko has a characteristic eyespot above the shoulder.

Darren Pietersen

Plated Lizards
Family Gerrhosauridae

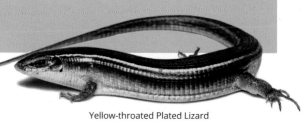

Yellow-throated Plated Lizard

These specialised lizards are covered in thick armoured scales that overlie bony plates in the skin (osteoderms). The dorsal, ventral and caudal scales are square to rectangular in shape and are arranged in straight longitudinal and transverse rows. A well-defined ventrolateral skin fold extends the length of the body. The head is short and often robust, and the ear opening is prominent. Both prefrontal and frontoparietal scales are present and the lower eyelid is scaly. The nostril is pierced between the two nasals and the 1st supralabial. Femoral pores may be present in both sexes but are better developed in males.

These lizards are diurnal and predominantly terrestrial. Many species inhabit burrows which they dig themselves or which are dug by other animals. Some species are rupicolous and scamper into the nearest crevice when disturbed. Most species are solitary, but rupicolous species often form small colonies where conditions are suitable. The tail is used to store fat and can be shed, although the larger species rarely do so. The female lays eggs in earthen burrows or in rock crevices. These lizards feed predominantly on large invertebrates (beetles, millipedes and snails being their favourite prey) although the larger species will also eat small vertebrates, as well as plant matter. Prey is actively hunted, with leaves and other debris scraped away in the search for food.

Seven genera and 37 species occur widely in sub-Saharan Africa and Madagascar. Seven species in four genera have been recorded in the region.

ROUGH-SCALED PLATED LIZARDS   *Broadleysaurus*

A monotypic genus containing a stout-bodied species of terrestrial lizard with a moderately sized head. The head scales are rough. The rostral may be in contact with or separated from the frontonasal, which may be entire or longitudinally divided. Prefrontals are usually in broad, occasionally narrow, contact (rarely separated). There are four (rarely three) supraoculars and five (rarely three, four or six) supraciliaries. The tympanic scale is narrow and band-like. The body is slightly flattened and covered in strongly keeled, ridged or rough scales. The dorsals are in 14–21 longitudinal and 31–38 transverse rows. The ventrals (sometimes termed plates) are large and in 10 (rarely nine) longitudinal and 28–35 transverse rows.

Rough-scaled Plated Lizard   *Broadleysaurus major*

SVL 170–200mm; max. SVL 245mm
A large, stout plated lizard with a cylindrical body and large head that is not distinct from the neck. Rostral and frontonasal in narrow contact; prefrontals in narrow to broad contact. 5 supraciliaries; 3–4 supralabials anterior to subocular, which borders lip; 4 infralabials. Dorsals strongly keeled (particularly on tail), rough, in 14–19 longitudinal and 31–33 transverse rows. Ventrals large, in 10 longitudinal rows. 8–17 femoral pores on thigh in both

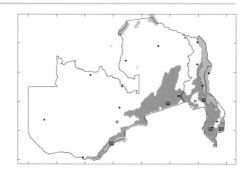

sexes, better developed and more obvious in males. Head yellow-brown to pale brown; back brown to straw-coloured, each scale with a black mark that may form irregular longitudinal lines. Longitudinal pale line arises above eye, fades out on body, may be indistinct. Flanks same colour as back, or dark with paler spots or blotches. Chin, throat and chest yellowish white; rest of ventrum dark with paler scale margins. Males develop pinkish throat in the breeding season. Juveniles dark with yellow speckling. **Habitat:** Arid and mesic savannas. **Behaviour:** Predominantly terrestrial, although also entering small, well-wooded rocky outcrops. A shy lizard that will retreat into cover at the least disturbance. Usually takes refuge in moribund termitaria, but also shelters under rocks, in disused burrows and under rubble. Males actively defend a territory, fighting with rivals by biting their hind legs and trying to flip them onto their back. **Prey and Predators:** Feeds predominantly on beetles, grasshoppers and millipedes, but will also eat other invertebrates, small lizards and other small vertebrates. Soft fruit and flowers are also eaten. It is regularly preyed on by Wahlberg's Eagles. **Reproduction:** Female lays 2–6 large, oval eggs (43–58mm x 23–28mm) in mid-summer. Incubation takes 70–81 days. Hatchlings measure 120–185mm in TL. **Range:** Southern Zambia and central and southern Malawi. Elsewhere southwards to South Africa and northwards through East Africa to the Horn of Africa, with scattered populations in Central and West Africa.

The Rough-scaled Plated Lizard will take shelter at the slightest disturbance.

GIANT PLATED LIZARDS   *Matobosaurus*

Large, rupicolous lizards with a medium-sized, depressed head and a depressed body. The head scales are smooth in juveniles, becoming ridged in subadults and rough in adults. The rostral is separated from (occasionally in contact with) the frontonasal and the prefrontals are in broad contact. They have four supraoculars and five (rarely four or six) supraciliaries. The subocular may be excluded from the lip by a supralabial scale or may be in contact with it. The tympanic scale is narrow and band-like in juveniles, becoming broad and sub-triangular in adults. The body is covered in large, keeled scales that have a single median keel in juveniles, three keels in subadults and multiple keels in adults. The dorsals are in 25–34 longitudinal and 49–58 transverse rows, and the ventrals in 12–20 longitudinal and 34–45 transverse rows.

These lizards often inhabit well-wooded rocky hills where they may form small colonies. They feed on a variety of invertebrates and plant matter, while small vertebrates are occasionally also eaten.

Two species occur widely across southern Africa. One species is found in the region.

Common Giant Plated Lizard *Matobosaurus validus*

The Common Giant Plated Lizard occurs exclusively on rock outcrops.

SVL 200–230mm; max. SVL 285mm
A large plated lizard with a dorsoventrally flattened body and a tapered head. Supranasals in contact behind rostral (rarely separated), separating rostral from frontonasal. Prefrontals in broad contact; 4–6 (usually 5) supraciliaries. Subocular does not reach lip. 7–11 (usually 8–9) supralabials; 4–9 (usually 6–7) infralabials. Dorsals fairly small, square in shape, with multiple keels, in 28–34 longitudinal and 49–56 transverse rows. Ventrals large, slightly overlapping, in 14–20 rows. 15–25 (mostly 18–22) femoral pores on thigh in both sexes. Back dark brown to black; each scale with pale spot, giving speckled appearance. Pair of broad, pale, yellowish dorsolateral stripes may be present. Head variegated, spotted with yellow. Chin, throat and upper chest pale grey-brown to white, becoming dark brown towards cloaca. Juveniles black with distinct series of yellow spots on back and barred flanks. Breeding males develop a reddish chin, throat and sides of head. **Habitat:** Large rock outcrops, especially granitic outcrops, in savanna. **Behaviour:** Exclusively rupicolous, it takes refuge under large boulders, rock plates and in rock fissures. It may wander onto ground adjoining these rock plates but

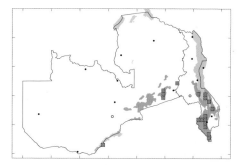

Juveniles are more boldly patterned than adults.

will rush back to cover with much noise if disturbed. If harassed, it will inflate its body, firmly wedging itself into the rock crevice. Usually found in family groups consisting of several adults and numerous juveniles. **Prey and Predators:** Feeds on a large variety of insects, including beetles, and will also feed on plant matter such as flowers, figs and berries. It has also been recorded eating small lizards and even young tortoises. It is a favourite prey of Wahlberg's Eagle. **Reproduction:** Female lays 2–5 (usually 4) large, oval eggs (44–46mm x 24–26mm) in a soil-filled rock crevice in mid-summer. Hatchlings measure 150–170mm in TL. **Range:** Southern and south-eastern Zambia, and southern Malawi. Elsewhere through Mozambique, Zimbabwe and Botswana to South Africa.

SEPS *Tetradactylus*

Small, serpentine plated lizards with a small head and long tail. The lower eyelids are scaly. The limbs are greatly reduced, with some species lacking forelimbs entirely and having only small hind limb buds. There is a prominent ventrolateral fold. The body scales are square in shape and arranged in regular rows. Femoral pores may be present or absent.

These fast, diurnal lizards 'swim' through the grass using their long tail and streamlined body to propel themselves forward. The tail is readily shed but is quickly regenerated, as it is essential for locomotion. They prey on grasshoppers and other insects, which are captured after a short dash. They retreat into grass tussocks or under rocks at night. All species are oviparous.

There are eight species in the genus, one of which occurs in the region.

Ellenberger's Long-tailed Seps *Tetradactylus ellenbergeri*

Ellenberger's Long-tailed Seps superficially resembles a snake.

SVL 55–65mm; max. SVL ♂ 69mm ♀ 72mm
A small plated lizard with reduced limbs and a serpentiform body. Forelimbs absent; hind limbs reduced to small (about 2mm) buds. Tail long, at least three times SVL. Head small. Prefrontals in broad contact. Head scales have fine ridges. Scales on back strongly ridged with single median keel, in 12–14 longitudinal and 65 transverse rows. Ventrals large, arranged in 6 longitudinal rows. Femoral pores absent. Tail easily shed, but regrows rapidly. Olive-blue to dark brown above, with pair of dark vertebral stripes running length of body and onto tail. Alternating dark and pale vertical bars on sides of head and anterior portion of body, rapidly fading posteriorly. Ventrum white to pale olive. **Habitat:** Moist savanna, swamp grassland and dambos. **Behaviour:** Usually seen basking on

top of grass tussocks. If disturbed, It may dive into water and hide amongst the vegetation. **Prey:** A variety of invertebrates, including grasshoppers, ants, beetles, caterpillars, spiders and snails. **Reproduction:** Female lays two eggs (11–12mm x 5–6mm), apparently during autumn and winter. **Range:** Scattered records from north-western, south-central and north-eastern Zambia. Elsewhere it occurs in Tanzania, the southern DRC and eastern Angola.

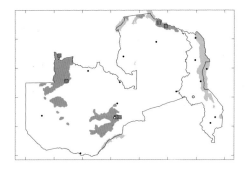

PLATED LIZARDS   *Gerrhosaurus*

Medium-sized diurnal, terrestrial lizards with a small to medium-sized head. The rostral may be in contact with, or separated from, the frontonasals. Prefrontals may be well separated, slightly separated or in narrow or broad contact. There are four supraoculars and four to five (rarely three or six) supraciliaries. The tympanic scale is narrow and band-like to broad and crescent-shaped. The body is cylindrical to almost square in shape and may appear slightly depressed. The head scales are smooth or weakly ridged, while the dorsals are weakly to strongly keeled, ridged or smooth. The dorsals are in 20–35 longitudinal and 49–67 transverse rows; the ventrals are in 8–10 longitudinal and 30–42 transverse rows.

The seven recognised species occur widely in sub-equatorial Africa. Five species enter the region.

KEY   Regional *Gerrhosaurus* species

1a Pair of well-defined black-edged pale dorsolateral stripes present;
  body relatively slender **2**
  b Black-edged pale dorsolateral stripes absent; body stout **4**

2a 5 supraciliaries; prefrontals in narrow contact or separated;
  SVL 5.3–8 times head length . . . . **G. flavigularis** (p. 232)
  b. 4 supraciliaries; prefrontals in broad contact; SVL 4–5 times head length **3**

3a Flank scales strongly keeled; plantar scales moderately to distinctly
  keeled; pale vertebral stripe usually absent in adults (but may be
  present in juveniles) . . . . **G. intermedius** (p. 233)
  b. Flank scales weakly to moderately keeled; plantar scales smooth
  to weakly keeled; pale vertebral stripe often present in adults . . . . **G. nigrolineatus** (p. 235)

4a Body plain golden-brown to grey; flanks same colour as the back or
  rusty red, often with darker infusions on the sides of the neck . . . . **G. multilineatus** (p. 234)
  b Body pale brown to red-brown, usually with darker flecks on head; scales on
  back and tail each with a yellow spot, giving rise to a flecked appearance . . . . **G. auritus** (p. 231)

Kalahari Plated Lizard   *Gerrhosaurus auritus*

SVL 150–180mm; max. SVL 215mm
A large, thick-bodied plated lizard with a medium-sized head. Nasals in contact, separating rostral from frontonasal. Prefrontals in broad contact. 4 supraciliaries; tympanic scale broad, crescent-shaped, covers large portion of ear opening. Dorsals strongly keeled, in 26 longitudinal and 51–54 transverse rows; lateral scales smooth. Ventrals in 8 longitudinal rows. 14–18 femoral pores on thigh in both sexes. Body pale brown to red-brown, usually with darker flecks on

head. Scales on back and tail each with yellow spot, giving flecked appearance. 3–4 narrow, dark-edged pale dorsolateral stripes may be present. Flanks lighter; each scale usually dark-centred. Limbs have dark-edged spots; pale spots usually present on thighs. Ventrum cream-white. Adults develop blue infusions on flanks, throat and upper lip during breeding season. Juveniles darker above with more distinct spotting. **Habitat:** Kalahari sandveld and bushveld. **Behaviour:** Diurnal. Shelters in holes which it digs at the base of bushes, or may use holes dug by other animals (especially rodents). Also takes

shelter in exposed tree roots. **Prey:** Feeds on grasshoppers, beetles, termites, scorpions and plant matter (including berries). **Reproduction:** Female lays eggs in late summer. **Range:** Northern Namibia and Angola, entering western Zambia. Elsewhere it occurs in central and northern Botswana, just entering western Zimbabwe and north-western South Africa.

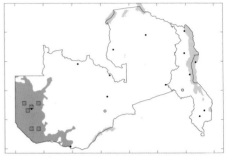

The Kalahari Plated Lizard has a distinct flecked appearance. INSERT The side of the head usually has dark flecks.

Yellow-throated Plated Lizard *Gerrhosaurus flavigularis*

SVL 100–120mm; max. SVL 142mm
A medium-sized, slender-bodied plated lizard with a fairly narrow head. Supranasals in narrow contact behind rostral; latter separated from frontonasal. Prefrontals in narrow contact or separated. 5 supraciliaries; 6 supralabials; 4 infralabials; subocular does not border lip. Dorsals square in shape, strongly keeled, in 20–24 longitudinal and 54–65 transverse rows. Scales on flanks usually smooth; those on tail strongly overlapping, keeled dorsally, smooth

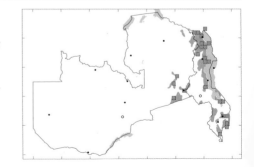

ventrally. Ventrals in 8 longitudinal rows. Plantar scales smooth, tubercular. 10–18 femoral pores on thigh in males; females lack femoral pores. Back red-brown to grey-brown, with pair of pronounced dark-edged yellow dorsolateral stripes extending from above eyes onto tail, fading posteriorly. Flanks grey-brown with irregular dark spots, often with faint yellowish bars. Lower portions of flanks off-white, merging with cream-white ventrum. Tail may have some dark flecking, white underneath. Chin, throat, chest and sides of head of breeding males become orange-red to yellow; some males develop a blue-grey throat. **Habitat:** Inhabits a range of habitats including moist savanna, open woodland and grassland. **Behaviour:** Terrestrial and diurnal. Shelters in holes that it digs at the base of bushes or under rubble. Surprisingly fast and difficult to catch, escaping into dense cover if pursued. The tail is easily shed and grows back fairly rapidly. **Prey:** Feeds on a variety of invertebrate prey, including grasshoppers, beetles, crickets and millipedes, as well as plant matter. **Reproduction:** Female lays 2–8 oval, soft-shelled eggs (16–22mm x 9–14mm) in a hole dug in the soil or under a rock in summer. Incubation takes 74–86 days. Hatchlings measure 105–120mm in TL. **Range:** Throughout eastern Africa from Sudan and Ethiopia through Malawi and eastern Zambia to South Africa.

Luke Verburgt

The Yellow-throated Plated Lizard closely resembles the Black-lined Plated Lizard. INSERT It has five supraciliaries.

Eastern Black-lined Plated Lizard   *Gerrhosaurus intermedius*

SVL 140–170mm; max. SVL 183mm
A large plated lizard with a slender, cylindrical body and a wedge-shaped head. Supranasals in broad contact behind rostral, separating it from frontonasal. Prefrontals in broad contact; 4 supraciliaries; 3–4 supralabials anterior to subocular, which borders lip; 3–4 infralabials. Dorsal and lateral scales strongly keeled, in 20–26 (usually 22–24) longitudinal and 54–64 transverse rows. Ventrals smooth, in 8 longitudinal rows. Plantar scales moderately to strongly keeled, spiny. Scales on tail strongly keeled above, with keeling becoming less pronounced on sides and underneath. 15–20 femoral pores on thigh in both sexes. Back brown to reddish brown with each scale dark-spotted, sometimes forming

irregular longitudinal lines. Pair of pronounced dark-edged white dorsolateral stripes extend from above eyes onto tail. Broken series of pale spots may extend from between shoulders to base of tail, especially in juveniles. Flanks orange-red to red-brown, fading ventrolaterally, with numerous irregular pale spots. Ventrum white to dirty white. Breeding males develop a deep blue or red throat. Juveniles often have dark transverse bars dorsally. **Taxonomic note:** This species was recently separated from the Western Black-lined Plated Lizard (*G. nigrolineatus*) on genetic and morphological grounds. **Habitat:** Bushveld and savanna. **Behaviour:** Terrestrial and diurnal. If disturbed, it will take refuge in rodent burrows or holes in moribund termitaria. **Prey:** Feeds on a variety of insects, including grasshoppers, beetles and millipedes Also eats plant matter. **Reproduction:** Female lays 4–9 eggs (22–30mm x 12–18mm) in an abandoned rodent burrow. Incubation takes 70–80 days. Hatchlings measure 160–180mm in TL. **Range:** Occurs widely in eastern and southern Africa, and throughout Malawi and southern, central and eastern Zambia.

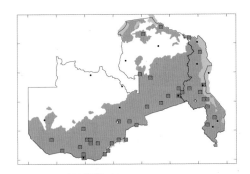

The breeding male develops a red or blue throat.

The Eastern Black-lined Plated Lizard resembles both Yellow-throated and Western Black-lined plated lizards.

Bocage's Plated Lizard *Gerrhosaurus multilineatus*

SVL 150–180mm; max. SVL ♂ 181mm ♀ 200mm
A large, thick-bodied plated lizard. Prefrontals in broad contact; nasals in contact, separating rostral from frontonasal. 4 supraciliaries; 3 supralabials anterior to subocular, which borders lip. Dorsals strongly keeled, in 22–26

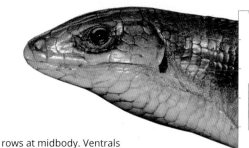

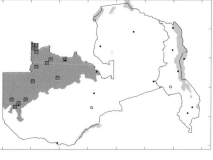

rows at midbody. Ventrals in 8 longitudinal rows. 14–18 femoral pores on thigh in both sexes. Scales at base of tail usually strongly overlapping and spinose, rarely just keeled. Back golden-brown to grey, flanks same colour as back or rusty red, often with darker infusions on sides of neck. Chin, throat and ventrum white. Breeding males develop blue sides to head and neck. **Taxonomic note:** Populations in Zambia and the DRC were previously treated as a separate species, Laurent's Plated Lizard (*G. bulsi*), although recent studies suggest that these two species are synonymous. **Habitat:** Woodland. **Behaviour:** Terrestrial and diurnal, often seen basking near its burrows or old termitaria. **Prey:** Feeds on plant material and invertebrates, including grasshoppers, beetles and termites. **Reproduction:** Female lays 3–6 eggs (up to 27mm x 12mm), in summer. **Range:** Central and north-eastern Angola, through western and north-western Zambia, to the extreme southern DRC.

TOP The forebody lacks pale stripes in Bocage's Plated Lizard. ABOVE This species favours woodland.

Western Black-lined Plated Lizard   *Gerrhosaurus nigrolineatus*

SVL 140–170mm; max. SVL 183mm
A large plated lizard with a slender, cylindrical body and wedge-shaped head. Supranasals in broad contact behind rostral, separating it from frontonasal. Prefrontals in broad contact. 4 supraciliaries; 3–4 supralabials anterior to

subocular, which borders lip; 3–4 infralabials. Dorsals strongly keeled; scales on flanks weakly to moderately keeled. Dorsals in 24–28 (rarely 23) longitudinal and 54–64 transverse rows. Ventrals smooth, in 8 longitudinal rows. Plantar scales smooth or weakly keeled. Scales on tail strongly keeled above; keeling becoming less pronounced on sides and underneath. 15–20 femoral pores on thigh in both sexes. Back olive to light brown, with pair of distinct dark-edged, cream-coloured dorsolateral stripes extending from above eyes onto tail. Black-bordered, cream vertebral stripe may be continuous or broken into discrete short stripes, or occasionally absent. Flanks may be plain olive to light-brown or have scattered black and wwhite scales. Ventrum white to dirty white.

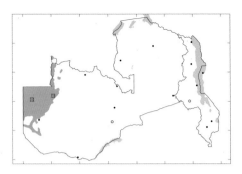

Taxonomic note: This species was recently separated from the Eastern Black-lined Plated Lizard (*G. intermedius*) based on genetic and morphological differences. **Habitat:** Bushveld and savanna. **Behaviour:** Terrestrial and diurnal. Often shelters in rodent burrows or holes in moribund termitaria. **Prey:** Feeds on a variety of insects including grasshoppers, beetles and millipedes, and will also eat plant matter. **Reproduction:** Female lays 4–9 eggs (22–30mm x 12–18mm) in an abandoned rodent burrow. Incubation takes 70–80 days. Hatchlings measure about 160–180mm in TL. **Range:** Occurs widely in central and west Africa, from Gabon to the southern DRC and north-western Zambia, although its exact distribution still needs to be determined.

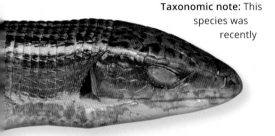

The Western Black-lined Plated Lizard closely resembles the Eastern Black-lined Plated Lizard. INSERT A pair of dark-edged, cream-coloured dorsolateral stripes originates above the eyes.

Girdled Lizards
Family Cordylidae

Nyika Girdled Lizard

Small to large lizards that are endemic to mainland Africa. The body shape varies from cylindrical and serpentine to dorsoventrally flattened with well-developed limbs. The body scales are large and either granular or in regular transverse rows. The ventrals are large, rectangular to quadrangular in shape, and arranged in regular rows. The parietals are large and square. Cranial osteoderms are always present. The scales on the tail are often spiny and arranged in whorls, but may be smooth or faintly keeled. Femoral pores are present.

These lizards are diurnal, with the majority of species being rupicolous, while some are terrestrial or arboreal. Most species are insectivorous and territorial, ambushing their prey from a stationary position.

Ten genera and more than 63 species have been described, of which three genera and six species have been recorded in the region.

Flat Lizards
Subfamily Platysaurinae

This subfamily contains a single genus and 16 species, all of which are oviparous. It is a predominantly eastern group, its range extending from extreme southern Tanzania through Mozambique, Zimbabwe and extreme south-eastern Botswana to eastern South Africa. Three isolated species occur in western southern Africa.

FLAT LIZARDS *Platysaurus*

Medium- to large-sized lizards with an extremely dorsoventrally flattened body. The limbs are long and the digits are well developed. The dorsals are granular, while the ventrals are large, smooth and juxtaposed, and either square or quadrangular in shape. The ventrals are arranged in regular longitudinal and transverse rows. The scales on the tail are non-spinose. Adult males are brightly coloured while females and juveniles are dull, usually with three longitudinal pale stripes on the dorsum. Males usually display by turning to face an intruder while lifting the forebody, displaying the bright gular region and ventrum. Mitchell's Flat Lizard (*P. mitchelli*) has a lateral display, presenting the side of the body to an intruder while simultaneously inflating itself to showcase the vivid colours to best effect. This behaviour has occasionally been recorded in other species.

These diurnal lizards inhabit large rock outcrops, particularly gneiss, sandstone and granite outcrops that weather to form narrow fissures. They take refuge in crevices and emerge to bask and forage when the sun heats up the rocks, and will rapidly retreat into a nearby fissure at the first sign of danger. Males defend territories during the breeding season, chasing off rivals. Subadult males are usually tolerated. Individuals become sexually mature after 2–3 years. The female lays 1–2 eggs in summer, sometimes in communal sites. These lizards prey on a variety of small insects and also occasionally eat small fruit and other plant matter.

A total of 16 species and 15 subspecies are recognised, although many of the subspecies likely represent valid species. Three species and one subspecies have been recorded in the region.

Common Flat Lizard *Platysaurus intermedius*

The male Common Flat Lizard has a bright orange tail.

The female is dark with three pale stripes.

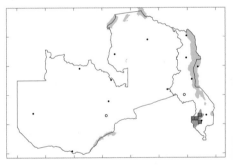

SVL 80–95mm; max. SVL ♂ 105mm ♀ 91mm
A medium-sized flat lizard with supranasals that are fused with the nasals. Nasals in contact behind rostral, or occasionally separated by internasal. Interparietal usually not in contact with occipital. Usually 5 supralabials anterior to subocular. Enlarged scales on side of neck granular; scales on flanks larger than those on back. Collar curved, consists of 7–12 scales. Ventrals large, square to rectangular in shape, in 16–20 longitudinal and 35–41 transverse rows. 18–23 femoral pores on thigh in males. Adult males dark olive-green above, becoming brown posteriorly, with faint pale dorsal spots; tail orange; throat dull blue or bright orange; chest and belly purplish black, suffused with orange

laterally. Females and juveniles dark brown to black above, with three well-defined narrow pale longitudinal stripes extending from top of head to base of tail; no light spots between stripes; large, diffuse pale spots often present on flanks. Ventrum predominantly white, with central orange band on belly in females and juveniles. Sides of tail pale anteriorly; anterior margin of each scale whorl becoming dark towards tail tip, creating dark bands. Dark central stripe present on dorsal surface of tail anteriorly, fading towards tip. **Subspecies:** Nine subspecies are recognised, most distinguishable by coloration, geographic distribution and differences in scalation. Only the Malawi Common Flat Lizard (*P. i. nyassae*) enters the region. **Habitat:** Large, flat rock outcrops in woodland and savanna. **Behaviour:** Diurnal. Usually found in small colonies. **Prey:** Various small invertebrates, including ants and beetles and their larvae. Plant matter also forms an important component of its diet. **Reproduction:** Presumably similar to other flat lizards. **Range:** Southern Malawi and adjacent central Mozambique.

Mitchell's Flat Lizard *Platysaurus mitchelli* Endemic

Gary Brown

Mitchell's Flat Lizard is endemic to Mount Mulanje.

SVL 60–100mm; max. SVL ♂ 112mm ♀ 81mm
A large flat lizard with a discrete pair of supranasals, which are in contact behind the rostral. Interparietal usually separated from occipital. Usually 4 supralabials anterior to subocular. Scales on side of neck, flanks and dorsum uniform in size; those on side of neck also spinose. 8–13 collar scales arranged in chevron, many only slightly developed. Ventrals in 12–14 longitudinal and 36–40 transverse rows. 17–22 well-developed femoral pores on thigh in males. Adult males olive-brown above; top of head dark brown with light spots; side of head yellow-green, extending as broad band onto side of neck (sometimes to tail tip); flanks dull purple with large pale green spots; sides of tail bright blue-green; throat white, infused with magenta medially, or entirely brick-red; collar broad, black; chest dark blue; lower chest and belly brick-red; large blue-black patch in centre of abdomen extends to base of tail; limbs transversely banded in dark blue and pale blue or green; tail light bluish green. Females and juveniles dark brown to black above with three longitudinal pale yellow stripes originating on head and extending to base of tail, which

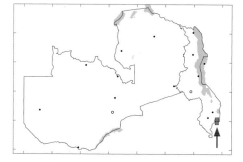

Werner Conradie

The female is dark brown to black above and closely resembles other female flat lizards.

occasionally break up into discrete spots; no pale spots between stripes; limbs, flanks and side of tail have indistinct pale spots; lower limbs covered with pale crossbars; ventral coloration similar to that of the male, but much lighter. **Habitat:** Syenite rock faces and cliffs on the lower slopes of Mount Mulanje. **Behaviour:** Usually forms small colonies. Adults are most often found on vertical cliffs, but also inhabit boulders at the forest edge and in grassland on the valley floor. Displaying males turn side-on to an intruder and inflate the neck and body to display the bright coloration to full effect. **Prey:** Small invertebrates, including ants, spiders and beetles and their larvae. A fair amount of plant matter is also eaten. **Reproduction:** Presumably similar to other flat lizards. **Range:** Endemic to Mount Mulanje.

Striped Flat Lizard *Platysaurus torquatus*

SVL 65–70mm; max. SVL ♂ 76mm ♀ 72mm
A small flat lizard with supranasals that are fused with the nasals, the latter in contact behind the rostral. Interparietal large, bordered posteriorly by occipital, which may be fragmented into 2–3 smaller scales. Usually 4–5 supralabials anterior to subocular. Scales on side of neck flattened and enlarged; scales on flanks larger than those on back. Collar curved, consists of 5–10 scales. Ventrals in 16–20 longitudinal and 34–47 transverse rows. 15–22 femoral pores on thigh in males. Adult males dark brown above, with three buffy longitudinal stripes and scattered buff spots; flanks bright orange to dull green, with pale yellowish-green spots; tail bright orange to coral-red; throat white with broad black collar; limbs greyish brown; chest orange or yellow, suffused with bright green, becoming dark blue on belly and blue-black towards cloaca. Females and juveniles blackish brown above with three pale longitudinal stripes with very few or no pale spots in between them; limbs greyish

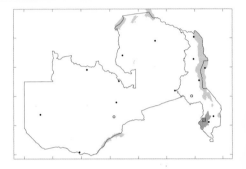

brown; tail blue, with a dark median stripe; throat white, sometimes suffused with yellow or grey; chest white; belly and base of tail orange. **Habitat:** Flat rock outcrops in woodland and savanna, particularly along rivers. **Behaviour:** Diurnal. Often forms large colonies. **Prey:** Predominantly ants, beetles and caterpillars. **Reproduction:** Female lays two eggs (about 19mm x 7mm), in summer. **Range:** Southern Malawi, extending through west-central Mozambique to north-eastern Zimbabwe.

The male Striped Flat Lizard has three faint stripes on the back.

Girdled lizards and relatives
Subfamily Cordylinae

This subfamily contains nine genera and 48 species, which occur predominantly in southern Africa. The body is moderately dorsoventrally flattened with well-developed limbs, or cylindrical and serpentiform. All species are viviparous.

GRASS LIZARDS   *Chamaesaura*

Large lizards with a very slender, serpentine body, narrow head and greatly reduced or absent limbs. The tail is extremely long (3–4 times SVL) and used to propel individuals forward as they 'swim' through grass. The dorsals are large, strongly keeled and arranged in regular rows.

These lizards are diurnal and insectivorous. They occur in grassland in central, eastern and southern Africa. Females give birth to 5–17 neonates, with reproduction being aseasonal in at least one species.

Five species and two subspecies are recognised, one of which occurs in the region.

Zambian Grass Lizard   *Chamaesaura miopropus*

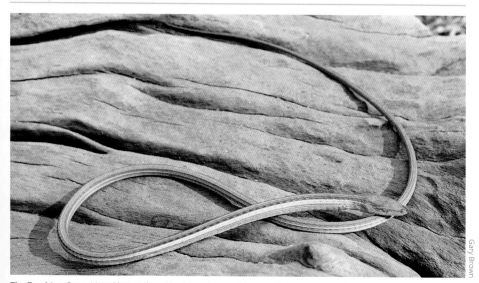

Gary Brown

The Zambian Grass Lizard has reduced limbs and resembles a snake.

SVL 90–140mm; max. SVL 180mm

A medium-sized lizard with a slender, elongate body and reduced limbs, thus resembling a snake. Head pointed, flattened. 2–3 supralabials anterior to subocular. Tail very long, 70% of TL, gently tapering. Forelimbs reduced to small buds; hind limbs resemble spikes, ending in a single toe. Body scales keeled, in 22–24 rows at midbody. Coloration pale yellowish tan on back with two darker dorsolateral stripes, which may break up into series of dark spots. Flanks

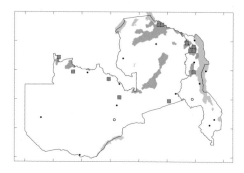

lighter, merging with white ventrum. **Habitat:** Montane grassland and grassy savanna, most often at high elevations. **Behaviour:** Diurnal and terrestrial. 'Swims' through grass like a snake. If threatened, it will take refuge in the nearest grass tuft or rapidly escape through the grass. **Prey:** A variety of insects, including grasshoppers and wasps. **Reproduction:** Female gives birth to up to four live neonates (140–145mm in TL) in summer. **Range:** Northern and eastern Zambia and central and northern Malawi, including the Nyika Plateau, north-east to Tanzania and just entering the southern DRC and Angola.

GIRDLED LIZARDS *Cordylus*

Small to medium-sized lizards with a moderately dorsoventrally flattened and robust body. The head is broad and triangular. The limbs are of moderate length and the digits are well developed. The dorsals are small, smooth to keeled, and in regular rows. The scales on the tail are enlarged and spiny.

Some species are exclusively rupicolous, while others are terrestrial or semi-arboreal. They feed on insects, which are ambushed from a stationary position, but also eat plant matter. Females give birth to 1–6 live neonates.

This genus occurs widely in southern and eastern Africa. A total of 22 species are recognised, of which two occur in the region.

KEY Regional *Cordylus* species

1a Head and body depressed; dorsals weakly keeled, not drawn into a posterior spine; scales on flanks same size as those on back; rupicolous . . . . . . *C. nyikae* (p. 242)
 b Head and body weakly depressed; dorsals strongly keeled, drawn into a posterior spine; scales on flanks smaller than those on back; mainly arboreal . . . . *C. tropidosternum* (p. 243)

Nyika Girdled Lizard *Cordylus nyikae*   Endemic

The Nyika Girdled Lizard is endemic to high-elevation areas in northern Malawi and Zambia.

SVL 70–80mm; max. SVL ♂ 94mm ♀ 95mm
A medium-sized cordylid with a stocky body and broad, triangular head. Head and body flattened; head scales rough. Nasals large, slightly swollen, nostril pierced in lower posterior corner, separated from 1st supralabial by narrow ridge. 6 rugose occipitals, outermost pair smallest. 5–7 (usually

6) supralabials, 4th and 5th weakly keeled; 6 (rarely 5) infralabials, the posterior-most weakly keeled. Dorsals uniform in size, very weakly keeled, not drawn into spine. Lateral scales weakly keeled, overlapping, with granular interstitial spaces. Dorsal and lateral scales in 27–30 transverse and 19–23 longitudinal rows. Median ventral scale rows smooth; outer row feebly keeled (outer 3 scale rows keeled in juveniles); in 12–16 (usually 14) longitudinal and 22–27 transverse rows. 5–8 femoral pores on thigh in males, preceded anteriorly by 12–20 glandular scales. Tail covered in whorls of large, elongate spines. Back light to dark brown; lighter mottling on body. Tail and labials light brown. Ventrum buffy. **Habitat:** Small rock outcrops in montane grassland. **Behaviour:** A diurnal, rupicolous

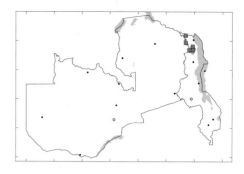

lizard that inhabits narrow rock cracks. **Prey:** Feeds mainly on beetles and moths, but will eat almost any invertebrate. **Reproduction:** Female gives birth to 2–4 live neonates in mid-summer. **Range:** Endemic to the Nyika Plateau and Misuku Hills in northern Malawi.

Tropical Girdled Lizard   *Cordylus tropidosternum*

The Tropical Girdled Lizard has a rounder body than the Nyika Girdled Lizard.

SVL 70–85mm; max. SVL 107mm
A stocky-bodied cordylid with a slightly flattened head and body. Head scales with numerous raised ridges. Nasals large; nostril pierced in lower posterior corner. 6 rugose occipitals. 6 (rarely 7) supralabials, posterior 3 keeled; 6 (rarely 5 or 7) infralabials, posterior 4 keeled. Dorsals strongly keeled, overlapping, drawn into posterior spine. Lateral scales smaller than dorsals, strongly keeled, overlapping with granular interspaces. Dorsal and lateral scales

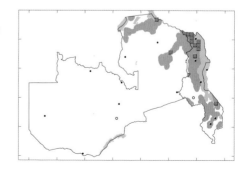

in 22–30 transverse and 18–24 longitudinal rows. All ventral rows keeled in juveniles, only outer 3–4 scale rows weakly keeled in adults. Ventrals arranged in 12–16 (usually 14) longitudinal and 21–28 transverse rows. Pair of slightly enlarged precloacal scales followed posteriorly by series of small scales. 3–7 femoral pores on thigh in males, preceded anteriorly by 3 rows of glandular scales. Tail covered in large, elongate spines arranged in whorls. Back dark brown to reddish brown, usually with darker and paler spots and mottling. Darker stripe often extends from above ear opening to beyond shoulder. Labials and ventrum white to yellowish white. **Habitat:** Moist woodland, forest and well-wooded savanna. **Behaviour:** A predominantly arboreal lizard, usually found under exfoliating bark and in tree hollows. Individuals may also be found on fallen tree trunks and occasionally sheltering under logs or exceptionally in rock crevices. **Prey:** Beetles, termites, millipedes, spiders and a variety of other invertebrates. **Reproduction:** Viviparous, the female gives birth to 2–5 neonates (60–70mm in TL), in mid-summer. **Range:** Northeastern Zambia and northern and southern Malawi, although probably in the central regions as well. Elsewhere it is found from the southern DRC to Kenya and southwards to Zimbabwe and central Mozambique.

Legless Skinks
Family Acontidae

These fossorial lizards lack all external traces of limbs and have smooth scales that are often shiny and

Barotse Legless Skink

close-fitting. The rostral and mental are enlarged and the frontal bone is divided. The nostrils are usually situated near the front of the rostral and in most species are connected to the posterior margin of the rostral by a nasal groove. These lizards lack pterygoid teeth and have a complex secondary palate. The eye may be exposed or covered by the dorsal head scales, and there is no external ear opening. The tail is short and bluntly rounded, and only a single enlarged cloacal scale is usually present.

Legless skinks are most common in sandy soils, where they inhabit the leaf litter or top layer of soil, descending to deeper depths during winter and prolonged dry periods. Some of the larger-bodied species occur in heavy clay soils. They prey on termites, beetle larvae and earthworms. All species are viviparous, with clutches of 1–4 (but up to 14) neonates being born, usually in summer.

The 27 recognised species in two genera occur predominantly in southern Africa, with two species in one genus entering the region.

LEGLESS SKINKS *Acontias*

This large group of lizards is characterized by medium- to large-sized skinks that lack all external limbs. They usually have a relatively slender body and a short, rounded tail that ends rather abruptly. Some species have exposed eyes that can be covered with a movable lower eyelid, while other species have the eye reduced and completely covered by the ocular scale, being invisible or visible only as a dark spot. The rostral is large, with the nostrils pierced within it and connected to its posterior border by a nasal groove. The head scales are fused to varying degrees in the different species and even within species there is often variation in head scale fusions, including fusions on only one side of the head. There are no external ear openings. The body scales are smooth and close-fitting, which is an adaptation to their fossorial lifestyle.

All species are fossorial and occur in a number of habitats, including deep Kalahari sands, coastal alluvium, heavy clay soils and rocky montane habitats. They feed on invertebrates and their larvae, while the larger species opportunistically eat other burrowing reptiles as well. They are often preyed on by other burrowing reptiles and small carnivores, while gamebirds may also be important predators in some areas. All species are viviparous, giving birth to a single clutch of 1–4 (but up to 14) neonates in late summer.

Currently, 21 species and six subspecies are recognised, of which two species occur in the region.

KEY Regional *Acontias* species

1a 3 sublinguals border mental; yellow above with two dark dorsal stripes . . . . **A. jappi** (p. 245)
  b 4 sublinguals border mental; blue-grey to dark grey above, lower
    flanks and ventrum orange-yellow . . . . **A. schmitzi** (p. 246)

Barotse Legless Skink   *Acontias jappi*

The Barotse Legless Skink is found west of the Zambezi River, and favours Kalahari sands.

SVL 150–170mm; max. SVL 188mm
A medium-sized, robust legless skink with a strongly depressed and pointed snout. Eye reduced, covered by ocular, visible as dark spot (occasionally visible as well-developed eye). Prefrontal relatively large, in contact with loreals laterally and subpentagonal frontal posteriorly. Single pair of parietals, 1 temporal, 1 nuchal and usually 2 supraciliaries on each side of head. Ocular much longer than high; 3 sublinguals border mental. Upper border

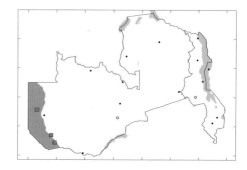

of ocular incompletely fused with anterior supraciliary, resulting in narrow slit that is continuous with orbit (i.e. an immovable lower eyelid). 14 scale rows at midbody; 176–186 ventrals; 22–27 subcaudals. Golden-yellow in colour. Two broad, black vertebral stripes originate on head, extending to tip of tail. These may become faint on tail or may persist and be accompanied by remnants of a further two dark lateral stripes on tail (i.e. four stripes on tail). Juveniles may have traces of four black dorsal stripes; tail unpigmented. Head often infused with darker markings, especially on rostral and parietal and between oculars. **Habitat:** Kalahari sands in woodland. **Behaviour:** Relatively common, usually found under rotting logs, in bush clumps and in loose sand just below the leaf litter. Apparently descends to deeper depths below the soil surface during winter, although some evidence suggests that it ascends to the top layer of soil during winter to mate. **Prey:** Feeds predominantly on termites and beetle larvae, but probably eats other invertebrates as well. **Reproduction:** One or two neonates are born in mid- to late summer. **Range:** Restricted to western Zambia and adjacent regions of eastern Angola.

Schmitz's Legless Skink   *Acontias schmitzi*   Endemic

Schmitz's Legless Skink occurs east of the Zambezi River.

Max. SVL 176mm

A medium-sized legless skink with a flattened and pointed snout. Eye reduced, covered by subocular, preocular and postocular. Rostral large; nostril pierced within rostral, connected with posterior border of rostral by straight nasal groove. 2 enlarged, azygous scales posterior to rostral. Parietals in broad contact behind frontal. 4 supralabials, 1st being the largest and in contact with subocular and preocular; 3 infralabials. 4 sublinguals border enlarged mental. 14 rows of smooth, close-fitting scales at midbody; 173–178 ventrals; 26 subcaudals. Back blue-grey to dark grey, this coloration extending onto flanks; sharp

transition to lower half of flanks and ventrum, which are yellow-white to light orange. Ragged, discontinuous dark grey median stripe may be present on ventrum; anterior two-thirds of the tail may be darkly pigmented below. Rostral and regenerated tail portions pale white. **Habitat:** Appears to favour deep Kalahari sands in miombo woodland. **Behaviour:** Only known from three specimens. Biology likely similar to other legless skinks. **Prey:** Probably similar to other legless skinks. **Reproduction:** Probably gives birth to 1–2 neonates in summer. **Range:** Probably restricted to deep Kalahari sands on the east bank of the Zambezi River.

Old World Skinks
Family Scincidae

Angola Burrowing Skink

These skinks usually have a cylindrical body and small, often vestigial limbs which may be entirely absent. Both the frontal and nasal bones are divided. The body scales are usually smooth and overlapping. Two or more enlarged precloacal plates are present. The tail is cylindrical and can be shed and regenerated in some genera, but cannot be shed in others.

The majority of species are fossorial or live in the leaf litter. Reproduction is oviparous, although some species retain the eggs in their body until the embryos are fully developed.

Of the 279 recognised species in 34 genera, seven species in four genera occur in the region.

BURROWING SKINKS   *Sepsina*

An African genus of burrowing skinks with small limbs and 3–5 digits on each limb. The supranasals are in contact behind the rostral. The interparietal is small and separated from the supraoculars, and external ear openings are present.

Very little is known about the biology or reproduction of these rare skinks, all of which are restricted to the southern half of Africa.

Five species are recognised, two of which occur in the region.

KEY   Regional *Sepsina* species

1a All limbs tridactyle . . . . **S. angolensis** (p. 247)
 b Forelimbs tetradactyle; hind limbs pentadactyle . . . . **S. tetradactyla** (p. 248)

Angola Burrowing Skink   *Sepsina angolensis*

SVL 70–80mm; max. SVL 91mm
A small but stout-bodied burrowing skink with a rounded snout. Lower eyelid transparent, scaly. Ear opening small. Nostril pierced between rostral, 1st supralabial, supranasal and small postnasal, latter separating supranasal and 1st supralabial. Frontal large, bordered anteriorly by smaller prefrontal and posteriorly by smaller interparietal. Interparietal bordered posteriorly by pair of parietals, latter in broad contact behind interparietal. 4 supraoculars,

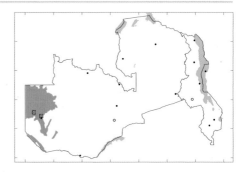

becoming progressively smaller posteriorly. 4–5 supraciliaries; 6 supralabials (4th entering orbit); 7 infralabials. Scales smooth, in 22–24 rows at midbody. Median 2 precloacal scales slightly enlarged. Limbs small, tridactyle; middle digits being the longest; toes slightly longer than fingers. Hind limbs 2–3 times larger than forelimbs. Tail fat, rounded, about two-thirds of SVL. Light brown to brown above; each scale dark-edged, forming reticulated pattern; or with each scale dark-centred, forming continuous longitudinal stripes. Ventrum creamy to yellowish white. **Habitat:** Mesic savanna. **Behaviour:** Fossorial. Actively forages in leaf litter and sandy soils. **Prey and Predators:** Unknown. **Reproduction:** Unknown. **Range:** From the lower Congo through Angola and western Zambia to northern Namibia.

The small but stout-bodied Angola Burrowing Skink has tridactyle limbs.

Four-toed Burrowing Skink *Sepsina tetradactyla*

SVL 65–75mm; max. SVL 80mm
A small, blunt-headed burrowing skink with a rounded snout. Lower eyelid transparent, divided into septa. Ear opening small. Nostril pierced between rostral, 1st supralabial, supranasal and small postnasal, latter separating supranasal and 1st supralabial. Frontal large, bordered anteriorly by smaller prefrontal and posteriorly by small interparietal. Parietals moderately enlarged, in broad contact behind interparietal. 4 supraoculars, 1st being the largest, becoming progressively smaller until 4th, which is the smallest. 4–5 supraciliaries; 6 supralabials (4th entering orbit); 7 infralabials. Scales smooth, in 24 rows at midbody. Median 2 precloacal scales slightly enlarged. Limbs small; forelimbs tetradactyle; hind limbs pentadactyle. Hind

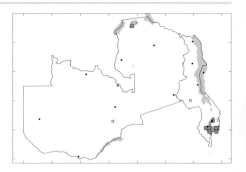

limbs longer than forelimbs. Tail fat, rounded, about two-thirds of SVL. Body grey or brown above, usually with pink infusions around limb insertions. Ventrum cream to yellowish white. Tail blue, sometimes with dark speckling. **Habitat:**

Sandy soils in dry to mesic savanna. **Behaviour:** A fossorial, probably diurnal species that actively forages in leaf litter. Seen after heavy rains, retreating under logs and piles of debris at other times. **Prey:** Termites and other invertebrates.

Reproduction: Unknown. **Range:** Recorded in southern Malawi and north-eastern Zambia. Elsewhere it is found from the south-eastern DRC to central-western and south-eastern Tanzania. Probably also occurs in northern Mozambique.

The tetradactyle forelimbs of the Four-toed Burrowing Skink are smaller than the pentadactyle hind limbs.

DART SKINKS *Typhlacontias*

Lizards in this genus generally lack external limbs, although remnants of external limbs are retained in FitzSimons' Dart Skink (*T. brevipes*) and in some Speckled Dart Skink (*T. punctatissimus*) individuals. The snout is flattened and projecting, and covered by a large rostral scale, with the nostrils pierced in the side of the rostral and linked to the posterior border of the rostral via a nasal groove. A small to minute nasal is enclosed within the nasal groove. There are three large, unpaired head scales between the rostral and the interparietal, and the pineal eye is usually distinctly visible. The eyes are small and may be completely exposed or partly covered and external ear openings are absent. There are 18 rows of smooth, imbricate scales at midbody.

These small, active skinks are usually found in loose sand and leaf litter, where they hunt for termites, beetle larvae and other invertebrates. They may be found under logs and other plant debris and are quite active near the soil surface at night. Little is known about the biology of members of this genus, although some retain the eggs within their bodies until the embryos are fully developed, giving birth to live young.

Six species and three subspecies are recognised, two of which are present in the region.

KEY Regional *Typhlacontias* species

1a 5 supralabials, 2nd entering orbit; frontoparietal and prefrontal in contact . . . . **T. rohani** (p. 250)

  b 6 supralabials, 3rd entering orbit; frontoparietal and prefrontal separated
  by 3rd supraocular . . . . **T. gracilis** (p. 250)

Roux's Dart Skink   *Typhlacontias gracilis*

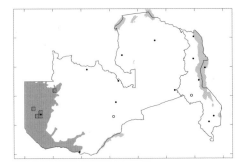

SVL 60–75mm; max. SVL 86mm

A small, slender skink that lacks external limbs. Rostral large, only slightly notched laterally. Frontonasal slightly larger than internasal and frontal. Frontal narrow, separated from frontonasal and 2 supraoculars by prefrontal. Frontoparietal present between frontal and interparietal. 3 supraoculars, first 2 in contact with eye, 3rd separated from eye by upper postocular. Frontoparietal separated from prefrontal by 3rd supraocular. 2 preoculars; 1–3 postoculars. 6 supralabials, 3rd entering orbit; 4 infralabials, 4th slender, horizontal, sometimes obscured by mandible. Tail about half of SVL. Scales small, tight-fitting, in 18 rows at midbody. 121–147 ventrals; 56–68 subcaudals. Coloration varied, ranging from buff to straw-coloured. Each scale often dark-centred; dark spots vary in size, may form two dark longitudinal stripes that originate as dark marks on head and extend onto tail. Dark brown lateral line may be present, originating in ocular region and extending to tail tip. **Habitat:** Woodland on Kalahari sands, including *Baikiaea* woodland. Compared to other species in this genus, it prefers areas with a higher rainfall. These areas may be susceptible to periodic flooding. **Behaviour:** Usually found singly under fallen logs and other suitable cover. **Prey:** Probably small invertebrates. **Reproduction:** Reproductive biology unknown, but it is probably oviparous and retains the eggs in its body until the embryos complete their development. **Range:** Endemic to western Zambia, but probably occurs in adjacent regions of Angola as well.

Rohan's Dart Skink   *Typhlacontias rohani*

Rohan's Dart Skink closely resembles Roux's Dart Skink.

SVL 65–80mm; max. SVL 90mm

A small skink with a flattened snout that projects forward. Small lateral notch in rostral; nasal groove encloses small postnasal. Frontoparietal and prefrontal in contact, excluding 2 enlarged supraoculars from frontal. 1–2 small preoculars may be fused or entirely absent; 2 postoculars, lowest separating lower anterior temporal and 2nd supralabial. 5 supralabials, 2nd entering orbit; 4 infralabials, posterior-most horizontally elongate, may be obscured by mandible. Tail about half SVL. Scales close-fitting, in 18 rows at midbody. 124–146 ventrals; 64–84 subcaudals. Coloration varied, ranges from dark buff to straw-coloured. Each scale dark-centred, with dark spots occasionally forming two dark longitudinal lines that originate on head and extend onto tail. Dark brown lateral line may be present. Dark centres of scales more developed in some regions, resulting in an overall dark appearance, including darker flanks; head, and especially snout, also dark in these individuals. **Habitat:** Prefers woodland on Kalahari sands with an average rainfall exceeding 400mm per annum. These areas are susceptible to sudden flooding events, especially flooding of annual pans. **Behaviour:** May be common under logs and other plant matter. Active just below the soil surface at night; its thin, undulating subterranean tracks are a common sight in the morning. **Prey and Predators:** Eats mostly small insects, including termites and beetle larvae. The

The rostral is enlarged and encompasses the nostril.

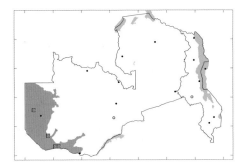

high proportion of individuals with regenerating tails suggests a high predation rate, probably by fossorial snakes such as quill-snouted snakes (*Xenocalamus*) and purple-glossed snakes (*Amblyodipsas*). **Reproduction:** Oviparous, the female retains the eggs in her body until the embryos complete their development, giving birth to 3–4 neonates. **Range:** Western Zambia, south-eastern Angola, northern Namibia, northern Botswana and western Zimbabwe.

LIMBLESS SKINKS *Melanoseps*

These burrowing skinks lack all traces of external limbs and ear openings as an adaptation to their fossorial lifestyle. The eyes are reduced and there is no upper eyelid, although an elongate, scaly lower eyelid is present. The rostral is not enlarged and the nostrils are pierced in the posterior edge of the rostral and adjoining the 1st supralabial. The supranasals are in broad contact behind the rostral and the interparietal is very large and in contact with the supraoculars. Prefrontal and frontoparietal are lacking. The fairly large interparietal is situated between the frontal and two pairs of parietals; the median parietal pair is in contact behind the interparietal. There is a reduction in the number of scale rows near midbody, resulting in a large variation in the number of midbody scale rows within species.

Eight species are recognised, two of which occur in the region.

KEY Regional *Melanoseps* species

1a 20–24 midbody scale rows; 144–164 ventrals; SVL >140mm . . . . **M. ater** (p. 252)
 b 17–22 midbody scale rows; 130–149 ventrals; SVL <140mm . . . . **M. loveridgei** (p. 253)

Black Limbless Skink *Melanoseps ater*

In northern populations the Black Limbless Skink is dark above and paler below.

Southern populations are uniformly dark.

SVL 140–170mm; max. SVL 185mm

A relatively large legless skink. Nostrils pierced within posterior border of rostral, bordered posteriorly by 1st supralabial. Nasal and postnasals absent, supranasal contacts 1st supralabial. 3 supraoculars; 4 supraciliaries. 5 supralabials, 1st being the largest; 6 infralabials. 20–24 scale rows at midbody, 144–164 ventrals; 42–61 subcaudals. Southern populations uniform black above and below; northern populations uniform black above with uniform yellow, pink or white ventrum that may have each scale dark-centred, resulting in chequered ventrum. Longitudinal stripes may be present on ventrum in juveniles. Tail uniform black or with heavy black mottling. **Habitat:** Edge of evergreen montane forest and surrounding woodland at high elevations. **Behaviour:** Often found under logs and stones. **Prey:** Unknown. Probably feeds on small invertebrates. **Reproduction:** Female retains the eggs in her body until the embryos complete their development, giving birth to 3–5 neonates in mid- to late summer. **Range:** Montane forest of the Rift Valley from Rungwe Mountain in southern Tanzania to high-elevation regions of north-eastern Zambia and Malawi, to Mulanje Mountain in the south.

Loveridge's Limbless Skink   *Melanoseps loveridgei*

SVL 120–135mm; max. SVL 142mm
A medium-sized burrowing skink that has
the nostril pierced in the posterior border
of the rostral and bordered posteriorly by
the 1st supralabial. No nasal or postnasals;
supranasal in contact with 1st supralabial behind
rostral. 3 supraoculars; 4 supraciliaries. 5
supralabials, 1st being the largest; 6 infralabials.
17–22 midbody scale rows. 130–149 ventrals;
42–52 subcaudals. Dark grey to black above;
ventrum uniformly dark, or pale with rows
of dark spots. Tail dark brown. Rarely dark
above with lateral stripes and white ventrum.
Habitat: Moist miombo woodland and savanna,
occasionally occurring at the edge of montane
forest. **Behaviour:** Very little is known about
this skink. It is presumed to be diurnal and
fossorial, and may favour moist localities.
Prey: Probably feeds on small insects and their
larvae. **Reproduction:** Female retains the eggs
in her body until the embryos complete their
development, giving birth to 2–8 neonates
(about 55mm SVL) in mid- to late summer.
Range: Eastern Tanzania, extending westwards
through north-eastern Zambia and the extreme
southern DRC, and southwards into northern
Mozambique. Probably occurs in northern
Malawi as well.

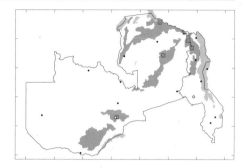

Loveridge's Limbless Skink usually occurs at lower elevations than the Black Limbless Skink.

SLENDER SKINKS   *Proscelotes*

Small, slender skinks with smooth scales and short, pentadactyle limbs. The eyes are small
and external ear openings are present. The supranasals are in contact behind the rostral. The
interparietal is small and not in contact with the supraoculars.

Four species are recognised, occurring in isolated populations in moist habitats in East and south-
east Africa. Only one species enters the region.

The Mulanje Montane Skink is endemic to Mount Mulanje.

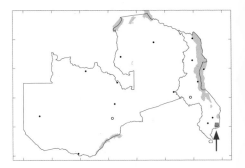

SVL 60–80mm; max. SVL 95mm
A small skink with smooth, close-fitting scales. Limbs reduced in size, pentadactyle. Nostril pierced between rostral and small, ring-like scale. 22–24 scale rows at midbody. 11–12 lamellae beneath 4th toe. Tail about equal to SVL. Uniform brown, or with dark spot on each scale which may form longitudinal lines. Distinct, grey dorsolateral stripe often present. Ventrum light pink. Tail bright blue in juveniles. **Habitat:** Montane grassland and evergreen forest. **Behaviour:** Fossorial and probably diurnal. Hunts in leaf litter and under rotting logs. **Prey and Predators:** Feeds on invertebrates. Preyed on by Grey-bellied Grass Snakes (*Psammophylax variabilis*). **Reproduction:** Probably retains the eggs in its body until the embryos complete their development, although Arnold's Montane Skink (*P. arnoldi*), of which *P. mlanjensis* was previously treated as a subspecies, can employ both this reproductive strategy and lay eggs. **Range:** Endemic to Mount Mulanje in Malawi.

Pacific Skinks
Family Eugongylidae

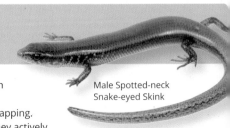

Male Spotted-neck
Snake-eyed Skink

A group of predominantly small-bodied skinks with small limbs. The eye may be unblinking or have a functional eyelid. The scales are smooth and overlapping.

These skinks are common in leaf litter, where they actively search for small invertebrates.

The family has a predominantly African and Australasian distribution. A total of 418 species in 37 genera are recognised, of which four species in two genera occur in the region.

SNAKE-EYED SKINKS   *Panaspis*

Small- to medium-bodied skinks with small, pentadactyle limbs. The eyes are small, with fixed, unblinking eyelids. There is a single, large transparent window in the lower eyelid and 2–4 supraoculars. Prefrontals are large and in contact or narrowly separated. The frontoparietals and interparietals are discrete. The ear openings are large. The limbs are reduced but fully developed. A pineal eye is present. The scales on the body are small and smooth. These active, diurnal skinks hunt in leaf litter and other debris. All species are oviparous, laying small clutches of hard-shelled eggs.

The genus is restricted to sub-Saharan Africa with seven species recognised at present, however genetic studies have indicated that numerous undescribed species exist within the *P. wahlbergii* species complex. Three of the seven described species have been recorded in the region, with additional undescribed species also occurring in the region.

Spotted-neck Snake-eyed Skink   *Panaspis maculicollis*

The male Spotted-neck Snake-eyed Skink has a series of pale spots on the neck.

The female lacks pale neck spots.

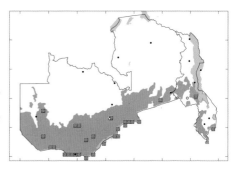

SVL 30–40mm; max. SVL 45mm
A small skink with reduced, pentadactyle limbs and unblinking eyes. Body and tail elongate, cylindrical. Tail slightly longer than body. Prefrontals widely separated; frontoparietals fused. 3–4 supraoculars. 5–6 supraciliaries;

6–7 supralabials, 4 anterior to subocular; 5–6 infralabials. Dorsals smooth and imbricate, in 22–26 rows at midbody. Palmar tubercles feebly conical. Dorsum olive-brown to golden-brown, sometimes with each scale dark-tipped. Tail may be paler; labials may have alternating light and dark banding. Side of neck dark with distinct white spots in males. Ventrum white, except in breeding males, which develop pinkish-orange chin and throat. **Habitat:** Arid and mesic savanna and woodland. **Behaviour:** An active, diurnal skink that frequents leaf litter but may also be found under logs, rocks and other suitable debris. Often seen foraging around grass tussocks, in leaf litter and at the base of bushes, disappearing into leaf litter when disturbed. **Prey:** Feeds predominantly on termites, although other invertebrates are also eaten. **Reproduction:** Female lays 1–5 eggs (7–8mm x 3–4mm) in mid-summer. Hatchlings measure about 40mm in TL. **Range:** Southern Zambia and southern Malawi, southwards to South Africa and eastwards to central Mozambique.

Seydel's Snake-eyed Skink *Panaspis seydeli*

Size unknown
A small skink with an elongate, cylindrical body and unblinking eyes. Limbs reduced in size, pentadactyle. Ear opening small, round. Prefrontals in broad contact; frontoparietals paired. 2–3 supraoculars. 4 supraciliaries; 4–5 supralabials anterior to subocular. 20–22 midbody scale rows. Plantar scales obtusely keeled. Dorsum brown; flanks darker, with darker longitudinal lines. White spots present on sides of head and neck. White lateral stripes present; supralabials and infralabials each have a dark spot. Ventrum greyish white. **Habitat:** Woodland and mesic savannas. **Behaviour:** Only known from four specimens. Frequents leaf litter.

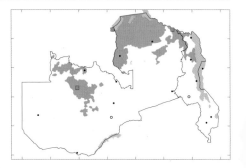

Prey: Invertebrates. **Reproduction:** Unknown. **Range:** Northern Zambia and the southern DRC. Possibly occurs in northern Malawi as well.

Wahlberg's Snake-eyed Skink *Panaspis wahlbergii*

SVL 40–50mm; max. SVL ♂ 64mm ♀ 50mm
A small skink with reduced, pentadactyle limbs and unblinking eyes. Body elongate, cylindrical; tail slightly longer than SVL. Prefrontals widely separated; frontoparietals fused. 3 supraoculars. 4–5 supraciliaries; 5–8 supralabials, 4–5 (rarely 3) anterior to subocular; 5–6 infralabials. Dorsals smooth and imbricate, in 22–29 rows at midbody. Coloration varied; uniformly dark brown to grey above, or with six longitudinal dark stripes. Median stripes close together, may fuse to form single median line extending onto base of tail. Pale dorsolateral stripe extends from nostril through eye and onto base of tail. Sides of head and flanks black to grey-black, fading out on tail. Pale spots and mottling

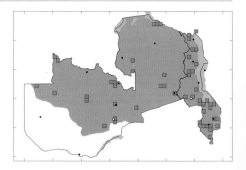

may be present anteriorly. Pale ventrolateral stripe, originating on supralabials, extends to at least shoulder but often to groin. Ventrum white to bluish white. Breeding males develop a reddish-pink throat and belly. **Taxonomic** note: *P. wahlbergii* as presently understood consists of a species complex and genetic studies indicate that a number of cryptic species exist within it. Some of these cryptic species are known to occur in the region, but their exact distributions and distinguishing morphological characteristics are not known at present. **Habitat:** Grassland, woodland and arid and mesic savannas at a wide range of elevations. **Behaviour:** Fairly common in leaf litter and under logs, rocks and other suitable debris. Very fast, often disappearing into leaf litter when pursued. **Prey and Predators:** Feeds on a variety of invertebrates, including spiders, termites and ants. Preyed on by various snakes and birds, including Brown-hooded Kingfishers. **Reproduction:** Female lays 2–6 eggs (7–9mm x 3–6mm) in mid-summer. Neonates are born after 40–50 days and measure 30–40mm in TL. **Range:** Widespread in Malawi and central and northern Zambia. Elsewhere to South Africa, the southern DRC and Tanzania.

Wahlberg's Snake-eyed Skink has a pale ventrolateral stripe.

The white ventrolateral stripe is reduced in females.

The throat and belly is reddish pink in breeding males.

FOUR- AND FIVE-TOED SKINKS *Leptosiaphos*

These medium-sized skinks usually have an elongate, slender body (robust in the Udzungwa Five-toed Skink [*L. rhomboidalis*]). The limbs are small with 3–5 digits. The lower eyelid is moveable and covered in transparent scales or a single transparent window. There are 4–5 supraoculars and the frontoparietals and interparietal are usually discrete. Supranasals are usually absent and the prefrontals are small and widely separated. There is no pineal eye. There are 5–6 supralabials, the 4th situated below the eye. The ear opening is small and the tympanum is not visible. The body scales are smooth, while the scales on the sides of the tail base are strongly keeled in males. The cloacal scale is not, or is only slightly, enlarged.

These skinks are fossorial, spending most of their time in leaf litter in forest and montane grassland. A total of 18 species are recognised, with a single species occurring in the region.

De Witte's Five-toed Skink   *Leptosiaphos dewittei*

Frank Willems

In the region, De Witte's Five-toed Skink has been recorded only in extreme north-western Zambia.

Luke Verburgt

The female is duller than the male.

SVL 50–60mm; max. SVL 67mm
A medium-sized skink with a slender, elongate body. Limbs reduced in size, pentadactyle; digits small. Lower eyelid moveable, covered by single transparent window. Body and tail cylindrical; tail about two-thirds of TL (when regenerated, only about half of TL and laterally compressed with series of transversely enlarged subcaudals). Prefrontals widely separated; frontoparietals discrete. 4 supraoculars. 6–7 (exceptionally 5 or 8) supraciliaries; 6 supralabials, 4th situated below the eye; 7 infralabials. Dorsals smooth, imbricate, in 22–24 rows at midbody. 11–14 lamellae beneath 4th toe. Males olive-brown to golden-brown above, becoming golden-yellow on flanks. Each scale may be dark-centred, forming a series of lines extending from nape to level of hind limbs. Darker speckling often present on labials. Throat pale yellowish white, becoming pale yellow on belly. Tail uniformly coral-red above, becoming slightly paler below. Females grey-brown with dark longitudinal stripes; tail bluish. **Habitat:** Forest, especially among the buttress roots of large trees. **Behaviour:** Diurnal, spends most of its time burrowing in leaf litter and top layer of soil. Also found under logs. **Prey and Predators:** Probably feeds on various invertebrates. Believed to be preyed on by wolf snakes (*Lycophidion*). **Reproduction:** Female lays 4 eggs (13–14mm x 11mm) in leaf litter, apparently in July. **Range:** From western Angola through the southern DRC to the Upemba National Park in the south-east. In the region, it has been recorded only in north-western Zambia.

Advanced Skinks
Family Lygosomidae

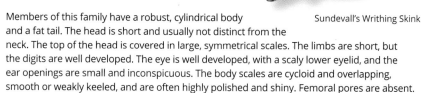

Sundevall's Writhing Skink

Members of this family have a robust, cylindrical body and a fat tail. The head is short and usually not distinct from the neck. The top of the head is covered in large, symmetrical scales. The limbs are short, but the digits are well developed. The eye is well developed, with a scaly lower eyelid, and the ear openings are small and inconspicuous. The body scales are cycloid and overlapping, smooth or weakly keeled, and are often highly polished and shiny. Femoral pores are absent.

Most African species frequent leaf litter or can be found under cover on sandy soils. They are occasionally active on the soil surface, especially after heavy rains. Most species are insectivorous. They are widespread in Africa and Australasia, occupying habitats that range from semi-desert to tropical forest.

54 species in six genera are recognised, of which two species in one genus occur in the region.

AFRICAN WRITHING SKINKS   *Mochlus*

This genus is endemic to Africa and contains small to large skinks with a robust, cylindrical body and a fat tail. The body is moderately to relatively elongate, the limbs are reduced in size and pentadactyle. A small but well-defined external ear opening is visible. The eyes are fully developed and the lower eyelid is scaly or has a transparent window. The snout is relatively pointed and the supranasals are usually in medial contact (occasionally partially or completely fused with the nasals). Prefrontals are not in medial contact but are occasionally fused with the frontonasal. There are two frontoparietals and the parietals are in medial contact behind the interparietal. The body scales are smooth, cycloid and overlapping, giving the body a shiny appearance. There are no enlarged precloacal scales.

These skinks are subterranean, spending most of their time in leaf litter or loose soil, often just below the surface. They may also be found under suitable cover on heavy clay soils and are active on the surface after heavy rains. They prey on small insects and their larvae. The female lays 2–6 soft-shelled eggs, although these may be retained in her body until the embryos complete their development.

The genus contains 19 species, two of which occur in the region.

KEY   Regional *Mochlus* species

1a 4–5 supralabials anterior to subocular; body predominantly red to red-brown with black crossbands . . . . *M. hinkeli* (p. 259)

 b 3 supralabials anterior to the subocular; body olive, grey, brown or black, sometimes with white or yellow blotching and streaking . . . . *M. sundevalli* (p. 260)

Eastern Red-flanked Writhing Skink   *Mochlus hinkeli*

SVL 110–120mm; max. SVL 145mm
A fairly large skink with a stout body and well-developed, pentadactyle limbs. Ear opening oval, with 2 scales projecting from anterior margin. Lower eyelid with 2 rows of scales. Nasal divided; nostril pierced in single postnasal. 4–5 supralabials anterior to subocular scale, which borders lip. Dorsal body scales tricarinate (rarely quadricarinate); lateral body and tail scales smooth; dorsal tail scales weakly tricarinate to smooth. 34–37 scale rows at midbody; ventrals in 63–75 transverse rows. Head and back red-brown to brown, with numerous transverse black bands that

are disrupted along dorsal midline (posterior 2 rows meet on dorsal midline) and continue onto flanks. Flanks red, often with black bands edged with white spots. White-edged black patches present on sides of neck anterior to forearm insertion. Sides of head red; infralabials red with a white dot, or white with dark spot. Alternating white and black bands on sides of tail. Ventrum white. Juveniles have the red coloration restricted to the head and the flanks are white with dark bars. Tail has alternating black-and-blue coloration, black bars being broadest. **Subspecies:** Two subspecies are recognised, with only the typical form entering the region. **Habitat:** Rainforest or forest edges. **Behaviour:** Poorly known. Believed to be terrestrial and diurnal, although some nocturnal and crepuscular activity has been recorded.

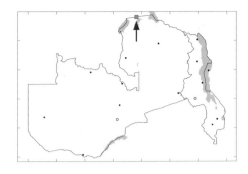

It digs its own holes, into which it flees at the first sign of danger. **Prey:** Beetles and arthropods, which are actively hunted in leaf litter. **Reproduction:** Female lays up to 12 eggs. **Range:** Central and East Africa, just entering extreme northern Zambia.

The Eastern Red-flanked Writhing Skink has diagnostic coloration.

Sundevall's Writhing Skink *Mochlus sundevalli*

SVL 100–120mm; max. SVL 140mm
A medium- to large-sized, robust writhing skink with a cylindrical body and tail. Lower eyelid scaly. Nasal divided; single supranasal (which may fuse with anterior nasal in northern Zambian populations); nostril usually

pierced between 3 scales. Prefrontals small, widely separated. 3 supralabials anterior to subocular. Ear opening small, deeply sunk. Limbs reduced in size, pentadactyle. Dorsals smooth throughout life, in 24–30 rows at midbody. Tail as long as (rarely slightly longer than) SVL. Coloration variable. Dorsum may be light brown to grey, each scale often with dark base, giving speckled appearance; flanks usually same colour. Dorsum may also be pale to dark brown, with varying degrees of irregularly scattered pale spots and streaks. In this colour form the flanks are yellow anteriorly fading to white posteriorly, with darker flecks. Tail more conspicuously spotted, these spots often extending onto ventral portion of tail as well. Intermediate colour forms common. Ventrum dirty white, sometimes with darker speckling. **Habitat:** Woodland and arid and mesic savannas. **Behaviour:** More common in leaf litter on sandy soils but also shelters under logs and rocks on heavy clay soils. Occasionally seen on the surface, especially after heavy rains. **Prey and Predators:** Preys on a variety of small invertebrates including beetles, ants and termites. Predators are varied, including small carnivores, raptors and a variety of snake species including the Black File Snake (*Gracililima nyassae*). **Reproduction:** Female lays 2–7 oval eggs (16–19mm x 9–11mm) in summer, often in a moribund termitarium. Neonates measure 50–55mm in TL. **Range:** Widespread from South Africa northward to Angola and eastward to Somalia.

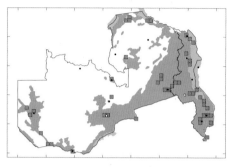

Some populations are dark above, with barred flanks.

Sundevall's Writhing Skink has short but fully formed limbs.

True Skinks
Family Mabuyidae

Female Rainbow Skink

True skinks are among the most commonly seen reptile species in the region. This large family consists of small to large lizards with a cylindrical body. Most species have well-developed pentadactyle limbs, except for some species that have reduced limbs and digits. The head is short and is indistinct or only barely distinct from the neck. The top of the head is covered in large scales. The parietals are in contact behind the interparietal and are bordered along their posterior edges by secondary temporals and transversely enlarged nuchals. The body scales are smooth to keeled (usually strongly carinated in species occurring in the region) and are cycloid and overlapping. The outer precloacal scales overlap the inner precloacal scales. The eyes are well developed. There is a transparent window (rarely scaly) in the lower eyelid, which is moveable. The ear openings are conspicuous and usually have lobes or scales projecting over the anterior margin. Each nostril is pierced in a single, discrete nasal. Femoral pores are absent, although at least one pair of enlarged precloacal scales is present in most species. The tail is usually longer than the SVL in the species occurring in the region.

Most species are diurnal and active. They occupy a wide range of habitats and elevations: from valleys to mountain tops and from deserts to forests. They may be terrestrial, arboreal or rupicolous, with the rock-living species often forming colonies, each with its own hierarchy. The rupicolous species are generally characterised by different colour patterns between the sexes, while the rest are usually various combinations of browns, greys and blacks. True skinks are active hunters, preying on a variety of insects and other invertebrates. Reproduction varies from oviparous to viviparous (sometimes even from place to place within a single species).

This family is widespread and is most common in sub-Saharan Africa and Australasia. Some 190 species are recognised in 22 genera, with new species continually being described. At present 16 species in two genera are known to occur in the region.

SERPENTIFORM SKINKS *Eumecia*

Large skinks with an elongate, cylindrical body and vestigial bud-like limbs that are not used for locomotion. The head is relatively short and the scales are smooth to faintly keeled.

These skinks are diurnal and use their serpentine body to 'swim' through the grass, their movements appearing snake-like. They prey on a variety of invertebrates, which are probably actively hunted. Beyond that, they are poorly known. Females are matrotrophic, ovulating small eggs and supplying the developing embryo with nutrients secreted from uterine cells.

There are two species in this genus, both of which occur in the region.

KEY Regional *Eumecia* species

1a 2–3 digits on each forelimb; hind limbs tridactyle . . . . *E. anchietae* (p. 263)
 b Forelimbs monodactyle; hind limbs didactyle . . . . *E. johnstoni* (p. 263)

Western Serpentiform Skink *Eumecia anchietae*

SVL 100–200mm; max. SVL 300mm

A long, serpentine skink with a relatively short head, pointed snout and cylindrical body. Tail as long as, or slightly longer than, SVL. Limbs greatly reduced in size; 2–3 minute digits on forelimbs; hind limbs tridactyle. Transparent window in lower eyelid. Ear opening large, oval, with two pointed lobes on anterior edge. Supranasals in contact behind rostral. 7 supralabials; 5th being the largest, entering orbit. 4 supraoculars; 5 supraciliaries. Dorsals smooth to faintly keeled, in 22–24 rows at midbody. Olive-brown above with white-edged dark spots. Light dorsal midline and narrower light paravertebral line present. Flanks grey-brown with vertical olive-brown bars. Large white-edged black cross on top of head. Ventrum greyish white. **Habitat:** Dense woodland, savanna, grassland, dambos and

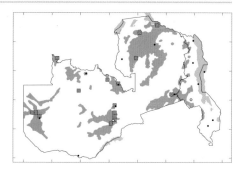

other marshy areas. **Behaviour:** Terrestrial and diurnal. 'Swims' through dense grass. **Prey:** A variety of invertebrates, including grasshoppers, mantids and beetles. **Reproduction:** Matrotrophic. Female gives birth to 6–9 young. **Range:** Central and northern Zambia, westwards to Angola and eastwards to Kenya and Tanzania.

The Western Serpentiform Skink has small limbs and resembles a snake.

Werner Conradie

Nyika Serpentiform Skink *Eumecia johnstoni*   Endemic

Max. SVL 263mm

A long, serpentine skink with a short head, moderately pointed snout and cylindrical body. Tail longer than body. Limbs greatly reduced; forelimbs half the size of hind limbs. Forelimbs monodactyle, digit minute; hind limbs didactyle. Transparent window in lower eyelid. Ear opening large, oval, with two lobes on anterior margin. Supranasals in contact behind rostral. 7 supralabials; 5th being the largest, entering orbit. Body scales smooth, in 22 rows at

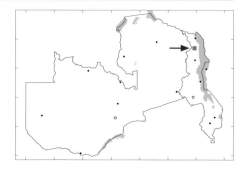

midbody. Dark olive above and greenish white below; series of small white-edged dark spots run from nostril to ear. **Habitat:** Presumably high-elevation grassland. Known only from the type specimen collected in 1896. **Behaviour:** Unknown. **Prey:** Unknown. **Reproduction:** Unknown. **Range:** Reportedly collected on the Nyika Plateau, although some authorities believe that it was collected in the region of Livingstonia at 1,800–2,100m a.s.l.

AQUATIC SKINKS   *Lubuya*

Large, robust skinks with an elongate body and a tail that is about twice as long as the SVL. The limbs are short and pentadactyle and the subdigital lamellae are keeled. The nostrils are situated on top of the snout and the nasals are elongate and in contact behind the rostral.

These skinks are usually encountered in moist locations in grassland or woodland. Semi-aquatic, they will readily take to water if disturbed. Their diet is varied but consists predominantly of invertebrates. Females are matrotrophic, ovulating small eggs and supplying the developing embryo with nutrients secreted from uterine cells.

This monotypic genus occurs at scattered localities ranging from central Angola to eastern Zambia, and just entering the southern DRC.

Iven's Skink   *Lubuya ivensii*

Iven's Skink is semi-aquatic and will dive into water when disturbed.

SVL 90–115mm; max. SVL ♂ 120mm ♀ 148mm
A large, robust skink with an elongate body and a long tail that is about twice the SVL. Single transparent window in lower eyelid, about half the diameter of eye. Nasals elongate, in contact behind rostral. Supranasals in contact behind nasals. Prefrontals usually in broad contact (rarely in narrow contact or separated). 3 supraoculars; 4–5 supraciliaries, 1st greatly enlarged and elongate. 4 (rarely 5) supralabials anterior to subocular; latter borders lip.

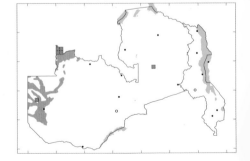

Nostrils situated on top of snout; postnasal elongate. 2–3 (rarely 4) triangular lobules on anterior border of ear opening. Scales on back tricarinate (rarely bicarinate), in 28–32 rows at midbody. Body dark brown with paler, relatively broad dorsal stripe and two narrower, pale dorsolateral stripes bordered on each side by thin black stripe. Flanks light brown. Clear white stripe originates behind rostral, passes over supralabials and extends to groin, bordered above and below by thin black stripes. Second pale ventrolateral stripe, which may also be black-bordered, arises just anterior to front limb insertion and extends onto tail. Ventrum plain white to dirty white. Posterior surfaces of hind limbs have a horizontal clear white stripe, bordered above and below by thin black stripes, which divides posterior surface in half. **Habitat:** Dambos, grassland and woodland, often in or near moist environments, as well as moist locations along forest margins. **Behaviour:** Semi aquatic. If disturbed, it will dive into the nearest water and swim submerged, using undulating body motions to propel itself, or take refuge in submerged vegetation. It shelters in holes that it digs in moist soil near the water. **Prey:** Beetles, grasshoppers, bugs, caterpillars, spiders and other invertebrates. Occasionally eats frogs. **Reproduction:** Viviparous, the female ovulates tiny eggs which are supplied with nutrients via a placenta. A female examined in October contained four well-developed embryos. **Range:** Widespread in central Angola, entering western and north-western Zambia and the adjacent south-western DRC. A potentially isolated population occurs in Lavushi Manda National Park in eastern Zambia.

TYPICAL SKINKS *Trachylepis*

Medium- to large-sized lizards with a cylindrical body and well-developed, pentadactyle limbs. The tail is at least as long as the SVL (and may be substantially longer in some species) and tapers to a point. The dorsal head scales are large and supranasals and prefrontals are present. The nostril is pierced in a single nasal. The lower eyelid is moveable, and has a single transparent scale. The ear opening is distinct and deeply sunk, usually with cones or scales projecting from the anterior margin. The body scales are cycloid and overlapping, the dorsals usually carinated (smooth in some species). The dorsals and ventrals are similar in shape and size and there is no clear distinction between the gulars and ventrals. There are no femoral or precloacal pores.

These diurnal lizards are very common and are among the most oft-seen reptiles. They occur in almost all habitats: from sea-level to mountain top and from desert to tropical forest. They may be terrestrial, arboreal or rupicolous. The rock-living species often show sexual dichromatism and form colonies of various sizes, each with its own hierarchy. Juveniles usually have a similar coloration to adults: often shades of grey, brown and black (although some species, particularly those that are rupicolous, may be quite brightly coloured). They prey on a variety of insects and other invertebrates, which are actively hunted. Reproduction is oviparous or viviparous, occasionally varying geographically within the same species.

This genus is widespread in Africa, Madagascar and parts of south-western Asia (a single species occurs on an island off the coast of Brazil). At present 78 species are recognised, 16 of which have been recorded in the region.

KEY Regional *Trachylepis* species

1a	Plantar scales smooth, non-spinose or tubercular	2
b	Plantar scales keeled, spinose	6
2a	Dorsals smooth or with 3 faint keels; tail 2.5–3 times SVL; ear opening diagonally elongate	*T. megalura* (p. 274)
b	Dorsals keeled (occasionally smooth in juveniles); tail less than 2.5 times SVL; ear opening round or vertically elongate	3

3a 38–52 midbody scale rows; rupicolous; males greenish, orange-brown or dark above with numerous pale spots, tail usually bright orange; females and juveniles dark with 3 pale longitudinal dorsal stripes, tail blue . . . . *T. margaritifer* (p. 273)
b 25–36 midbody scale rows; arboreal or terrestrial **4**

4a Dorsals weakly tricarinate (occasionally with 5 weak keels); prefrontals in contact . . . . *T. planifrons* (p. 275)
b Dorsals with 4–11 keels; prefrontals not (or rarely) in contact **5**

5a Slender build; 4 (occasionally 5) supraciliaries; dorsals usually with 7–9 (range 5–11) keels; tail more than twice SVL; back and flanks of similar coloration . . . . *T. boulengeri* (p. 267)
b Robust build; 5 (occasionally 6) supraciliaries; dorsals usually with 4–6 (range 4–11) keels; tail approximately 1.5 times SVL; flanks usually darker than back . . . . *T. maculilabris* (p. 272)

6a No lobes on anterior margin of ear opening; subocular not narrowed below, in contact with lip; restricted to Liuwa Plains . . . . *T. capensis* (p. 268)
b Lobes present on anterior margin of ear opening; subocular distinctly narrowed below or excluded from lip **7**

7a Dorsals on 4th toe in single row almost to base; skin very fragile **8**
b Dorsals on 4th toe in 2 rows on proximal phalanx; skin not very fragile **14**

8a Short triangular lobes on anterior border of ear opening; distinct white ventrolateral stripe **9**
b Well-developed lanceolate lobes on anterior margin of ear opening; no pale ventrolateral stripe **12**

9a Flanks usually darker than dorsum **10**
b Flanks usually same colour as dorsum **11**

10a Lower margin of 2nd loreal much longer than anterior margin; lobes on anterior margin of ear opening usually directed slightly downwards; occurs in western Zambia . . . . *T. damarana* (p. 269)
b Lower margin of 2nd loreal subequal to anterior margin; lobes on anterior margin of ear opening usually directed slightly upwards; occurs in Malawi and eastern Zambia . . . . *T. varia* (p. 279)

11a Pale vertebral stripe often present; no dark longitudinal stripes on back; widespread in central and northern Zambia . . . . *T. albopunctata* (p. 267)
b No pale vertebral stripe; dark longitudinal stripes often present on back; occurs in extreme north-eastern and north-western Zambia . . . . *T. 'Central Africa'* (p. 277)

12a 36–42 midbody scale rows; rupicolous; occurs in southern Malawi and southern Zambia . . . . *T. lacertiformis* (p. 271)
b 30–36 midbody scale rows; terrestrial; occurs in western Zambia or Lavushi Manda National Park and surrounding area **13**

13a Occurs in western Zambia . . . . *T. punctulata* (p. 276)
b Occurs in Lavushi Manda National Park and surrounding area . . . . *T. 'Lavushi Manda'* (p. 277)

14a Dorsals bicarinate, or with poorly developed 3rd median keel; 11–14 lamellae beneath 4th finger; flanks with large white spots; restricted to Nyika Plateau . . . . . . *T. hildae* (p. 270)
b Dorsals at least tricarinate; 14–20 lamellae beneath 4th finger; flanks usually without large white spots **15**

15a 2 rows of scales above window in lower eyelid; restricted to Mulanje and Dedza mountains . . . . *T. mlanjensis* (p. 275)
b 3–4 rows of scales above window in lower eyelid; widespread **16**

16a Dorsum red-brown with pair of well-defined pale dorsolateral stripes; no black lateral band . . . . *T. striata* (p. 278)
b Dorsum olive-brown to pale grey-brown; pale dorsolateral stripes absent or poorly defined; black lateral band extends from eye to shoulder, occasionally onto flank . . . . *T. wahlbergii* (p. 280)

White-spotted Variable Skink   *Trachylepis albopunctata*

The White-spotted Variable Skink closely resembles other variable skinks.

SVL 55–60mm; max. SVL 65mm

A small skink that is very similar to Common Variable Skink (*T. varia*) and Damara Variable Skink (*T. damarana*). Snout moderately pointed. Transparent window in lower eyelid, bordered above by 2 rows of scales. Supranasals usually separated (occasionally in contact); prefrontals usually separated (rarely in narrow contact). 4–6 supraciliaries. 8 supralabials, first 4–5 anterior to subocular. Ear opening oval, with 3–4 small, subtriangular scales projecting from anterior margin. 30–36 midbody scale rows. Dorsals and lamellae tricarinate. Plantar scales spiny; 19–20 lamellae beneath 4th toe. Skin fragile. Dorsum dark blackish brown, olive or red-brown, often with pale vertebral stripe. White flecks rarely present on dorsum; dark transverse bars or blotches often present on dorsum and flanks. Flanks same colour as dorsum, usually with distinct pale lateral stripe that extends from below eye to groin. Ventrum pale. **Taxonomic note:** This species was recently separated from

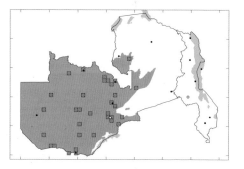

T. varia based on genetic and morphological evidence. **Habitat:** Savanna and woodland. **Behaviour:** An active, diurnal and predominantly terrestrial skink. **Prey:** A variety of insects, spiders and other invertebrates, which it seizes after a short dash from cover. **Reproduction:** Unknown. **Range:** Widespread in Angola and western, central and northern Zambia, just entering the southern DRC. Its exact distribution has not been determined.

Boulenger's Skink   *Trachylepis boulengeri*

SVL 60–80mm; max. SVL 93mm

A large, slender skink with a short head and a tail that is more than twice the SVL. Transparent window in lower eyelid, bordered above by single scale row. Prefrontals usually not in contact. 4–5 supraciliaries. 4 supralabials

anterior to subocular. 28–32 midbody scale rows; dorsals with 5–11 (usually 7–9) keels, number of keels increasing with age. Plantar scales and those beneath toes smooth; 12–16 lamellae beneath 4th finger; 15–20 lamellae beneath 4th toe. Dorsal and lateral coloration plain grey-brown, usually with a few scattered dark spots dorsally. Narrow dark line extends from just in front of eye to ear opening. Tail flecked with dark brown. Ventrum yellow. **Habitat:** Savanna, bamboo thickets, edges of wetlands and thatched roofs. Often sleeps above the water in submerged aquatic vegetation or in Lala Palm leaves near water. **Behaviour:** An unobtrusive, terrestrial skink that is usually seen foraging on logs and in leaf litter, often at the edges of wetlands. **Prey:** Insectivorous, feeding on insects and spiders. **Reproduction:** Oviparous, the female lays up to eight eggs (14mm x 10mm) in May. **Range:** From southern Tanzania south to central Mozambique, eastern

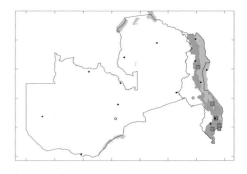

Zimbabwe and southern Malawi, although likely to occur throughout Malawi in suitable habitat along the western shore of Lake Malawi.

In the region, Boulenger's Skink occurs at low elevations in Malawi.

Cape Skink *Trachylepis capensis*

SVL 80–120mm; max. SVL 136mm
A large, robust skink with a very short head. Large transparent window in lower eyelid; bordered above by 2 scale rows. Prefrontals in contact or separated. Usually 5 (sometimes 4) supraciliaries. Usually 4 supralabials anterior to subocular; latter reaches lip. No enlarged, projecting scales on anterior margin of ear opening. Scales tricarinate dorsally, in 30–36 rows at midbody. Plantar scales weakly keeled; 10–15 keeled lamellae beneath 4th finger; 14–22

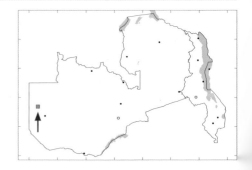

lamellae beneath 4th toe. Olive-brown to light greyish brown above, with broad pale vertebral stripe flanked by black streaks and pair of narrow pale dorsolateral stripes. Flanks mottled dark and light. Ventrum uniform dirty white to grey. **Habitat:** Open plains. **Behaviour:** Terrestrial, living in short burrows that it digs in soft sand at the base of a bush or stone. Also found under logs and rocks. **Prey:** Hunts large insects in open sandy areas and other clearings. Will gorge itself on termites when available. **Reproduction:** Viviparous. 5–18 young (60–75mm in TL) are born in late summer. **Range:** Largely restricted to South Africa, Botswana and southern Namibia, with relict populations in the eastern highlands of Zimbabwe and Liuwa Plains in Zambia.

The Cape Skink has a very stocky body and short head.

Damara Variable Skink   *Trachylepis damarana*

The Damara Variable Skink has an elongate second loreal.

SVL 55–65mm; max. SVL 68mm

A relatively small skink with a moderately pointed snout. Transparent window in lower eyelid, bordered above by 2 scale rows. Supranasals usually in contact (rarely separated); prefrontals usually separated (rarely in narrow contact). 4–6 supraciliaries. Lower margin of second loreal much longer than anterior margin. 8 supralabials, 4–5 anterior to subocular. Ear opening oval, with 2–4 short, subtriangular scales that project posteriorly, and usually slightly downwards, from anterior margin. Skin fragile. Dorsals and lamellae tricarinate. 30–36 midbody scale rows; 46–56 ventrals. Plantar scales spiny; 19–26 lamellae beneath 4th toe. Dorsum dark blackish brown, olive or red-brown, without pale vertebral stripe. Dark bars often present on body; white flecks often present dorsally. Flanks often darker, usually with well-defined white lateral stripe that runs from below eye to groin. Ventrum bluish white. **Taxonomic note:** This species was recently separated from *T. varia* on genetic and morphological grounds. **Habitat:** Savanna and bushveld. **Behaviour:** A common, active, diurnal skink often seen foraging on logs and rocks and on broken ground. Although predominantly terrestrial, it may be rupicolous in some areas. **Prey:** Insects, spiders and other invertebrates. **Reproduction:** Both oviparous and viviparous populations occur. The female lays 6–13 eggs in spring and summer. Hatchlings measure 40–50 mm in TL. **Range:** Its exact distribution

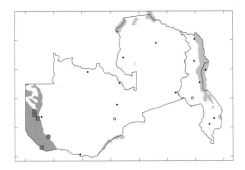

has not been determined. Known to occur from northern Namibia through southern Angola, western Zambia (west of the Zambezi River), Botswana, Zimbabwe and north-eastern South Africa, just entering western Mozambique.

Montane Three-striped Skink *Trachylepis hildae* Endemic

The Montane Three-striped Skink is endemic to the Nyika Plateau.

SVL 65–75mm; max. SVL 87mm
A small, robust skink with a short head and cylindrical body. Small transparent window in lower eyelid, bordered above by 2–3 scale rows. Nostril pierced at level of, or just posterior to, vertical suture between rostral and 1st supralabial. Prefrontals usually separated, occasionally in contact. Subocular only slightly narrowed below, excluded from lip by supralabials. 4–5 supraciliaries. 2–3 scales projecting from anterior border of ear opening. 38–40 midbody scale rows. Dorsals usually bicarinate, with faint median keel occasionally present. Plantar scales keeled and spinose;

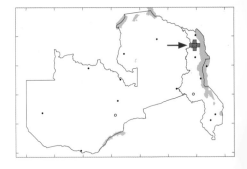

subdigital lamellae with single keel; 11–14 lamellae beneath 4th finger; 14–20 lamellae beneath 4th toe. Tail slightly longer than SVL. Light brown to olive-brown above, with numerous dark speckles and streaks that usually form two broad bands either side of vertebral midline. Three pale dorsal stripes usually distinguishable, which may be light green. Flanks and limbs light brown with numerous white spots. Chin and throat sometimes spotted or streaked with black, may be tinged with light green. Belly white. **Habitat:** Open montane grassland and rock outcrops in montane grassland. **Behaviour:** Often seen basking on exposed rocks or logs after rain. It shelters in rodent burrows or under logs and rocks. **Prey and Predators:** Preys on a range of invertebrates. Predators include birds of prey and African Pipits. **Reproduction:** Unknown. **Range:** Endemic to the Nyika Plateau in northern Malawi and adjacent Zambia.

Bronze Rock Skink   *Trachylepis lacertiformis*

SVL 45–50mm; max. SVL 54mm

A small, slender skink with a relatively sharp snout. Large transparent window in lower eyelid, bordered above by 2 scale rows. Prefrontals usually separated. 5 supraciliaries. 3–4 lance-shaped scales projecting from anterior margin of ear opening. Skin fragile, tears easily. 36–42 midbody scale rows; each dorsal with 5–7 keels. Plantar scales keeled and spinose. 14–17 lamellae beneath 4th finger; 17–23 keeled, spinose scales beneath 4th toe. Lamellae beneath 4th toe has multiple keels. Uniform grey-brown to bronze above, occasionally with few scattered dark spots dorsally. Indistinct pale dorsolateral band on tail. Scales on chin and throat dark-bordered, forming dark longitudinal streaks. Belly white. **Habitat:** Rock outcrops in moist savanna. Weathered outcrops that provide narrow fissures for shelter are particularly favoured. **Behaviour:** Most active in the early morning

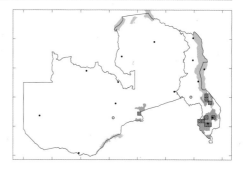

and late afternoon, when it can be seen running across boulders and foraging amongst accumulated leaves at the base of trees and boulders. **Prey:** A range of invertebrates. **Reproduction:** Viviparous. The female gives birth to 3–4 young in late summer. **Range:** Southern Zambia and southern Malawi, through central Mozambique and Zimbabwe, with an isolated population in south-western Angola.

Luke Verburg

The Bronze Rock Skink is uniform grey-brown to bronze above.

Speckle-lipped Skink   *Trachylepis maculilabris*

The eyelids and ear opening of the Speckle-lipped Skink are usually white, yellow or orange.

The sides of the head and neck are usually speckled.

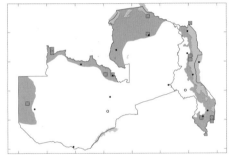

SVL 65–80mm; max. SVL ♂ 84mm ♀ 98mm
A large, relatively stout skink with a long tail and a pointed snout. Large transparent window in lower eyelid, bordered above by single row of scales. Prefrontals not in contact. 7 supralabials, 4 anterior to subocular. 5–6 supraciliaries. 29–36 midbody scale rows; dorsals with 4–11 (usually 4–6) keels. Plantar scales smooth; 13–16 lamellae beneath 4th finger; 14–20 smooth lamellae beneath 4th toe. Tail roughly 1.5 times SVL. Dorsum olive to grey-brown, with scattered dark flecks. Flanks darker than dorsum, with light and dark speckling, especially on side of head and neck. Eyelids and scales surrounding ear opening often bright yellow. Lip usually white with black speckling. Ventrum yellow to cream, occasionally with dark speckling, especially on throat. **Habitat:** Forest and moist savanna, especially at forest edges and in forest clearings. **Behaviour:** A predominantly arboreal skink found foraging on tree trunks, in hollow logs and in leaf litter. It regularly climbs onto thatched huts. **Prey:** Arthropods and snails. **Reproduction:** Female lays 6–11 eggs (10–14mm x 6–8mm) at any time during the year and may lay up to six clutches per year. **Range:** Southern Malawi and along the shore of Lake Malawi to northern Malawi, as well as northern and western Zambia. Probably occurs in the intervening regions as well. Elsewhere it occurs from West Africa through Central and East Africa to Angola and central Mozambique.

Rainbow Skink   *Trachylepis margaritifer*

The male Rainbow Skink is golden brown above, often with pale speckles.

The female has three pale bands and a blue tail.

SVL 90–110mm; max. SVL 120mm

A large skink with a short head and a moderately rounded snout. Small transparent window in lower eyelid, bordered above by two scale rows. Prefrontals in contact. 5 supraciliaries. 4–5 supralabials anterior to subocular; latter not narrowed below. Ear opening oval, with 2–5 anterior lobes. 38–52 midbody scale rows; dorsals tricarinate. Plantar scales tubercular; 12–19 lamellae beneath 4th finger; 17–26 smooth lamellae beneath 4th toe. Tail slightly longer than SVL. Adult males golden-brown above, each scale usually with a white spot; pale dorsal line often present; sides of neck black, may have narrow vertical white bars; tail bright orange to brown. Females and juveniles dark above, with three bluish-white dorsal stripes; tail bright blue. Ventrum white in both sexes. Chin and throat may be suffused with orange in breeding males. **Habitat:** Rock outcrops in moist savanna and at forest edges. **Behaviour:** An active, rupicolous skink. Males are territorial, conveying dominance by bright breeding colours. Rival males are fiercely engaged, but juvenile males are not attacked. **Prey:** Feeds on a variety of invertebrates, and even on smaller lizards. **Reproduction:** Sexual maturity is reached after 15–18 months. The female lays 6–10 eggs (17–21mm x 10–15mm) during summer. Incubation takes 61–62 days. Hatchlings measure 73–80mm in TL. **Range:** Widespread from south-eastern Kenya southwards through Malawi and eastern and southern Zambia to Zimbabwe, eastern Botswana and South Africa.

Long-tailed Skink   *Trachylepis megalura*

SVL 60–75mm; max. SVL 85mm

A large, fairly slim skink with a very long tail (2.5–3 times SVL) and a moderately rounded snout. Small transparent window in lower eyelid, bordered above by 2 scale rows. 4–5 supraciliaries. Usually 4 supralabials anterior to subocular. Prefrontals in contact. Ear opening lacks lobes. Dorsals smooth or faintly tricarinate; in 22–28 rows at midbody. Plantar scales smooth; 11–13 smooth lamellae beneath 4th finger; 16–19 smooth lamellae beneath 4th toe. Light orange-brown to grey-brown above. Flanks dark, usually bordered above by pale dorsolateral stripe. Narrow white lateral stripe usually present, running from upper lip to groin, sometimes extending onto tail and bordered below by narrow dark stripe. Dark-edged, pale vertebral stripe may also be present. Ventrum white to pale yellow. **Habitat:** Montane grassland and tall grass in savanna and woodland. **Behaviour:** Shy and secretive. 'Swims' through grass, aided by extremely

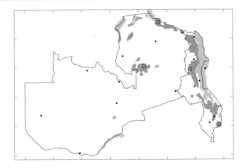

long tail. Forages beside clearings, from whence it dashes out to capture prey. **Prey:** Spiders, grasshoppers and other invertebrates. **Reproduction:** Female gives birth to 4–8 (up to 15) young. **Range:** Scattered localities in north-eastern Zambia and central and southern Malawi, although probably occurring in the intervening regions as well. Elsewhere it occurs from the eastern and southern DRC through central Mozambique and East Africa to Ethiopia.

The Long-tailed Skink occurs in montane grassland and tall grass in savanna and woodland.

Mulanje Skink   *Trachylepis mlanjensis*   Endemic

Gary Brown

The Mulanje Skink is endemic to the Dedza and Mulanje mountains.

SVL 60–70mm; max. SVL 78mm

A relatively small, montane skink. Prefrontals usually separated. 4–5 supraciliaries. Small transparent window in lower eyelid, bordered above by 2 scale rows. 5 (sometimes 6) supralabials anterior to subocular, which borders lip. 37–42 midbody scale rows; dorsals tricarinate. Plantar scales keeled, spinose; lamellae with single keel, numbering 15–17 beneath 4th finger and 17–22 beneath 4th toe. Back dark brown with numerous lighter flecks and three equally sized pale dorsal stripes. Median stripe divided on back of head; dorsal stripes merge on tail. Ventrum grey with white median patches. **Taxonomic note:** Preliminary genetic analyses suggest that this species may merely be a variant of the Eastern Striped Skink (*T. striata*). **Habitat:** Montane grassland and

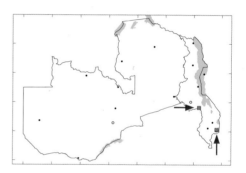

rock outcrops. **Behaviour:** An active, diurnal skink. **Prey:** Invertebrates. **Reproduction:** Female gives birth to 3–7 young in late winter, occasionally with a second breeding event in summer. **Range:** Endemic to Mulanje and Dedza mountains in southern Malawi.

Eastern Tree Skink   *Trachylepis planifrons*

SVL 65–80mm; max. SVL 116mm

A large, stout skink with a moderately pointed snout and a tail that is much longer than the SVL. Prefrontals in contact. 4 supralabials anterior to subocular. Ear opening lacks any projecting scales. 25–33 midbody scale rows; dorsals weakly tricarinate (5 weak keels occasionally present). Plantar scales smooth. 13 lamellae beneath 4th finger, 15 lamellae beneath 4th toe. Tail about twice as long as SVL. Back grey to brown with scattered pale spots dorsolaterally and dark

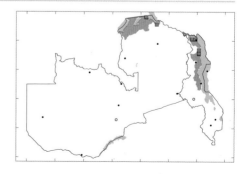

spots along dorsal midline. Broad, dark lateral band present, often fading out towards groin. Ventrum white to grey. **Habitat:** Mesic savanna or open woodland. **Behaviour:** Diurnal and arboreal. Usually seen on trees or in bushes. Its long tail enables it to climb on tree stems as well as fairly thin branches. It also climbs onto human-made structures, especially those built from natural materials. If pursued, it usually moves to the opposite side of the tree trunk and may jump if threatened. Usually descends to the ground only when moving between trees, but may occasionally hunt on the ground. **Prey:** Invertebrates. **Reproduction:** Oviparous. No further details known. **Range:** Northern Malawi and Zambia, eastwards to Kenya and Tanzania, northwards to Somalia and eastern Ethiopia and westwards to the south-eastern DRC.

Colin Tilbury

The Eastern Tree Skink resembles the Eastern Striped Skink, but has a longer tail.

Speckled Skink   *Trachylepis punctulata*

SVL 45–55mm; max. SVL 60mm

A small, terrestrial skink with a pointed snout. Transparent window in lower eyelid, bordered above by 2 scale rows. Prefrontals usually separated. 5 supraciliaries. 5 supralabials anterior to subocular. 2–4 lanceolate scales project from anterior border of ear opening. 30–36 midbody scale rows; each dorsal with 5–7 keels (3 in juveniles). Skin fragile, tears easily. Plantar scales spinose, keeled; 10–15 lamellae beneath 4th finger; 16–28 lamellae beneath 4th toe. Lamellae spinose, with multiple keels. Back usually uniform grey-brown with short white stripe running from below eye to ear opening. Paler vertebral, dorsolateral and lateral stripe may also be present, as may dark spots or streaks. Ventrum plain white. In breeding males, tail base and posterior surfaces of hind limbs become infused with red. **Habitat:** Arid and mesic savannas. **Behaviour:** Terrestrial and diurnal. Forages between grass tussocks in sandy regions. **Prey:** Insects and spiders. **Reproduction:** Female gives birth to 2–4 young in March. **Range:** Western Zambia. Elsewhere from south-western Angola through Namibia and Botswana to northern South Africa, north-western Zimbabwe and southern Mozambique.

Werner Conradie

A short pale stripe extends from the eye to the ear.

In the region, the Speckled Skink occurs in western Zambia, often on sandy soils.

Central African Variable Skink *Trachylepis* sp. 'Central Africa'

SVL 55–65mm; max. SVL 65mm

A relatively small skink with a moderately pointed snout. Transparent window in lower eyelid, bordered above by two scale rows. Supranasals in contact or separated; prefrontals usually separated (rarely in narrow contact); 5 (rarely 6) supraciliaries. 8 supralabials, 4–5 anterior to subocular. Ear opening oval with three short, subtriangular scales projecting from anterior border. Skin fragile. Dorsals tricarinate; 34–36 midbody scale rows; 52–61 ventrals. Plantar scales spiny; scales beneath toes keeled; 19–22 lamellae beneath 4th toe. Dorsum dark blackish brown, olive or red-brown, without pale vertebral stripe. Dark longitudinal stripes may be present, originating just behind head and fading out near base of tail. White spots often present dorsally; dark bars and blotches often present on body and flanks. No dark lateral band; well-defined pale lateral stripe usually extends from below eye to groin. Ventrum white. **Taxonomic note:** This species was recently separated from *T. varia*

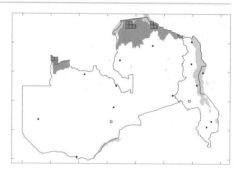

based on genetic and morphological evidence. It is yet to be formally named. **Habitat:** Savanna and woodland. **Behaviour:** A predominantly terrestrial, active diurnal skink often seen foraging on logs and rocks or between grass tussocks. **Prey:** Insects, spiders and other invertebrates. **Reproduction:** Probably viviparous. **Range:** Its exact range is yet to be determined. Known to occur in the Eastern DRC, entering extreme north-eastern and north-western Zambia.

Lavushi Manda Skink *Trachylepis* sp. 'Lavushi Manda'

Size unknown

A fairly small, terrestrial skink with a moderately pointed snout. Prefrontals separated. 5 supraciliaries and 5 supralabials

anterior to subocular. 3 prominent lanceolate scales project from anterior border of ear opening. Back reddish brown, plain or with scattered dark blotches posteriorly. Top and sides of head sometimes light grey, merging into reddish-brown back. Pale dorsolateral stripe faint to obvious, originating above ear opening and extending onto sides of tail, becoming more prominent posteriorly. Flanks same colour as dorsum or mottled in black. Dark sutures usually present on supralabials. Dark speckling on throat. Hind limbs may be covered in large, pale spots. Ventrum dirty white to light grey. **Taxonomic note:** This species is known only from photographs. Though clearly a distinct species, it is undescribed at present. The well-developed lanceolate scales on the anterior border of the ear opening indicate that it is a member of the *T. punctulata* species group. **Habitat:** Woodland. **Behaviour:** Predominantly terrestrial, clambering onto rocks and logs to forage and bask. **Prey:** Probably small invertebrates. **Reproduction:** Unknown. **Range:** Only recorded in Lavushi Manda National Park in eastern Zambia. May be more widespread in the region, possibly extending into southern DRC as well.

Frank Willems

The Lavushi Manda Skink is an undescribed species known only from Lavushi Manda.

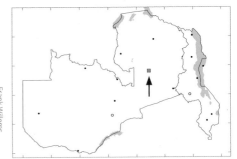

Eastern Striped Skink *Trachylepis striata*

The Eastern Striped Skink can be confused with Wahlberg's Striped Skink or the Eastern Tree Skink.

SVL 80–110mm; max. SVL 113mm

A medium-sized skink with a bluntly rounded snout and a tail that is only slightly longer than the body. Prefrontals usually separated. 5 supraciliaries. Transparent window in lower eyelid fairly small, bordered above by 3–4 scale rows. Subocular narrowed below, excluded from lip (rarely in contact with lip). Lobes present on anterior margin of ear opening. Dorsals have 3–7 keels; 34–42 midbody scale rows. Plantar scales spinose, keeled. Lamellae have single keel, number 15–19 beneath 4th finger and 15–25 beneath 4th toe. Back dark to red-brown with well-defined pair of pale to yellow dorsolateral stripes that run the length of the body. Pale spots occasionally present between dorsolateral stripes. Flanks dark, frequently with pale spots, which may also extend onto limbs. Grey, black or orange markings often present on chin and throat. Belly white. **Taxonomic note:** Preliminary genetic results suggest that Wahlberg's Striped Skink (*T. wahlbergii*) may be a colour variant of this species. **Habitat:** Savanna and human settlements in savanna. **Behaviour:** Predominantly arboreal. Common on both anthropogenic structures and trees. **Prey and Predators:** Feeds on a wide variety of insects and other invertebrates. Occasionally eats small vertebrates, such as Common Dwarf Gecko

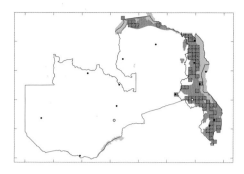

(*Lygodactylus capensis*) and Common Tropical House Gecko (*Hemidactylus mabouia*). Predators include Mozambique Spitting Cobra (*Naja mossambica*), Western Stripe-bellied Sand Snake (*Psammophis subtaeniatus*) and other sand snakes, Eastern Bark Snake (*Hemirhagerrhis nototaenia*), Common Wolf Snake (*Lycophidion capense*), Rufous-chested Sparrowhawk, Black-headed Heron, Brown-hooded Kingfisher and Pearl-spotted Owlet. **Reproduction:** Female gives birth to three clutches of 4–9 young throughout the year. Growth is relatively fast and sexual maturity is reached in 15–18 months. **Range:** Throughout East Africa, south to eastern South Africa and westwards through Malawi and north-eastern Zambia to the eastern DRC.

Common Variable Skink   *Trachylepis varia*

SVL 55–65mm; max. SVL 66mm

A relatively small skink with a moderately pointed snout. Supranasals may be in contact or separated. Prefrontals usually separated (rarely in narrow contact). 5 supraciliaries (rarely 3, 4 or 6). Transparent window in lower eyelid, bordered above by 2 scale rows. Anterior margin of 2nd loreal about same length as lower margin. 8 supralabials, 4–5 anterior to subocular. Ear opening oval, smaller than eye, with 2–4 short, usually upwards-directed subtriangular lobes on anterior margin. Skin fragile. Dorsals and lamellae tricarinate; 31–36 midbody scale rows; 46–55 ventrals. Plantar scales spiny; 18–23 keeled lamellae beneath 4th toe. Dorsum dark blackish brown, olive or red-brown above, sometimes with pale vertebral and dorsolateral stripes. Flanks darker, usually with well-defined

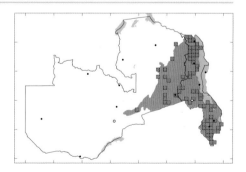

white lateral stripe running from below eye to groin. Ventrum bluish white. Individuals from Nyika Plateau are usually darker overall with a black throat. **Taxonomic note:** The widespread *T. varia* species complex was recently separated into eight species. **Habitat:** Savanna, montane

Inspection of the second loreal is necessary to distinguish the Common Variable Skink from other variable skinks.

grassland and bushveld. **Behaviour:** An active diurnal skink, often seen foraging on logs and rocks and in broken ground. Predominantly terrestrial, but rupicolous in rocky areas. Short-lived, males usually only survive for 15–16 months and females for 16–17 months. **Prey and Predators:** Feeds on insects, spiders and other invertebrates, which are seized after a short dash from cover. They are preyed on by a variety of snakes, including Common Wolf Snake (*Lycophidion c. capense*), sand snakes (*Psammophis*) and vine snakes (*Thelotornis*). **Reproduction:** Viviparous, the female gives birth to 2–4 young. Sexual maturity is reached in eight months. A female from the Nyika Plateau was found to contain four eggs (each measuring 7mm in diameter) in spring. **Range:** The exact distribution has not yet been determined. Known to occur from Mozambique (and possibly southern Tanzania), through Malawi and eastern and south-eastern Zambia to Zimbabwe and eastern South Africa.

Wahlberg's Striped Skink   *Trachylepis wahlbergii*

SVL 80–100mm; max. SVL 107mm
A relatively large, stout skink with a bluntly rounded head. Prefrontals usually not in contact. Usually 5 supraciliaries. Transparent window in lower eyelid relatively small, bordered above by 3–4 scale rows. Subocular may be in contact with lip or separated from it by supralabials; 5–6 supralabials anterior to subocular. 32–43 midbody scale rows; each dorsal with 3–7 keels. Plantar scales keeled, spiny; 15–18 lamellae beneath 4th finger; 17–24 lamellae beneath 4th toe; each lamella with single keel. Tail 1.5 times the length of the body. Grey-brown to olive-brown above and laterally, occasionally with five dark longitudinal lines dorsally. Broad, pale dorsolateral stripes may be distinct to ill defined, restricted to neck or completely absent. Median dorsals occasionally dark-edged,

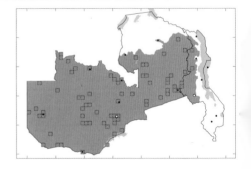

giving rise to faint longitudinal lines. Broad, dark lateral band extends from eye to anterior front limb insertion, rarely extending to groin. Ventrum and lower portions of flanks pale blue to white. Breeding males have orange or yellow throat and top of head becomes orange-brown.

Wahlberg's Striped Skink has a dark patch on the side of the neck.

Taxonomic note: Preliminary genetic results suggest that this species may merely be a colour variant of *T. striata*. **Habitat:** Dry woodland and savanna. Particularly common in mopane woodland. **Behaviour:** A predominantly arboreal skink that shelters in hollow tree trunks, under loose bark or under logs when disturbed. It is also found on buildings and isolated rock outcrops. **Prey:** A variety of invertebrates. **Reproduction:** Female gives birth to 3–6 live young throughout the year. **Range:** Southern Angola through Zambia and western Malawi, southwards through Namibia and Botswana to western South Africa.

Worm Lizards
Family Amphisbaenidae

These lizards are entirely fossorial and lack all traces of external limbs. This family contains both round-headed and spade-snouted forms, both of which occur in the region. The head is small and strongly ossified, an adaptation to their burrowing lifestyle. The head scales are large and reduced in number – in some genera a single large scale covers the head. This enlarged head scale often develops into a horizontal spade that may have a sharp horizontal edge to facilitate digging. The nasals face backwards, a further adaptation to their fossorial lifestyle. In two genera the nasals are situated on the ventral surface of the head. The lower jaw is set back, resulting in the small mouth being located ventrally. The eyes are situated beneath the head scales and are usually visible as dark spots, and external ear openings are absent. The body is covered in rings of rectangular, non-overlapping scales that are soft to the touch, but incredibly tough. The dorsals and ventrals are separated by a faint longitudinal groove. The skin is loose and is attached to each vertebra by only three sets of muscles. This allows the tubular body extensive movement within the skin 'sheath', enabling a ramming motion necessary for burrowing. The tail is usually very short and bluntly rounded. This adaptation helps to guide individuals when moving backwards in their tunnels. The body is usually pale pink to

Maurice's Worm Lizard

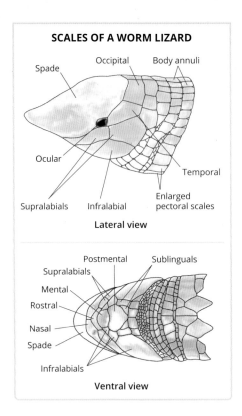

SCALES OF A WORM LIZARD

Spade · Occipital · Body annuli

Ocular

Temporal

Supralabials · Infralabial · Enlarged pectoral scales

Lateral view

Postmental · Sublinguals

Supralabials

Mental

Rostral

Nasal

Spade

Infralabials

Ventral view

purple, occasionally with alternating light and dark bands.

Worm lizards inhabit a wide range of habitats, from heavy clay soils to deep sands, but are most numerous in sandy areas. They are very rarely seen on the soil surface, usually emerging only after heavy rains. They use peristaltic locomotion to move in a straight line and can easily move forwards and backwards in their burrows and on soil. They prey on a variety of subterranean invertebrates, especially termites. Many species will wave their tail in the air as a defence mechanism, thus drawing attention away from the head. As a result many individuals have scarred or truncated tails. Many smaller species have an autotomy constriction site – a circular band where the tail is distinctly narrower than the rest of the tail and where the tail breaks if it has to be shed, though it cannot be regenerated. Most species are oviparous, with a few species apparently being viviparous.

By far the largest family of worm lizards, it occurs widely in Africa and South America. A total of 11 genera and 173 species are currently recognised, of which 11 species in three genera occur in the region.

DWARF WORM LIZARDS   *Zygaspis*

Relatively small, limbless fossorial lizards with a rounded head, distinct nasal shields, prefrontals and ocular scales. The body is relatively stout and of approximately equal girth throughout. The tail is rounded. Scale fusions are common in some species, resulting in a variable number of head scales.

They are most common in alluvial sands but some species also inhabit rocky regions. They are often found under suitable cover or in the top layer of soil. They are oviparous and insectivorous, preying predominantly on termites.

This genus occurs from the north-western DRC to northern South Africa and from Angola to Mozambique. Eight species are recognised. Three species enter the region.

KEY Regional *Zygaspis* species

1a 3rd supralabial bordered posteriorly by single large temporal (temporal fused with postsupralabials); body annuli dark anteriorly and white posteriorly, resulting in alternating light and dark bands . . . . *Z. nigra* (p. 283)

b 3rd supralabial bordered posteriorly by temporal and at least 1 postsupralabial; uniform purple-brown above, paler below 2

2a 3rd supralabial followed by 3 (2–4) temporals and 2 postsupralabials; short blind sulcus extends from anterior margin of preocular towards nostril . . . . . . *Z. kafuensis* (p. 283)

b 3rd supralabial followed by 1 or 2 (1–5) temporals and 1 postsupralabial; no sulcus extending from anterior margin of preocular towards nostril . . . . . . *Z. quadrifrons* (p. 284)

Kafue Dwarf Worm Lizard   *Zygaspis kafuensis*   Endemic

Joseph Zulu

The Kafue Dwarf Worm Lizard appears more robust than other dwarf worm lizards.

SVL 180–200mm; max. SVL 220mm
A large worm lizard with a rounded head, a fairly long tail and discrete preoculars. Short, blind-ending sulcus extends from anterior edge of preocular towards nostril. 4 parietals; 2 postoculars; 3 (occasionally 2 or 4) temporals. 3 supralabials; 2 postsupralabials; 3 infralabials, 2nd being the largest. 198–205 body annuli; 30–43 caudal annuli. 12–18 dorsal and 12–18 ventral segments per body annulus. Lateral sulci well defined. Four precloacal pores. Uniform purple-brown above; paler below, with anterior half of each ventral segment pigmented, posterior half white. **Habitat:** Miombo woodland. **Behaviour:** Biology is probably similar to the Kalahari Dwarf Worm

Lizard (*Z. quadrifrons*). **Prey:** Termites and other invertebrates. **Reproduction:** One female was found to contain four eggs (20mm x 5mm). **Range:** Restricted to central Zambia.

Black Dwarf Worm Lizard   *Zygaspis nigra*

SVL 200–250mm; max. SVL 280mm
A large, round-headed worm lizard with discrete preoculars that are not fused with the prefrontals. No parietals (1–3 parietals rarely present); 1 postocular; 1 large temporal. No postsupralabials; 3 infralabials, 2nd being by far the largest. 183–205 body annuli; 40–54 caudal annuli. 14–24 dorsal and 12–16 ventral

segments per body annulus. Lateral sulci well defined. Four precloacal pores. Predominantly black; back portion of each annulus usually pale, giving banded effect. Up to 90% of dorsals and 60% of ventrals black in adults, chin and throat remaining white. Scattered white subcaudals may be present. Juveniles paler, with brown coloration restricted to front half of annuli; ventrum white anteriorly, usually with some brown pigmentation on the leading edges of the subcaudals. **Habitat:** *Baikiaea* woodland on Kalahari sands, occasionally entering miombo woodland. **Behaviour:** Similar to the Kalahari Dwarf Worm Lizard (*Z. quadrifrons*). **Prey:** Various invertebrates. **Reproduction:**

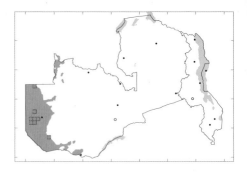

Unknown. **Range:** Eastern Angola, Zambia west of the Zambezi River and just entering northern Namibia in the Zambezi Region.

The Black Dwarf Worm Lizard has a characteristic finely banded pattern.

Kalahari Dwarf Worm Lizard   *Zygaspis quadrifrons*

This species is common and widespread.

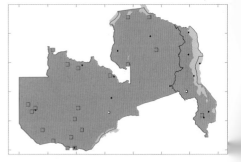

SVL 170–210mm; max. SVL 245mm
A medium-sized worm lizard with a rounded snout, fairly long tail and preoculars that are not

fused with prefrontals. Number of head scales varies due to fusions: usually 2 parietals (0–5); 2 postoculars (rarely 1 or 3–5); 1–2 temporals (rarely 3–5); 3 supralabials; 1–2 postsupralabials (rarely none or 3); 3 infralabials, 2nd much larger than 1st or 3rd. 195–245 body annuli; 32–50 caudal annuli. 12–23 dorsal and 10-22 ventral segments per body annulus. Lateral sulci well defined. Four precloacal pores. Light purple-brown dorsally, darkening towards tail, fading out on flanks. Ventrum white anteriorly, becoming darker towards tail; subcaudals as dark as dorsum. Pre- and postcloacal scales usually white. **Habitat:** Woodland and bushveld, where it is most common in deep Kalahari sands and rocky habitats on hills. **Behaviour:** May be locally common. Fossorial, it is often found under logs, rocks and other suitable cover, in decomposing logs, or under leaf litter in the top layer of soil. Individuals are occasionally seen on the surface after heavy rains. **Prey:** Feeds predominantly on ants and termites, although other invertebrates and their larvae are probably also eaten. **Reproduction:** Female lays 3–4 eggs (17–19mm x 3.5–4mm) in mid- to late summer. **Range:** Wide-ranging: from the southern DRC to the northern parts of South Africa and from south-western Angola to central Mozambique.

The Kalahari Dwarf Worm Lizard ranges from pink to brownish in colour.

SPADE-SNOUTED WORM LIZARDS *Monopeltis*

Medium-sized worm lizards that have 1–2 enlarged, bony scales covering the head. The head is strongly dorsoventrally flattened, with the anterior edge drawn into a sharp cutting edge. The nasals are separated by the rostral. The scales in the pectoral region are modified, with 4–6 enlarged pectoral scales being present laterally and ventrally. The body is cylindrical and the tail is smoothly rounded and covered with somewhat irregular segments. The tail may be shed in long-tailed species, but cannot be regenerated. Precloacal pores are always present in species in the region. Body annuli are counted from the 3rd infralabial, over the top of the enlarged pectorals and along the lower margin of the lateral sulcus (i.e. along the ventrum), as 'extra' dorsal half-annuli are often present.

Although these lizards may be locally common, they are rarely encountered owing to their fossorial habits. They are most frequently observed in sandy areas, but are capable of burrowing in hard soils as well, and thus occur in a variety of habitats (although they are absent from forests). They probably have stable burrow systems that are used for extended periods of time. Most specimens are exposed by earthmoving activities, road construction and ploughing, although individuals are occasionally found on or just beneath the soil surface sheltering under logs, rocks and any other suitable cover (even large animal carcasses). Individuals are occasionally forced to the surface after heavy rains have flooded their burrows or following attacks from predatory ants, at which stage they are vulnerable to attack from a variety of birds and mammals. Burrowing reptiles, especially quill-snouted snakes (*Xenocalamus*), frequently prey on them. These lizards prey exclusively on invertebrates and their larvae, displaying a preference for termites. Their reproductive biology is poorly known owing to their secretive nature, but at least one species gives birth to live young.

Twenty species are recognised, which occur throughout central and southern Africa. Four species occur in the region.

KEY Regional *Monopeltis* species

1a	Two enlarged head scales; body robust	*M. anchietae* (p. 286)
b	Single large head scale, sometimes with lateral sutures; body not robust	2
2a	Ocular very small or absent; postocular absent	*M. rhodesianus* (p. 288)
b	Ocular elongate; postocular present	3
3a	276–316 body annuli; ocular in contact with nasal or postnasal; 8–12 caudal annuli	*M. mauricei* (p. 287)
b	214–263 body annuli; ocular not in contact with nasal or postnasal; 6–8 caudal annuli	*M. zambezensis* (p. 288)

Anchieta's Worm Lizard   *Monopeltis anchietae*

Anchieta's Worm Lizard has a robust body.

SVL 200–300mm; max. SVL 345mm
A medium-sized, robust worm lizard with two enlarged head scales, with the anterior one being the larger of the two. Nasals short, not in contact with each other, oculars or lip. Ocular wedged laterally between two head scales, well separated from 2nd supralabial, usually bordered posteriorly by postocular. 3 supralabials, 3rd being the largest; 3 infralabials, 3rd being the largest. Preoculars absent. 4–6 elongate pectoral scales. 170–198 body annuli; 5–9 caudal annuli. 18–19 dorsal and 11–27 ventral segments per body annulus. Number of dorsal segments usually far greater than number of ventral segments. Lateral sulci well defined. 6–28 'extra' dorsal half-annuli. Two precloacal pores, rarely absent. Tail short, bluntly rounded, cannot be shed. Head and tail particularly well pigmented in reddish brown; intervening dorsal surface slightly paler, this coloration usually extending to below lateral sulcus. Ventrum white, except for tail, which may be pigmented below as well. **Habitat:** Deep sandy areas in moist savanna, entering mesic environments. **Behaviour:**

Fossorial. Adults usually occur deep in soil, although occasionally seen on the surface after heavy rains. Juveniles tend to be present closer to the surface and are occasionally found under logs and rocks. One adult was spotted under an elephant carcass where it was presumably feeding on the abundant termites. **Prey and Predators:** Termites, small beetles and butterfly larvae. Other invertebrates and their larvae are probably also eaten. It is preyed on by various fossorial snakes, including Common Purple-glossed Snake (*Amblyodipsas polylepis*), Bicoloured Quill-snouted Snake (*Xenocalamus bicolor*) and Bibron's Burrowing Asp (*Atractaspis bibronii*). **Reproduction:** Unknown. **Range:** Extreme

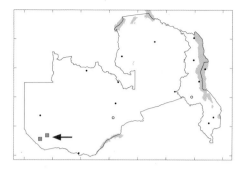

south-western Zambia, but possibly more widespread. Elsewhere it ranges from northern Botswana through northern Namibia and into southern Angola.

Maurice's Worm Lizard   *Monopeltis mauricei*

Maurice's Worm Lizard is long and slender.

Darren Pietersen

SVL 250–350mm; max. SVL 365mm

A medium-sized, slender worm lizard with a single enlarged head scale, although some juveniles may have the head scale transversely divided. Nasals elongate, in contact with ocular. Nasal may be divided into discrete nasal and postnasal. Nasals not in contact with one another or lip. Ocular elongate, very narrow, usually curved, in contact with both postnasal and 2nd supralabial anteriorly, and medial parietal pair posteriorly. Triangular subocular wedged between ocular and 3rd supralabial. 3 supralabials, 3rd being the largest; 3 infralabials,

3rd greatly enlarged. 6 elongate pectoral scales. 276–316 body annuli; 8–12 caudal annuli. 30–42 dorsal and 16–29 ventral segments per midbody annulus. Number of dorsal segments always greater than and usually nearly twice the number of ventral segments in a body annulus. Lateral sulci poorly developed. 'Extra' dorsal half-annuli usually lacking. Two precloacal pores. Tail short, smoothly rounded. Uniform pink to pinkish white, occasionally with scattered darker spots. **Habitat:** Prefers deep Kalahari sands. **Behaviour:** Fossorial. Rarely comes to the surface or found under surface cover. Occasionally found on the soil surface after heavy rain. **Prey and Predators:** Feeds on ants, termites, small beetles and butterfly larvae. Other invertebrates and their larvae are probably also eaten. Predators include quill-snouted snakes (*Xenocalamus*). **Reproduction:** Unknown. **Range:** South-western Zambia. Elsewhere it occurs through eastern Namibia, western and central Botswana and extreme north-western South Africa and north-eastern Zimbabwe, probably occurring in southern Angola as well.

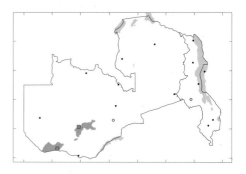

Zimbabwe Worm Lizard   *Monopeltis rhodesianus*

SVL 180–250mm; max. SVL 290mm

A medium-sized worm lizard with a single enlarged head scale that usually lacks lateral sutures. Nasals fairly short, well separated from oculars and one another. Nasals may be in broad contact with, or well separated from, lip. Ocular reduced in size or absent; when present, ocular does not contact 2nd supralabial and usually does not contact nasal. 2–3 supralabials, 3rd greatly enlarged, first 2 may be fused or the 1st fused with nasal; 3 infralabials, 3rd greatly enlarged, first 2 may be fused. 4–6 elongate pectoral scales. 172–223 body annuli; 5–9 caudal annuli. 13–26 dorsal and 10–22 ventral segments per body annulus. Number of dorsal and ventral segments per body annulus usually about equal. 6–16 (usually fewer than 10) dorsal half-annuli, majority being restricted to anterior portions of body. Two precloacal pores. Tail short, smoothly rounded. Lateral sulci well developed over posterior two-thirds of body, but absent or only weakly developed on anterior third. Body uniform pink-white; darker pigmentation largely restricted to dorsal regions of posterior half of body, becoming more pronounced on dorsal and ventral

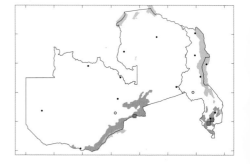

portions of tail. **Habitat:** Prefers deep sandy soils in mesic savanna. **Behaviour:** Fossorial. Rarely, individuals may be seen above ground following heavy rain and under logs or rocks. **Prey and Predators:** Poorly known. Probably feeds on a variety of invertebrates. Predators include quill-snouted snakes (*Xenocalamus*), jackals, hornbills and birds of prey. **Reproduction:** Unknown. **Range:** Extreme southern Zambia and southern Malawi. Elsewhere it occurs in eastern and northern Zimbabwe, with isolated records from central Mozambique, although these populations are probably continuous.

Zambezi Worm Lizard   *Monopeltis zambezensis*

SVL 150–200mm; max. SVL 275mm

A very small, slender worm lizard with a single large head scale that may have short lateral sutures in juveniles. Nasals short, not in contact with oculars, lip or each other. Ocular elongate, in contact with 2nd supralabial anteriorly and bordered posteriorly

by parietals. Slight lateral indentation to accommodate ocular; no preoculars. Triangular postocular usually present. 3 supralabials, 3rd by far the largest; 3 infralabials, 3rd being the largest. 6 enlarged pectoral scales. 214–263 body annuli; 6–8 caudal annuli. 15–26 dorsal and 14–22 ventral segments per body annulus.

Usually slightly more dorsal than ventral segments in any given annulus. Lateral sulci well developed. Tail short, smoothly rounded. Two precloacal pores. Pinkish white, with diffuse speckling restricted to the posterior two-thirds of the back, extending to below the lateral sulci. This speckling often restricted along the dorsal midline, resulting in mid-dorsal stripe. Tail often darker above and below. **Habitat:** Mopane woodland, usually on red soils. **Behaviour:** Fossorial, often inhabiting comparatively dry regions. **Prey:** Probably similar to other worm lizards. **Reproduction:** Unknown. **Range:** Only recorded from the

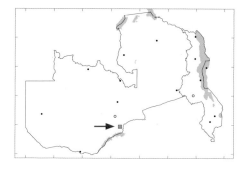

vicinity of Lake Kariba in extreme southern Zambia and extreme northern Zimbabwe.

BLUNT-TAILED WORM LIZARDS *Dalophia*

Medium- to large-bodied worm lizards with usually only a single, very large bony scale covering the head. The head scale has a sharp anterior edge, which is used for digging. The nasals are nearly always in contact with each other anteriorly, sometimes narrowly separated. There are 4–6 enlarged, smooth scales in the pectoral region. The body is long, cylindrical and relatively slender. The tail is relatively long and always ends abruptly in a single large, calloused pad. Precloacal pores are absent.

These lizards are entirely fossorial, being very rarely encountered on or near the soil surface. Their biology is poorly known, but they appear to occur deeper in the soil than do spade-snouted worm lizards (*Monopeltis*), or may occur in lower densities. Their reproductive biology is poorly known, but at least two species lay eggs. They prey more readily on beetles and their larvae than do spade-snouted worm lizards, although termites and other invertebrates are also regularly eaten. The blunt tail pad is believed to be an anti-predatory mechanism, effectively blocking access to the rest of the body when in a burrow.

Seven species are recognised, all of which are restricted to central and southern Africa. Four species enter the region.

KEY Regional *Dalophia* species

1a	No constricted caudal autotomy site	**2**
b	Constricted caudal autotomy site present	**3**
2a	19–33 caudal annuli; dorsal caudal scales usually do not form 'herringbone' pattern	**D. pistillum** (p. 292)
b	33–42 caudal annuli; dorsal caudal scales form 'herringbone' pattern	**D. longicauda** (p. 291)
3a	20–28 caudal annuli	**D. angolensis** (p. 289)
b	30–45 caudal annuli	**D. ellenbergeri** (p. 290)

Angolan Worm Lizard *Dalophia angolensis*

SVL 300–350mm; max. SVL 362mm
A slender, medium-sized worm lizard with a single fused head scale that usually has lateral sutures. Preoculars absent. Ocular in contact dorsally and anteriorly with enlarged head scale, bordered below by 2nd and narrowly by 3rd supralabials. Nasals elongate, in narrow contact medially and with oculars posteriorly, not contacting lip. 3 supralabials, 2nd being the longest, 3rd being the largest; 3 infralabials,

first 2 small, 3rd greatly enlarged. 6 elongate pectoral scales. 302–324 body annuli; few 'extra' dorsal half-annuli. 16–24 dorsal and 12–18 ventral segments per body annulus. The number of dorsal segments is greater than the number of ventral segments per annulus. Lateral sulci well developed. No precloacal pores. Tail long, ending in a slightly projecting, unsegmented calloused pad. 20–28 caudal annuli; autotomy constriction site on 6th or 7th caudal annulus. Body unpigmented, uniformly pinkish white. **Habitat:** Kalahari sands in mesic savanna. **Behaviour:** Fossorial and rarely seen. **Prey and Predators:** Probably preys on invertebrates. The first Zambian specimen was found in the stomach of an Elongate

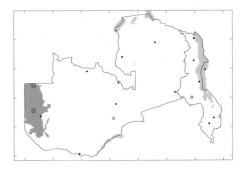

Quill-snouted Snake (*Xenocalamus mechowii*). **Reproduction:** Unknown. **Range:** Upper Zambezi River and Liuwa Plains National Park. It is also found in Angola.

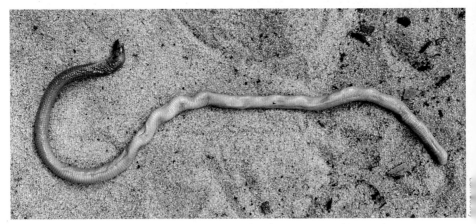

In the region, the Angolan Worm Lizard is restricted to sandy soils in western Zambia.

Barotse Worm Lizard   *Dalophia ellenbergeri*

SVL 350–400mm; max. SVL 420mm
A fairly large, slender worm lizard with a single large head scale that has lateral sutures. Preoculars and postoculars absent. Nasals elongate, in contact with each other anteriorly (rarely narrowly separated) and with oculars posteriorly, not in contact with lip. 3 supralabials, 2nd longest; 3 infralabials, 3rd greatly enlarged. 6 enlarged pectoral scales. Lateral sulci well developed; few or no 'extra' dorsal half-annuli. 312–344 body annuli; 14–21 dorsal and 11–14 ventral segments per body annulus. Precloacal pores absent. Tail long (30–43 caudal annuli), ends abruptly in flat,

calloused pad. Autotomy constriction site on 6th, 7th or 8th caudal annulus. Body uniformly pinkish white. **Habitat:** Deep Kalahari sands in mesic savanna, especially near large, permanent rivers. **Behaviour:** Fossorial, rarely seen on soil surface. May be more common in vicinity of large termitaria. **Prey and Predators:** Probably feeds on termites and other invertebrates. Preyed on by Rufous Beaked Snake (*Rhamphiophis rostratus*). **Reproduction:** Female lays two eggs (30mm x 5mm). **Range:** Occurs widely in western Zambia, with a single record from eastern Angola, although these populations are probably continuous.

The head is covered with a single bony scale.

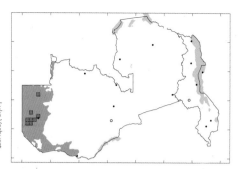

Like all worm lizards in this genus, the tail of the Barotse Worm Lizard ends in a hard, blunt pad.

Long-tailed Worm Lizard   *Dalophia longicauda*

SVL 350–450mm; max. SVL 520mm

A medium- to large-sized worm lizard with a single large scale (with lateral sutures) covering the head. Nasals elongate, in contact anteriorly, narrowly separated from lip. Nasals may be divided posteriorly (forming discrete nasal and postnasal), in contact with oculars. Preoculars absent. Ocular scale situated in lateral notch in large head scale. Postocular elongate, triangular, in contact with 3rd supralabial. 3 supralabials, 2nd being the longest; 3 infralabials, 3rd greatly enlarged. 6 enlarged pectoral scales. 307–338 body annuli; 33–42 caudal annuli.18–24 dorsal and 12–16 ventral segments per body annulus. Few 'extra' dorsal half annuli. Precloacal pores absent. Tail long, ending abruptly in hard, calloused pad. Dorsal caudal annuli directed obliquely backwards, forming 'herringbone' pattern. Caudal autotomy site absent. Body pinkish white, sometimes with

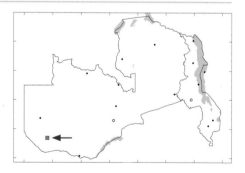

grey speckling on dorsal and lateral surfaces (to the level of lateral sulci) posteriorly, which may be concentrated around annular edges. Tail may be uniformly dark. **Habitat:** Moist alluvial sands along permanent rivers. **Behaviour:** Fossorial. Only rarely seen on the soil surface, usually after heavy rains. **Prey and Predators:** Feeds on ants and beetle larvae and probably other invertebrates. Preyed on by quill-snouted snakes (*Xenocalamus*). **Reproduction:** Unknown. **Range:** Western Zambia, west of the Zambezi River. Elsewhere it occurs in extreme north-eastern Namibia, extreme northern Botswana and extreme north-western Zimbabwe.

Errol Pietersen

The Long-tailed Worm Lizard has a diagnostic 'herringbone' pattern on the tail.

Pestle-tailed Worm Lizard   *Dalophia pistillum*

SVL 350–500mm; max. SVL 560mm
A medium- to large-sized worm lizard with a single large head scale that has lateral sutures. Nasals in contact anteriorly, narrowly separated from lip, in contact with oculars posteriorly. Nasals may be asymmetrically divided into discrete nasal and postnasal. Preoculars absent. Postocular elongate, triangular, in contact with 3rd supralabial. 3 supralabials, 2nd being the longest; 3 infralabials, 3rd greatly enlarged. 6 enlarged pectoral scales. 280–352 body annuli; 19–33 caudal annuli. 17–30 dorsal and 12–17 ventral segments per body annulus. Few or no 'extra' dorsal half-annuli. Caudal autotomy site absent. Precloacal pores absent. Annuli on tail often form backward-pointing chevron pattern. Anterior portions of body pale pinkish white; posterior portions light grey dorsally, extending to just below the lateral sulci (rarely more ventrally); tail may be uniformly grey. Ventrum plain white. **Habitat:** Most prevalent in deep Kalahari sands, but also found in harder soils. **Behaviour:** Fossorial, possibly preferring deeper depths than spade-snouted

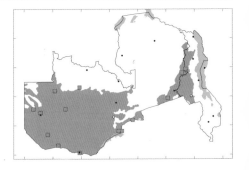

worm lizards (*Monopeltis*). Rarely seen on the soil surface. **Prey and Predators:** Feeds on beetles (adults and larvae), ants and termites, although other invertebrates are probably also eaten. Predators include quill-snouted snakes (*Xenocalamus*), Honey Badgers and Striped Polecats. **Reproduction:** Female lays four eggs (26–35mm x 8–10mm) in spring. **Range:** Widespread in western, southern and eastern Zambia. Elsewhere it occurs through Angola, Namibia, northern South Africa, Botswana and northern Zimbabwe to central Mozambique.

Old World Lizards or Lacertids
Family Lacertidae

This family is comprised of small to medium-sized lizards with a slender body, long tail and well-developed limbs. The large scales on top of the head usually have osteoderms and are often interspersed with small scales or granules. An external ear opening is present, occasionally completely covered by a fold of skin or

Holub's Scrub Lizard

obscured by lobes projecting from the anterior border. The body scales range from small granules to moderately sized scales. The ventrals are large, quadrangular in shape, and are arranged in regular longitudinal rows. The toes are long, each with a sharp claw. Femoral pores are usually present. The tail is usually long and quite thin, with numerous whorls of keeled scales. It is easily shed but can be readily regenerated. These lizards are often brightly coloured, especially breeding males, and juveniles often have a very different coloration from adults.

These active, diurnal lizards occupy a wide range of habitats: from desert to forest and from sea level to mountain tops. Most are terrestrial, although some species are rupicolous or arboreal. They prey on a variety of invertebrate species, including scorpions. Many terrestrial species dig a short burrow at the base of a grass tussock or under a log or stone, while the rupicolous species shelter in rock crevices and the arboreal species in tree hollows or under loose bark. Most species are oviparous, with some European species giving birth to live young.

This family occurs in Africa, Europe and Asia. There are 321 species in 42 genera, of which 10 species in six genera occur in the region.

SCRUB LIZARDS *Nucras*

Small lizards with a rounded snout, cylindrical body and very long tail. The nostril is pierced between 2–3 nasals and is well separated from the supralabials. The lower eyelid is scaly and the subocular borders the lip. A distinct collar is present. Dorsals are small, smooth and juxtaposed. The subdigital lamellae are smooth and there are no lateral fringes on the toes. Femoral pores are present.

These common terrestrial lizards occur widely in tropical and southern Africa, being most prevalent on sandy soils in arid and mesic savanna. They are most active in the early mornings and late afternoons, but are generally secretive unless feeding at a termite alate eruption. They are active foragers, feeding on a variety of invertebrate species. Some species specialise on scorpions. They may store fat in the long tail. Some species are brightly coloured and many have brightly coloured tails, which is believed to be an anti-predatory strategy as the tail attracts attention away from the head. They are preyed on by various raptors and snakes. All species are oviparous, the female laying 2–9 eggs in summer.

A total of 12 species are recognised, three of which occur in the region.

KEY Regional *Nucras* species

1a Pineal eye present; usually 5–8 enlarged scales beneath forearm . . . . **N. holubi** (p. 295)
 b Pineal eye absent; usually 7–11 enlarged scales beneath forearm 2

2a No granules separating supraoculars from supraciliaries; 16–24 lamellae
   beneath 4th toe; pale bars on side of head . . . . **N. boulengeri** (p. 294)
 b 2–9 granules separating supraoculars from supraciliaries; 20–33 lamellae
   beneath 4th toe; no pale bars on side of head . . . . **N. ornata** (p. 296)

Boulenger's Scrub Lizard *Nucras boulengeri*

In the region, Boulenger's Scrub Lizard occurs only in north-eastern Zambia.

SVL 50–60mm; max. SVL 65mm

A medium-sized lacertid with a blunt snout, well-developed collar and scaly lower eyelid. Nostril pierced between 3 nasals, latter not enlarged (or only slightly so). Lower nasal excluded from rostral. 2 prefrontals; 4–6 supraoculars. Tympanic scale large, curved; temple covered with large granules. 4 supraciliaries and 4 supralabials anterior to subocular; latter borders lip. Collar consists of 9 (rarely 6) scales. 16–24 lamellae beneath 4th toe. Dorsals small, juxtaposed, keeled, in 40–56 rows at midbody. Ventrals in 6–8 longitudinal and 27–31 transverse rows; 2 enlarged precloacal scales. Foot as long as, or slightly longer than, head. 11–13 femoral pores on thigh. Tail about twice the SVL, usually more than twice the SVL in females. Back brown, with scattered, indistinct dark spots that may be absent or fuse into dark blotches. Head, limbs and upper surface of tail

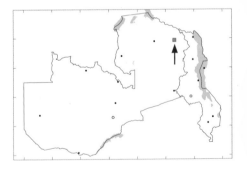

red. Narrow yellow dorsal stripe, which may be bordered with black, extends from top of head to base of tail. Pair of pale yellow dorsolateral stripes extend from back of head to base of tail. 1–2 rows of yellow dots and dashes present on flanks. White or yellowish-white lateral line extends from lips through ear opening to hind limb, often breaking up into discrete spots

Stephen Spawls

posteriorly. Dorsal surfaces of males become spotted with yellow and white during breeding. Ventrum immaculate. Posterior portion of tail rufous in males. **Subspecies:** Two subspecies are recognised. Only *N. b. kilosae* enters the region. It occurs in extreme north-eastern Zambia and eastern and central Tanzania. **Habitat:** Mesic savanna. **Behaviour:** Active and diurnal. Individuals take refuge in a hole dug at the base of a bush. **Prey:** A variety of invertebrates, including crickets and bugs. **Reproduction:** Female lays up to four eggs (about 5mm). **Range:** North-eastern Zambia, through Tanzania to Kenya.

Holub's Scrub Lizard   *Nucras holubi*

Holub's Scrub Lizard has pale spots, not bars, on the flanks.

Luke Kemp

SVL 55–65mm; max. SVL 73mm
A medium-sized lacertid with an elongate head and a cylindrical body and tail. 3 nasals; nostril pierced at the posterior edge of anterior nasal. Anterior nasals in narrow to broad contact behind rostral. Pineal eye present on crown of head. 4 supraoculars; 6–8 supraciliaries. Supraoculars separated from supraciliaries by series of 2–9 (usually 3–7) granules. Lower eyelid scaly. 2–12 (usually 5–8) enlarged scales beneath forearm. Dorsals granular, flattened, in 41–65 rows at midbody. Ventrals in 8 longitudinal and 26–34 transverse rows. 10–21 femoral pores on thigh. Tail more than twice the SVL. Back grey to reddish brown, becoming darker dorsolaterally, with a series of three pale longitudinal stripes extending from head to base of tail. Flanks black, with two rows of yellow or white spots, lower row of spots merging to form pale ventrolateral line.

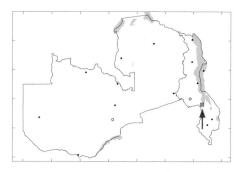

Ventrolateral region grey, abutting with white to creamy white ventrals. Tail reddish brown to coral-red. Juveniles more distinctly striped; white flank spots and blotches do not merge into stripe. **Habitat:** Frequents broken, rocky ground in mesic savanna. **Behaviour:** Active, diurnal and terrestrial, often seen foraging between grass tussocks or the base of bushes.

Takes refuge in holes dug in the ground or under rocks and other suitable debris. **Prey:** Predominantly small beetles and termites, although other small insects are also eaten.

Reproduction: Oviparous, the female lays 1–7 eggs in mid-summer. Hatchlings measure 50–60mm in TL. **Range:** From southern Malawi through Zimbabwe to South Africa.

Ornate Scrub Lizard   *Nucras ornata*

The Ornate Scrub Lizard has pale bars on the side of the head and flanks.

SVL 60–85mm; max. SVL 114mm
A large, robust scrub lizard with a cylindrical body and tail and a blunt snout. Nostril pierced in suture between 3 nasals. Anterior nasals in narrow contact behind rostral. 2 prefrontals, in broad contact; 4 supraoculars; 6 supraciliaries. Supraoculars separated from supraciliaries by series of 2–8 granules (usually 2–5, rarely absent). Pineal eye absent. Lower eyelid scaly. 7–9 supralabials (4–5 anterior to subocular, which borders lip); 6–7 infralabials. Collar well developed. Dorsals granular and juxtaposed, in 39–60 rows at midbody. Ventrals broad, imbricate, in 6–8 longitudinal and 25–34 transverse rows. 5–13 (usually 7–11) enlarged scales beneath forearm. 11–19 femoral pores on thigh. Foot longer than head. Tail more than twice the SVL. Brown above with numerous irregular black spots and blotches. Two thin pale dorsolateral stripes, occasionally bordered by black stripes that may be interrupted, originate behind head and extend over most of body, fading posteriorly. Top of tail heavily marked

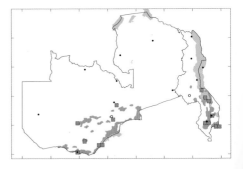

Juveniles have a coral-red tail.

with black. Flanks brown, with numerous vertical black-edged white bars, becoming spotted ventrolaterally. Continuous black-edged, white vertical stripes on sides of neck. Ventrum white. Tail brown above, white below. Juveniles black above and laterally, with narrow white median and dorsolateral stripes extending from back of head to base of tail; sides of neck have vertical white bars that are narrowest dorsally, widening ventrally; flanks have irregular series of white spots which may fuse with white ventrum or fuse with each other to form diffuse lateral stripe. Tail coral-red. **Habitat:** Montane grassland and mesic savanna, most often on sandy soils. **Behaviour:** Diurnal and terrestrial. Often seen foraging amongst grass tussocks and in leaf litter. Digs holes at the base of a bush, into which it retreats if threatened. Often found sheltering under rocks on rocky hillsides. **Prey and Predators:** Preys on centipedes, grasshoppers and other large insects. It is eaten by various snake species, including Olive Grass Snake (*Psammophis mossambicus*) and other grass snake species and Rufous Beaked Snake (*Rhamphiophis rostratus*), which catch it while it is active during the day. Bibron's Burrowing Asp (*Atractaspis bibronii*), Common Purple-glossed Snake (*Amblyodipsas polylepis*) and Common Wolf Snake (*Lycophidion capense capense*) capture it while it is sleeping in its burrow at night. **Reproduction:** Female lays 5–7 eggs in mid-summer. **Range:** From south-eastern Tanzania through southern Malawi and southern Zambia to Mozambique and South Africa.

LONG-TAILED LIZARDS *Latastia*

Medium- to large-sized terrestrial lizards with very long tails. The nostril is pierced between 3–5 nasals and in contact with, or very narrowly separated from, the 1st supralabial. The dorsals are small, close-fitting and usually uniform in size. The collar is well developed and the subdigital lamellae are keeled.

These diurnal lizards are capable of high speeds and are very difficult to catch. They prey on small invertebrates and are believed to be oviparous.

They are endemic to Africa, occurring from Senegal to Somalia and southwards to Zambia and Malawi. Ten species are recognised, of which a single species has been recorded in the region.

Johnston's Long-tailed Lizard *Latastia johnstonii*

SVL 45–55mm; max. SVL 60mm
A slender, medium-sized lizard with a tail that is more than twice the SVL. Head small, fairly elongate; snout pointed. Limbs relatively short; toes long. Nostril pierced between 3–4 nasals and 1st supralabial (sometimes separated from latter by narrow ridge). 2 large supraoculars bordered anteriorly and posteriorly by few small scales, separated from 5–7 supraciliaries by series of small granules. Tympanic scale narrow, crescent-shaped. Subocular borders lip; 4–6 supralabials anterior to subocular. Collar well developed. Dorsals small, weakly to strongly keeled, in 39–52 rows at midbody. Ventrals smooth, in 6 longitudinal and 24–25 transverse rows, with the two median scale rows being narrowest. 2 large precloacal scales present, the posterior scale sometimes divided. 11–17 femoral pores on thigh. Breeding males reddish brown above, this coloration fading

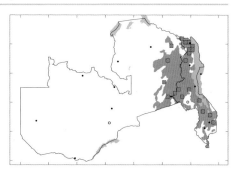

posteriorly; several bright yellow spots present on flanks anteriorly, the remaining flank spots being pale blue-white to pale green; lips, neck and ventrum bright yellow. Females have black-edged yellow dorsal stripe and yellow dorsolateral stripe originating just behind head and extending to base of tail; yellow lateral stripe also present; numerous irregular vertical black bars on sides of neck and flanks; lower flanks and ventrum white. Juveniles more vividly coloured, with bright orange tails; lack barred flanks. **Habitat:** Mesic savanna and high-elevation grassland. **Behaviour:** Poorly known. Diurnal and terrestrial; believed to be an active hunter, preferring open areas and taking refuge in a hole dug at the base of a bush. **Prey:** Insects. **Reproduction:** Female lays 2–3 eggs, measuring 12mm x 7mm. **Range:** Throughout Malawi and eastern Zambia, to the south-eastern DRC and Tanzania.

Johnston's Long-tailed Lizard has several yellow or green spots on the flanks.

ROUGH-SCALED LIZARDS   *Ichnotropis*

These medium-sized lizards have large head scales which are rough, ridged or keeled. The tail is long. The nostril is pierced between three nasals and the lower eyelid is scaly. There is no collar, although a short fold is present in front of the arm. The dorsals are large, lanceolate or rhomboid, strongly keeled, and overlapping. The ventrals are smooth and imbricate. The subdigital lamellae are sharply keeled and spinose. Femoral pores are present.

These active terrestrial lizards are most common on sandy soils in mesic savanna. They are oviparous. Some species are 'annuals' – they live just long enough to mature (5–8 months) and lay one, or rarely two, clutches of 3–12 eggs before they die. Thus, for a period of time each year these species are present only in the form of eggs.

This genus contains six species which occur widely in tropical and southern Africa. Three species occur in the region.

KEY Regional *Ichnotropis* species

1a 44–47 midbody scale rows; occipital does not extend beyond parietals;
    dark dorsolateral band, if present, not bordered by pale stripes . . . . *I. grandiceps* (p. 301)
 b 28–43 midbody scale rows; occipital often extends beyond parietals;
    dark dorsolateral band bordered above and below by pale stripes **2**

2a Prefrontal in contact with anterior supraocular; head scales strongly keeled
    with few secondary fine ridges . . . . *I. bivittata* (p. 299)
 b Prefrontal not in contact with anterior supraocular; head scales not strongly
    keeled, but with numerous fine ridges . . . . *I. capensis* (p. 300)

Angolan Rough-scaled Lizard   *Ichnotropis bivittata*

Luke Verburgt

In the region, the Angolan Rough-scaled Lizard occurs only in northern Zambia and northern Malawi.

SVL 65–75mm; max. SVL 78mm
A medium-sized, slender lizard with a pointed snout. Single, undivided frontonasal. Prefrontal separated from supraciliary by 1–2 rows of small scales; subocular borders lip. 8 supralabials, usually 4 anterior to subocular. Body scales enlarged, mucronate, strongly keeled, in 32–40 rows at midbody. Ventrals in 8–10 longitudinal and 27–33 transverse rows. 9–13 femoral pores on thigh. Top of head and back coppery red to bronze, this coloration extending to tail tip. Dorsum bordered laterally by pale dorsolateral stripe approximately two scales wide, originating at eye and extending onto tail. Flanks dark, bordered below by another pale stripe that extends from supralabials through ear opening to base of tail. Second dark stripe extends from lower portions of supralabials and upper edges of infralabials to forearm. Breeding males develop rusty red flanks between front and hind limbs; white stripes on anterior portion of body become bright yellow. Ventrum usually plain white. Juveniles less well-marked than adults and may be patternless except for round white shoulder-patch. **Habitat:** Arid and mesic miombo woodland, favouring sandy, open areas. **Behaviour:** A diurnal, terrestrial lizard that actively hunts. **Prey:** Insects, including ants and grasshoppers. **Reproduction:** Unknown. **Range:** From southern Tanzania westwards through northern Malawi and northern Zambia to the DRC and Angola.

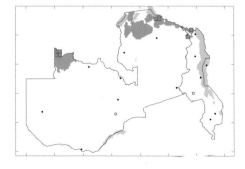

Common Rough-scaled Lizard *Ichnotropis capensis*

SVL 45–55mm; max. SVL ♂ 64mm; ♀ 68mm
A medium-sized, slender lizard with a narrow, pointed head. Frontonasal entire; subocular borders lip. 8 supralabials, 3–5 (usually 4) anterior to subocular. Dorsals keeled, strongly overlapping, in 28–43 scale rows at midbody. 8–14 femoral pores on thigh. Back uniform greyish, olive-brown to red-brown in adults. Narrow black dorsolateral stripe or series of dark spots, bordered below by pale stripe originate behind eye and extend onto tail. Flanks dark brown to black, bordered below by another pale stripe. Ventrum white; limbs spotted above and white below. Breeding males develop rust-red or orange stripe on anterior flanks and have the chin, throat and lateral stripe infused with bright yellow. Juveniles have pale grey-brown back with pale dorsolateral stripe. **Habitat:** Arid and mesic savannas. **Behaviour:** Active and diurnal. An 'annual' species, hatchlings mature rapidly (7–8 months) and reproduce before dying after 13–14 months.

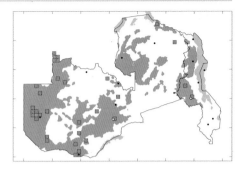

Prey: Termites, spiders, beetles, grasshoppers and other invertebrates. **Reproduction:** Mating occurs in October–December. The female lays 3–9 eggs (9–9.5mm x 6–7mm) in a burrow dug in soft sand shortly after mating. Incubation takes 56–77 days. Hatchlings emerge in January–March and measure 60–70mm in TL. The female may lay two clutches per season. **Range:** From South Africa northwards through Zambia to Angola and western Malawi.

In the Common Rough-scaled Lizard, the breeding male has a yellow throat and orange-red flanks.

Females and juveniles are plainer than adult males.

Subadult males have intermediate coloration.

Zambezi Rough-scaled Lizard   *Ichnotropis grandiceps*

Errol Pietersen

The Zambezi Rough-scaled Lizard is plain grey-brown above with a rust-red flank stripe.

SVL 50–65mm; max. SVL 70mm

A medium-sized lizard with a fairly large head. Scales on head weakly ridged; frontonasal undivided. Occipital does not project beyond parietals; subocular borders lip; 4–5 supralabials anterior to subocular. 3 supraoculars, 3rd being the smallest; 5 supraciliaries. Supraoculars separated from supraciliaries by single row of small scales. Narrow tympanic scale on upper anterior edge of ear opening. Dorsals small, strongly keeled, overlapping; ventrals smooth, rounded, in 10 longitudinal and 30 transverse rows. Scales in 44–47 rows at midbody. 12–14 femoral pores on thigh. Head and back pale grey-brown to olive-brown anteriorly, becoming olive-yellow posteriorly and with scattered darker spots throughout. Thin, pale dorsolateral stripe may be present. Limbs reddish orange, with small pale spots sometimes present on

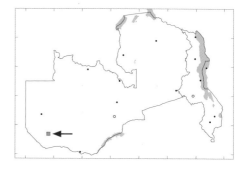

hind limbs. Rust-red lateral stripe originates just behind eye and extends for entire length of body, fading on base of tail (occasionally absent). Flanks light grey below lateral stripe, frequently with large white spots. Tail uniformly grey-brown to pinkish, with dorsolateral series of paired dark and white spots. Ventrum white. **Habitat:** *Baikiaea* woodland on Kalahari sands and hard limey soils in open woodland. **Behaviour:** A diurnal lizard that actively forages for invertebrates. Appears to be regionally common, especially in *Baikiaea* woodland. **Prey:** Invertebrates. **Reproduction:** Unknown. It is suspected that this is not an 'annual' species, as adults and juveniles have been collected together. **Range:** South-western Zambia. Elsewhere it occurs in the Zambezi Region of Namibia and adjacent sections of northern Botswana and north-eastern Namibia.

DESERT AND SAVANNA LIZARDS *Meroles*

Medium-sized terrestrial lizards with large head scales that are usually smooth (rough in one species). Tail long and usually cylindrical, but may be slightly depressed basally or laterally. The occipital scale is usually reduced in size or absent. The nostril is pierced between three nasals and is widely separated from the 1st supralabial. The subocular does not reach the lip. The lower eyelid is scaly and lacks a transparent window. The collar is distinct (absent in one species) while the gular fold is absent. The body scales are small and granular, juxtaposed or weakly imbricate (rhombic, imbricate and strongly keeled in one species). The ventrals are smooth and not, or only slightly, imbricate. The fingers and toes have lateral serrations or fringes, while the subdigital lamellae are smooth, keeled or spinose. Femoral pores are present.

These active, diurnal lizards are most common on deep, sandy soils in desert, with one species occurring in mesic savanna. They prey on various invertebrates. All species lay eggs.

The genus contains eight species, one of which occurs in the region.

Rough-scaled Savanna Lizard *Meroles squamulosus*

The Rough-scaled Savanna Lizard has pale stripes and scattered dark blotches.

SVL 60–70mm; max. SVL 77mm
A medium-sized lizard with a fairly robust body and a small head. Frontonasal divided; subocular does not reach lip. Body scales small, strongly keeled, overlapping, in 42–62 rows at midbody. Ventrals in 10–12 longitudinal and 28–34 transverse rows. 11–18 femoral pores on thigh. Body pale buff to dark coppery brown, usually with narrow, broken, dark crossbands or blotches and six longitudinal rows of pale spots. Pale, dark-edged spots usually present on limbs. Ventrum white to grey, sometimes with yellowish tinge. Adult males have dark speckling on infralabials

and sublinguals, and develop a bright orange to orange-red chest and throat when breeding. Juveniles usually have pale median, dorsolateral and lateral stripes and are tinged with pink posteriorly. **Habitat:** Open areas in arid and mesic savannas. **Behaviour:** An active diurnal lizard. It digs extensive burrows at the base of trees (often thorn trees), which may be shared by several individuals. Sexual maturity is reached in 4–5 months and individuals die off after 10–12 months. Populations survive as eggs during winter (when all adults have already died off). **Prey:** Predominantly termites and grasshoppers, although beetles and other invertebrates are also eaten. **Reproduction:** Female lays 8–12 eggs (10–12mm x 6–7mm) in April–May. These

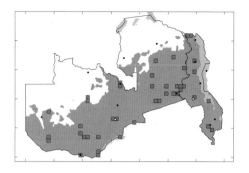

hatch in October–November and hatchlings measure 70–80mm in TL. **Range:** From South Africa northwards to southern Angola, throughout most of Zambia and Malawi and eastwards to Tanzania.

SAW-TAILED LIZARDS   *Holaspis*

These lizards have a pointed snout and a dorsoventrally flattened body. The tail is also dorsoventrally compressed, with a fringe of flat scales. The lower eyelid is scaly and a well-developed collar is present. Femoral pores are present. Pale longitudinal stripes are present on the body, which is black, and the tail is bright blue.

They are predominantly arboreal, sheltering in tree hollows and under dead bark. They prey on spiders and ants, and probably other invertebrates. These unique lacertids are able to flatten their ribs, thus increasing their surface area, and are able to glide for long distances between trees. They are oviparous.

They occur quite widely in tropical Africa, often inhabiting forest, but also entering open woodland. Two species are recognised, of which one occurs in the region.

Eastern Saw-tailed Lizard   *Holaspis laevis*

SVL 43–48mm; max. SVL 51mm
A fairly small, arboreal lizard with a flattened body and tail. Tail longer than body, with fringe of flat scales. Head long, pointed. Collar well developed. Lower eyelids scaly, with 3–5 enlarged, semi-transparent scales in centre. Toes long, with fringe of flattened scales. Dorsals in 74–84 rows at midbody. Ventrals in 6 longitudinal rows. 17–25 femoral pores on thigh. Back and sides black. Broad, cream-coloured stripe present on head. Two pale dorsolateral stripes originate on head, running along length of body and fading out at base of tail. Lateral pale stripe originates on supralabials, extends along entire length of body and most of tail, fading posteriorly. Top of tail covered in bright blue enlarged scales on

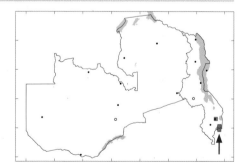

black background; lower surfaces blue to black, fringe of flat scales yellow. Throat, limbs and cloacal region cream-coloured. Rest of ventrum orange to yellow. **Habitat:** Forest and closed to fairly open woodlands. **Behaviour:** A diurnal, arboreal lizard that shows a preference for vertical tree trunks. It is not easy to approach, quickly darting to the opposite side of the tree

Luke Verburgt

The body is black with pale stripes.

trunk when threatened. It is agile and may leap between tree trunks and sometimes also uses its flattened body to glide for distances of up to 10m between trees. Usually takes refuge in the tree canopy, under loose bark, or in holes in the tree trunk. **Prey:** Forages on tree trunks for cockroaches, spiders and ants. **Reproduction:** Female lays two relatively small eggs (9–11mm x 5–6mm) under loose bark or in leaf litter. **Range:** From eastern Zimbabwe eastwards through southern Malawi and central Mozambique and northwards to Tanzania.

Luke Verburgt

The Eastern Saw-tailed Lizard has a diagnostic blue and black tail.

FOREST AND MEADOW LIZARDS   *Adolfus*

These medium- to large-sized lizards are characterised by various skeletal and internal features. The pineal eye is absent, a single postnasal is present and the frontoparietal is not fused to the occipital. The tail is cylindrical and as long as, or slightly longer than, the SVL. The lower eyelid is scaly and supraciliary granules are usually present. The body scales are usually of a more or less uniform small size, except for the Multi-scaled Forest Lizard (*A. africanus*), whose lateral scales are distinctly smaller than the middorsals. The ventrals are smooth and arranged in 6–8 longitudinal rows (the outermost row is keeled and constricted anteriorly in one species). Femoral pores are present. Ventral coloration ranges from yellow or orange to green or blue.

These lizards are semi-arboreal and most common in forest, but are also found in grassland and forest clearings. Their reproductive biology is poorly known, but all species are believed to be oviparous.

Four species are currently recognised, but numerous species are believed to await formal description. One species enters the region.

Multi-scaled Forest Lizard   *Adolfus africanus*

SVL 45–55mm; max. SVL 64mm
A medium-sized, slender lizard with rhombic body scales. Nostril separated from 1st supralabial. 7–8 supralabials; 6–10

In the region, the Multi-scaled Forest Lizard occurs only in the Ikelenge Pedicle.

Luke Verburgt

infralabials; 4 supraoculars; 5–6 supraciliaries. Collar distinct, consisting of 7–9 scales.
Each scale has well-developed keel directed diagonally in towards the backbone; scales along dorsal midline distinctly larger than those on flanks. 18–26 midbody scale rows. Ventrals in 6 longitudinal rows, outermost row strongly reduced in size and weakly keeled anteriorly. 17–19 lamellae beneath 4th toe. Median and outermost ventral scale rows narrower than other ventrals. 12–17 femoral pores on thigh. Top of head metallic copper-bronze, extending as broad dorsal stripe to tip of tail; scattered black spots may be present within dorsal stripe. Dorsal stripe often bordered by pale yellow spots that may fuse into narrow yellow stripes on tail. Side of head and flanks dark brown to black; pale yellow stripe originates on supralabials, extends to shoulder, may continue as series of large pale spots along length of body. Ventrum bright lime-green. **Habitat:** Frequents small clearings in primary forest where sunlight is able to penetrate the canopy. **Behaviour:** Usually seen basking in dappled shade on fallen tree trunks and limbs and exposed roots in forest clearings. **Prey:** Forages for arthropods in leaf litter. **Reproduction:** Probably lays eggs. **Range:** Extreme north-western Zambia. Elsewhere it occurs from Kenya to Cameroon.

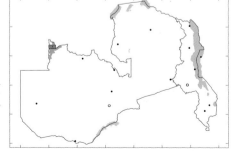

Monitors
Family Varanidae

White-throated Monitor

Large to very large lizards with large limbs and long, strong claws. The tail is long, tough and usually laterally depressed, and cannot be shed or regenerated. The neck is distinct, flexible and longer than in most other lizard taxa. The scales on the head are small, while those on the body are bead-like and non-overlapping. Belly scales are quadrangular and arranged in transverse rows. A single pair of precloacal pores are usually present. The ear openings are distinct. The tongue is long and forked and used to smell by capturing particles in the air before being inserted into Jacobson's Organ, which is situated in the roof of the mouth. These lizards have large, conical teeth.

Most members of the family are semi-aquatic, with some species being terrestrial or arboreal. The family also includes the largest terrestrial lizard, the Komodo Dragon (*V. komodoensis*), which can reach lengths of up to 3.1m and weigh as much as 160kg. Most species in this family are carnivorous (two species are herbivorous) and will eat anything that they can overpower, including crustaceans, molluscs, insects, eggs, baby birds, small mammals, tortoises and even snakes. The larger species may scavenge. Two Australasian species possess venom glands and have venom in their saliva, but none of the African species are venomous. When threatened, monitors inflate their body and may expel the air with an audible hiss. They often stand on 'high legs' and will lash out with the hard tail in defence. They readily bite and will also expel the contents of their bowels on any would-be predator. Males of some species engage in ritualised combat to establish dominance. The female lays clutches of 7–60 large, oval, leathery-shelled eggs in a hole that she digs in the ground or in a termite mound.

The greatest number of species are found in Australia, but members of this family are also widespread in Africa (excluding Madagascar and the Indian Ocean islands), India and Asia. There is only one genus in the family, containing 80 species.

MONITORS *Varanus*

These large lizards have well-developed limbs and long, strong claws on each digit. The scales on the head are small, while those on the body are bead-like and close-fitting. The tail is long, hard and relatively thin and cannot be shed or regenerated.

Most members of this genus are semi-aquatic, with some species being terrestrial or arboreal. All but two species are carnivorous and will eat anything they can overpower, including snakes. Monitors are often preyed on by large raptors, especially Martial Eagles and snake eagles, as well as cobras (*Naja*). The female lays large, oval eggs with soft, leathery shells in a hole dug in the ground or in a termite mound, the latter sealed up by the termite workers.

There are 80 species in this genus, two of which occur in the region.

KEY Regional *Varanus* species

1a Body thickset; nostrils oblique slits, located much nearer to eye than to tip of snout; terrestrial . . . . **V. albigularis** (p. 307)
 b Body fairly slender; nostrils oval, located slightly closer to eye than to tip of snout; semi-aquatic . . . . **V. niloticus** (p. 308)

White-throated Monitor *Varanus albigularis*

Darren Pietersen

The White-throated Monitor has a broad head and a mottled brown colour.

SVL 300–600mm; max. SVL 850mm
A very large lizard with a heavyset body and a powerful head. Snout bulbous, slightly depressed above. Nostrils oblique slits, located much closer to eye than to tip of snout. Limbs short, stout, with well-developed claws. Tail longer than SVL, muscular, tapers to thin, hard tip. Dorsals small, coarse, in 110–167 rows at midbody. Body olive or grey-brown through dark brown to black, with series of 5–6 pale, dark-edged patches along dorsal midline. Top of head and neck dark; sides of head and throat white or black (see Subspecies). Numerous broad concentric dark and pale rings on tail. Limbs dark with numerous pale spots. Ventrum grey to off-white, usually with scattered dark spots. Juveniles more vividly coloured. Body often covered in dirt and unshed skin. **Subspecies:** Three poorly defined subspecies are recognised. *V. a. albigularis* has 119–167 (mostly 130–154) scale rows at midbody and a white throat, often suffused with grey or grey-brown. Juveniles often have a dark patch on the throat. The nuchal scales are not larger than the scales on the head and back. It occurs widely in Zambia and Malawi, and southwards throughout Zimbabwe, South Africa, Mozambique and parts of Botswana and Namibia. *V. a. angolensis* has 110–138 scale rows at midbody, 74–86 ventrals and a vertebral series of enlarged scales extending

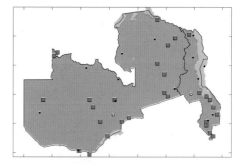

Tyrone Ping

This large lizard often climbs trees.

from behind the head to the base of the tail. Adults have a black throat. It occurs in north-western Zambia, adjacent Angola and the southern DRC. In *V. a. microstictus* the nuchals (excluding their surrounding discs) are distinctly larger than the scales on the top of the head and back. It is restricted to East Africa, just entering Malawi. **Habitat:** Arid and mesic savannas, rocky outcrops and open woodland. **Behaviour:** Equally at home on the ground, on rocks and in trees. Takes refuge in any suitable structure, including holes in the ground, moribund termitaria, tree stumps, tree hollows and rock outcrops. Adults have fixed home ranges that may be as large as 28km². Usually slow-moving, but can escape with a dash of speed if threatened. If it cannot escape, it raises itself up on its limbs, inflates the neck and body and hisses, simultaneously lashing out at the attacker with its tail. It readily bites, and despite having rounded, cusped teeth, it can inflict a powerful and painful bite. If continuously harassed, it may evacuate its bowels on the attacker, extrude its hemipenes (if male) and even adopt tonic immobility. Moves slowly while foraging, continuously flicking the forked tongue while searching for prey. Lives for at least 15 years in the wild. **Prey and Predators:**

Will feed on almost any animal, including invertebrates (beetles, millipedes, scorpions, snails, slugs), small birds, bird eggs, rodents, carrion, amphibians (including Giant Bullfrogs), young tortoises (including Leopard Tortoises [*Stigmochelys pardalis*] and Speke's Hinged Tortoises [*Kinixys spekii*]), lizards and even snakes (such as Puff Adders [*Bitis a. arietans*]). Adults are preyed on by Martial Eagles, African Crowned Eagles, Black-chested Snake Eagles and Honey Badgers, while many egg clutches are raided by Banded Mongoose. It is also preyed on by some of the larger cobras (*Naja*). **Reproduction:** Mating occurs in August–September and the female lays 8–51 large (55–61mm x 35–39mm) eggs in a hole dug in moist sand in mid-summer. She may occasionally lay her eggs in an active termite mound or tree hollow. Incubation is prolonged (about four months, but up to 10 months depending on conditions). Hatchlings measure 220–280mm in TL. **Range:** Widespread throughout southern and East Africa, and northwards to Somalia and Ethiopia.

Water Monitor   *Varanus niloticus*

SVL 600–800mm; max. SVL 980mm
A very large lizard with a relatively slender body and a flattened, obtusely pointed head. Nostrils oval, located slightly closer to eye than to tip of snout. Scales on body small, smooth, bead-like, in 128–183 (usually 137–165) rows at midbody. Tail much longer than SVL, cylindrical anteriorly, becoming laterally flattened posteriorly. Very low toothed dorsal crest present on tail. Limbs moderately long, with well-developed, sharp claws. Juveniles have sharp teeth; these become bluntly rounded in adults, although sharp teeth are retained in front of jaw. Adults grey-brown to dark olive-brown above, with darker markings and 6–11 light yellow bands or series of spots. Lower flanks and ventrum yellowish white, usually with indistinct darker transverse bands. Tail has 10–18 alternating light and dark bands. Juveniles black above, with transverse yellow bands that may break up into spots. Top of head and limbs black with numerous yellow spots. Labials alternately banded in black and yellow. Broad yellow bands

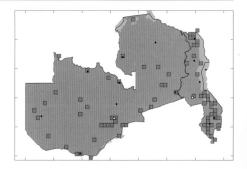

separated by narrower black lines on side of neck and lower flanks. Concentric broad black bands separated by narrower yellow bands on tail. **Habitat:** Usually found in close proximity to rivers, dams and other permanent or temporary waterbodies. **Behaviour:** This semi-aquatic lizard will shelter in any suitable cover, including dense aquatic vegetation, rock crevices, tree hollows and holes in the riverbank. Juveniles often sleep partially submerged in aquatic vegetation or on protruding logs just above the surface of the water. It is an adept climber and may scale trees and cliffs in search of food or shelter. It swims beneath the surface for quite a way, usually re-emerging in suitable cover, such as reeds. It may also dive off cliffs or overhanging trees into the water if surprised. It propels itself through the water with the limbs tightly adpressed to the body to streamline its shape, using the flattened tail as an oar. Although mostly foraging near the water's edge, it may on occasion wander far from water in search of food. If disturbed while on land, it rushes towards the water with great speed, noisily splashing into its refuge. When waterbodies dry up, it may move great distances across land in search of another water source and is just as adept on land as it is in water. If cornered, it will raise itself up on all four limbs, inflate the body, hiss and lash at its attacker with its tail, often with the head pointed diagonally down. The strong, sharp claws are also used in self-defence and it may bite as well. If these defences fail, it may adopt tonic immobility. **Prey and Predators:** Omnivorous, it feeds on plant matter, crabs, amphibians, birds (particularly fledglings), eggs (including terrapin and crocodile eggs), fish, small rodents, millipedes, gastropods and carrion. It is preyed on by Martial Eagles, Southern African Pythons (*Python natalensis*), Nile Crocodiles (*Crocodylus niloticus*) and some of the larger cobra (*Naja*) species. **Reproduction:** Female lays 16–60 large eggs (52–64mm x 30–45mm) in late winter to mid-summer in a hole dug into the riverbank or an active termite mound, with the latter nests being sealed in by the termites. Incubation is prolonged and may take up to 12 months. Hatchlings dig their way out of the rain-softened nest the following summer, and measure 200–300mm in TL. Hatchlings remain in the relative safety of shallow water, where they forage for frogs and insects. **Range:** Widespread throughout sub-Saharan Africa, extending into Egypt along the Nile River.

The Water Monitor has a narrow head and a laterally compressed tail.

Chameleons
Family Chamaeleonidae

These interesting, unique lizards are largely adapted to an arboreal lifestyle. They have four well-developed limbs and a unique foot structure, with the toes usually bound together and positioned in two opposing pairs. The tail may be long and prehensile, or short and non-prehensile, and

Flap-necked Chameleon

cannot be shed or regenerated. The eyes are positioned in small turrets and can move independently of each other. The body scales are small and close-fitting. They lack external ear openings and their sense of hearing is poorly developed. A large casque often covers the dorsal portion of the head and enlarged occipital lobes (ear flaps) are often present. The tongue is extremely long and telescopic and can be propelled to a distance greatly exceeding the body length to capture prey. Precloacal and femoral pores are absent. Some species have inguinal pits (in the groin) or axillary pits (under the forearm) of unknown function, which are useful as identifying features. Dorsal, ventral and gular crests may be present. Males are often more brightly coloured than females, and in some species males have horns or other cranial ornamentations. In males, the hemipenes are withdrawn into sheaths at the base of the tail and consequently the tail base is broader than in females.

Most species are arboreal, although some species have adapted to life in grass or may even be completely terrestrial, favouring leaf litter. The laterally compressed body, prehensile tail and opposing toe clusters facilitate their arboreal lifestyle and enable them to traverse exceedingly thin branches and vines. The body shape, parietal crest, casque and occipital lobes all serve to break up their outline and enable them to blend into their surroundings. In addition, chameleons are renowned for their ability to rapidly change colour in relation to their background, a feat which is achieved by activating different layers of chromatophores (pigment cells) in the skin. These colour changes can also occur in relation to mood and temperature, with individuals often becoming darker when angry or during cold weather (to absorb the maximum amount of heat) and more brightly coloured during mating and territorial displays.

Both males and females live a predominantly solitary life, with territorial boundaries being established and maintained through ritualised combat, including head-butting, inflating the throat pouch and rapidly changing colour. Although physical fights are rare, individuals may resort to biting an intruder if the latter fails to leave the territory. They prey on a wide variety of invertebrates and the larger species may rarely eat small mammals, reptiles or birds as well. Chameleons in turn are preyed on by a large variety of predators, including snakes (boomslang [*Dispholidus*] and vine snakes [*Thelotornis*] in particular), raptors, other small carnivorous birds, small arboreal carnivores and primates. Most species lay large clutches of soft-shelled eggs, usually deposited in a hole that the female digs in moist ground. Some genera, especially those in montane regions and temperate environments, are viviparous.

This family contains 202 species in 12 genera and occurs throughout sub-Saharan Africa (including Madagascar) and Asia, with a few species entering Europe, India and associated offshore islands. Twelve species in six genera occur in the region.

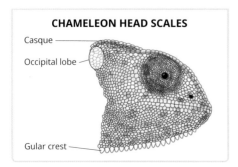

CHAMELEON HEAD SCALES

Casque

Occipital lobe

Gular crest

These relatively small chameleons have an elongate head that is longer than it is wide. The tail is significantly longer than the SVL. The casque is distinctly raised posteriorly in males but is usually less pronounced in females and juveniles. Rostral projections (absent in one species) are single or paired. There are no occipital lobes, gular or ventral crests. The scales on the body are slightly heterogenous and consist of fine granules or flattened polygonal tubercles. Some species have scattered enlarged tubercles, while in other species these tubercles may form rosettes on the flanks.

This genus is largely restricted to East Africa. These chameleons are confined to tropical and subtropical forests and often occur in relict montane and sub-montane forests. Twenty species are recognised, one of which occurs in the region.

Poroto Single-horned Chameleon   *Kinyongia vanheygeni*

Darren Pietersen

The Poroto Single-horned Chameleon occurs in the Misuku Mountains in extreme northern Malawi.

SVL 50–60mm; max. SVL 66mm
This small chameleon has a tail that is much longer than the SVL. Head fairly elongate. Occipital lobes absent. Parietal casque large, distinctly raised posteriorly. Two short, blade-like rostral appendages extend beyond level of mouth, each consisting of two parallel rows of three enlarged, conical scales. Row of enlarged, conical scales extends from rostral appendages to above eyes. No dorsal, gular or ventral crest. Head and casque covered with relatively large, flat scales. Body scales finely heterogenous, with clusters of enlarged scales interspersed between small body scales. Scales arranged in rosettes on lower flanks. Coloration varied, depending to an extent on mood, and includes various shades of grey, brown, green, blue and

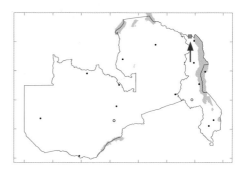

yellow. Male coloration normally pale grey to light yellow, with enlarged scales often green or yellow. Head olive-green. 3–4 darker saddles on body; several dark and light bands on tail (may be ill-defined). Females have lower parietal crest and lack rostral appendages. Females bright green, with dark border to parietal crest, below which is a large pale patch; two dark patches present on upper anterior portion of flanks; indistinct orange stripe usually present on flanks. **Habitat:** Montane forest. **Behaviour:** This recently described chameleon is poorly known. It is arboreal and inhabits the middle and possibly upper storeys. **Prey:** Probably feeds on a variety of insects. **Reproduction:** Probably lays eggs. **Range:** Restricted to the Poroto Mountains and the Rungwe volcanic complex in south-western Tanzania and the Misuku Mountains in extreme northern Malawi.

LEAF CHAMELEONS   *Rieppeleon*

Small chameleons with a noticeably laterally compressed body, giving them a leaf-like appearance. The tail is 14–40% of the TL and is not prehensile. The parietal bone is triangular, tapering posteriorly into a thin sagittal crest. There are no rostral processes or horns. The supraorbital crest is well developed and bony. The soles of the feet are covered in spines and the claws are weakly bicuspid. There are no accessory spines beneath the feet. A slightly raised skin ridge is present on the flanks. Body coloration consists of longitudinal stripes on a green or brown background.

Four species are currently recognised, restricted to eastern Africa from Malawi through East Africa to Somalia. One species enters the region.

Beardless Leaf Chameleon   *Rieppeleon brachyurus*

The Beardless Leaf Chameleon lacks an interorbital ridge.

SVL 30–40mm; max. SVL ♂ 46mm ♀ 50mm
A small chameleon with a laterally compressed body and short tail. No rostral process, dorsal or gular crest. Supraciliary ridges well developed, resulting in deeply concave interorbital space. No raised interorbital ridge of enlarged tubercles. Supraciliary ridges extend posteriorly, meeting at acute angle and merging with vertebral midline. Scales on body small, with scattered, slightly enlarged tubercles. Scales along vertebral midline may be enlarged and conical, but not grouped. Thin, slightly raised longitudinal ridge originates on temple, continuing over flanks to base

of tail. Body light yellow-tan to grey-brown. Three parallel dark lines may be present on flanks, the median line being the darkest and running just below raised skin ridge. Small axillary pit present; no inguinal pits. **Habitat:** Gallery forest and moist miombo woodland, sometimes entering surrounding grassland. **Behaviour:** Mainly terrestrial, foraging in leaf litter and grass, but occasionally also climbing into low shrubs, especially at night to sleep. It may be attracted to fruiting trees, presumably to capture insects that feed on fallen fruit. If harassed, it will inflate its body while 'vibrating' violently. **Prey:** Fruit flies, houseflies, termites, spiders, snails and other small invertebrates. **Reproduction:** Female lays 7–14 eggs (9.5mm

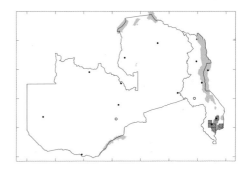

x 5mm) in late summer. Hatchlings measure 15mm in TL. **Range:** Malawi (east of the Shire River), northern Mozambique and south-eastern Tanzania.

MONTANE CHAMELEONS *Nadzikambia*

This small genus consists of only two species that lack a gular pouch and gular and ventral crests. The casque is small or absent and the dorsal crest is weakly defined. The body scales are heterogenous, with rosettes of tubercles present on the lower flanks. Reproduction is oviparous.

These medium-sized chameleons inhabit sub-montane forest. They frequent the mid-storey, but may also be seen on the ground on occasion. At night they sleep on thin branches on the outer limbs of trees and large shrubs. When a predator approaches along the branch, the movement of the twig alerts the chameleon, allowing it to drop to the ground and escape.

Mulanje Chameleon *Nadzikambia mlanjensis*   Endemic

SVL 70–75mm; max. SVL ♂ 81mm ♀ 84mm
A small chameleon that lacks a casque but has a cranial crest. Row of enlarged, tubercled scales present on back of head, arising behind eyes and forming parietal crest. Second row of enlarged, tubercled scales arise in front of eyes, running almost to tip of snout. Scales on crown enlarged, flat to slightly tubercled. Scales on body fairly homogenous, bead-like, separated by granular interspaces. Tail slightly longer than body. Body green to orange, usually with blue infusions on lower back and two pale triangular bars on each flank, which may be indistinct in males. Throat and sides of head bright lime-green, with scattered light blue spots. Male crown has mosaic of pale green and blue scales anteriorly, becoming orange or brown posteriorly. Crown orange-red to russet-brown in females. Tail green with orange or pale infusions, particularly dorsally. Ventrum and inner portions of limbs and feet light

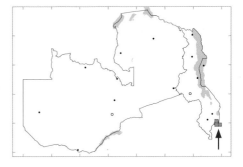

blue-green, sometimes with pale mid-ventral line. **Habitat:** Sub-montane evergreen forest. **Behaviour:** This arboreal chameleon perches on the outer extremities of trees to sleep. If disturbed, it will drop to the ground to escape. **Prey:** A variety of invertebrates. **Reproduction:** Female lays 6–8 eggs (15–16mm x 7–8mm) in summer. **Range:** Endemic to Mount Mulanje in south-eastern Malawi.

The Mulanje Chameleon has a cranial crest and is endemic to Mount Mulanje.

PYGMY CHAMELEONS   *Rhampholeon*

Small chameleons with a laterally compressed body, giving them a leaf-like appearance. The tail is short and not prehensile. Soft rostral processes are present, ranging in size from just discernible to obvious. The parietal bone is triangular, but lacks a posterior sagittal crest. The scales beneath the feet are conical, rounded and smooth, and accessory spines are usually present. The claws may be strongly bicuspid or simple. The supraorbital ridge is soft or absent. Most species have inguinal and axillary pits. The coloration includes various shades of brown and green, usually with two or three oblique lateral stripes.

These small chameleons are restricted to moist forest and forest edges. They are diurnal and terrestrial, capturing insects from amongst the leaf litter. At night they climb into low shrubs and bushes, favouring spindly plants and branches. This is a useful defence against predators, whose weight is generally to great to be supported by the flimsy branches. As the branch gives way, it alerts the chameleon, allowing it to fall to the ground and escape. When moulting, pygmy chameleons may ascend to greater heights and have been recorded up to three metres above the ground. All species are oviparous, the females laying small clutches of eggs in leaf litter or under logs.

Currently, 14 species are recognised, restricted to tropical East and Central Africa, with one species entering Nigeria. Three species have been recorded in the region.

KEY Regional *Rhampholeon* species

1a	Inguinal pits absent	*R. nchisiensis* (p. 316)
b	Inguinal pits present	2
2a	Scales on body heterogenous; endemic to Mount Mulanje	*R. platyceps* (p. 317)
b	Scales on body homogenous, with evenly spaced, enlarged tubercles; endemic to Malawi Hill in the Natundu Range	*R. chapmanorum* (p. 315)

Chapman's Pygmy Chameleon   *Rhampholeon chapmanorum*   Endemic

SVL 40–45mm; max. SVL ♂ 46mm ♀ 52mm
A small chameleon with a laterally compressed body and a very short tail. Prominent rostral process present. Top of head flattened; casque weakly developed, not raised posteriorly. Parietal crest consists of slightly enlarged tubercles; temporal crest prominent. Supraorbital ridge raised into small, soft peak, formed by cluster of tubercles above eye. Supraorbital peaks connected by V-shaped interorbital ridge consisting of 13–17 enlarged tubercles. Supraorbital ridges connected to rostral process by series of enlarged triangular tubercles. Dorsal crest most prominent mid-dorsally, composed of clumps of tubercles. No gular or ventral crest. Body scales fine, homogenous, with fairly evenly spaced enlarged conical tubercles. Deep axillary and inguinal pits present. Body mottled pale brown, becoming paler ventrolaterally. Six darker brown blotches evenly spaced along vertebral midline, sometimes extending as transverse dark bands that terminate in dark spot, with third dark spot embedded in band. Interstitial skin on throat white. Mouth lining bright orange. **Habitat:** Lowland seasonal rainforest. **Behaviour:** Usually encountered perched on leaves, twigs or moss in the understorey. Rival males flatten their body even more and stand perpendicular to their opponent while rhythmically swaying. This is usually accompanied by the head and neck becoming a pale powder-blue and the eyelids turning bright white. Males may also inflate their neck, exposing the white interstitial skin, and gape to show off the bright yellow mouth lining. Rival males produce vibrations, presumably through the controlled exhalation of air, and may bite the limbs of their opponent. **Prey:** Various invertebrates. **Reproduction:** A female was found to contain eight poorly developed eggs in February. **Range:** Restricted to the Natundu Hills Range in southern Malawi. A population has been introduced to a second location away from the Natundu Hills for conservation purposes.

The female has shorter rostral appendages.

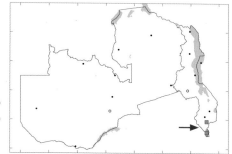

Chapman's Pygmy Chameleon (here a male) is endemic to extreme southern Malawi.

Pitless Pygmy Chameleon *Rhampholeon nchisiensis*

In the Pitless Pygmy Chameleon the male has a distinct rostral appendage.

The rostral appendage is shorter in the female.

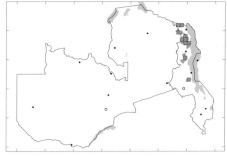

SVL 40–50mm; max. SVL ♂ 43mm ♀ 67mm
A small chameleon with a laterally compressed body and a very short tail. Flexible rostral process present. Casque flat. Supraciliary ridge consists of enlarged, pointed granules, one of which may be horn-like. Interorbital ridge elevated, backward-pointing, consists of enlarged tubercles. No gular, ventral or dorsal crests, although small, evenly spaced clumps of tubercles may be present along vertebral midline. Body scales homogenous, granular, with scattered enlarged tubercles. Axillary pits usually absent (very rarely present); no inguinal pits. Females larger than males. Body olive-grey to yellow or brown, usually with two or three thin, oblique darker stripes on flanks. 5–6 small, darker blotches on either side of vertebral keel. **Habitat:** Montane forest and forest edges. **Behaviour:** Spends most of its time in leaf litter, climbing into low shrubs at night to sleep. **Prey and Predators:** Feeds on a variety of invertebrates, including beetles, caterpillars and spiders. Preyed on by Eastern Vine Snakes (*Thelotornis mossambicanus*). **Reproduction:** Female lays 12–15 eggs (8–13mm x 5–7mm) in mid-summer. Eggs are laid solitary in the leaf litter, partially submerged in the soil or under fallen logs. **Range:** Nchisi Forest, Misuku Mountains, Viphya Plateau, Jembya Plateau, Mafinga Mountains and the Nyika Plateau, also entering southern Tanzania.

The Mulanje Pygmy Chameleon (here a male) is endemic to Mount Mulanje.

The tail is very short in both sexes (here a female).

SVL 50–60mm; max. SVL ♂ 70mm ♀ 66mm
A fairly large pygmy chameleon with a laterally compressed body, very short tail and rostral process (rarely absent). Casque flat. Supraciliary ridge present, consisting of enlarged granules and sometimes enlarged horn-like spine. Interorbital ridge, comprised of enlarged tubercles, present (may be indistinct). Raised parietal ridge, consisting of enlarged tubercles, arises just behind eye and meets at acute angle behind head, merging with dorsal crest. Remaining scales on head flattened. Dorsal crest present on back, poorly to well defined, consists of evenly spaced groups of slightly enlarged spines. No gular or ventral crest. Body scales strongly heterogenous.

Axillary and inguinal pits present. Body grey-brown to olive-brown, sometimes with darker head. Displaying males mottled grey and brown with black flank stripes and scattered green and yellow flecks. Females may be yellowish orange with darker head and dorsal crest. **Habitat:** Sub-montane and montane rainforests and riparian scrub. **Behaviour:** This terrestrial chameleon spends most of its time on leaf litter or in low shrubs during the day, climbing into low shrubs at night to sleep. **Prey:** Various invertebrates. **Reproduction:** Female lays up to 12 eggs (13mm x 6mm) in summer. **Range:** Endemic to Mount Mulanje and the nearby Mchese Mountain in southern Malawi.

TRUE CHAMELEONS *Chamaeleo*

This group of lizards is characterised by the relatively long, prehensile tail and are best known for their ability to change colour rapidly. True chameleons may have occipital lobes or prominent parietal crests, but lack all other head ornamentation. The gular-ventral crest is always present (although occasionally indistinct) and consists of a single row of cones. A temporal crest is absent. The casque is edged in a lateral parietal crest that originates as a posterior continuation of the supraorbital ridge. The scales on the flanks are homogenous to slightly heterogenous, granular and close-fitting. Tarsal spurs may be present.

They occur predominantly in arid and mesic savannas and woodland, although some species have adapted to desert, forest and high-elevation grasslands. The female is oviparous, usually laying a single clutch (but up to three) in a season.

This wide-ranging genus occurs over much of Africa and also enters Europe, the Middle East, Arabia, the Indian sub-continent and Socotra Island. There are 14 recognised species, three of which occur in the region.

KEY Regional *Chamaeleo* species

1a Occipital lobes present; parietal crest not continuous with dorsal crest . . . . ***C. dilepis*** (p. 319)
 b Occipital lobes absent; parietal crest continuous with dorsal crest **2**

2a Snout truncated; 2 rows of tubercles or enlarged granules along the
    vertebral midline; occurs in high-elevation grassland . . . . ***C. anchietae*** (p. 318)
 b Snout pointed; single row of tubercles or enlarged granules along
    vertebral midline; occurs in savanna . . . . ***C. laevigatus*** (p. 320)

Anchieta's Chameleon *Chamaeleo anchietae*

Anchieta's Chameleon lacks occipital lobes and has a fairly short tail.

SVL 60–70mm; max. SVL ♂ 71mm ♀ 90mm
This relatively large chameleon lacks occipital lobes and the parietal crest is continuous with the dorsal crest. Tail relatively short, 35–43% of TL, prehensile. Two rows of granules or enlarged tubercles along vertebral keel, latter not serrated. Continuous gular and ventral crest consists of white or pale triangular scales. Body scales homogenous. No tarsal spur. Body usually green, yellow or brown, with distinct or indistinct small, dark spots. Pale mid-ventral line usually extends from chin to

cloaca. **Habitat:** Scrubby plateau grassland at medium to high elevations. **Behaviour:** Perches on grasses and low shrubs, descending to ground to cross open areas. Males are territorial and will not tolerate smaller males in their territories. **Prey:** Diet probably includes a wide array of invertebrates. **Reproduction:** Female lays 10–15 eggs in a burrow which she excavates. Hatchlings measure 40–50mm in TL. **Range:** Occurs in a number of isolated populations along a narrow band from central Angola, through the southern DRC to the Udzungwa Mountains in Tanzania. In the region it has been recorded only on the Nyika Plateau, but it may occur in grassland in the Misuku Hills as well.

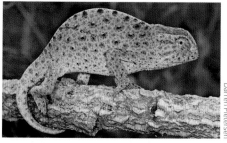

Some individuals have distinct dark spots.

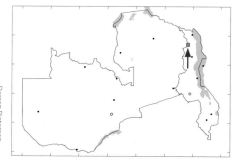

Flap-necked Chameleon   *Chamaeleo dilepis*

The Flap-necked Chameleon has well-developed occipital lobes.

SVL 100–130mm; max. SVL ♂ 172mm ♀ 193mm
A large chameleon with small to large occipital lobes. Casque slightly raised posteriorly. Tail as long as SVL, prehensile. Well-developed supraciliary ridge above each eye. Scales on throat small, more or less arranged in parallel longitudinal lines, latter separated by folds of bare skin. Body scales heterogenous; those on occipital lobes large. Serrated dorsal crest present anteriorly, gradually decreasing in size and vanishing on tail. Well-developed gular crest, consisting of spinose conical scales, extends from throat to just anterior to cloaca. Distinct tarsal spur present in males. Body normally green, with distinct broad white lateral line; various shades of brown and olive also common.

Small white lateral patch may be present just behind flap, with second patch just behind shoulder. Gular crest white. Interstitial skin on throat orange-yellow (particularly noticeable when puffed up during threat display), as is lining of mouth. Breeding males develop a white throat. When disturbed, it may become dark (almost black) and usually shows off inflated yellow throat while raising large occipital lobes. Juveniles light green or orange, with numerous darker spots and dark transverse bars.

Taxonomic note: Up to 11 subspecies have been recognised in the past, although the differences between these are typically slight and show extensive overlap. As such, the authors treat all these 'subspecies' as variants of a single species pending definitive genetic studies. **Habitat:** Arid and moist savannas and woodlands, absent from dense forest. **Behaviour:** Arboreal, but regularly descends to the ground to move between trees or to lay eggs. If threatened, it darkens the skin, raises the occipital lobes, inflates the throat and opens the mouth (showing the bright gular skin and mouth lining). It will readily hiss and bite. In some regions it undergoes torpor in winter, during which time it may shelter under rocks or other suitable cover. **Prey and Predators:** Feeds on virtually any invertebrates, especially flies, beetles, grasshoppers, crickets, moths and butterflies. It is a favourite prey of boomslangs (*Dispholidus*) and vine snakes (*Thelotornis*). Monkeys, hornbills (especially Crowned Hornbills), bush shrikes, African Cuckoo Hawks and Little Banded Goshawks also prey on it. **Reproduction:** Female lays 30–40 (range 19–77) small (13–16mm x 7–9mm), soft-shelled eggs in a hole dug in moist ground in summer. Incubation may take up to a year. Hatchlings measure 40–60mm in TL. **Range:** Widespread throughout sub-Saharan Africa, excluding West Africa.

Stressed individuals usually have a dark coloration.

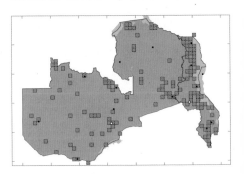

Smooth Chameleon   *Chamaeleo laevigatus*

SVL 90–120mm; max. SVL ♂ 108mm ♀ 135mm
A fairly large chameleon with a casque that is keeled and slightly raised posteriorly and lacks occipital lobes. Supraciliary ridge present. Dorsal crest small, often almost indiscernible, usually restricted to nape, disappearing posteriorly, composed of single row of tubercles or enlarged granules. Gular crest present, consisting of spinose enlarged scales that extend posteriorly to level of cloaca, and sometimes onto tail. Tail 44–47% of TL, prehensile. Body scales homogenous. Coloration variable, ranging from various shades of green to olive to shades of brown. Irregular darker spots and blotches also

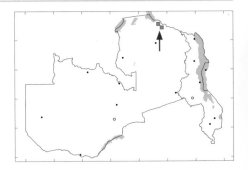

common, may form darker transverse bars along vertebral midline. When threatened, these darker markings increase in size and intensity. Some individuals light cream to grey, with darker spots. Gular and ventral crests white. **Habitat:** Arid and mesic savannas, occasionally entering reedbeds. **Behaviour:** Diurnal and arboreal. **Prey:** A variety of invertebrates, showing an apparent preference for grasshoppers. **Reproduction:** Female lays 15–30 (up to 60) eggs (about 7mm in diameter). Incubation takes 4–5 months. Hatchlings measure 25–30mm in TL. **Range:** North-eastern Zambia, extending through East Africa to Ethiopia and westwards to Cameroon.

Mike McLaren

The Smooth Chameleon lacks occipital lobes and has a relatively long tail.

WHISTLING CHAMELEONS *Trioceros*

This genus contains the largest chameleon species in Africa. In all species the tail is relatively long and prehensile. Some species possess cylindrical, bony horns, while occipital lobes and paired gular crests may also be present. The body scales may be nearly homogenous to strongly heterogenous and are usually granular.

This large genus occurs widely in tropical Africa, where members occur in moist evergreen forest and surrounds, while some species occur in moist woodland and savanna. Reproduction is oviparous, with some species retaining the eggs in their body until the embryos are fully developed.

Currently, 41 species are recognised, three of which occur in the region.

KEY Regional *Trioceros* species

1a Rostral crest or appendage present . . . . *T. melleri* (p. 324)
 b Rostral crest or appendage absent 2

2a Occipital lobes thin and rudimentary; background scales sub-uniform with
 scattered larger tubercles; tubercles in vertebral crest closely set;
 two pale stripes on each side of head . . . . *T. goetzei* (p. 322)
 b Occipital lobes well developed; background scales strongly heterogenous;
 tubercles in vertebral crest usually widely spaced; one pale stripe
 on each side of the head . . . . *T. incornutus* (p. 323)

Goetze's Whistling Chameleon *Trioceros goetzei*

Enlarged dorsal crest scales are closely spaced in Goetze's Whistling Chameleon.

SVL 55–80mm; max. SVL ♂ 60mm ♀ 90mm
A small chameleon that lacks a rostral process and horns. Casque slightly raised posteriorly. Occipital lobes small. Dorsal crest well developed, consists of enlarged, spinose, soft scales extending onto tail. Gular and ventral crests absent. Tail prehensile, slightly longer than SVL. Body scales homogenous, with scattered enlarged tubercles on flanks. Coloration very variable, usually includes shades of green, brown and grey, and sometimes purple-grey. 5–7 dark saddles common along vertebral midline. Pale stripe arises at postero-dorsal border of eye, extending along lateral crest of head, over flanks to at least base of tail. Area above this stripe usually darker grey-brown to purple-grey. Second pale stripe or series of pale blotches arises from posterior border of eye, fading out on neck, and becoming prominent again from above shoulder, extending from there to hind limb insertion. Dorsal crest often green; throat may be orange. **Subspecies:** Two subspecies are recognised, one of which occurs in the region. The Nyika Whistling Chameleon (*T. g. nyikae*) occurs on the Nyika Plateau in Malawi as well as in south-western Tanzania bordering Malawi. Slit-like gular pouches may be present or absent

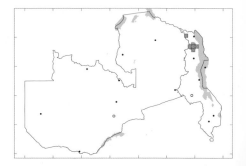

Coloration is very variable.

(orange if present). **Habitat:** Common in heath, bracken and montane swamp verges, as well as forest fringes and grassland. **Behaviour:** Usually found in low bushes and trees and regularly enters marshes and reedbeds, where it often sleeps in aquatic vegetation above water. When handled, it may utter an audible squeak or 'whistle' (actually the successive forceful exhalation and inhalation of air). **Prey:** Invertebrates, including flies, beetles and their larvae, bugs, ants, caterpillars, cockroaches and spiders. **Reproduction:** Female gives birth to 6–10 live young in summer. **Range:** In the region it is restricted to the Nyika Plateau in Malawi and adjoining Zambia. There are unconfirmed records from the Mafinga range and Chitipa district in northern Malawi. Elsewhere it occurs in southern Tanzania.

Ukinga Hornless Chameleon   *Trioceros incornutus*

Enlarged dorsal crest scales are widely spaced in the Ukinga Hornless Chameleon.

Colin Tilbury

SVL 60–80mm; max. SVL ♂ 93mm ♀ 93mm
A medium-sized chameleon that lacks horns and rostral appendages. Casque flattened. Occipital lobes large, covered with large scales. Dorsal crest consists of spinose scales; latter usually well spaced, extends onto anterior part of tail. Gular and ventral crests absent. Tail prehensile, about as long as SVL. Body scales heterogenous, with scattered enlarged scales on flanks. Coloration variable. Crown of head pale reddish brown to dark olive-brown, usually with three chestnut-red chevrons. Body shades of green or brown, with series of large, dark blotches along flanks. Series of pale patches extend from posterior border of eye, over dorsal third of body, to base of tail, may form weak dorsolateral band. **Habitat:** Montane woodland and forest. **Behaviour:** A rare chameleon that favours the mid- and upper storeys of shrubs, small trees and thickets. **Prey:** A variety of invertebrates,

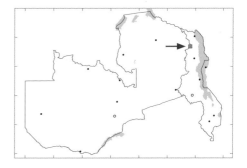

including beetles, caterpillars, cockroaches, flies, spiders and snails. **Reproduction:** Female gives birth to 11–16 live young in summer. **Range:** In the region it is restricted to the Nyika Plateau in Malawi and probably adjoining Zambia. Elsewhere it occurs in the Ukinga and Poroto mountain ranges and on Mounts Ngozi and Rungwe in Tanzania.

Giant One-horned Chameleon *Trioceros melleri*

The Giant One-horned Chameleon is the largest chameleon species on the African continent.

SVL 150–250mm; max. SVL ♂ 288mm ♀ 273mm
A massive chameleon, the largest species on the African continent. A scaly rostral horn is present in adults, while hatchlings and juveniles just have a rostral bump. Occipital lobes large. Casque slightly raised posteriorly. Dorsal crest conspicuous, undulating, extending entire length of body and over most of tail. Gular and ventral crests absent. Tail prehensile, usually slightly longer than SVL. Body scales finely heterogenous with numerous scattered large, flat, granular scales. Scales on occipital lobes greatly enlarged. Coloration variable, usually consists of shades of yellow, green, grey and black, often with scattered paler and/or darker spots. Usually 3–4 narrow transverse green-yellow bands on body and 10–11 on tail. Sides of head, nose and throat usually light green with darker spots. Longitudinal series of 4–5 dark spots often present on lower flanks. Juveniles mottled in grey-brown and black. **Habitat:** Well-wooded savanna and woodland, including miombo woodland. **Behaviour:** Mainly arboreal, frequently clambering to the tops of trees to heights in excess of 10m, but will descend to the ground to cross open areas or lay eggs. When harassed, it turns to face the threat while

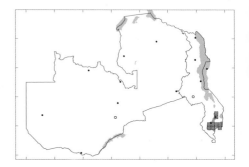

inflating the body and gaping the mouth, raises the occipital lobes, hisses and bites. Males are territorial and will defend their territory with their rostral horns and by biting. **Prey:** Its diet is varied and it will probably eat anything it can catch. Adults prey on grasshoppers, katydids, dragonflies, ants, flies and even small lizards, birds and other chameleons. **Reproduction:** Female lays 38–91 eggs (16–22mm x 13–17mm) in late summer. Incubation takes about 80 days. Hatchlings measure roughly 60mm in TL. Sexual maturity is reached at two years of age. **Range:** Southern Malawi, east of the Shire River. Elsewhere it occurs in north-eastern Mozambique and eastern Tanzania.

Agamas
Family Agamidae

Medium- to large-sized lizards with a cylindrical or dorsoventrally flattened body. The head is large and usually triangular, the neck is distinct, the limbs are well developed and the tail is long and tapering. The tail cannot be shed and does not regenerate. The ear openings are large and the tympanic membrane is often visible. The eyes are prominent, with moveable eyelids. The head is covered in small, irregular scales and the pineal eye is usually well developed and visible as a small circular depression on the top of the head. The body scales are keeled and overlapping and may be drawn into spines. Many species have enlarged scales scattered across the dorsum, or arranged in longitudinal or transverse rows. Clusters of small spines are often present near the ear openings.

Blue-headed Tree Agama

Agamas are diurnal and can often be highly visible and tolerant to the presence of people. They inhabit a variety of niches, being arboreal, rupicolous or terrestrial. Males often have a brightly coloured head and/or throat, particularly during the breeding season, while females, juveniles and non-breeding males are often drably coloured. Some species have complex social structures, with a dominant male protecting a harem of females and warding off potential intruders by displaying from a nearby vantage point or, exceptionally, physically attacking them. The dominance and courtship displays involve the male bobbing his brightly coloured head up and down while perched on a vantage point. Agamas are able to change their colour to a limited degree in response to temperature, light intensity and level of excitement, although these changes are not as pronounced as those seen in chameleons. The diet varies greatly between species. Some prey predominantly on ants and termites, others are mostly herbivorous, and some of the larger species prey on beetle larvae, myriad other invertebrates and even small vertebrates. Most species are oviparous. The female usually deposits her clutch of eggs in a hole dug in moist ground near her retreat. The sex of the young is determined by the incubation temperature.

This large family contains about 456 species in 54 genera that occur throughout Africa, Europe, Asia and Australia. Seven species in two genera occur in the region, although additional cryptic taxa may be described in due course.

WHORL-TAILED AGAMAS *Acanthocercus*

Large agamas that are dorsoventrally flattened and have well-developed limbs with thin toes. They lack an enlarged occipital scale. The body scales are heterogenous, with a series of enlarged scales along the dorsal midline and usually additional enlarged scales arranged in transverse rows. The tail is broad at its base and slowly tapers to a tip, with distinct whorls giving it the appearance of a pine cone. Males are brightly coloured, especially during the breeding season, when they develop a vividly coloured head. Females and juveniles usually have drab coloration.

These lizards prey on a variety of invertebrates, including ants, termites, caterpillars and beetles and their larvae. They are diurnal and arboreal and spend most of their time on large tree trunks, occasionally descending to the ground or inhabiting rock outcrops or buildings. The female lays relatively large clutches of eggs in a hole dug in moist soil, and the sex of the hatchlings is determined by the temperature in the nest during incubation.

The genus is predominantly restricted to southern and eastern Africa, with some species entering Western Asia. Of the 12 recognised species, four occur in the region.

Blue-headed Tree Agama   *Acanthocercus atricollis*

The tail of the Blue-headed Tree Agama is covered in discrete whorls.

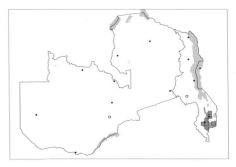

SVL 120–150mm, max. SVL ♂ 167mm ♀ 139mm
A large agama with a large, triangular head that is distinct from the body. Head larger in males. Nostrils round, directed outwards, pierced in posterior portion of elongate, slightly tubular nasal or just below *canthus rostralis*. Ear opening larger than eye; tympanum visible. Dorsals small, smooth and mucronate; those along dorsal midline larger, of varying size and strongly (larger scales) to weakly keeled or smooth (smaller scales). Enlarged scales become more scattered along flanks. 100–136 midbody scale rows. Ventrals smooth, larger than dorsal matrix scales, in 76–94 rows. Tail covered in discrete whorls; dorsals much larger than ventrals. 10–34 precloacal pores in 2 (rarely 3) rows in males. Breeding males have blue-green head and throat, blue fading out on chest; rear part of body reddish brown to yellow; tail yellowish anteriorly, grading to blue posteriorly; enlarged scales pale blue anteriorly, becoming yellow posteriorly; large black spot present in front of shoulder; broad pale vertebral stripe extends from back of head to base of tail; throat pale to brilliant blue, with dark blue reticulate

pattern; ventrum pale brown with irregular dull blue patterning. Females and non-breeding males olive-green to brown above with darker marbling and reticulations; large black spot present in front of shoulder, may be partially obscured by neck fold; throat infused with blue; ventrum off-white to cream with dark reticulations or vermiculation. Juveniles pale with broad, dark crossbands resembling series of X's on back; tail banded. Mouth lining bright orange in both sexes, used in threat displays. **Habitat:** Open savanna and woodland, often near human habitations. **Behaviour:** An arboreal lizard that is usually found in loose colonies consisting of a mature male and several females and juveniles. Diurnal, although some nocturnal activity has been noted. Often seen on tree trunks, where it clings conspicuously while bobbing the head up and down. At night it sleeps in bark fissures, in hollows, on open branches or under foliage. **Prey and Predators:** A generalist, it feeds on ants, caterpillars, beetles and their larvae, grasshoppers and other invertebrates, occasionally also eating thorn tree gum. It is preyed on by Brown House Snakes (*Boaedon capensis*), Savanna Vine Snakes (*Thelotornis capensis*), and various other snakes and birds of prey. **Reproduction:** Female lays 4–16 oval, leathery eggs (18–28mm x 10–22mm) in a hole dug in moist ground beneath a tree in spring to mid-summer. Incubation takes 75–90 days. Hatchlings measure 70–80mm in TL and become sexually mature in their second year. **Range:** Southern Malawi, through Mozambique and Zimbabwe to South Africa and southern Botswana. An apparently isolated population occurs in the southern and eastern DRC and possibly in northern Zambia, although this population may represent a distinct species.

Bill's Tree Agama   *Acanthocercus branchi*

Leslie Reynolds

In Bill's Tree Agama, breeding males attain a pinkish hue.

SVL 80–140mm; max. SVL ♂ 155mm ♀ 125mm
A medium- to large-sized, arboreal agama with a large, triangular head that is distinct from the body. Head distinctly broadened in males. Nostril round to pear-shaped, directed laterally, pierced within posterior portion of nasal. Ear opening about same size as eye, surrounded by small spines; tympanum visible. Dorsals small and smooth, interspersed with large, keeled scales that are usually pale and arranged in 4 indistinct to distinct transverse rows between limbs. Numerous scattered enlarged scales also present dorsally, keeled, more concentrated along the dorsal midline. 103–130 midbody

scale rows; 67–81 longitudinal rows along dorsal midline between middle of forearm and middle of hind limb insertions. Ventrals small and smooth or slightly imbricate, in 79–95 longitudinal rows. Gulars flat, smooth, becoming smaller towards gular fold. Males have 21–25 precloacal pores, in two rows. Females have fewer enlarged scales than males. Breeding males have blue head and forelimbs, which fade into dark brown to orange- or red-brown on back; enlarged scales on back paler, giving rise to coarsely speckled appearance; base of tail orange, becoming light blue towards tip, may have pale bands; large black patch present on shoulder; throat blue at base and medially, becoming paler on margins; ventrum dirty white. Non-breeding males and females paler on flanks, grading to brown or pinkish brown dorsally; occasionally with irregular dark transverse bands on flanks; network of orange or red markings often present on back; series of pale blotches may be present along dorsal midline; head pale brown to light blue; black shoulder patch present; alternating dark and pale bands on tail. Juveniles dirty brown, with four broad, pale-centred, dark transverse bars between limbs; head pale blue; tail banded. **Habitat:** Dense to open woodlands. **Behaviour:** Similar to other tree agamas. Arboreal and diurnal. **Prey:** Feeds on various invertebrates, and probably small vertebrates. **Reproduction:** Lays eggs, although details are unknown. **Range:** Malawi and eastern Zambia and southwards to Zimbabwe. An apparently isolated population occurs in the southern DRC.

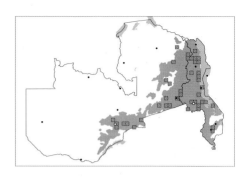

There are bands of enlarged, pale scales on the back.

Western Tree Agama   *Acanthocercus cyanocephalus*

SVL 120–140mm, max. SVL ♂ 147mm
A large agama with a large, triangular head that is distinct from the body, with males having a larger head than females. Nostrils round, situated just below *canthus rostralis*. Ear opening as large as, or slightly smaller than, eye; tympanum visible. Dorsals small and smooth, with relatively few enlarged, keeled scales scattered along dorsum and not forming clumps or transverse rows. Scales along dorsal midline large and keeled, interspersed with

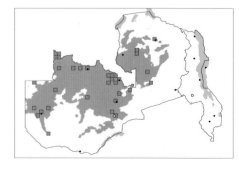

smaller scales. 100–119 midbody scale rows. Ventrals and gulars small, smooth, in 74–94 longitudinal rows; gulars decrease in size towards gular fold. Tail covered in discrete whorls. Males have 24–26 precloacal pores, in two rows. Breeding males have a dark blue head, throat and shoulders, with some light blue patches; body black with numerous pale scales, giving rise to speckled effect; dark transverse bands occasionally present on body; ventrum pale brown with irregular dark

The tail has dark and pale bands.

flecks; anterior part of tail brownish yellow; posterior half dark blue with alternating dark and blue bands. Females and non-breeding males uniform brownish above with 4–5 dark saddles, latter usually interrupted centrally by pale blotches; pale and dark bands on tail; throat white with blue reticulate pattern; ventrum off-white, usually stippled with grey. Black spot usually present just anterior to front limb insertion. **Habitat:** Prefers open woodland, but also enters urban gardens and plantations. **Behaviour:** Diurnal and predominantly arboreal, but just as comfortable on man-made structures. **Prey and Predators:** Feeds on a wide variety of invertebrates, including spiders, caterpillars, ants, termites, flies, bees, wasps, grasshoppers and beetles. Preyed on by Forest Vine Snakes (*Thelotornis kirtlandii*). **Reproduction:** Lays eggs, but details unknown. **Range:** Northern Namibia, through Angola and Zambia into the southern DRC.

In the Western Tree Agama, the enlarged dorsal scales are randomly scattered on the body.

Eastern Tree Agama *Acanthocercus gregorii*

SVL 90–130mm, max. SVL ♂ 138mm ♀ 120mm
A large agama with a large, triangular head that is distinct from the neck, with males having a larger head than females. Nostrils round, situated just below *canthus rostralis*. Ear opening as large as eye; tympanum visible. Dorsals small, keeled, becoming larger along dorsal midline, in 88–126 rows at midbody. Scattered enlarged scales on back and flanks, becoming more concentrated along dorsal midline. Ventrals smooth, small, larger than

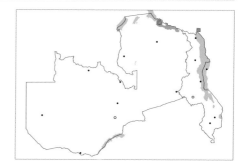

Females and non-breeding males are grey-brown.

In the region, the Eastern Tree Agama occurs in extreme north-eastern Zambia and northern Malawi.

dorsal matrix scales, in 77–92 longitudinal rows. Gulars small and smooth to feebly keeled, but erect and about the same size as ventrals. Tail covered in discrete whorls. 7–37 precloacal pores in males, in 2–3 rows; precloacal pores absent in females. Breeding males have a blue-green to yellow head; body bluish with numerous scattered pale tubercles, giving rise to speckled effect; throat dark blue, becoming paler laterally, may be covered in a blue reticulate pattern, which may extend onto the chest and belly; tail yellowish at base and darker posteriorly. Females and non-breeding males grey-brown with darker marbling and reticulations; throat and belly off-white, may be infused with blue or have a blue reticulate pattern; tail pale anteriorly, dark posteriorly. **Habitat:** Open savanna and woodland. **Behaviour:** Diurnal and predominantly terrestrial, but also found on rock outcrops and in trees. **Prey:** A variety of invertebrates. **Reproduction:** Gravid females were recorded in mid-summer. **Range:** Widely distributed in East Africa, just entering northern Mozambique and extreme northern Malawi and north-eastern Zambia.

AGAMAS *Agama*

Dorsoventrally flattened lizards with well-developed limbs and long, thin toes. The head is triangular, the neck is narrow and distinct, and the tail is thin. The eyes are large, with scaly eyelids, and the ear openings are large with the tympanum usually visible. The head is covered in small, irregular scales, with an enlarged occipital scale overlying the pineal eye. Two enlarged teeth are present in the front of the upper jaw. Males have precloacal pores and are often more vividly coloured than females and juveniles. Breeding males usually develop a bright head, while breeding females may also become brighter, usually in the form of red infusions on the body.

These lizards are largely diurnal, although some nocturnal activity has been recorded. They may be arboreal, rupicolous or terrestrial, and may be solitary or form small harems. Males grow larger than females and will defend a territory from rival males, usually through elaborate territorial displays. They prey predominantly on ants and termites, occasionally supplementing their diet with other insects. Females lay relatively large clutches of soft shelled eggs in a hole that they usually dig in moist ground near their retreat. The sex of the hatchlings is determined by the incubation temperature.

The genus is widespread in and endemic to Africa, with 46 species currently recognised, although new species are continually being described. Three species occur in the region.

KEY Regional *Agama* species

1a Dorsals generally small; scattered or clumped; distinctly enlarged scales
    arranged in rows or scattered across dorsum . . . . **A. armata** (p. 331)
 b Dorsals more or less equal in size; enlarged dorsals lacking or restricted
    to the dorsal midline **2**

2a Scales on back (excluding scales along dorsal midline) as large as, or only slightly
    larger than, those on belly; ventrals smooth; predominantly rupicolous . . . . **A. kirkii** (p. 333)
 b Scales on back much larger than those on belly; ventrals keeled; terrestrial
    or arboreal . . . . **A. mossambica** (p. 334)

Peter's Ground Agama   *Agama armata*

Peter's Ground Agama has six rows of enlarged scales on the body.

SVL 70–80mm; max. SVL ♂ 82mm ♀ 94mm
A fairly small agama with a triangular head that is longer than it is wide. Nostril pierced beneath very short *canthus rostralis*. Dorsal head scales heterogenous, keeled, overlap towards snout, with 2–4 enlarged scales in middle of snout.

10–13 supralabials. Body scales strongly keeled, shortly mucronate, directed obliquely in towards backbone, interspersed with 6 rows (8–10 rows in individuals from Malawi) of enlarged scales arranged in longitudinal rows. 73–105 midbody scale rows. Vertebral crest poorly developed on nape, becoming more pronounced on back. Gulars and ventrals keeled, mucronate. Upper surfaces of limbs covered in approximately equal-sized scales. Tail spiny, slightly longer than SVL. 3rd and 4th toes equal in size, with 14–20 subdigital lamellae beneath each. 1 (rarely 2) rows of 9–18 precloacal pores in males. Grey or reddish brown above, with 4–5 pale-centred transverse dark bands or spots across back. Pale vertebral streak runs from base of head to base of tail. Bright red spots sometimes present dorsally. Head dark above and blue on sides (particularly pronounced in breeding males), with two dark interorbital bars usually present. Limbs and tail have dark transverse bands. Ventral surfaces cream to greyish white, with darker patterning on chin and throat that may extend over chest

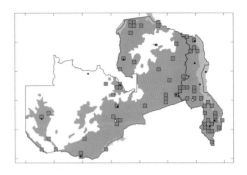

and belly. Males have a dark spot at base of throat. **Habitat:** Mesic and sandveld savannas. **Behaviour:** Terrestrial, individuals take refuge in short burrows often located at the base of a bush. Occasionally takes shelter in rodent burrows. **Prey:** Feeds predominantly on ants and beetles. Other invertebrates, such as wasps and termites, are also eaten. **Reproduction:** Female lays 9–16 oval eggs (13–15mm x 8–10mm) in summer. **Range:** Eastern South Africa, through Mozambique northwards to Malawi, Zambia and the southern DRC.

The breeding female develops an orange-red back and pale blue head.

Kirk's Rock Agama   *Agama kirkii*

In Kirk's Rock Agama, breeding males have a coral-red to yellow head.

This large agama favours large rock outcrops.

SVL 80–100mm; max. SVL 115mm

A large agama with a fairly flat body and long limbs. Head longer than broad; snout fairly pointed. Nostril pierced in posterior portion of small tubular nasal on, or just below, the *canthus rostralis*, directed upwards and outwards. Ear opening exposed, slightly smaller than eye. Scales on the head are smooth, slightly convex and heterogenous. 2–3 enlarged scales in middle of snout. Groups of small spines surround ear opening, also present on sides of neck. 8–11 supralabials. Dorsals on body small, strongly keeled, imbricate, shortly mucronate (although less so in females),

directed obliquely in towards backbone. Dorsal crest on nape well developed in males, becomes low but distinct on back and well developed on tail. Dorsal crest from nape to base of tail short and distinct in females and juveniles. Gulars and ventrals smooth, about same size as those on back; 99–114 midbody scale rows. 4th finger and 4th toe the longest; 19–23 subdigital lamellae beneath 4th toe. Tail flattened, nearly twice the SVL (about 1.5 times SVL in females), covered in large, strongly keeled mucronate scales arranged into segments. 1 (sometimes 2) row of 10–14 precloacal pores in males. Males have a coral-red to yellowish head; back blue-black to purple; pale dorsal midline runs from nape to base of tail; throat coral-red to orange, with pale lines running parallel to jawline anteriorly, merging into single median line at base of throat; limbs and tail paler than back; chest and belly navy-blue; narrow pale blue-green bands on tail. Breeding females have a blue-green head; back maroon, covered in bluish-grey blotches. Immature males olive-brown above, with darker markings often enclosing paler blotches; ventrum white with dark brown infusions or vermiculation on throat and chest that sometimes extends onto belly. Non-breeding adults and juveniles mottled grey-black. **Habitat:** Granitic and paragneiss outcrops in arid and mesic savannas. **Behaviour:** Rupicolous, preferring large rock outcrops although also occurring in boulder-fields and occasionally climbing into trees. Juveniles have been observed sand-bathing, using all four limbs to shower their body with sand. **Prey:** Feeds predominantly on ants, occasionally preying on beetles and other invertebrates. **Reproduction:** Female lays about 10 eggs in a hole dug in soft soil or beneath a rock slab in summer. **Range:** Central, southern and eastern Zambia and southern Malawi, entering northern Malawi at Vwaza Marsh. Elsewhere it occurs through Mozambique to Zimbabwe and extreme eastern Botswana.

Mozambique Agama   *Agama mossambica*

The Mozambique Agama has a distinct dorsal crest on the nape and tail.

SVL 80–100mm; max. SVL ♂ 115mm ♀ 105mm
A large agama with a head that is longer than it is broad. Nostril directed upwards and backwards, pierced in posterior portion of small, tubular nasal on *canthus rostralis*. Ear opening exposed, larger than diameter of eye. Dorsal head scales feebly keeled; clusters of small spines around ear opening and on sides of neck. 9–10 supralabials. Body moderately depressed. Body scales strongly keeled, mucronate, imbricate, directed diagonally inwards towards dorsal midline. Dorsal crest distinct on nape, low on back and distinct again on tail. Ventrals imbricate, shortly mucronate, distinctly keeled (only faintly keeled in some populations), smaller than dorsals. 69–94 midbody scale rows. 3rd and 4th fingers subequal in length, or 4th finger slightly longer; 4th toe

longest, or approximately equal in length to 3rd. 22–23 subdigital lamellae beneath 4th toe. Tail slightly depressed basally, compressed posteriorly, just over 1.5 times SVL. Tail covered in large, strongly keeled mucronate scales that are much larger than scales on back. 12–15 precloacal pores in males. Adult males grey to olive-brown above, may have 4–5 large, elongate brick-red to blackish spots on either side of dorsal midline, which may fuse into bands. Broad pale blue to white vertebral stripe often present. Head olive to dark brown above with darker markings on sides and distinct reddish bar running across forehead in front of eyes. Large reddish spot present just above shoulder. Ventrum dirty white to pinkish with bright blue patterning on chin and throat that merges into blue patch at base of throat. Breeding males develop a dark blue head and throat, with bright yellow forehead and eyebrow; body grey, may be mottled with maroon. Breeding females have an orange back. Non-breeding adults mottled grey-brown, usually with olive to dark brown head, reddish forehead stripe, red patch above shoulder and 4–5 brick-red to blackish spots along flanks. Both sexes usually have a dark diagonal stripe extending from posterior margin of eye to ear opening. Juveniles more distinctly marked above, with a yellowish vertebral streak and dark crossbars; head olive-brown, becoming bluish green posteriorly; yellow spots may be present above and below the ear openings, as may a yellowish stripe on the flanks. **Habitat:** Woodland, moist lowland savanna and forest fringes. **Behaviour:** Equally at home on the ground and in trees, usually scampering up the nearest tree at the first sign of danger. **Prey:** Feeds predominantly on ants, supplementing this diet with termites, beetles, grasshoppers and other insects. **Reproduction:** Female lays eggs during spring or summer. **Range:** From Tanzania through southern Malawi to Zimbabwe and Mozambique.

This agama (here a juvenile) is equally at home in trees and on the ground.

Luke Verburgt

CHELONIANS
Order Testudines

CHELONIANS

CHELONIANS include tortoises, terrapins and turtles. Their bodies are generally covered by a hard, protective shell (a few species have a greatly reduced shell and are covered by soft, leathery skin instead). All chelonians have an anapsid skull (i.e. lacking temporal openings). These reptiles occur in a variety of habitats: tortoises live on land, terrapins inhabit fresh waterbodies and turtles, the largest species of the group, inhabit the oceans.

The shell consists of the upper carapace and the lower plastron, linked by the bridge. The various bony plates constituting the shell are joined by tooth-like sutures, although some species have distinct plates joined by cartilaginous interspaces. In most species the shell is covered in thin, horny plates (called scutes) that may become detached if injured or subjected to fire, exposing the underlying bone plate. The scutes grow with the animal: a new layer of keratin is deposited underneath the existing plate and extends beyond its margin, creating annual growth rings and gradually increasing plate thickness. In most species the shell is immovable, although two genera have hinges: hinged terrapins (*Pelusios*) have a hinge on the anterior portion of the plastron, while hinged tortoises (*Kinixys*) have a hinge at the posterior portion of the carapace, allowing the shell to be partially or wholly closed for protection. The Pancake Tortoise (*Malacochersus tornieri*) has persistent fenestrations between the bones of the shell, resulting in a comparatively soft and pliable shell. The shell of soft-shelled terrapins is covered by a thick, leathery skin and is not hard to the touch.

Chelonians have a highly specialised skeleton, with the ribs, vertebrae and sternum fused to the bony interior of the carapace. The scapula and pelvis are located on the inside of the rib cage. Most chelonians have a parrot-like beak, although some species have lips. The head and neck are highly flexible and retractile, being withdrawn either straight back (suborder Cryptodira) or sideways (suborder Pleurodira). Tortoises and terrapins are able to withdraw their limbs as well, whereas turtles are not able to. The limbs are usually short and thick, and aquatic species have webbing between their toes. The limbs of turtles are modified into large flippers for swimming.

Owing to their heavy shell, most chelonians are slow-moving (turtles and terrapins in water are notable exceptions). Most are herbivorous, although many terrapins are omnivorous and some turtles prey on invertebrates and fish, which are often captured from an ambush position. All chelonians lay their eggs in holes dug on land (even female turtles haul out onto beaches to deposit their egg clutches above the high-water level). Turtles and most terrapins lay soft-shelled eggs, whereas tortoises and soft-shelled terrapins lay hard-shelled eggs. The female finds a sunny, moist location to dig a hole using her hind legs and may use urine or cloacal water to soften the ground before and during the excavation process. The eggs are deposited into the freshly dug nest and the soil is carefully replaced. There is no maternal care: the eggs are abandoned and hatchlings are left to fend for themselves. Incubation can take 4–15 months and is in part dependent on the season and prevailing weather conditions. Chelonian eggs enter a condition called diapause during winter and very little embryonic development occurs until the following spring, when temperatures increase. Diapause slows embryonic development down to such an extent that eggs laid the previous autumn hatch with those laid the following spring. In many species the sex of the hatchlings is determined by the incubation temperature, with males developing at lower temperatures and females at higher ones.

There are 348 species and an additional 119 subspecies of chelonians in 90 genera, of which 13 species in six genera have been recorded in the region.

Eastern Hinged Tortoise

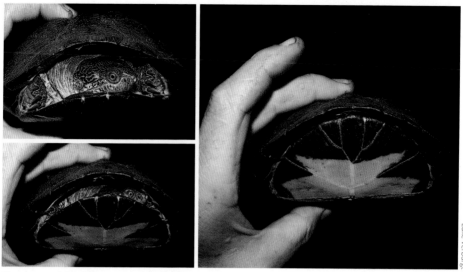

The anterior plastral hinge of a Serrated Hinged Terrapin in action.

Luke Verburgt

CHELONIAN SHELL AND SCUTES

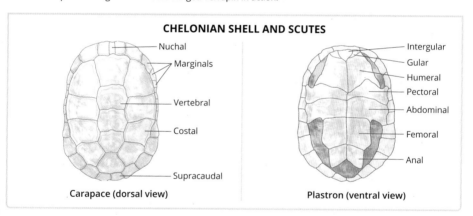

Carapace (dorsal view)
- Nuchal
- Marginals
- Vertebral
- Costal
- Supracaudal

Plastron (ventral view)
- Intergular
- Gular
- Humeral
- Pectoral
- Abdominal
- Femoral
- Anal

KEY Genera of Testudines

1a Shell flattened, disc-like, covered in leathery skin .... *Cycloderma* (p. 349)
  b Shell covered in distinct hard scutes **2**

2a Neck withdrawn sideways into shell; aquatic **3**
  b Neck withdrawn straight back into shell; terrestrial **4**

3a Anterior plastral hinge absent; shell thin; head with distinct bi-toned
    coloration, being dark above and pale below .... *Pelomedusa* (p. 340)
  b Anterior plastral hinge present; shell usually thick .... *Pelusios* (p. 342)

4a Shell broad, very flattened, soft, flexible .... *Malacochersus* (p. 351)
  b Shell dome-shaped or depressed (but not flattened), hard, inflexible **5**

5a Postero-lateral hinge present; nuchal present; carapace noticeably depressed .... *Kinixys* (p. 352)
  b Postero-lateral hinge absent; nuchal absent; carapace dome-shaped ...... *Stigmochelys* (p. 356)

Side-necked Terrapins
Suborder Pleurodira

A group of aquatic terrapins with webbed hind feet. The head is withdrawn sideways into the shell, always leaving one eye exposed to monitor for threats. The shell is usually hard and dorsoventrally flattened, with an unpaired intergular at the front of the plastron. These reptiles occur throughout South America, Africa, Madagascar and Australia.

African Terrapins
Family Pelomedusidae

A large group of primitive, medium-sized terrapins. The shell is hard and an anterior plastral hinge can be present (*Pelusios*) or absent (*Pelomedusa*). Nuchals and supracaudals are absent and an intergular is present. The head and neck are completely retractable beneath the carapace edge. The nostrils are located at the tip of the snout to facilitate breathing at the water's surface while the majority of the body remains submerged. The feet are depressed and paddle-like to aid with swimming, while the front claws are strong and used to shred food grasped in the mouth before it is ingested. Coloration is typically dull brown, green or black.

Central Marsh Terrapin

When threatened, these terrapins will bite and scratch and are also capable of exuding a foul-smelling fluid from glands near the base of the limbs. They are predominantly carnivorous, but will also feed on plant material and readily scavenge. Females lay 8–50 soft-shelled eggs in a hole dug above the flood level, and incubation usually takes 50–100 days.

This family occurs widely across sub-Saharan Africa, including Madagascar, and contains two genera and 27 recognised species.

MARSH OR HELMETED TERRAPINS   *Pelomedusa*

Medium-sized terrapins with a moderately depressed carapace and no plastral hinge.

They frequent temporary waterbodies, as their thin shells afford them little protection against the crocodiles and other predators in more permanent water sources. When the waterbodies dry out, these terrapins bury themselves below ground and may remain dormant for up to six years until conditions are suitably moist. They can cover large distances on land, usually at night after good rainfall, and are therefore able to travel between temporary waterbodies in arid environments.

Ten species are recognised, with another four requiring verification. One occurs in the region.

Central Marsh Terrapin   *Pelomedusa subrufa*

TL 100–140mm; max. TL 197mm
A small to medium-sized terrapin with a hard, flat, thin shell and no plastral hinge. Head large; temporal scale on side of head large, undivided.

Two small skin processes present under chin. Pectorals usually in broad contact at plastral midseam (rarely in narrow contact, or triangular and not in contact). Four small musk glands near edge of carapace opposite 4th and 8th marginals. Limbs well webbed, broad, with sharp claws. Carapace uniformly light to dark brown. Plastron predominantly light-coloured in adults; often with dark markings in juveniles. Head distinctly two-toned, darkly vermiculated above, pale below and on sides (including jaws). **Habitat:** Inhabits temporary pans, dams, marshes and small streams. Rarely enters larger rivers or permanent waterbodies owing to the presence of large Nile Crocodiles (*Crocodylus niloticus*), against which the thin shell does not offer protection. **Behaviour:** Regularly basks on rocks or logs exposed above the surface of the water, at the water's edge or while drifting on the water surface. Adults may travel long distances between suitable waterbodies. During drought periods, this species aestivates in a burrow which it digs in moist soil, often far away from the nearest temporary water source.

Prey and Predators: Omnivorous, feeding on aquatic plants, insects, tadpoles and amphibians. Regularly ambushes smaller bird species (especially doves and sandgrouse) at the water's edge. Many wading birds are seen with a foot bitten off, probably as a result of a predation event by a terrapin species. It will regularly scavenge. While aestivating, it may be dug up and eaten by jackals and Honey Badgers. **Reproduction:** Mating takes place in the water during summer. The female lays 10–30 (occasionally more than 40) soft-shelled eggs (30–40mm x 18–28mm) in moist soil above the high-water level. If the ground is dry, the female may urinate on the nest site before excavation commences. Incubation takes 90–110 days and eggs usually hatch after rain has softened the soil above the nest, easing the emergence of the hatchlings. **Range:** Widespread but patchily distributed throughout the region. Elsewhere it ranges to southern Angola and Namibia, the south-eastern DRC, northern Tanzania, Mozambique and extreme north-eastern South Africa. It has been introduced to Madagascar.

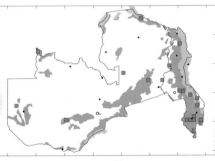

Derek Solomon

TOP The Central Marsh Terrapin lacks a plastral hinge. ABOVE The head is two-toned.

HINGED TERRAPINS *Pelusios*

Medium-sized to large terrapins with a moderately flattened to domed carapace. A well-developed anterior plastral hinge is present and closes when the head is withdrawn, providing protection. The shell is thick and some species have serrations on the dorsal and/or posterior surfaces, especially in juveniles. The colour of the plastron is an important local distinguishing feature.

The genus occurs widely in sub-Saharan Africa, as well as on Madagascar and various islands in the Indian Ocean. Its taxonomy is not well understood and 17 species are recognised at present, six of which enter the region.

KEY Regional *Pelusios* species

1a Plastral hinge poorly developed; anterior lobe of plastron more than twice the length of suture between abdominals .... *P. nanus* (p. 344)
b Plastral hinge well developed; anterior lobe of plastron less than twice the length of suture between abdominals **2**

2a Axillary present; posterior margin of carapace usually serrated; plastron yellow with symmetrical black angular pattern along margins .... *P. sinuatus* (p. 346)
b Axillary absent; posterior margin of carapace smoothly rounded; plastron dark or yellow, without dark angular pattern along margins, may have yellow patterning medially **3**

3a Carapace yellow to brown, uniform or with black blotches; plastron yellow, uniform or with some peripheral sulci black, especially on anterior lobe of plastron; head with yellow and brown vermiculation; skin on limbs yellow ... *P. castanoides* (p. 343)
b Carapace not yellow; plastron usually not uniform yellow; skin on limbs grey to black **4**

4a Carapace brown; plastral scutes yellow medially, dark at joins, forming symmetrical pattern; neck and limbs grey-black; inhabits temporary waterbodies .... *P. subniger* (p. 348)
b Carapace black (rarely brown); plastron predominantly black, sometimes with broad yellow median band; inhabits permanent waterbodies **5**

5a Plastron uniform black or black with broad yellow-brown medial band; head black above with distinct symmetrical yellow patterning; neck and limbs dark grey; beak unicuspid .... *P. bechuanicus* (p. 342)
b Plastron black, occasionally yellow medially (very rarely uniform yellow); head uniform dark above, pale yellow on sides or dark with bold yellow vermiculations; skin on neck and limbs grey-brown; beak bicuspid .... *P. rhodesianus* (p. 345)

Okavango Hinged Terrapin *Pelusios bechuanicus*

TL 250–300mm; max. TL 330mm
A large terrapin with an elongate, thick, domed carapace that is wider posteriorly than anteriorly. Plastral hinge well developed. Head large; beak unicuspid. Three skin processes usually present under chin. Posterior border of carapace smoothly rounded. Vertebrals slightly keeled in juveniles, not keeled in adults. Lateral marginals obtusely keeled in subadults, becoming smooth in adults; posterior marginals not notched or projecting. Anterior lobe of plastron less than twice the length of suture between abdominals; plastron moderately constricted at hind limb level. Weakly developed crescent-shaped scales present on anterior surface of the forelimbs. Axillary absent. Growth rings poorly defined. Carapace and plastron uniformly black; plastron occasionally pale yellow medially or with white sutures. Head black with symmetrical yellow markings, latter more prominent in juveniles. Neck and limbs yellowish grey; outer surface of limbs grey. **Habitat:** Deep, clear waterways. **Behaviour:** Unknown. **Prey:** Invertebrates and fish, and probably amphibians as well. **Reproduction:**

Female lays 21–48 soft-shelled eggs (35–39mm x 21–23mm) in moist soil in late spring. **Range:** Zambezi River and southwards to the Greater Okavango basin in northern Botswana. Also occurs in other large watercourses and marshes in south-central Zambia.

The plastron is predominantly black.

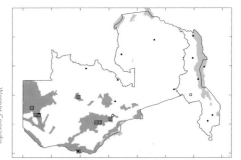

The Okavango Hinged Terrapin has bold yellow patterning on its head.

Yellow-bellied Hinged Terrapin *Pelusios castanoides*

TL 170–200mm; max. TL 223mm

A medium-sized terrapin with an elongate, domed shell that is wider posteriorly than anteriorly. Plastral hinge well developed. Head of moderate size; beak bicuspid. Two skin processes usually present under chin. Posterior border of carapace smooth, round, or slightly serrated. Vertebrals lack keels; small projection often present on 4th vertebral. Anterior lobe of plastron less than twice the length of suture between abdominals. Plastron weakly constricted at hind limb level. Several transverse rows of enlarged, crescent-shaped scales present on front limbs. Axillary absent. Growth rings usually visible. Carapace olive-brown to dark brown or yellowish, may have marbled appearance. Plastron yellow, usually with faint dark markings along sutures of anterior scutes. Head dark brown, with fine yellow vermiculation; rest of skin yellow or yellow-brown. **Habitat:** Frequents seasonal pans, swamps, marshes, lakes and quiet backwaters, preferring weedy areas. **Behaviour:** Buries itself in soft mud when waterbodies dry up, aestivating until good rains. Individuals may also aestivate away from waterbodies, resulting in many having scars on their shells caused by fires. **Prey:** Feeds on aquatic plants, insects, amphibians and freshwater snails. **Reproduction:** Female lays up to 25 eggs (30–33mm x 21–23mm) in spring or early summer. **Range:** From East Africa, southwards through Mozambique and Malawi to eastern South Africa, with isolated populations on Madagascar and the Seychelles.

The plastron is predominantly yellow.

The limbs of the Yellow-bellied Hinged Terrapin are covered in yellow skin.

Dwarf Hinged Terrapin   *Pelusios nanus*

TL 80–100mm; max. TL 120mm
A small terrapin with a poorly developed plastral hinge. Head of moderate size; snout blunt; beak unicuspid. Two skin processes present under chin. Carapace narrow, oval, but elongate in males. Vertebrals not, or only faintly, keeled. Posterior pair of marginals notched at their suture, with the median portions of these marginals often projecting posteriorly. Anterior lobe of plastron more than twice the length of suture between

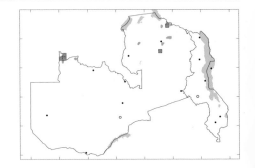

abdominals. Posterior lobe of plastron only slightly constricted at hind limb level and between hind limbs and posterior border. No enlarged scales on forelimbs. Axillary and inguinal absent. Growth rings well defined. Carapace brown, occasionally with black streaks; bridge black; plastron yellow with a black margin. Head black with brown vermiculation dorsally. Skin on neck and limbs yellow; outer surfaces of limbs dark brown. **Habitat:** Probably inhabits perennial waterbodies. Found in small waterbodies in moist savanna and forest–savanna mosaic along the southern edge of the Congo basin. **Behaviour:** Unknown. **Prey and Predators:** Unknown. **Reproduction:** A captive female laid five viable eggs (28–30mm x 15–17mm) 10 months after capture. **Range:** From northern and central Angola eastwards to northern Zambia and the southern DRC.

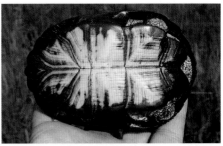

The plastral hinge is poorly developed.

The Dwarf Hinged Terrapin is the smallest terrapin species found in the region.

Mashona Hinged Terrapin *Pelusios rhodesianus*

TL 150–200mm; max. TL 255mm
A small to medium-sized terrapin with a domed carapace that is wider posteriorly than anteriorly. Plastral hinge well developed. Head small; beak bicuspid. Two skin processes present under chin. Posterior border of carapace smooth, rounded; no notch in posterior pair of marginals. Vertebrals weakly keeled in juveniles, becoming smooth with age; adults often retain keel on 4th vertebral. Anterior lobe of plastron less than twice the length of suture between abdominals. Posterior lobe of plastron not constricted at hind limb level. Scales on anterior surface of forelimbs well developed, crescent-shaped. Axillary absent. Growth rings usually distinct.

Carapace uniform black or dark grey. Plastron uniform black or with irregular yellow patches medially, rarely uniform yellow. Head dark brown above, creamy yellow on sides and below, or brown with yellow vermiculation. Neck and limbs pale yellow, but limbs grey-brown on the outer surfaces. **Habitat:** Inhabits quiet, weed-choked backwaters of dams, lakes and swamps. **Behaviour:** May enter grassland surrounding waterbodies after rain, presumably to lay eggs. **Prey:** Feeds on aquatic snails and insects, frogs, small fish and aquatic vegetation. **Reproduction:** Female lays 11–14 soft-shelled eggs (33–37mm x 20–23mm) between September and April and may lay more than one clutch per season. Hatchlings have been observed in December and January. **Range:** Widespread from East Africa through Central Africa, extending westwards to Angola and southwards to eastern Zimbabwe, Mozambique and the Okavango Swamps in Botswana. A relict population is present in South Africa.

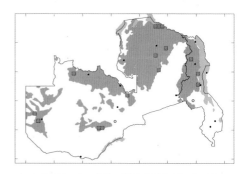

The plastron is predominantly black.

The head of the Mashona Hinged Terrapin can be two-toned (seen above) or vermiculated.

Serrated Hinged Terrapin   *Pelusios sinuatus*

TL 300–400mm; max. TL 465mm

A large terrapin with a domed carapace that is wider posteriorly than anteriorly. Plastral hinge large, well developed. Head relatively small; snout somewhat pointed; beak weakly bicuspid. Two skin processes present under chin. Vertebrals keeled, particularly in juveniles. Posterior marginals enlarged, serrated, upturned. Anterior lobe of plastron about as long as suture between abdominals; shorter than this suture in large adults. Posterior lobe of plastron moderately constricted at hind limb level. Axillary present (may be absent in individuals smaller than 70mm in TL). Growth rings usually distinct. Carapace uniformly dark. Plastron yellow medially with symmetrical black angular pattern around edges, rarely uniformly reddish brown (especially in juveniles). Head dark brown with yellow or light brown vermiculation; may be darker dorsally, gradually fading to dirty white on chin and throat. Neck and limbs pale olive-grey; outer surfaces of limbs dark grey. Juveniles orange-brown to greenish grey dorsally, with fine, dark markings radiating outwards from centre of scutes; plastron mottled in salmon and grey. **Habitat:** Permanent waterbodies, including large rivers, lakes and dams. **Behaviour:** Basks on logs and rocks exposed above the water surface, or on the shoreline. **Prey and Predators:** Readily feeds on mussels, snails, invertebrates, fish and amphibians. Opportunistically scavenges on carcasses in the water and may pick ticks off the legs of large animals while they are drinking or wallowing. Occasionally eats floating fruits. This species is regularly preyed on by Nile Crocodiles (*Crocodylus niloticus*). Juveniles are eaten by African Fish-Eagles and Southern Ground Hornbills. Its nests are raided by Water Monitors (*Varanus niloticus*) and mongooses. **Reproduction:** Female lays 7–30 eggs (42–45mm x 24–26mm), in soft sand up to 500m from the water's edge between October and January. Hatchlings emerge between March and April and measure 40–51mm in TL. **Range:** Widespread through tropical East Africa, and from Somalia through Kenya, Tanzania, Malawi and eastern and southern Zambia to north-eastern South Africa.

Dark angular markings are present on the plastron.

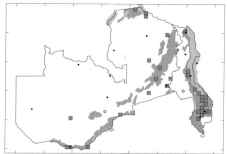

The posterior scutes of the Serrated Hinged Terrapin are upturned and often project.

Pan Hinged Terrapin *Pelusios subniger*

The Pan Hinged Terrapin has dark skin and a yellow bridge.

The plastron is yellow with dark sutures.

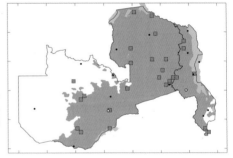

TL 130–180mm; max. TL 195mm

A small to medium-sized terrapin with a rounded carapace and a small but well-developed plastral hinge. Head large; snout blunt; beak unicuspid. Two skin processes usually present under chin. Vertebrals not keeled; 3rd vertebral usually wider than long. Posterior pair of marginals not notched or projecting. Anterior lobe of plastron less than twice the length of suture between abdominals. Posterior lobe of plastron strongly constricted at hind limb level. No axillary. Carapace uniformly brown to reddish brown; alternating yellow and brown pattern on bridge. Plastral scutes dark with pale yellow centres. Head uniformly brown to blue-grey, occasionally with black spots, but not vermiculated. Neck and limbs dark grey to black. **Habitat:** Temporary pans and other small, temporary waterbodies. **Behaviour:** Often aestivates away from water during droughts. As a result, many individuals have scars on their shells from fires. **Prey:** Omnivorous; it feeds on small frogs, tadpoles, invertebrates, crabs and vegetable matter. **Reproduction:** Female lays 8–12 soft-shelled eggs (roughly 35–36mm x 20–21mm) in summer. Incubation takes 104–107 days. Hatchlings measure 30–35mm in TL. **Range:** East Africa, through Malawi and Zambia to northern Botswana and eastern South Africa. Elsewhere it has been introduced to Madagascar and various Indian Ocean islands, including the Seychelles.

Modern Chelonians
Suborder Cryptodira

This is the largest suborder of chelonians and includes land tortoises and most terrapins. In this group the head is withdrawn straight into the shell by bending the neck into an S-shape. The limbs are often simultaneously withdrawn for protection, with the hard, scaly exterior surface of the limbs providing additional protection for the head.

Soft-shelled Terrapins
Family Trionychidae

These terrapins have a flattened, disc-like, soft shell with flexible cartilaginous edges. The body is covered in leathery skin with no external trace of a hard shell. There are only three claws on each forefoot and the limbs are well webbed and paddle-like. The neck is very long and extendible, and the snout is tubular.

Zambezi Soft-shelled Terrapin

They feed on fish, frogs and aquatic insects, and occasionally eat plant material. They come ashore to lay eggs and occasionally to bask. Juveniles may be seen walking long distances after rain or between waterbodies as these dry up.

There are 31 species in 13 genera occurring mainly in south-east Asia and North America, with five species in three genera found in Africa.

AFRICAN SOFT-SHELLED TERRAPINS *Cycloderma*

A genus of unusual terrapins with a soft shell that is covered in skin rather than scutes. The carapace is large, flat and oval. The limbs are paddle-like and modified for swimming. Large, flexible skin flaps are present posteriorly on either side of the plastron, which are used to cover the hind feet when they are withdrawn. The neck is long, and the snout is a pointed and tubular.

Two species are recognised, with only one entering the region.

Zambezi Soft-shelled Terrapin *Cycloderma frenatum*

TL 300–500mm; max. TL 560mm
A large, flat-shelled terrapin with a smooth, soft shell and a flexible flap that covers the hind legs. Adults may reach a mass of 18kg. Head elongate, flattened; snout pointed, tubular. Eyes bright yellow, especially in juveniles. Neck long, can be completely withdrawn into carapace, partially closing front of shell. Feet broad, well webbed; each front foot with 4–5 sharp-edged crescent-shaped skin flaps; each hind foot with single skin fold under the heel. Claws

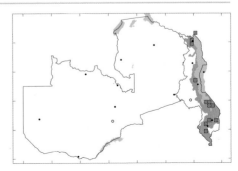

long, sharp, black. Juveniles have a moderately developed vertebral keel and numerous wavy lines of tubercles on carapace. Adults uniform pale brown to dark olive dorsally, occasionally with faint blotching. Plastron ranges from white to fleshy pink in coloration, sometimes with grey infusions (especially in juveniles). Juveniles pale grey to pale green with carapace edged with white and head and neck grey, with broad pale stripes. Neck vividly striped with cream and black in juveniles, becoming uniformly dull olive or with dark longitudinal stripes in adults. **Habitat:** Streams, rivers, lakes and swamps.

The snout is pointed and tubular.

Juveniles prefer smaller waterbodies where they are comparatively safe from predators, particularly Nile Crocodiles (*Crocodylus niloticus*). **Behaviour:** Shy. Basks on the water surface and on shorelines; swims on the water surface in muddy waters. Juveniles may travel long distances between waterbodies as these dry up or fill up after rains. It appears to aestivate during winter. **Prey and Predators:** The powerful forelegs are used to dig into soft mud for crustaceans, but it will also eat fish, frogs and aquatic insects. It is preyed on by crocodiles and otters. Juveniles are preyed on by Southern Ground Hornbills while migrating between pans. Along Lake Malawi, local fishermen raid nests for freshly laid eggs, reducing the fecundity of this population. Adults are also collected for food, predominantly for the overseas market. **Reproduction:** Female lays 15–25 hard-shelled eggs (30–35mm in diameter) from December to March. Hatchlings emerge after approximately 12 months. **Range:** Occurs along the length of Lake Malawi and the southern portions of Lake Tanganyika. Elsewhere it is found from East Africa southwards to the Save River in central Mozambique, entering extreme eastern Zimbabwe.

The Zambezi Soft-shelled Terrapin lacks a bony exterior shell.

Land Tortoises
Family Testudinidae

Leopard Tortoise

This family comprises species that have modifications for life on land. Most tortoises have a thick, domed carapace and a hard ventral plastron, which are joined laterally by bridges. The Pancake Tortoise (*Malacochersus tornieri*) has a flat, soft shell to facilitate a rupicolous lifestyle. Some species have hinges near the hind legs which allow for limited closing of the hind carapace to further protect the back legs. In all species the head is globular, with a horny beak, and the neck is thick and retractile. The top of the head is covered in large scales. The hind feet are columnar, while the front feet are weakly spatulate. The front legs are covered in large scales, which provide protection for the limbs and head when these are withdrawn. The tail is short and fat. They are usually mottled in shades of yellow, tan, brown and black, affording them effective camouflage in savanna.

The diet consists predominantly of vegetable matter, although land tortoises are also geophagous and may occasionally chew on bones for their calcium. Many species also prey on small invertebrates, including millipedes, beetles, snails and termite alates. They usually aestivate during winter, entering thickets, earthen burrows or rock crevices for protection.

These tortoises occur in the temperate and tropical regions of all continents, including Madagascar and many Indian Ocean Islands and the Galapagos Islands, but do not occur in Australia. As many as 59 species in 16 genera occur globally, of which five species in three genera are found in the region.

PANCAKE TORTOISES   *Malacochersus*

A monotypic genus that is nearly endemic to East Africa, just entering north-eastern Zambia. This genus is unique amongst African tortoises in that the carapace is very soft and flexible throughout life, caused by persistent fenestrations between the bones of the carapace. The costal and peripheral bones are thin and some reabsorption of the endochondral ribs also occurs, providing further flexibility. Unlike most other chelonians, pancake tortoises are agile and can easily right themselves if they land on their back.

Pancake Tortoise   *Malacochersus tornieri*

TL 130–160mm; max. TL 180mm
A small tortoise with a broad, flat, soft and flexible carapace that lacks a hinge. Snout rounded; beak weakly to moderately hooked, bicuspid or tricuspid. Posterior marginals weakly recurved, slightly serrated. 4–7 (usually 5) vertebrals, with 4th and 5th usually only in narrow contact. 4 (rarely 5) costals; 22–24 (usually 22) marginals; supracaudal divided (rarely entire). Anterior margin of plastron notched. Gulars together as wide as, or wider than, long; intergular rarely present. 2 (rarely 3) small axillaries; 2–4 inguinals. Front limbs covered with large, overlapping, pointed scales. Carapace slightly domed in hatchlings,

becoming gradually depressed as they grow. Carapace scutes brown or tan-centred in adults, with dark bands radiating out to scute border. Large adults often become uniform brown, sometimes with darker speckling. Juveniles more vividly coloured than adults, being dark yellow with dark markings covering both the carapace and plastron. Plastron colour highly variable, uniformly pale yellow in hatchlings, grading to yellow with black radial bands or dark smudges in adults. **Habitat:** Small rocky hills in dry *Vachellia–Commiphora* savanna at higher elevations. **Behaviour:** Diurnal, but shows crepuscular tendencies. Relies on speed to attain cover, rather than withdrawing its extremities into the shell. It takes refuge under rocks and in rock crevices, a habit that is greatly assisted by the soft and flexible shell. It is an adept climber. If threatened, it will wedge itself into a rock crevice, using its strong claws for extra anchorage, and will also inflate its body, wedging it even further. If disturbed while away from cover, it will either climb rapidly or launch itself and slide. **Prey:** Feeds on a variety of plants, including succulents, herbs and flowers. Will also eat beetles. **Reproduction:** Mating occurs in mid-summer and a single large egg (47–50mm x 25–31mm) is laid at the beginning of the rainy season. Incubation takes

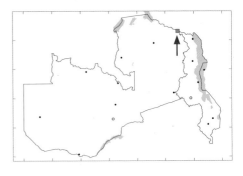

5–6 (but up to eight) months. **Range:** Extreme north-eastern Zambia and neighbouring Kenya and Tanzania.

The Pancake Tortoise has a soft, flat shell and inhabits rock outcrops.

HINGED TORTOISES *Kinixys*

Medium-sized tortoises with a hinge present posteriorly on the carapace between the 7th and 8th marginals and extending upwards to separate the 3rd and 4th costals. Fibrous cartilage deposited along the sutures lends flexibility to this hinge. The hinge develops with age and is absent in juveniles (and rarely in some adults). Nuchals and submarginals are present and the gulars are greatly thickened anteriorly. The outer margin of the 3rd costal is shorter than that of the 4th.

Hinged tortoises are omnivorous, feeding on a variety of plant material and various invertebrates, including millipedes and snails. Females lay clutches of 2–10 eggs in summer, with incubation taking 3–12 months.

Eight species are recognised worldwide, which range from West Africa through Central and East Africa to southern Africa. They have been introduced to Madagascar. Three species occur in the region.

Bell's Hinged Tortoise *Kinixys belliana*

Stephen Spawls

Bell's Hinged Tortoise has a well-developed hinge on the posterior portion of the carapace.

TL 130–170mm; max. TL 200mm

A large hinged tortoise that is morphologically very similar to the Eastern Hinged Tortoise (*K. zombensis*). Beak unicuspid. Carapace slightly convex, highest posteriorly, reaching highest point between 4th and 5th vertebrals. Straight carapace length usually less than 2.3 times shell height, more than 1.4 times carapace width. Hinge well developed. 5 vertebrals; 4 (rarely 5) costals; usually 24 marginals; 1 axillary; 1 inguinal. Posterior marginals slightly

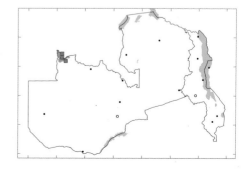

recurved, may be weakly serrated. Gulars not forked anteriorly; combined these are less than twice as wide as they are long. Supracaudal entire. Front limbs covered with enlarged scales. Tail short, thick. Carapace yellow, with 4–6 broad, black radial bands extending from pale areola to scute margin. Males often less well marked, may be uniform grey-brown to brown. Zonary pattern present in juveniles, breaks up into radial pattern in adults. Faint black radial pattern usually present on plastron in adults. **Habitat:** Forested regions in north-western Zambia. **Behaviour:** Diurnal; most active in the early morning and late afternoon during moist weather. During winter it aestivates under logs and in holes. **Prey:** The diet consists predominantly of vegetation, but is supplemented with millipedes, snails and carrion. **Reproduction:** Female lays 5–8 eggs in summer. **Range:** In the region it has been recorded only in the Mwinilunga District in north-western Zambia. Elsewhere it occurs from Angola through the DRC to Sudan and Ethiopia.

Speke's Hinged Tortoise   *Kinixys spekii*

Stephen Spawls

Speke's Hinged Tortoise is common and widespread across the region.

TL 140–160mm; max. TL 183mm
A medium-sized tortoise with a unicuspid beak and a flattened carapace. Carapace highest anteriorly, reaching highest point between 1st and 2nd vertebrals. Straight carapace length usually more than 2.3 times shell height. Carapace scutes not raised. Hinge moderately to well developed. 5 (rarely 6) vertebrals; 3–5 (usually 4) costals; 23 (rarely 22 or 24) marginals; 2 axillaries of moderate size; 1 large inguinal. Posterior marginals slightly recurved, but never serrated. Gulars frequently forked anteriorly, especially in males; combined these are less than twice as wide as they are

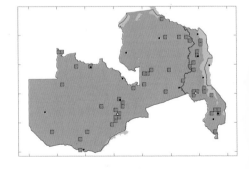

long. Supracaudal usually distinctly narrowed towards the middle; anterior margin often concave. Anterior margin of plastron projects well beyond anterior margin of carapace. Front limbs covered in enlarged, pointed scales. Carapace consists of alternating dark and light zonary pattern, with scutes dark-centred. Adult males often uniformly brown. Plastron yellow or tan, occasionally with darker speckling. **Habitat:** Mesic savanna and bushveld. **Behaviour:** Diurnal; most active in the early mornings and late afternoons after rainstorms, sheltering under shrubs during hot weather. During winter it aestivates, taking shelter under and between rocks, under logs and in disused termitaria, often partially burying itself. **Prey and Predators:** Feeds predominantly on vegetable matter, although beetles, millipedes and even giant land snails are also eaten. Juveniles and adults are eaten by African Lions, Southern Ground Hornbills and White-throated Monitors (*Varanus albigularis*). **Reproduction:** Mating occurs in late summer. 2–6 eggs (33–47mm x 28–34mm) are laid in late summer and incubation takes 10–12 months. **Range:** Throughout Zambia and Malawi. Elsewhere it occurs from South Africa through East Africa to southern Ethiopia.

Eastern Hinged Tortoise   *Kinixys zombensis*

The Eastern Hinged Tortoise has a radial dorsal pattern.

TL 140–180mm; max. TL 211mm
The largest species of hinged tortoise in the region, with a slightly convex carapace and a unicuspid beak. Carapace highest posteriorly, reaching highest point between 3rd and 4th vertebrals. Straight carapace length usually less than 2.3 times shell height, less than 1.4 times carapace width. Hinge well developed. 5 vertebrals; 4 (rarely 5) costals; usually 23 marginals; 2–3 axillaries; 1 large inguinal. Posterior marginals may be slightly recurved, never serrated. Gulars unforked anteriorly, combined these are less than twice as wide as they are long. Supracaudal entire, not narrowed in middle, may have a shallow central depression towards its lower margin. Front margin of plastron usually projects beyond anterior margin of carapace, especially in

males. Forelimbs covered in enlarged, pointed scales. Carapace yellow with 4–6 dark radial bands extending from pale centre to scute margin. Males often less well marked, becoming uniformly grey-brown to brown with age. Juveniles have black plastron with yellow median band, which gradually breaks up with age; adults usually have faint black radial pattern. **Habitat:** Prefers sandy substrates in mesic and moderately arid savannas. **Behaviour:** Diurnal; most active in the early morning and late afternoon during moist weather. During winter it aestivates under rocks, logs and in holes. **Prey and Predators:** Diet consists predominantly of vegetation but is supplemented with millipedes, snails and carrion. Adults and juveniles are preyed upon by Southern Ground Hornbills. **Reproduction:** Female lays 2–10 eggs (39–48mm

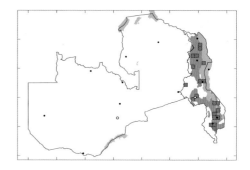

x 32–36mm) in summer. **Range:** Throughout Malawi. Elsewhere from Kenya through Tanzania and Mozambique to eastern South Africa, just entering eastern Zimbabwe. An isolated population on Madagascar is believed to be an anthropogenic introduction.

LEOPARD TORTOISES *Stigmochelys*

Large tortoises with a strongly convex carapace and no lateral hinge. The outer border of the 3rd costal is as long as, or slightly longer than, the outer margin of the 4th costal. Submarginals are absent. The gulars are paired, as long as they are wide and slightly thickened anteriorly. The nuchal is absent and the supracaudal entire. Carapace scutes are often raised, but smooth in juveniles and usually in very old individuals too. Buttock tubercles are present.

Only a single species is recognised, occurring widely through East and southern Africa.

Leopard Tortoise *Stigmochelys pardalis*

TL 300–400mm; max. TL 750mm
The largest species of tortoise in the region; adults may weigh in excess of 8kg. Beak unicuspid, often serrated, sometimes hooked. Gulars paired, as long as they are wide, not notched or only slightly notched anteriorly. 5 (rarely 6) vertebrals; 4 (rarely 5) costals; 10–12 marginals; 2 axillaries (1 large and 1 much reduced); 1 large inguinal. 2–3 buttock tubercles present on each side. Posterior marginals usually serrated, upturned. Anterior plastron margin not noticeably projecting. Plastron concave in adult males. Forelimbs covered in large, scattered scales that sometimes overlap. Hatchlings dull yellow, with each carapace scute dark-edged and often containing dark central spot. Plastron yellow with darker edges and scattered dark mottling. Adults yellowish to light brown dorsally, with numerous darker spots and

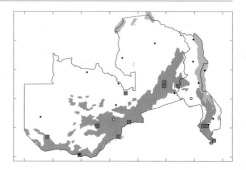

radiations on scutes. Plastron uniformly pale yellow, may have darker stippling and radiations. Old individuals usually become uniformly dark grey-brown. **Habitat:** Occurs widely in nearly all habitat types, but absent from forests and true desert, as well as very high elevations. **Behaviour:** Slow-growing initially. The growth rate becomes quite rapid after 7–8 years and from then on is rapid until sexual maturity is reached at about 15 years. Predominantly diurnal, although nocturnal behaviour has been recorded and may be in response to recent rain events or high diurnal temperatures. It practises both geophagy and osteophagy on occasion. This behaviour is believed to help meet the calcium demands for shell growth as well as egg development. **Prey and Predators:** Predominantly herbivorous, although it also eats bone fragments and carnivore faeces to supplement calcium intake, which is essential for shell formation during growth. Individuals may rarely scavenge carcasses. Its eggs are preyed on by ants, monitor lizards (*Varanus*) and various small carnivores. The juveniles are extensively preyed on by monitor lizards, large birds (including crows, storks, hornbills and raptors), Puff Adders (*Bitis a. arietans*) and Snouted Cobras (*Naja annulifera*) as well as various mammalian carnivores, including Leopard and African Lions. Adults mainly succumb in veld fires, but may occasionally be eaten by Nile Crocodiles (*Crocodylus niloticus*), Spotted Hyenas and African Lions. **Reproduction:**

Copulation is elaborate, with the male following the female for an extended period of time, regularly butting her with the anterior margin of his plastron. During copulation, the male extends his neck while uttering hoarse, hissing sounds. The female digs a flask-shaped pit in which she lays 6–15 (exceptionally up to 30) hard-shelled eggs (32–41mm x 35–44mm). Under optimal conditions, the female may lay as many as six clutches in a season at roughly one-month intervals. Incubation takes 10–15 months, depending on the temperature. **Range:** Southern Malawi and southern and central Zambia. Elsewhere from East Africa to southern Africa.

In juveniles the scutes are pale with dark margins.

The Leopard Tortoise has characteristic light and dark mottling.

CROCODYLIANS
Order Crocodylia

Crocodylians

are small to very large reptiles with well-developed limbs that may be webbed or partially webbed. The head is large and narrow to broad. The back is covered in large horny or bony scutes, the flanks are leathery, and the scales on the belly are soft and smooth. The tail is relatively long, laterally compressed and used for swimming. The cloaca is orientated longitudinally, and males have a single penis.

Crocodiles are unique amongst reptiles in that they possess a four-chambered heart, affording them more efficient blood oxygenation than other reptiles with a three-chambered heart. They also possess a third eyelid, or nictitating membrane, which removes dirt from the surface of the eye. Other adaptations include a hard palate in the roof of the mouth and better limb articulation compared to other reptiles. Despite their large size, they are just as fast on land as in the water, and can gallop, walk on extended legs, or propel themselves along on their bellies. Crocodiles can smell, see and hear well. The nostrils, eyes and ears are all situated in a line at the top of the head, allowing exposure to the surface (for breathing, vision and hearing, respectively) while the majority of the head and body remains concealed below the water. When submerged, crocodiles are able to close their nostrils and ears with specialised skin flaps to prevent water from entering.

These reptiles are quite vocal, particularly so when juveniles call to mothers and when males compete for mating opportunities.

Crocodiles are extensively hunted for their skin, which is used in the leather industry, and are also often persecuted for eating livestock and people. All crocodiles are aquatic and occur widely in the tropics. There are 25 species and nine genera in two families.

Crocodiles
Family Crocodylidae

Reptiles in this family have a head that is narrow to moderately broad and elongate. The back is covered in large horny or bony scutes, the flanks are leathery and the belly scales are fairly flat and soft. The fourth tooth in the upper jaw is visible when the jaws close. The feet are webbed.

There are 18 species in four genera, which occur widely in the tropics. Six African species in three genera are recognised, of which two species in two genera enter the region.

Young Nile Crocodile

KEY Genera of Crocodylidae

1a	Jaws slender; head five times as long as broad	*Mecistops* (p. 362)
b	Jaws broad; head twice as long as broad	*Crocodylus* (p. 363)

A crocodile's nostrils, eyes and ears are all positioned on top of the head, allowing it to breathe, see and hear while exposing only a very small part of the head.

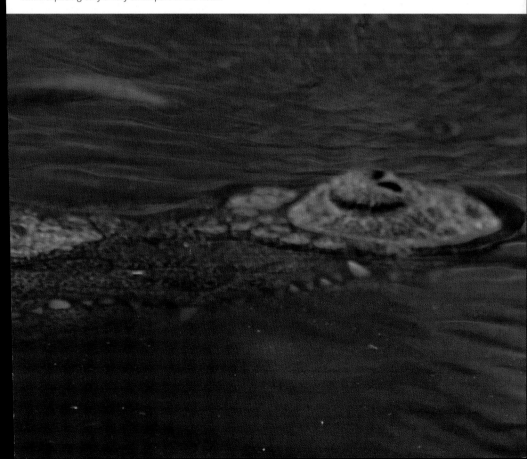

SLENDER-SNOUTED CROCODILES *Mecistops*

Medium-sized crocodiles with long, slender jaws that are dorsoventrally flattened and end in a bulbous tip. The nostrils are located dorsally near the tip of the snout, which lacks dorsal ridges. In both jaws the teeth are prominent and visible even when the mouth is closed. The limbs are large and well developed, the hind feet are webbed, and the tail is laterally flattened and used for swimming. The back is covered in large, bony or horny scutes, which are weakly to strongly keeled. The scales on the flanks are leathery, while those on the belly are small and soft.

Their diet consists predominantly of fish, reptiles, amphibians and invertebrates, although small mammals are also occasionally eaten.

This genus is endemic to Africa. Two species are recognised, one of which enters the region.

Eastern Slender-snouted Crocodile *Mecistops leptorhynchus*

Stephen Spawls

In the region, the Eastern Slender-snouted Crocodile occurs only in Lake Mweru.

TL 1,500–2,500mm; max. TL 3,500mm
A medium-sized crocodile with a long, slender snout that ends in a bulbous tip. Teeth of both jaws very prominent, visible even when jaws close. Squamosal bosses absent. Back covered in weakly keeled osteoderms, latter arranged in 6–8 longitudinal and 19 transverse rows. Flanks leathery, with 1–3 (usually 2) rows of enlarged scales. 25–28 ventral scale rows. Limbs large, muscular, with slight webbing between toes of hind limbs. Tail comprises 30–40% of TL, laterally compressed, muscular, with paired raised dorsal keels posteriorly. Juveniles short-snouted. Coloration variable, consisting of various shades of grey, brown and olive; usually

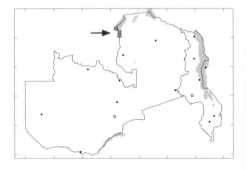

light yellowish brown with darker bands or blotches. Ventrum white to light creamy yellow. Juveniles grey-green with vivid irregular black blotches and crossbars. **Habitat:** Medium-sized to large lakes, rivers and streams in forests and forest–savanna mosaics, or large rivers with well-developed riparian vegetation. Also occurs in flooded forests, swamps and baïs. **Behaviour:** A fast and agile swimmer. Basks on secluded sand banks and logs protruding above the water during the day. Shy and secretive by nature, it rapidly retreats at any sign of danger. If harassed, it will attempt to hide in waterside vegetation rather than diving into water. If grasped, juveniles emit a loud distress call. Adults emit a low growl, especially at the start of the rainy season, believed to serve a territorial function and also for attracting potential mates. One individual lived for 30 years in captivity. This species is not dangerous to humans. **Prey and Predators:** Adults prey mainly on fish (including catfish, bream and cichlids), but will opportunistically feed on crabs, shrimps, swimming birds (including Pink-backed Pelicans), reptiles (including Ornate Water Snakes [*Grayia ornata*] and flap-shelled terrapins [*Cycloderma*]), amphibians and small mammals (including Aquatic Chevrotain). Juveniles prey on frogs, tadpoles and insects, including grasshoppers and dragonflies. Adults are hunted for food, the pet trade and, to a lesser extent, for leather. All age classes are negatively affected by overfishing and accidental capture in nets, as well as habitat loss. Water Monitors (*Varanus niloticus*) and primates raid its nests. **Reproduction:** Females reach sexual maturity at about two metres in TL. Mating is believed to take place in November and December, with nest construction occurring between November and February. The female constructs a nest of vegetable material (averaging 1.25m in diameter and 45cm deep) on an elevated bank, usually at the base of a large tree, and always under closed-canopy forest (including riparian forest). These nests are often shielded by vegetation and sited on river inlets or flooded areas away from the main river. The female lays 13–21 eggs between late January and early March, covering them with a layer of vegetation of up to 30cm deep. Incubation takes about 100 days. The female usually remains in the water near her nest, emerging to guard it only every 2–7 days. Hatchlings emerge in April and May, corresponding with peak water levels. They measure 310–350mm in TL and enter the water soon after hatching, favouring shallow waters and backwaters, especially where floating vegetation is prevalent. The female guards them for about three months. **Range:** In the region, it has been recorded only in Lake Mweru. Elsewhere, it occurs in Lake Tanganyika in East Africa, westwards to Angola and northwards to Gabon.

TRUE CROCODILES *Crocodylus*

True crocodiles can attain lengths in excess of six metres and weigh more than a ton. All species are similar in appearance, having a large, robust body, well-developed limbs and a laterally compressed tail that is used for swimming. The snout is moderately broad and elongate, with the teeth of both jaws visible when the mouth is closed. The nostrils are located dorsally near the tip of the snout. The scales on the back are hard and horny or bony and many have a raised median ridge. The scales on the flanks are leathery, while those on the belly are nearly square in shape, flat and soft.

The larger species hunt large animals and may also opportunistically eat humans. The smaller species prey on small mammals, birds and fish. They are widespread in the tropics, although are largely replaced in Amazonia by caimans (*Caiman*).

There are 13 species, two of which occur in Africa and one of which enters the region.

Nile Crocodile *Crocodylus niloticus*

TL 2,000–3,500mm; max. TL 5,900mm
A large to very large lizard-like reptile with a robust body, well-developed limbs and a laterally compressed tail. Snout moderately broad, elongate, with valved nostrils situated dorsally towards the tip. Teeth of both jaws visible even when jaws close. Raised ridges present above eyes. Eyes yellow; pupils

vertical. Back covered with geometric horny osteoderms; many with pronounced median ridges. Scutes on head relatively flat, fused to skull. Tail long (40% of SVL), laterally compressed, with two rows of raised dorsal scutes proximally, these fusing to form single median row posteriorly. Hind feet webbed. Juveniles greenish with irregular black markings over back, sides and tail. Adults dark olive-green to olive-grey, occasionally with some darker markings. Ventrum uniform pale yellow to yellow. Lining of mouth yellow to orange-yellow. **Habitat:** Usually inhabits permanent waterbodies, but may occasionally be found far from water, especially during the rainy season, when it migrates between waterbodies. Juveniles prefer quieter backwaters or temporary waterbodies, especially those with waterside or submerged vegetation. **Behaviour:** Almost entirely aquatic, it is a fast, powerful swimmer, using its large tail for propulsion with the limbs tucked against the body. Often lies on sandbanks to bask. It may remain submerged below the water surface for over 45 minutes. Young crocodiles may use their jaws to dig a burrow (up to three metres deep) in a bank, sometimes communally, in which they shelter for the first 4–5 years. All age classes are able to produce sounds, ranging from the squeaks of hatchlings and yelps of juveniles to the various roars, hisses and growls of adults. This species has lived for more than 60 years in captivity and is believed to exceed 100 years of age in the wild. **Prey and Predators:** Hatchlings prey on insects, tadpoles and small frogs, while juveniles prey on frogs, fish, terrapins, snakes, birds and small mammals. The prey selected gradually increases with the size of the individual, and adults prey on fish, large snakes, large mammals (mostly antelope, but sometimes zebra and buffalo and even young elephants and adult rhino), waterfowl, domestic animals and even humans. Prey is often ambushed at a favourite drinking site or may be silently approached from a distance with the body submerged below the water and only the eyes and nostrils above the surface (or entirely submerged). Once seized, large prey is dragged below water, where it is held until it drowns.

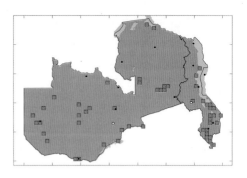

Carrion is also regularly eaten. Chunks of flesh are ripped out of large prey by grasping the flesh and spinning. Large food items may be softened by repeated biting before being swallowed. The valved nostrils and gular flap can be closed when submerged, allowing it to feed underwater. Nests are predated by monitor lizards (*Varanus*), baboons, hyenas and even other Nile Crocodiles, while hatchlings are eaten by pythons (*Python*), large fish, birds of prey and other Nile Crocodiles. Hippopotamuses have been recorded biting crocodiles in two during acts of aggression. **Reproduction:** Males establish a hierarchy in May and mating occurs in the water during July and August. Egg deposition usually occurs in November (August–December). The female uses her hind feet to dig a hole (30–45cm deep) on a well-drained, sunny sandbank above the flood level. She may re-use the same nesting beach for her entire life. 16–95 (usually 30–50) hard-shelled eggs (70–78mm x 50–56mm) are deposited and she often remains near the nest, protecting it from potential predators and leaving the nest only to drink. Incubation takes 84–90 days. The hatchlings emit a high-pitched noise while still in the egg, signalling the female to carefully excavate the nest. She then gathers the hatchlings in her mouth and transports them to the water's edge, where she releases them. Hatchlings measure 280–320mm in TL and remain together in a stretch of shallow water for the first 6–8 weeks. Sexual maturity is reached at 12–15 years at a TL of 2–3m. **Range:** Widespread in eastern and southern Africa, being replaced in Central and West Africa by the West African Crocodile (*C. suchus*). Also present on Madagascar.

The Nile Crocodile often basks on sandy riverbanks.

Young Nile Crocodiles are usually more boldly patterned than adults.

Glossary

Addressed: Lying closely against. Used in reference to the limbs, which in some lacertid species can be pressed against the body to get a relative indication of limb length.

Alate: Having wings. Used in reference to ants and termites who, during parts of their lifecycle, develop wings prior to leaving the nest and dispersing; also called flying ants.

Anaphylaxis: A severe allergic reaction that can result in lowered blood pressure, shock, breathing difficulties and neurological distress. It may prove fatal if left untreated.

Anapsid: An organism that has no temporal openings in the skull (chelonians).

Annulus (plural Annuli): A ring-shaped structure or region. In worm lizards, used to describe the circular body segments.

Anterior: Referring to the front.

Anthropogenic: Relating to, or as a result of, human activities.

Antivenom: A serum containing antibodies against specific venoms. Used in the treatment of severe snake bites. Snake antivenom is produced by injecting small quantities of snake venom into horses over an extended period of time, and then harvesting these antibodies from the horses' blood. Because of the way that antivenom is produced, some people show a severe allergic reaction when antivenom is administered, which can result in anaphylactic shock and death. For this reason, antivenom should only be administered by a medical practitioner.

Arboreal: Living in trees.

Areola: The central part of a chelonian scute, also marking the original horny plate that the tortoise was hatched with.

a.s.l.: Above sea level.

Autotomy: The intentional shedding of a body part (usually a tail) in defence.

Axillary: In reference to the region of the armpit. In chelonians, refers to the scale(s) present in the region of the front limb.

Azygous: Single, not paired.

Baïs: Natural openings in the forest that usually consist of flooded grassland and open water of varying depths, sometimes with other aquatic vegetation.

Bicarinate: Having two keels or ridges.

Bicuspid: Having two points; in tortoises it refers to the two point-like projections on the beak.

Bifurcated: Forked; divided into two portions.

Biogeography: The study of the geographic distribution of animals and the historical or geological factors that shaped the currently known geographic distribution.

Canthus rostralis: The angular region between the top of the head (crown) and the side of the head, between the eye and the snout.

Carapace: The upper portion of a chelonian shell.

Cardiotoxic: Pertaining to a venom that affects the heart, weakening it and reducing its ability to pump blood.

Carinate: Having keels or ridges. Usually used to describe the dorsal surface of a scale.

Casque: The raised, helmet-like structure found on the back of the head of some chameleon species.

Castes: The division of a social insect colony based on the work performed by each (e.g. workers, soldiers).

Caudal: In reference to the tail.

Chelonian: A member of the reptile order Testudines (tortoises, terrapins and turtles).

Chemical crypsis: A method whereby an organism excretes chemicals, often pheromones, with which to disguise itself, thereby avoiding detection.

Chevron: A V-shaped mark, either inverted or right-way up.

Chromatophores: Pigment-containing and light-reflecting cells, usually located in the skin of various animals.

Circumorbitals: The scales around the periphery of the eye that are in contact with the eye opening, and in contact with the eye, in the snake family Viperidae.

Cloaca: The common cavity at the end of the digestive system that is used to excrete waste products (urine and faeces) as well as provide access to the genitalia (females). The outer opening is usually called the vent, through which the male hemipenes protrude during mating.

Colubrid: A member of the snake family Colubridae.

Costal: A scale on the side of a chelonian shell (see figure on p. 339).

Crepuscular: Being most active at sunrise and sunset.

Cryptic species: A species that is morphologically very similar or identical to another species, and which can often only be told apart using genetics and/or behavioural characteristics.

Cuneate: Wedge-shaped. Often used in relation to a small scale on the lips of snakes.

Cytotoxic: Pertaining to a venom that affects the soft tissue cells and blood vessel walls, resulting in leakage of fluid into the intra-cellular space which results in swelling; may also lead to local necrosis.

Dambo: A shallow, seasonally inundated wetland usually devoid of trees. One or more poorly defined stream channels may be present, and they are often surrounded by woodland.

Diapsid: An organism that has two temporal openings in the skull (in reference to reptiles, this includes lizards, skinks, geckos, snakes and crocodiles).

Diastema: A gap separating teeth, and usually separating teeth of different functions (e.g. a gap separating the fangs from the remaining teeth).

Dichromatism: The occurrence of two different colour phases or varieties.

Didactyle: Having two digits at the end of a limb.

Digit: A finger or toe.

Discrete: Individually separate; distinct.

Diurnal: Active entirely or predominantly during the day.

Dorsal: Pertaining to the upper side of the body or back.

Dorsals: The scales on the upper side of the body or back.

Dorsolateral: Referring to the region where the dorsal and lateral surfaces meet (the junction between the back and the sides).

Dorsoventrally: Relating to the axis joining the dorsal and ventral surfaces (i.e. top to bottom).

Dorsum: The upper side of the body; the back.

DRC: Democratic Republic of the Congo.

Elapid: A member of the snake family Elapidae.

Endemic: Naturally occurring in, and restricted to, a particular region.

Eustachian tube: A narrow canal linking the pharynx to the middle ear, allowing for the equalisation of pressure on either side of the eardrum.

Exfoliating: Material (usually rock or tree bark) being shed or peeling away from an underlying surface in layers of varying dimensions.

Extant: Living; still in existence.

Extralimital: Occurring or situated outside of a particular geographical area.

Femoral: Relating to the femur or thigh; relating to the upper portion of the hind limb.

Femoral pores: Pores situated ventrally in the scales on the upper leg of some lizards. The scales containing the femoral pores are often enlarged.

Fenestrations: Small perforations or holes.

Flounce: A raised structure on the surface of a hemipenis, arranged transversely along it.

Forciples: A pair of modified front legs that are used as powerful venomous forceps.

Fossorial: Burrowing; living predominantly underground.

Frontonasal: A single or paired scale on the head of a reptile, situated between the frontal and nasal scales (see figure on p. 203).

Frontoparietal: A single or paired scale on the head of a reptile, situated between the frontal and parietal scales (see figure on p. 203).

Geophagous (Geophagy): Eating soil.

Gravid: Carrying eggs or young. The reptile equivalent of being pregnant.

Gular: Referring to the throat region; also a scale on the plastron of the chelonian shell (see figure on p. 339).

Haemorrhaging: Excessive bleeding either subcutaneously and/or from orifices and other open wounds.

Haemotoxic: Pertaining to a venom that causes the destruction of red blood cells and prevents blood clotting, resulting in haemorrhaging.

Half-annuli: Many worm lizards have dorsal annuli (segments) that are narrower than the ventral annuli. This results in there being more annuli if counted along the dorsum compared to ventral counts. This difference is expressed as the difference in half-annuli.

Hemipenes (singular: Hemipenis): The paired copulatory organs present in all male squamate reptiles.

Herbivorous: Pertaining to a diet consisting predominantly or exclusively of vegetable matter.

Heterogenous: Consisting of different shapes and sizes (e.g. scales); not uniform.

Homogenous: Consisting of approximately the same shapes and sizes (e.g. scales); uniform.

Hypapophysis (plural Hypapophyses): A process or projection on the lower surface of a vertebra.

Ikelenge Pedicle: The portion of Zambia that is wedged between Angola and the DRC in north-western Zambia, north of Mwinilunga.

Imbricate: Overlapping; often used to describe scales.

Inferior: Lower.

Infralabial: Referring to the scales along the lower lips that are usually enlarged and are in direct contact with the mouth (see figures on p. 39 and p. 203).

Infranasal: The lower of two nasals.

Inguinal: Referring to the groin; also a scale on the plastron of chelonians.

Intergular: A scale on the plastron of some chelonian species (see figure on p. 339).

Internarial distance: The distance between the nostrils, measured in a straight line.

Internasal: One or more scales on the head of a reptile, situated between the nasals (see figure on p. 39).

Interocular distance: The head width measured at the level of the eyes.

Interorbital: The dorsal area between the eyes.

Interparietal: A scale on the head of a reptile, situated between the parietals (see figure on p. 203).

Interphalangeal: Referring to the region (typically a joint) between the different phalanges or segments of a finger or toe.

Invertebrate: An animal that lacks a backbone (e.g. insects, snails, spiders, etc.).

Jacobson's Organ: A scent organ situated in the roof of the mouth of many reptiles, consisting of two tubes or sacs. Scent particles in the air are collected by the forked tongue, and the tongue is then inserted into the Jacobson's Organ, where the particles are analysed and 'smelled'.

Keel: A prominent ridge occurring on the scales of some snakes and lizards, and on the scutes of some chelonians.

Keratin: A hard, tough, fibrous non-soluble protein that is the main constituent of nails, horns and claws.

Keratinised: Pertaining to an object that has become hard owing to the presence of keratin.

Keratinous: Containing or made up of keratin.

Lacertid: A lizard belonging to the family Lacertidae.

Lamella (plural Lamellae): Any thin plate-like or scale-like structure.

Lanceolate: Having a narrow, tapering oval shape that ends in a point.

Lateral: Referring to the sides of the body.

Loreal: A scale on the side of the head of a reptile, situated between the nostril and the eye but not being in contact with either (see figures on p. 39 and p. 203).

Mandible: The lower jaw.

Marginal: A scale on the edge of the carapace of a chelonian (see figure on p. 339).

Matrotrophic: Pertaining to the provisioning of nutrients directly from the mother to the developing embryo that supplement or replace a yolk sac; a form of viviparity.

Medial: Referring to the region in the middle of the body or scale.

Median: Referring to the region in the middle of the body or scale.

Melanistic: Pertaining to an individual that appears darker or blacker than usual (usually appearing all-black) owing to the increased presence of melanin in the skin.

Mental: The foremost scale on the lower jaw of a reptile, bordered above by the mouth and bordered on each side by infralabials (see figures on p. 39 and p. 203).

Mesic: Containing a moderate amount of moisture.

Mesocarnivore: An animal whose diet consists predominantly of meat, but also includes invertebrates and some plant material.

Monodactyle: Having a single digit at the end of a limb.

Monophyly: All the descendants of a common ancestor; all members of a closely related group.

Moribund: Inactive; close to death.

Mucronate: Strongly overlapping and drawn into a spine.

Mushitu: Swamp forest.

Nape: The back of the neck.

Nasal: Pertaining to the region of the nose; a scale on the head of a reptile that either adjoins or encloses the nostril (see figures on p. 39 and p. 203).

Nictitating membrane: A transparent or semi-transparent membrane that forms an additional, inner eyelid and which can be drawn across the eye to protect it (for example from dust) and also assists with keeping the eye moist.

Necrosis: The death of a portion of tissue.

Neonate: A hatchling or newborn.

Neurotoxic: Pertaining to a venom or poison that predominantly affects the nervous system, although it usually affects other tissues to a lesser extent as well.

Nuchal: The frontmost scute on a chelonian carapace when present (see figure on p. 339); also the scale(s) bordering the parietals posteriorly on the head of some lizards.

Occipital: Pertaining to the region at the back of the skull; also a scale on the head of some reptiles which borders the parietals (see figure on p. 203).

Ocular: A scale in contact with the eye (see figures on p. 39 and p. 203). In some snake and lizard families, it is the scale covering the eye.

Omnivorous: Pertaining to a diet that contains food of both plant and animal origin.

Orbit: The eye socket.

Ossified: Turned into bone or bony tissue.

Osteoderm: A bony plate in the skin of some reptiles.

Osteophagy: The act of eating bones.

Oviparous: A mode of reproduction that involves depositing eggs that later hatch outside the maternal body.

Palmar: Relating to the palm of the hand.

Parietal: Referring to the region on the crown of the head; also a scale on the back of the head of reptiles (see figures on p. 39 and p. 203).

Pectorals: Enlarged scales situated laterally and ventrally on the 'neck' of worm lizards, between the head and the body annuli.

Pentadactyle: Having five digits at the end of a limb.

Peristaltic: Pertaining to wave-like alternating contraction and relaxation of muscles in tubular structures.

Pheromone: A chemical substance that is released by an individual, which in turn affects the behaviour of another individual of the same or different species.

Pineal eye: A round structure on the crown of the head, especially in lizards, that is photo-receptive and used to control circadian rhythm. Also called a parietal eye or parietal foramen.

Plantar: Relating to the sole of the foot.

Plastron: The lower surface of the chelonian shell.

Plumbeus: Being lead-coloured; light to dark grey.

Poisonous: Pertaining to a substance that is capable of causing illness or death when ingested.

Polyvalent antivenom: Antivenom that is effective in the treatment of a bite from several different snake species, as it is manufactured using the venom from several different snake species.

Posterior: Towards the rear.

Postero-dorsal: Situated at the top, rear border of an object.

Postero-lateral: Situated on the flanks and towards the rear.

Postmental: A scale bordering the mental posteriorly (see figure on p. 207).

Postnasal: A scale bordering the nasal posteriorly (see figure on p. 39).

Postocular: A scale bordering the eye posteriorly (see figure on p. 39); in some reptile families it is the scale that borders the ocular posteriorly.

Postsupralabial: A scale bordering the supralabial posteriorly.

Precloacal pores: Pores situated in the scales directly anterior to the cloaca (sometimes called preanal pores); the precloacal scales are often enlarged.

Precloaco-femoral pores: Precloacal and femoral pores joined together in a continuous line.

Prefrontal: A scale on the head of a reptile, situated immediately in front of the frontal scale (see figures on p. 39 and p. 203).

Prehensile: Adapted for grasping or holding, especially by wrapping around an object.

Preocular: A scale bordering the eye anteriorly (see figure on p. 39); in some reptile families it is the scale that borders the ocular anteriorly.

Preoral: In front of the mouth.

Presubocular: A scale on the side of the head of blind snakes, situated anterior to the subocular scale.

Quadricarinate: Having four keels or ridges.

Retractile: Capable of being drawn inwards.

Rhomboidal: More or less diamond-shaped.

Rostral: Pertaining to the nose; a scale at the foremost point of the head of a reptile (see figures on p. 39 and p. 203).

Rugose: Wrinkled or corrugated; often used to describe a scale that has a raised area that is not keeled.

Rupicolous: Living on or amongst rocks.

Sagittal crest: A raised, bony projection extending from the posterior border of the skull, in line with the vertebral midline.

Saurid: A member of the suborder Sauria, which includes all the reptiles traditionally referred to as lizards.

Septum (plural Septa): A partition separating two cavities or masses of tissue.

Scalation: The arrangement of scales.

Scansor: A specialised pad on the underside of the toe of many geckos composed of thousands of minute hairs and which allow the animal to climb vertical and even inverted surfaces.

Scute: One of the individual hard plates composing a chelonian shell.

Slough: To shed the old skin to reveal the new layer of skin which has formed underneath.

Spatulate: Having a broad, rounded end.

Species complex: A group of closely related species; sometimes these are not yet formally recognised as separate species.

Spinose: Having spines; appearing spiny.

Squamate: A member of the order Squamata; all snakes and lizards.

Subcaudals: The scales on the underside of the tail.

Subdigital: Occurring on the underside of the finger or toe.

Subequal: Of similar, but not identical, size.

Subhexagonal: Appearing nearly hexagonal in shape; an object with six sides that are approximately straight and with opposing sides of similar length.

Sublingual: Pertaining to the area beneath the tongue; a scale on the underside of the head of a reptile, situated behind the mental and bordering the infralabial scales along their lateral margin. Also referred to as chin scales.

Submarginal: Pertaining to the area near the margin; the scales on the underside of some chelonians, situated between the carapace and plastron.

Subocular: A scale on the head of a reptile, situated below the eye.

Subpentagonal: Appearing nearly pentagonal in shape; an object with five sides that are approximately straight and with opposing sides of similar length.

Subtriangular: Appearing nearly triangular in shape.

Sulcus (plural Sulci): A groove or furrow in the surface of an object. In worm lizards, this refers to the groove running along the side of the body that separates the dorsal annuli from the ventral annuli.

In chelonians, it refers to the point where two scales meet. With reference to a hemipenis, it is the central groove along which semen is transferred during mating.

Superior: Upper.

Supracaudal: Situated above the tail; one of the marginal scales on the carapace of chelonians, situated in the middle at the rear of the carapace (see figure on p. 339).

Supraciliary: Pertaining to the area above the eyelid; a scale on the head of a lizard (see figure on p. 203).

Supralabial: Referring to the scales along the upper lips that are usually enlarged and are in direct contact with the mouth (see figures on p. 39 and p. 203).

Supranasal: The upper of two nasal scales.

Supraocular: A scale on the head of a reptile, situated above the eye (see figures on p. 39 and p. 203).

Supraorbital: Situated above the eye.

Suprarostral: A scale on the head of some vipers, situated between the rostral anteriorly and the nasal and internasals posteriorly.

SVL: Snout–vent length; the length of a squamate reptile or crocodile measured ventrally from the tip of the snout to the posterior border of the cloacal scale.

Sympatric: Occurring in the same geographical area.

Synanthropic: Pertaining to a species that lives in close proximity to humans and benefits from the artificial habitats that are created by humans.

Tarsal: Pertaining to the lower part of the hind limb, above the foot.

Taxonomy: The branch of science that deals with describing and naming new species, and describing how species are related to each other.

Temporal: Pertaining to the side of the forehead; also a scale on the side of the head of a reptile, situated towards the rear margin of the head (see figure on p. 39).

Termitarium (plural Termitaria): The colonial nest made by termites, usually using mud and their own faeces and extending both above and below ground level.

Terrestrial: Living on the ground.

Testudine: A member of the order Testudines; all chelonians.

TL: Total length; the length of a squamate reptile or crocodile measured from the tip of the snout to the tip of the tail; the length of a chelonian measured in a straight line from the anterior-most portion of the shell to the posterior-most point of the shell.

Tonic immobility: A behaviour in which animals remain motionless and appear to be dead, usually to avoid predation. Also known as playing dead or thanatosis.

Tricarinate: Having three keels or ridges.

Tricuspid: Having three points; in tortoises it refers to the three point-like projections on the beak.

Tridactyle: Having three digits at the end of a limb.

Tubercle: A rounded scale that is larger and higher than the surrounding scales.

Tubercular: Pertaining to scales that are enlarged and rounded.

Tympanic scale: A scale on the head of a reptile, situated at the anterior border of the tympanum or ear opening.

Tympanum: The ear drum.

Unicuspid: Having a single point; in tortoises it refers to the point-like projection on the beak.

Venom: A substance that is capable of causing illness or death when injected into the body.

Venomous: Being able to produce venom.

Ventral: Pertaining to the belly or undersurface of the body. In snakes, ventral scales (called ventrals) are defined as those scales that are bordered by a dorsal scale on each side. In lizards, ventral scales (also called ventrals) are defined as all the belly scale rows that are bordered by dorsal scales on each side.

Ventrolateral: Referring to the region where the ventral and lateral surfaces meet (the junction between the belly and the sides).

Ventrum: The belly or undersurface of a reptile.

Vertebral: Pertaining to the mid-back or spinal region of an animal; also referring to the central row of scutes in chelonians (see figure on page 339).

Verticil: A whorl or circular arrangement of scales.

Vestigial: Pertaining to a very small remnant of something that used to be obvious or well developed in an evolutionary ancestor, and often no longer performing any function.

Viviparous: A mode of reproduction that involves giving birth to live young which develop within the mother's body and which are directly nurtured by the female's body during development.

Voucher specimen: A dead animal that is retained and preserved indefinitely, and usually deposited in a publicly accessible national institution such as a museum. Voucher specimens are used to record the morphological variation of organisms, maximum lengths attained, geographic distribution, etc. When a new species is described, a voucher specimen must be designated.

Xanthic: Appearing yellow or yellowish owing to the absence of certain colour pigments in the skin.

Zonary: Pertaining to concentric circles or zones of lighter and darker pigment on the scutes of some chelonians.

References

Bates, M.F., Branch, W.R., Bauer, A.M., Burger, M., Marais, J., Alexander, G.J. and de Villiers, M.S. (Eds). 2014. Atlas and red list of the reptiles of South Africa, Lesotho and Swaziland. *Suricata 1.* South African National Biodiversity Institute, Pretoria, South Africa.

Branch, W.R. 1998. *Field guide to snakes and other reptiles of southern Africa.* Struik Publishers, Cape Town, South Africa.

Broadley, D.G., Doria, C. and Wigge, J. 2003. *Snakes of Zambia: an atlas and field guide.* Edition Chimaira. Frankfurt, Germany.

Broadley, D.G. and Blaylock, R. 2013. *The snakes of Zimbabwe and Botswana.* Edition Chimaira, Frankfurt, Germany.

Brown, G. and Wilkey, R. 2019. *Reptiles of Malawi: a photographic guide to 145 species.* Biddles, United Kingdom. ISBN: 9780954298357.

Figueroa, A., McKelvy, A.D., Grismer, L.L., Bell, C.D. and Lailvaux, S.P. 2016. A species-level phylogeny of extant snakes with description of a new colubrid subfamily and genus. *PloS ONE* 11(9): e0161070.

Marais, J. 2014. *Snakes and snakebite in southern Africa.* Struik Nature, Cape Town, South Africa.

Olson, D.M., Dinerstein, E., Wikramanayake, E.D., Burgess, N.D., Powell, G.V.N., Underwood, E.C., D'Amico, J.A., Itoua, I., Strand, H.E., Morrison, J.C., Loucks, C.J., Allnutt, T.F., Ricketts, T.H., Kura, Y., Lamoreux, J.F., Wettengel, W.W., Hedao, P. and

Kassem, K. R. 2001. Terrestrial ecoregions of the world: a new map of life on Earth. *Bioscience* 51(11): 933–938.

Pyron R.A., Burbrink, F.T. and Wiens, J.J. 2013. A phylogeny and revised classification of Squamata, including 4161 species of lizards and snakes. *BMC Evolutionary Biology* 13: 93.

Rhodin, A.G.J., Iverson, J.B., Bour, R., Fritz, U., Georges, A., Shaffer, H.B. and van Dijk, P.P. 2017. Turtles of the World: Annotated checklist and atlas of taxonomy, synonymy, distribution, and conservation status (8th ed.). *Chelonian Research Monographs* 7: 1–292.

Spawls, S., Howell, K., Hinkel, H. and Menegon, M. 2018. *Field guide to East African reptiles.* Bloomsbury Publishing, London, UK.

Van Breugel, P., Kindt, R., Lillesø, J.P.B., Bingham, M., Demissew, S., Dudley, C., Friis, I., Gachathi, F., Kalema, J., Mbago, F., Moshi, H.N., Mulumba, J., Namaganda, M., Ndangalasi, H.J., Ruffo, C.K., Védaste, M., Jamnadass, R. and Graudal, L. 2015. *Potential natural vegetation map of eastern Africa (Burundi, Ethiopia, Kenya, Malawi, Rwanda, Tanzania, Uganda and Zambia).* Version 2.0. Forest & Landscape Denmark and World Agroforestry Centre (ICRAF). URL: http://vegetationmap4africa.org.

Wilkey, R. 2019. *Snakes of Malawi: a field guide to the snake species of Malawi.* Njoka Books. ISBN: 9781912804887.

Photographic credits

Key: a = all, b = bottom, l = left, m = middle, r = right, t = top

Photographers: CT = Colin Tilbury; DP = Darren Pietersen; FP = Fabio Pupin; FW = Frank Willems; GB = Gary Brown; GN = Gary Nicolau; HM = Harith Morgadinho; JM = Johan Marais; LK = Luke Kemp; LV = Luke Verburgt; PL = Paul Lloyd; SS = Stephen Spawls; TP = Tyrone Ping; WC = Werner Conradie

p1: LK; **p2:** LV; **p6:** LV; **p7:** LV; **p10 t:** LV; **p10 b:** DP; **p12 l:** LV; **p12 r:** GN; **p13:** LV; **p21:** LV; **p24:** GB; **p25:** DP; **p26 a:** LV; **p27 a:** LV; **p28:** DP; **p29 tl:** LK; **p29 tr:** LV; **p29 ml:** LV; **p29 mr:** FP; **p29 bl:** LV; **p29 br:** DP; **p30:** LV; **p31:** LV; **p34:** LV; **p36 t:** GN; **p36 b:** LV; **p37:** LV; **p38:** LV; **p43:** GN; **p45:** GN; **p50:** GN; **p55:** DP; **p57:** DP; **p59:** LV; **p62:** LV; **p66:** LV; **p69:** PL; **p79:** LV; **p81:** LV; **p82:** LV; **p92:** LV; **p95:** LV; **p100:** LV; **p102:** LV; **p107:** LV; **p108:** LV; **p109:** LV; **p121:** LK; **p126:** HM; **p137:** DP; **p138:** LV; **p143:** LV; **p145:** LV; **p154:** GB; **p156:** SS; **p161:** LV; **p168:** CT; **p171:** CT; **p175:** LV; **p178:** WC; **p179:** GB; **p200:** DP; **p201:** LV; **p206:** LK; **p207 a:** LV; **p210:** LV; **p227:** GN; **p232:** LV; **p233:** LV; **p235:** CT; **p236:** LV; **p237:** LV; **p244:** DP; **p247:** LV; **p251:** LV; **p254:** LK; **p259:** LV; **p262:** CT; **p281:** DP; **p293:** LV; **p306:** LV; **p310:** LV; **p325:** TP; **p336:** LV; **p338:** TP; **p340:** LV; **p 349:** DP; **p351:** LV; **p358:** JM; **p360:** LV; **p361:** LV

Useful contacts

Museums

Livingstone Museum
Website: livingstonemuseum.org
Email: info@livingstonemuseum.org
Facebook: @livingstone.museum
Phone: +260 213 324 429
Physical address: Plot 567, Mosi-Oa-Tunya Road,
Livingstone, Zambia

Chichiri Museum (Museum of Malawi)
Email: chichirimuseum@malawi.net
Phone: +265 1 873 258
Physical address: Kasungu Crescent, Chichiri,
Blantyre 3, Blantyre, Malawi

Organisations

Helping Hands in Snake Safety
Website: www.hhiss.com
Email: info@hhiss.com
Facebook: @helpingsnakes
Phone: +260 974 248 144

Kalimba Reptile Park
Website: kalimbazambia.com
Email: kalimbareptiles@gmail.com
Facebook: @kalimbareptilepark
Phone: +260 967 213 272
Physical address: Ngwere Road, Ngwerere,
Lusaka, Zambia

Herpetological Association of Africa
Website: africanherpetology.org
Email: secretary@africanherpetology.org
Facebook: @HerpetologicalAssociationofAfrica

Livingstone Crocodile Park
Website: www.livingstonecrocodilepark.com
Email: gwemsaf@gmail.com
Facebook: @livingstonecrocpark
Phone: +260 213 321 733
Physical address: Mosi-Oa-Tunya Road,
Livingstone, Zambia

Snakes Alive Zambia
Website: infobwana.com/orgs/snakes-alive-zambia
Email: snakesalivezambia@gmail.com
Facebook: Paul Lloyd (Snakes Alive Zambia)
Phone: +260 770 794 662
Physical address: 8 Villa Victoria, Mulungushi Road,
Roma, Lusaka, Zambia

Citizen Science Platforms

Citizen science is an incredibly valuable tool to researchers and conservationists, as it harnesses the power of the public to generate geographic distribution data on a much wider scale than scientists can ever hope to achieve alone. If you find a species where it has not been recorded before, consider taking a photograph and uploading it to a citizen science platform. By doing this, you will be helping to map the current distribution of the species and this will in turn be used for conservation assessments, research and field guides.

ReptileMAP Virtual Museum
Website: vmus.adu.org.za

iNaturalist
Website: www.inaturalist.org

Index to scientific names

Index to common names